To Walt
whose love of nature
and
gifted teaching of science
inspired so many

SECONDARY SCIENCE INSTRUCTION
An Integrated Approach

SECONDARY SCIENCE INSTRUCTION

An Integrated Approach

Walter A. Farmer

Margaret A. Farrell

Jeffrey R. Lehman

 JANSON PUBLICATIONS, INC. Providence, Rhode Island

ACKNOWLEDGMENTS

The authors wish to thank the copyright holder for permission to reprint in this text the following figure:

Fig. 3.7: From *Science teaching and the development of reasoning* (Volumes for Biology, Chemistry, Earth Science, General Science and Physics), by Karplus, R., Lawson, A. E., Wollman, W., Appel, M., Bernoff, R., Howe, A., Rusch, J. J., & Sullivan, F. (Berkeley, CA: The University of California, 1977). By permission of The Regents of the University of California.

Secondary Science Instruction: An Integrated Approach is a completely revised edition of *Systematic Instruction in Science for the Middle and High School Years*, copyright © 1980 by Addison-Wesley Publishing Company, Reading Massachusetts.

CONTENTS

TO THE STUDENT

(This introduction was written with the preservice teacher in mind. Inservice teachers might compare our list of the basic ingredients needed to enter science teaching with their own experience. The final paragraphs on the instructional model serve as an introduction to the text itself. We recommend that all readers carefully review that section.)

So you want to be a teacher? Are you *sure* that secondary school science teaching is for you and that you are for it? No expert can tell you the answer. Nor is there any evidence to support the notion that teaching skills are passed on by heredity. The fact that Dad and Aunt Sally are teachers is in the realm of interesting, but unrelated information. Neither will the mere reading of this book in and of itself provide you with the answer. What this book is designed to do is to promote an interaction of your talents with real-world classroom situations in a systematic way so that you will find an answer and so that you will know when you have found it.

The term *interaction* was deliberately chosen. Becoming a teacher depends on your willingness and ability to learn the complex background necessary for teaching and to implement that background in meaningful ways in the classroom. A science methods instructor, a college supervisor of student teaching, and a school cooperating teacher can and will help in many important ways and at crucial points in the process. However, no one person or combination of these persons can do your part. What is your part? Our cumulative experience in working with hundreds of young men and women in methods courses and student teaching points to several things *you must bring* to the situation.

Comprehension of subject matter is certainly one key ingredient. No one expects you to recall all the detailed information you have learned in many semester hours of coursework in your major subject field. In fact, much of this information will find only the most limited use in teaching secondary school students. What is important is that your command of the fundamental concepts and basic principles enables you to apply those concepts to unique or novel situations and to treat them on various levels of sophistication while maintaining the integrity of the academic content.

Courage is also vital. Inexperienced teachers are generally "tested" by secondary school students who want to determine what they can get away with in class. Novice teachers who cannot bring themselves to consistently insist on adherence to some simple rules of conduct—and thus risk temporary dislike by their students—don't last very long. Little things overlooked in the hope that they will go away soon grow into big things; confrontations follow, and growing disrespect for the teacher breeds overt hatred. When situations progress to this point, the odds (25 students versus 1 teacher) are almost always insurmountable, and another teacher is lost to the profession.

You must genuinely like young people! Even the dullest of students can sense a teacher's dislike in spite of the teacher's best efforts to conceal the feeling. Even professional actors or actresses would be hard pressed to present a facade for five class periods a day, five days a week, throughout the entire school year. When students perceive a teacher's dislike of them as young people, problems are certain to develop. Then, too, consider how such teachers must feel having to work closely for extended periods of time each day with age groups they do not like. The start of each teaching day must seem like the beginning of a familiar bad dream.

Physical endurance is often overlooked. Beginning teachers are constantly amazed to discover how physically exhausted they are at the end of a teaching day. All the years you spent sitting in class as a student have done little to prepare your muscles for the amount of standing and walking required by teaching. On top of physical strain in the classroom, teachers have to face correction of papers and preparation of lesson materials after dinner. This proves too much for some to endure.

A realistic view of self is another prerequisite for success. All of us bring strengths and weaknesses to the teaching situation. You must learn how to capitalize on your strengths and be determined to shore up your weaknesses as rapidly as possible. This means that you must learn to be receptive to constructive criticism offered by supervisors and you must develop the skills of self-criticism. After all, shouldn't the main goal of teacher education be to help novices progress to the point where they can succeed in the classroom and continue to learn about instruction on their own throughout their teaching careers? Because we firmly believe that it is, the main purpose of this book is to assist you in becoming a life-long student of teaching.

If what we have said thus far makes sense to you and if you are determined to give teaching your best shot, you are our kind of person and this book was written with you in mind. Teaching can and should be an intellectually stimulating and ever-changing challenge. It should also be an endless source of satisfaction.

Note that the word *instruction* instead of the word *teaching* appears in the title of this book. Our choice of words indicates emphasis on producing learning according to specific intents of the teacher (objectives) by purposefully controlling those variables known to affect various types of learning. No doubt your students will learn in your classes things other than those you intended to convey. We pay some attention to these byproducts of instruction, but we decided to focus on an integrated approach to instruction in science.

Obviously, there are many aspects of instruction that generalize across any subject matter. However, our experience indicates that novices learn best by starting to think about the specifics of their own discipline, to apply these specifics in particular instances, and to derive generalizations *after* a critical mass of first-hand experience has been accumulated. Further, each subject matter discipline has its own type of conceptual framework (structure of ideas) and its own kinds of processes for generating ways of finding out that system of ideas. Analyzing the discipline in terms of these process and product aspects reveals its potential as a source of objectives (specific goals to be attained by learners).

Does one teach *content* or *kids?* Think this over for a minute and see if you believe that question is really worth considering as an either/or proposition. Practitioners almost universally agree on a response such as "Both," or "One teaches subject matter to students," or "One teaches students the subject matter." As experienced secondary school teachers, we long ago abandoned any inclination to consider either/or responses to this perennial question. This point of view should be obvious in the instructional model schema that precedes each chapter of the text.

Note that this schematic model incorporates both a planning and an implementation vector. Both the nature of the content to be learned and the intellectual development of students are treated as essential prerequisites to the specification of objectives. Once realistic and valid aims have been specified, knowledge about how humans learn various categories of content can be used as a basis for designing instructional strategies. The strategies must include plans for *giving feedback to students* so they will know how they are progressing toward the objectives during the implementation stage. It is also vital to *plan for and collect feedback from students* so that planned strategies can be intelligently altered during the same stage. Similarly, the feedback loop that goes back to the specified objectives can function only if knowledge of student attainment of these objectives is obtained regularly and systematically.

Does this model of instruction make some sense to you? It should, because we have developed it by working with hundreds of preservice and inservice teachers. However, don't worry if all its ramifications are not clear at this point. That's what this book is all about. Read it, but don't stop there. Interact with the ideas, perform the activities, then apply the integrated approach with your students and *believe the data.*

PREFACE

The outline for the revision of this second edition was planned by the original, authors, Walter A. Farmer and Margaret A. Farrell, who first completed a revision of a parallel text in mathematics education: Farrell, M. A., & Farmer, W. A. (1988). Secondary mathematics instruction: An integrated approach. Providence, RI: Janson Publications, Inc. With the death of Professor Farmer, our colleague Jeffrey R. Lehman was asked to collaborate in the work leading to publication. Jeffrey Lehman joined the faculty of the Department of Teacher Education at the State University of New York at Albany just one year after the completion of his doctorate at the University of Florida. For the next several years, he worked closely with Professor Farmer, used the previous edition of the text in his own classes, and developed his own lines of expertise in science education research. His contributions to the revision of this second edition have been invaluable.

Margaret A. Farrell

The first edition of this text evolved over a ten year period as authors, Walter A. Farmer and Margaret A. Farrell, collaborated to improve key parts of the undergraduate program for the education of science and mathematics teachers. Sample chapters were used in an intensive professional semester program in which special methodology and clinical experiences reflected the emphasis on the integration of theory, research, and practice. The book also has been used as a source book, or required text, in graduate science education curriculum, supervision, and perspectives of science education courses. Secondary school department chairs have used it to assist their new teachers, and experienced teachers have praised the text for serving as a catalyst to help them reflect on their own teaching. Doctoral students have found that the integration of psychology and science instruction, as well as the emphasis on the structure of the discipline of science, serves as a good basis for their research in science education.

We have been gratified by these positive responses to the first edition. In the second edition, we used the word *integrated* in the title of the text to highlight the integration of theory, practice and research that occurs at several levels. There is the thought model of instruction on the first page of each chapter. In each chapter, we relate one or more components of that thought model to the subject of the chapter and, always, to the real world of teaching. The schema of the thought model of the discipline of science found in Chapter 4 is of major importance. That model reflects a dynamic view of science, its products and processes. We emphasize the thought models of science that can be introduced by the teacher with concrete models and hands-on activities, and encourage the reader to contrast the model of science with that of its sister discipline, mathematics. Thought models are used to illustrate aspects of psychology, as in the nested stages model in Chapter 3 and the information processing model in Chapter 6. Yet, with this emphasis on theory and research, a hallmark of the text is its practical validity as a guide to the science teacher who is in the real world of the classroom. We take the approach that learning is a constructivist activity and thus, the text is written in an interactive manner. We also take the view that teaching is a complex, problem-solving task and we continually challenge the reader to reflect on the nature of this task.

In this second edition, we have included many references to research supporting specific suggestions or results. All of these sources are listed at the end of the text in a single list, References. We have updated the Suggestions for Further Study section at the end of each chapter, but have continued to try to keep these of the kind that could be read with profit by the preservice teacher and the inservice teacher new to the topic. Expanded indices, both name and subject, are responses to needs voiced by students who used the first edition. There are major revisions in some chapters, particularly Chapter 3, where we no longer introduce Piagetian psychology as if to a beginner. The emphasis is now on the application of research and theory in cognitive developmental psychology to instruction in science. Next, we consider recent research on the learning of science by secondary school students and also introduce the reader to individual differences, under the categories of cognitive style, information processing, gender differences, and the talented and the slow learner. Chapter 9 has also been substantively rewritten and now provides a more extensive base on historical perspectives that affect instruction and curriculum in science, as well as a look at the future implications of issues, such as the applications of science/technology/society and the role of discussion of critical issues—*e.g.*, the ozone layer, dissection, evolution versus creationism—by science teachers. Throughout the text, attention has been given to the integration of microcomputers and other aspects of technology into the science classroom. All other chapters have been updated.

Each chapter begins with an introductory section written with the college student in mind; we later characterize these sections as *advance organizers*. A few chapters have a section on definitions, and all have an introductory activity that we have found indispensable to learning. Some are paper-and-pencil activities, but most are laboratory or interview tasks. Each chapter concludes with a summary and self-check, a set of simulation or practice activities, and a collection of annotated readings.

There are several possible orderings of chapters that might be used by an instructor of a science methods class. We have found that Chapter 1 is an ideal place to start since college students relate to the material in that chapter. Since our students concurrently spend part of their time in a clinical experience, we like to move rather quickly to Chapter 3. Because they are observing and working with adolescents, they have a base of data to reflect on as they study Chapter 3. Chapters 7 and 8 include sections on short- and long-range planning and testing. We have found that it makes little sense to study the later sections until our students need to work with long-range activities. Each of these chapters is rich in material and is most profitably assigned in small doses. For example, we assign the section on Planning for Concepts from Chapter 7, then have students in small groups analyze the sample plan, next consider their ideas in a question/answer session, and have students apply their understandings by drafting a concept plan. That plan is then analyzed and compared to the model by student-pairs and by the instructor. Chapter 10 and parts of 11 can be threaded throughout the course. In fact, we assign the Resource File Module in the Appendix on the first day of class and check parts of it at various times throughout the course. When we use the text as a source in a graduate course, we use other orderings of chapters to fit the needs and the expertise of the audience.

We offer particular thanks to Dr. Joseph Kelly, who provided us with a most helpful synopsis of the literature in one area of science education, and to Dr. Alan Osborne, who helped us track down a citation, given a small number of clues. We appreciate the helpful comments of Alan Fiero, Dr. Raymond O'Connell, and Ronald Porter, who read sections of the revision, and of Christopher Farmer, who tried out, and reacted to, one of the new Introductory Activities. Ronald Porter also provided first draft diagrams for one of the Introductory Activities. We are grateful for the insightful comments and notes of our regular proofreader, Mrs. Norah Davis; and we especially thank our substitute proofreader, Mrs. Yvonne Farmer. Finally, we note, with deepest appreciation, the support and encouragement from so many of our colleagues and from the many former science students and science teachers who had worked with Walter A. Farmer.

February, 1990   M. A. Farrell
                                                    J. R. Lehman

CHAPTER ONE

MODES OF INSTRUCTION

Instructional Moves by the Teacher

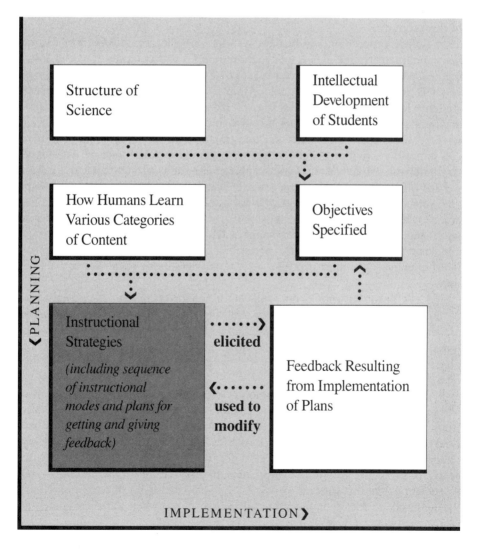

As explained in the introduction, we view teaching as a complex problem-solving task, one whose components are highlighted by the instructional model on the title page of this chapter. Note the shaded box that illustrates the place where *Modes of Instruction* fit into the total picture. Why begin with components of instructional strategies? Certainly there are several logical alternatives. Why was the decision made to begin with modes?

We begin with modes of instruction because we believe it is the most psychologically sound beginning point for students who are preparing to teach. It is an area where you have a wealth of concrete experiences upon which to draw. Your teachers have used some or all of these modes since the day you entered kindergarten, so your experiences with modes are readily available in your memory and will enable you to interact with the information and ideas to be presented in this section.

Before proceeding any further, let's be sure the phrase *Modes of Instruction* communicates the idea intended. Some prefer to call these behaviors *Teaching/Learning Activities*. Either term means essentially the same thing. Just ask yourself the question, "What kinds of things do teachers do in an effort to help students learn the content of science?" If you reflect upon your own experiences as a student, certain things are sure to come to mind. Most students recall lecture, discussion, homework, and question/answer. Some of you will also recall hands-on activities or laboratory work, demonstrations, audiovisual aids, or computer-related activities. If you came up with an assortment similar to these, we are off to a good start. Now consider whether you, each of your classmates, and your instructor all mean exactly the same thing when using each of these labels or terms. Our experience tells us that such is not the case. This is not at all surprising, since we tend to use several of these terms very loosely in our speech and since most textbooks do little better on this point. If we are to communicate ideas effectively, we must first give operational definitions of the key terms to be used.

Let's begin with an operational definition of *operational*. A definition is of the *operational* type if *it refers to key observable traits and, wherever possible and appropriate, how these are measured.* Unlike most dictionary definitions, our definition does *not* describe the new entity in terms of abstractions (nonobservables). Do you have the idea? The only way to be sure is to try to use that idea in appropriate ways.

You will get feedback as you interact with the main part of the next section, where we consider the most commonly employed modes, their operational definitions, their uses in instruction, and their potential for getting and giving feedback (knowledge of results). We begin with the lecture mode because it is the one that college students have experienced most frequently. The sequence of others that follow was selected according to a preconceived pattern of verbal interaction. See if you can detect this pattern as you read. Above all else, be sure to interact with the material, as rote memorization will be of no use when the time comes for you to step into the role of teacher.

1.1 DEFINITIONS OF COMMON INSTRUCTIONAL MODES

Lecture   During most of the time you spent in college classrooms you were expected to sit quietly and listen to the professor talk about the subject matter. Often you were expected to take notes, and sometimes your teacher used the chalkboard. Frequently at the end of such a class period the teacher asked, "Any questions?" Questions from students may not have been either expected or desired, and such questions were seldom forthcoming. What, then, is a brief operational definition for *lecture*? *The teacher talks, perhaps with some use of the chalkboard, while the students listen quietly and sometimes take notes.* Check this definition to be sure that it communicates meaning in terms of observables. Can you tell one when you see one? If so, this is a bona fide operational definition. Note that no time requirement is made in the definition, so this mode may occur for either an entire class period (as is frequently the case in college classes) or for smaller segments of a class session (as is more frequently the case in secondary schools).

Question/Answer   This is one of the most common modes employed at the secondary school level. Novice observers are usually amazed at the results of keeping tally of the number of questions asked by the teacher during a 40-minute class period. The total often exceeds one hundred and not infrequently approaches two hundred! The pattern typically begins with the teacher asking a question and then recognizing one student, who answers. Next the teacher reacts verbally in some way to the student's response and asks a question of another student, who then responds. Again the teacher handles the student's response and poses another question, which in turn is answered by a third student, and so the pattern continues. As in the lecture mode, the teacher may write some things on the chalkboard and the students may take notes. Thus the operational definition for *question/answer* is: *The teacher asks a question; one student answers; the teacher reacts and asks another question which is responded to by a second student, and so forth.* Again note that the definition does *not* specify a time limit, so the mode may continue for all or any part of a class period.

Discussion   This term is used very loosely by many teachers, students, and textbook writers. We have all observed instructors who began class with "Today we are going to discuss the very important applications of _____ " and who then followed with 40 minutes of lecture on the topic. Textbook writers are also prone to make the same error, as evidenced by a host of chapters that begin with something akin to "The following topics will be *discussed.*"

   Throughout this book we use the term *discuss* to refer to *planned student-to-student talk with occasional verbal intervention by the teacher.* Think back to the last time you were involved in a buzz-group session. Your most recent participation was probably in the dorm rather than in a college classroom, for this mode is rarely employed by college teachers. If your last experience was an actual discussion, most or all of the participants contributed information and ideas *without* filtering them through the leader of the group every time. Have you caught the essential difference that discriminates this mode from the question/answer mode? If so, you are doing well. If you are not so sure, talk it out with a few classmates and refer back to the operational definition. Note that no time limit is implied, nor is the size of the group narrowly prescribed. However, the entire class is rarely involved as a single discussion group. On the other hand, one person can hardly constitute a discussion group. A group consisting of four to six participants is the size recommended as optimal for effective discussion. Some proponents of cooperative learning (see Davidson, 1990) say that group size should be limited to four participants so that all members have an opportunity to participate and to cooperate, rather than compete. We recommend that no hard-and-fast rule be applied, but that the teacher pay particular attention to the composition of the group to ensure that one person does not dominate the discussion.

Have you caught on to the pattern we had in mind as we sequenced the presentation of the three modes defined (not *discussed*) thus far? If so, try to verify your conjecture as you read about the next three modes.

Demonstration   The literal meaning of this word is "show" and that meaning pinpoints the operational definition of the mode. Typically, but not always, *the teacher shows something, such as a specimen or a model, while students watch.* In some instances, one student may do the showing while other students and the teacher watch. You may be thinking at this point that usually some talking (such as lecture or question/answer) is used with a demonstration. Some talking usually is involved, but silent demonstrations can be used very effectively. What do we call a situation where demonstration, short lecture, and question/answer are used in an integrated fashion? This is one example of an *instructional strategy.*

We consider the design of strategies in Chapter 7. If you reflect on your own experiences as a secondary school student, you are probably about to conclude that, with rare exceptions, modes are usually combined into a strategy. This is good thinking. For now, however, let's focus attention on the individual modes, since this background will serve you well when all other prerequisites to strategy design have been mastered.

Laboratory   This mode does not refer to a place nor a special class period in the weekly schedule, but to an activity. This activity may occur in a regular classroom, a specially equipped room, at home, or outdoors. The key idea is that *students manipulate concrete objects or equipment under the direction of the teacher.* Junior high students may be taking samples of ten M & M's from a large bag and counting the number of brown, green, yellow and red candies in each sample as part of a probability lab. Chemistry students may be engaged with molecular models and asked to observe and write down the name and formula of the compound that each model represents. This is in clear contrast to demonstrations in which only one individual does the manipulation and in which all others watch. (The word *manipulation* is frequently used by mathematics teachers to mean "calculation." This is not the sense in which we refer to manipulative tasks.)

The three modes that follow include other activities used by teachers to help students achieve objectives. While these are not completely distinct from the five presented earlier, they have their own advantages and limitations that need to be emphasized.

Individual student projects   At first glance, this may look like the laboratory mode. The critical differences are that here the *students are all doing different manipulative activities or varied library research, or different problem-solving tasks on an individual basis.* Note that all students are *not* doing the same things in the same place at the same time as so often is the case in the laboratory mode. Some student choice of activity is also implied by this mode.

By now you have probably discerned the pattern of sequencing of modes presented thus far. We began with the "talking" modes, placing the most teacher-dominated mode first (lecture) and moving through to the least teacher-dominated mode (discussion). Next we considered the "showing" and "doing" modes, again moving from the most to the least teacher-dominated mode.

Audiovisual and technological activities (ATAs)   Actually all modes involve hearing, seeing, or both and a few involve touching in combination with seeing, and sometimes hearing. However, this mode typically means that *students look at, listen to, or touch specific kinds of equipment. Equipment typically known as audiovisual includes projectors for films, film strips or loop films, video cassette recorders, audio tape recorders and compact disc recorders, and overhead or opaque projectors. Equipment that is usually classified as technological includes mini, micro, and mainframe computers and programmable and non-programmable calculators.* It is easy to think of examples of this mode being used as an integral part of another mode, rather than in addition to it. For example, a biology teacher may demonstrate the effect of background noise on auditory reaction time by using a computer to generate audio signals and to time subsequent responses.

Supervised practice   This mode involves having *students try to perform some practice tasks, often at their seats or at the chalkboard, while the teacher observes their progress and gives help and reinforcement as needed.* Like all other modes, this one has an important role to play in effective and efficient strategy design. However, novices often either overlook its importance or carry out this mode in an ineffective manner. We outline more about this later, but think about the relationship of this mode to the mode that follows. Perhaps you can get the jump on us.

Homework   "Boo, Hiss!" is the typical student reaction to homework. Could this be due in part to the narrow definition given to the mode by typical teacher use? Let's not limit the possibilities to the odd-numbered problems for tonight. (Guess what is coming for tomorrow night?) We prefer to define the homework mode as *any activity relevant to the achievement of objectives, that students perform outside of the scheduled class sessions.* This definition encompasses such potentially meaningful activities as spending 15 minutes in the supermarket after school to get data from labels on competing brands of the same product, getting data for growth curves on plants grown over a two-week period, and interviewing a random sample of people to elicit their beliefs on a science-related topic. It also leaves room for doing the even-numbered problems from a textbook when this makes pedagogical sense.

Although we might try to identify and operationally define a few more modes, the nine defined thus far are the common ones and will suffice for our purposes. By now if you have been interacting with the text, you should be anxious to get on to meatier questions of what each mode has to offer as input into strategy design and what the potential of each mode is for getting feedback (finding out how well each student is doing) and giving feedback (letting students know how they are progressing).

1.2 INTRODUCTORY ACTIVITY

There's no observation without an observer.

A. With at least one other classmate, observe a junior high or senior high science class. As the class progresses, record data following the format shown in Figure 1.1. Record instances of feedback the teacher got and any reactions by the teacher to that feedback. Be specific—for instance, list the approximate number of hands raised.

Use of the following shorthand will save time:

T: teacher   Q/A: question/answer
S(Ss): student (students)   Demo: demonstration
HWPM: Homework post-mortem ("going over" last night's homework)

Time	Subject/Grade: **Chemistry 11**	Topic: **Atomic Structure**
	Names of modes observed	Samples of feedback observed during the use of each mode
8:10 am to 8:15 am	1. T lectures on atom.	1. 3 Ss have heads on desk; all others look front, are quiet, and take notes.
8:15 am	2. T: Q/A on content of lecture	2. 10–12 Ss volunteer and T calls on 4 in front, praises ans., and clarifies.

Fig. 1.1

B. Meet with one or more of your classmates who observed the same lesson. Compare the data collected and check for agreements/disagreements as to the modes observed and the related feedback. Account for any discrepancies in the data that might have resulted from lack of consistency in use of the operational definitions of the modes (consult Section 1.1).

C. Consult with classmates who observed other lessons and look for any common patterns, such as number of changes of modes used within a single class period and amount and kinds of feedback given or received by the teacher. (Note: This activity can be carried out in a live classroom or while viewing a videotape of a class.)

1.3 USES OF MODES

Lecture

This mode provides an opportunity for the teacher to give verbal input at key times during the class period. (Remember, there is no time requirement in the definition of this mode.) Introduction to lessons, summaries of problem-solving strategies, information on the history of science or on applications of some scientific concept—all of these are important instances of times that the lecture mode might be used effectively. It is assumed that the words of the lecturer convey substantively the same meaning to all of the students. (Reflect on this assumption when you study differences in adolescent reasoning in Chapter 3.) It is also assumed that the students are listening with the intent to comprehend and remember, not just displaying the "lecture syndrome" (eye movements following the teacher, smiles on faces when the teacher tells a joke, and so on). Since it is difficult for most secondary school students to remain passive listeners for long periods of time, the lecturer should either keep it short or be a dynamic lecturer, or both. Few novices, if our experience is any guide, are dynamic lecturers. What has been your personal experience with lectures that extend for long periods of time? How long can you pay rapt attention? Does the lecturer seem to know when you are confused on a point, or does he or she continue to retread the same ground while you are anxious to get on to the next idea? What feedback is available to the lecturer? How can he or she interpret the feedback signs, particularly if the group is sophisticated in playing the game of school? Further, how do students find out if they are following the thinking of the lecturer? Obviously the feedback-giving and -getting potential of this mode is minimal and, along with the limited attention span problem, it is a strong argument for using lecture selectively and for brief time spans.

Question/Answer

Many novices, and some veterans, believe question/answer is a mode that enables the teacher to find out who knows what. Is it? Only one student responds at a time, a sample of only one out of twenty-five or thirty! So much for feedback potential—better than lecture, but still extremely limited. Furthermore, many a novice has been misled by apparently positive feedback from one segment of a diverse group of students in a question/answer sequence. Quiz scores subsequently reveal far less success with the topic. Consider the following illustration: Jack answered question 1; Mary, question 2; Sam, question 3; and so on. That's right! Mary and Sam may have been cued in by Jack's response, but may be unable to *begin* the problem. Other students may be unable to *complete* the solution. What, then, is the forte of question/answer?

The question/answer mode is extremely valuable as a way to guide developmental thinking, to stimulate creative problem solving, to initiate discussions, and to stimulate quick recall of prerequisites needed for the day's lesson. Indeed, the question/answer mode can be used effectively in combination with every other mode. The kind of question asked, the preamble to the question posed, and the variety of ways used to encourage and accept responses are all skills that make the difference between thoughtful interaction and humdrum, dull sequences.

There are three major components of the question/answer mode that need special attention: the questions themselves, the ways in which student responses can be obtained, and the ways in which student responses can be handled. Beginners can get disastrous results from trying to use the question/answer mode when a complex question is dropped on the class like a bomb. Lack of student response may also be a function of the teacher's inability to handle earlier responses. Ms. Goldberg complains that only Bill and Sara ever respond to her questions, but in Mr. Boswell's class, most or all members of the class mumble something whenever he asks a question. What can be done to help either of these teachers? A lot! But let's start at the beginning.

The following do's and don'ts are intended for the teacher whose difficulty seems to be related to the nature of the questions asked.

The question—do's and don'ts

1. Write down the major question in a developmental sequence and analyze the possible responses ahead of time.
2. Precede a question/answer by a brief lecture or demonstration designed to set the stage for the sequence.
3. Do not ask frequent yes-no questions or fill-in-the-blank questions, such as "Does anyone know the answer to number five?" (Students who answer "No" or "Yes" have answered the question.)
4. Increase the number of questions requiring a phrase or a sentence in response.
5. Do not try to elicit developmental thinking by the all-encompassing "What about" questions, such as "What about the atom?"
6. Use a variety of opening question-phrases, such as "How? Who knows? When is ... true? What is ... ? What seems to be ... ? Why?

Notice that suggestion 1 refers to your planning, as does suggestion 2; but all the other suggestions require some on-the-spot analysis. An observer can help gather appropriate data; so can a tape recorder. In either case, a teacher can begin to alter his or her questioning skills over time. Why is suggestion 2 made? As you read the section on the discussion mode, look for a parallel guideline. Try to imagine a classroom where the teacher regularly disregards suggestion 3. What kind of class response is likely to occur? If you conjectured that something like mumbled responses (or shouted responses) from a few would probably happen, then your conjecture matches reality. Now suggestion 3 takes on more significance, for even the newest student of teaching realizes that if wide and specific interaction does not occur, the teacher has no way of immediately assessing the extent to which the question/answer mode guided developmental thinking.

How do you get specific and wide interaction from students? The second set of suggestions deals with diverse ways of *getting* responses from students (the second critical ingredient in an effective question/answer mode); none should be used exclusively.

Getting responses from students—do's and don'ts

1. Pose the question *before* you call on someone.

2. Do not call on students in the same area of the room for all answers.

3. Help shyer or slower students gain confidence by asking them easy questions at first.

4. Don't bore bright students by always asking them recall questions.

5. Do not direct a series of quick questions to students row by row (or in any clear pattern).

6. Do not call *only* on students who volunteer.

7. Wait at least three to five seconds prior to accepting responses to high-level questions. Inform the students that you are going to do this.

8. Tell the students that there is no penalty for incorrect or partially correct answers. Tell them it is not a quiz, but a learning experience.

Several of the suggestions are again a part of your planning. Suggestions 3, 4, and 7 refer to easy and higher-level questions. A careful analysis of the science content *before* you begin the class will help you to plan several high-level questions. For example, in a lesson on solubility, a chemistry teacher might ask students to describe the process that they would use to separate each component from a mixture of several components. Depending on the quality of the answer, backup questions on the justification for the described procedure could help students to go beyond memorized routines. Beginning teachers have found that suggestion 7 is difficult to implement until they have established some control in the classroom. However, researchers (Budd-Rowe, 1978) have found that its effective use with a thought-provoking question has turned many a passive class into one which volunteers. One way to introduce a class to this questioning technique might be to say something like: "I am going to ask you a thought question and I won't take any answers for five seconds. Here's the question ... "

Since the teacher wants to optimize both the number and the quality of responses from the students, many of these suggestions must be used in combination with one another. Occasionally, the teacher should violate one of the guidelines to achieve an optimum result. For example, Mrs. Frost cannot implement suggestion 1 from the responses list. As soon as the end of her question is heard and before she is able to call on a student, her seventh-grade class shouts out responses. What should Mrs. Frost do? See if the next set of suggestions helps.

These suggestions deal with the third component of the question/answer mode—handling student responses.

Handling student responses—do's and don'ts

1. Ask another student to agree or disagree and give his or her reasons for doing so.

2. Take a "straw vote" ("Let me see the hands of those who agree with Jack, those who disagree, those who aren't sure."), and follow up with a request for justification.

3. Frown a bit and ask, "Are you sure?"

4. Ask other students to add to the answer of the first student.

5. Ask a student to explain how he or she arrived at the solution.

6. Ask if there is another way to solve the problem.

7. Do not accept *mixed* chorus responses.

8. If a student cannot answer a difficult question, ask a contingency (backup) question on a lower level.

9. Refuse to accept responses that are not audible to all students.

10. Give praise for partially correct responses to complicated questions.

Mrs. Frost, who has to deal with a "too eager" class, may now use one of these suggestions to direct attention to one student. One clear way to convince a class of the limitations of the mixed chorus response is to use suggestion 1 from this set of guidelines. That student's confusion as to what he or she is asked to defend is more convincing than a hundred reminders from the teacher. These suggestions must be used with some care and in combination with those listed earlier.

In addition to all the concerns noted so far, the physical location of the teacher can greatly influence the nature of the verbal interaction. Look at Figure 1.2 and analyze the flow of verbal interaction. Each number represents either a question or an answer, and it is clear that a large number of these occurred, but where? Why? Where was the teacher? (*T* designates teacher location.)

Chalkboard

T

1, 3, 5, 7, 10, 13, 15, 17, 19, 21, 23, 25,
27, 29, 31, 33, 35, 38, 41, 43, 45, 47, 49, 51,
53, 55, 57, 59, 61, 63, 65, 67, 69, 71, 73, 76, 79

	66	4, 64, 68	18, 34, 52, 54, 56	14, 32, 42, 44, 46, 48, 50
		24, 28	8, 11, 58, 70	9, 12, 26, 37, 40
2		30	36, 39, 74, 78	16, 60, 62, 75, 77
	6		72	20, 22

20 students present

Fig. 1.2 Flow of verbal interaction.

Now analyze Figure 1.3.

There is still only one teacher in the classroom, but that teacher has moved to four different locations during the sequence. Why? Compare the sequence of numerals in the box designated as teacher responses in each case. A different pattern of verbal interaction is occurring in these two classrooms. To what extent can the teacher control this pattern so that the broadest possible feedback sampling can occur? The teacher who stands next to a timid, soft-spoken student can encourage a louder voice by moving away from the speaker. The right-handed teacher may find that he or she frequently calls on students to the left of the teacher's desk. Your position is important and must be consciously varied to achieve optimum results.

Discussion

As noted earlier, most activities labeled "discussion" are really lecture or question/answer. In a discussion, as defined here, the teacher usually initiates the interaction, but is only sporadically heard from after that. What, then, is the first essential ingredient for a discussion? There must be a topic—a question, a problem, or a situation in which the students can share ideas and compare or contrast views. What are some suitable topics or situations that have been used effectively by science teachers in initiating discussion?

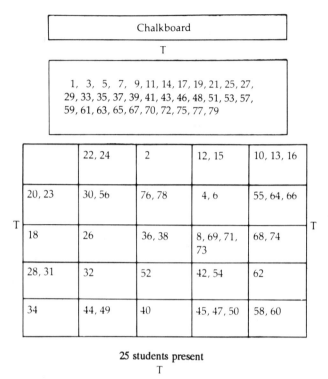

Fig. 1.3   Flow of verbal interaction.

Class	Topic	Procedure/Purposes
1. Science 9	Designing experiments	Small groups seek varied methods to test a given hypothesis and contrast practicality and adequacy of controls in each proposed design.
2. Biology	Air pollution	Groups to discuss ways of reducing air pollution in our community, including advantages and disadvantages of each method.
3. Any subject level	Test post-mortem when results range from very good to poor	Each group to be arranged by the teacher to reflect the range. Group to discuss all problems on which any member needs help, consider reasons behind errors, pinpoint strategies for correct solutions.

| 4. Science lab | Results of individual or group lab work | Groups to compare results, conjecture possible generalizations based on lab work, pose questions, analyze reasons for varied results. |

Obviously, a second major ingredient for a successful discussion is appropriate student prerequisites. In the first illustration, students who know only enough science to propose one way to test the hypothesis will have nothing to compare. If all or most students in the class are at this level, the "discussion" will degenerate into a practice session. For a similar reason the teacher must structure heterogeneous groups in the third illustration just given. If all the failing students are in the same group, you have the blind leading the blind. Of course, a teacher who attempts a discussion on air pollution before the students have learned concepts such as percentage composition of air or effects of various substances on plants, animals, and people is asking for a shared ignorance pool on the topic. (You may have experienced such ignorance pools in many out-of-school discussions.) Even given all of the student prerequisites mentioned with respect to the air pollution problem, the wise teacher would also prepare the way for an effective discussion by an appropriate pre-class assignment. In this case, the students might be asked to interview other students or family members about air pollution and identify common misconceptions, if any, from the collected responses. Such an assignment "sets up" the class with a common area of concern, on which each has gathered some data. Some discussions need this kind of pre-class assignment where a reading, the completion of a set of structured exercises, or the collection of survey data provides everyone with a common set of initial information to serve as a basis for discussion questions.

The necessary ingredients for the effective use of the discussion mode, then, are the suitability of the topic, the students' grasp of needed prerequisites, and pre-class assignments, when needed. But even with the presence of all of these, many discussions slump because the teacher ignores a simple structural ingredient. Compare Figures 1.2 and 1.3 with Figure 1.4. Students who see only their nearest neighbors and only the backs of heads are not likely to engage in useful interaction. Seating arrangement becomes of prime importance. Figure 1.4 offers two possible seating arrangements for the discussion mode. A teacher who makes considerable use of discussion may want to explore alternative seating arrangements *within* subgroups. Some guidelines that make a lot of sense have been verified by practitioners in the area of group interaction (Kell & Corts, 1980).

1. Communication tends to flow *across* a circle, not around it. Remember that a massive amount of communication is nonverbal and we can see more clearly the facial expressions of the person across the circle or table.

2. A corollary to the above guideline is the principle that communication is maximized between students who sit opposite each other and lessened between those who sit side by side.

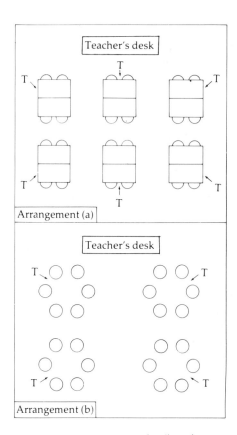

Fig. 1.4   Arrangements for discussion.

Although it is probably impractical to assign each student to a seat, you can use these guidelines to encourage a shy student to participate, or to discourage an overtalkative student from monopolizing the group.

Finally, where should you be during the discussion? To find the answer to that question, you must first answer several more important questions. What can a teacher find out *during* a discussion? How can a teacher contribute without altering the mode to Q/A?

If you've prepared the class for the discussion, carefully selected a suitable topic, structured the groups and seating arrangements thoughtfully, and clearly given all instructions *before* the students move into their groups, then your role in the first few minutes is that of a helpful overseer. You are making sure that all students follow those initial instructions by making a quick tour around the perimeter of the groups.

What next? If you're only interested in the end product of the discussion, you can hire a babysitter and take some time off. Be careful! You may scoff at that idea, and yet some teachers reward only the end product and neither attend to, nor reward, the steps students take to get to that end. You want to get feedback on each group's work and on as many individuals' work as possible. Who is contributing? How? Who agrees, disagrees? You must systematically circulate and look and listen carefully to get this kind of feedback. Furthermore, if students are to believe that their efforts in the discussion are worthwhile, you must give verbal and nonverbal praise to individuals and groups for such things as creativity, thoughtfulness, intelligent skepticism, and efficiency. However, you must be cautious that your praise isn't misconstrued as a closing off of discussion, because your other major role is to sustain the discussion by cuing students as to potentially useful avenues by answering some questions and by posing other questions. Take a long careful look at the various positions of the teacher in Figure 1.4 and notice the directions the teacher faces. Why are these directions and positions recommended? In what areas is the teacher never found in these diagrams?

When does a discussion end? When the attention of subgroup members starts wandering, the discussion mode has already continued too long. You should call a halt when all groups have made some inroads on the topic and when sharing of ideas seems desirable. After all the students have responded to the signal to end the discussion, each spokesperson can report on that group's findings. Then students from other groups can be asked to indicate agreements or disagreements. Finally, you can help all to summarize class results.

Notice that the feedback getting and giving of this mode has high potential. You may sample everyone a number of times under optimum conditions. The discussion mode also has been found to be especially effective in promoting the learning of problem solving in science classes (Seymour & Padberg, 1975). We'll reconsider the unique contribution of this mode and others where students interact with other students in Chapter 3, when we study adolescent reasoning.

Demonstration

Used in combination with lecture, question/answer, or laboratory, this mode can be remarkably effective. The following examples illustrate just a few of the ways in which demonstrations can be used to enhance science instruction. (See Chapters 10 and 11 for many more examples.)

Examples of effective demonstrations

Class (topic)	Demo	Use
1. Biology 10 (Symmetry in Living Things)	T cuts grapefruit in half.	To show model of radial symmetry

2. Life Science 7 (Nutrition)	T holds up can of soup, box of cereal.	To get attention on practical problems
3. Chemistry 11	T inserts flaming splint into a large test tube of hydrogen.	To illustrate a test for hydrogen
4. Physical Science 8	T lifts heaviest S off the floor with one hand by using a ten foot long 2 × 4 as a lever.	To show actual mechanical advantage (AMA) of simple machine

To focus student attention on a demonstration, you must first be sure that the object can be seen. (You'd be surprised at the number of teachers who ignore this "common sense" maxim!) The specimen must be large enough to be visible from the rear, or the teacher must move about the room with a smaller object. White cardboard sheets or the overhead screen can provide an effective backdrop. A model of the brain or a crystal can be highlighted by placing either of them on the stage of the overhead. The overhead light in a darkened room shines on the object as in a theater. What are the students to see? Do they know where to look and why? If not, the effectiveness of the demonstration will suffer.

Although demonstration is often used simultaneously with other modes, a silent demonstration can be very effective. Such a demonstration might be used either to set the stage for, or to further develop, a topic. One middle school teacher silently demonstrated step-by-step procedures for a laboratory, while the students observed and recorded safety violations. At the demonstration's conclusion, students identified safety violations and talked about them before performing the activity themselves.

What is the potential of this mode for feedback getting? Almost zero. Oh, experienced teachers learn to "read" the nonverbal signs—the alert gazes, the "aha" expressions, the scowl, or the worried look. Unfortunately, experienced students have also learned to play the game of school and many manage to put on the face the teacher wants to see.

Laboratory

Since the students are manipulating equipment or material in this mode, they are doing so to collect data. Therefore, you might employ this mode to help students reach a generalization, test a conjecture, observe the application of a rule, or learn and practice a psychomotor skill. Some examples follow.

Examples of effective laboratory exercises

Class	Materials	Activity	Purpose
1. Science 9	Triple beam balance and solid objects	Ss mass objects to within .01 gram and check against T's results.	To develop and practice motor skills of massing solid objects.
2. Physical Science	Grooved rulers, protractors, marbles, styrofoam cups	Ss roll marble down incline into a styrofoam cup and measure distance cup moves. Repeat with different angles of inclination.	To examine inclined plane.
3. Science 7	Microscopes, slides of varied animal and plant cells, and slides of tiny objects that are not cells	Ss manipulate slides and microscope and observe similarities and differences among cells and noncells.	To form biological concept of cell.
4. Chemistry	Test tubes containing a wide variety of acids, bases, and alcohols; litmus and pH paper	Ss are given 10 minutes to test and group substances according to reactions to litmus and pH paper.	To form concepts of acid and base.

How does a teacher implement the laboratory mode? Perhaps more than any other mode, this one requires careful preparation of materials, instruction in safety precautions, organization of equipment, and possible reorganization of the usual physical facilities in the classroom. Directions need to be pre-planned. Some teachers write directions on an overhead projection sheet so that all students can refer to them repeatedly. If the laboratory activity involves small groups, the teacher must decide on the nature of the groups. Again, it may save time to list group names and locations on an acetate sheet or the chalkboard. Don't forget the need to survive! If Marc and Tom fight continually, you're asking for trouble if you place them in the same group.

Is grouping a necessary part of the laboratory mode? In example 2, group work may be essential, with members of the group alternating the jobs of measuring, recording, and graphing. In example 1, on the other hand, each student needs to work independently on the massing of objects task and there is no real advantage in grouping. In either case, beware of being hypnotized by eager, active students who never attain the purpose of the lab because you forgot the most important ingredient of all. You must tell the students where they're headed, emphasize the need to look for patterns (as in example 3), insist on careful recording of data, and structure the follow-up to the lab so that the different observations can be shared. Here is a place where developmental questioning combined with lab can be used with profit.

What feedback potential is possible with this mode? Little or none if you are ill-prepared, must repeat directions often, or must continue to carry materials to different students. However, if you have done your job well, the students should be busy with the materials in a matter of minutes. Now you can move systematically to each individual or group, listening, asking questions, and observing the way in which the students are proceeding. In addition, you have unlimited opportunities to praise, to cue, and to correct intermediate errors.

Why use the lab mode with bright, older students who are well motivated? Isn't it a waste of time? Recall your own experience in recent college classes when a new concept was defined for you. Did you always grasp the concept? Have you sometimes been helped to understand the concept by a concrete example furnished by a peer? If so, then you already can appreciate the potential importance of the lab mode for all students. Indeed, it has been found that even the brightest students in advanced classes profit from well-designed hands-on activities introducing them to an unfamiliar, complex concept. There is much more about this in Chapter 3.

Some references to help the science teacher design interesting laboratory activities will be found in Chapter 11, and the emphasis on the use of the laboratory mode in various curriculum projects is described in Chapter 9.

Individual Student Projects

Projects can be initiated by students or by the teacher. Projects may be used to explore some topic in depth, to introduce relevant applications of the science topic being studied, or to investigate the historical background of the topic. Project work may occur during the class period, but most of the project work is usually carried on outside of class time. Student reports may be shared with the class, and student productions can be displayed.

Here are two examples of project directions used in senior high school science classes.

1. *Tenth Grade Biology Project*   *Date*: February 8
    (This would be suitable for one or two students. Additional projects related to plant physiology would be available to other students.)

    Construct three simple respirometers as described on pages 141–143 of *The Lore of Living Plants* by Johannes van Overbeek. Then design and conduct an experiment using these respirometers to compare the respiration rates among germinating bean, corn, and pea seeds. Check out your plan for experimental design with the teacher by February 23. The final oral report to the class is due on March 30 and should include attention to the functioning of the respirometer, experimental design employed, the data obtained, and the practical importance of the findings.

2. *Eleventh Grade Chemistry Project*   *Date*: October 1
(Each student in the class is to select one element as a subject for this project.)

Choose one of the elements #3 through #13. Construct an atomic model from common materials (such as gum drops, marshmallows, pipe cleaners, ping-pong balls, toothpicks, or dowel rods) in such a way as to make the best possible representation of the kind of atom selected. Bring your model to class on October 15, and plan to (1) demonstrate it to the class, (2) point out all the features of your model that accurately represent contemporary science knowledge, and (3) point out the limitations of your representation.

If students complain of the extra work involved in a project, then the teacher has goofed somewhere along the line. The project should be threaded into the coursework. It is up to the teacher to design assignments and daily work so that students see this mode as an alternative, but different, way of learning relevant aspects of science. The students soon learn that the teacher doesn't mean what is said if no class time is reserved for reports, or if the end of the project means little more than a grade in the teacher's record book.

Because much of the project work is completed outside of class time, the feedback potential prior to project completion is limited. However, the teacher is able to gather feedback on a host of student capabilities upon completion of the project, and can give feedback in the form of written or oral comments. Project work affords an excellent opportunity to encourage students to give feedback to each other—formally during oral reports, and informally as they inspect posted projects.

The first time students hand in completed projects, the teacher is faced with a new problem. How will the projects be graded? Twenty-four reports, models or posters may exhibit considerable artistic talent, or none at all. The teacher who hasn't thought about the evaluation aspect of the project work may be faced with a barrage of student criticism when the graded material is returned to the class. "This isn't art class!" "How did you judge the projects?" "What's my grade?" These are not easy questions to answer, but you must answer them if you assign projects. See if the material on all aspects of evaluation found later in this book meshes with your present response.

Audiovisual and Technological Activities (ATAs)

Lights out! Is it a signal for paper-wad battles or siesta time? All too often, even in an interested class, ATA time means neither the battle nor the nap but an extraneous short feature that is clever but hasn't much to do with the topic. Again teacher preparation is critical if this mode is to help students learn.

There are four major areas of preparation in the use of ATAs: (1) use of the equipment; (2) quality and suitability of the tape, slide, film, filmstrip, computer program, transparency, or video; (3) preparation of the students; and (4) follow-up and integration of the ATA into other modes. The suggestions listed below may seem to include the obvious, but our experience in the classrooms of novice teachers convinces us that the obvious is often overlooked.

ATAs—do's and don'ts

1. Use of the equipment:

   a) Check out your school's rules and regulations and follow them. (Some schools have student operators of equipment.)

   b) Dry-run equipment you will operate *in the classroom in which it will be used.* Check visibility and/or audibility from various areas of the room.

   c) When the equipment consists of multiple microcomputers and software to be used by students, there is a need not only to dry-run the equipment, but to teach the students to observe certain routines and precautions. The "Suggestions for Further Study" section at the end of this chapter includes a recent text that provides information on some of these cautions. However, given the constantly changing state of technology, we recommend that teachers take one of the many courses on the incorporation of the microcomputer into science instruction and follow that up by reading relevant articles in professional journals (see Chapter 11).

2. Quality and suitability of the materials:

   a) Review all material you hope to use and *do not* use material of poor quality or limited applicability, even if last year's teacher did order it.

   b) Be a ruler of, not a slave to, equipment and materials! If parts of a computer program are excellent for your purposes, run only those parts. (Be sure that you have keyboard control over such programs.) If you wonder how the students would have considered a question heard on a film before they hear the answer, stop the film, engage in Q/A, then start the film, and let it provide the reinforcement. The possibilities are unlimited.

3. Preparation of the students:

   a) Provide an introduction and an overview. Let the students know where and how this ATA contributes to the topic being studied.

   b) Explain to the students their responsibilities. Will you ask questions during, and/or after, the viewing/listening? Should they take notes? If so, make sure they can see. (Obvious, isn't it? But how many pitchblack classes have you sat in and been expected to take notes?)

4. Follow-up and integration of ATA mode:

   a) Plan alternative ways of combining this mode with others to get feedback, to give feedback, and to promote attention to the task. One route, the interspersing of Q/A with the ATA, was alluded to in 2b. Another effective route is to prepare an outline with questions or problems to be responded to either during the viewing/listening or after, or both. Hand this outline to the students prior to the viewing/listening.

   b) Keep the particular ATA material alive after the lights go on. Conduct Q/A or small-group discussions if suitable. Future lessons, assignments, tests, and quizzes should refer to examples from this use of an ATA whenever possible.

It is clear that all this time and effort should not be wasted on worthless materials. But the old saying "A picture is worth a thousand words" has been proven true too often for you to ignore the immense potential of the ATA mode. However, suppose you have equipment available for either a lab or a demo and have a video cassette or a computer program that portrays the same lesson. On what basis would you make a choice of mode? How would you rate this mode as to feedback potential? Why? Check out your conjectures against the ideas presented in Chapter 2.

Supervised Practice

Practice makes perfect—or does it? Have you ever practiced a golf swing with little improvement in your drive? It's probable that you learned an error to perfection. That's right. Practice must follow *relevant* instruction. You must know how to get feedback on the results of that instruction before and during the supervised practice. In fact, the word *supervised* suggests that intimate tie between this mode and feedback. In Chapter 2, several suggestions aimed at feedback getting and giving are detailed.

Here are a few suggestions that should help you implement supervised practice:

1. Use several short periods rather than one long, marathon session at the end of class. (Of course, this will keep students busy; but there is a more important reason. It has to do with feedback and learning. (Chapters 2, 6, and 7 have more on this.)

2. Sequence and cluster your practice examples so that all or almost all students can begin the work and so that no one is finished before you have some time to make a tour of most of the room. Tour of the room? That's right. "Supervise" does not mean that you monitor the group as if you were the guard in the tower of a prison yard.

3. Follow the arrows in Figure 1.5 *after* all the students are at work. The arrows illustrate the direction you should face. Why is it a good move to turn the body as diagrammed here? Remember, there are 25 students in those seats,

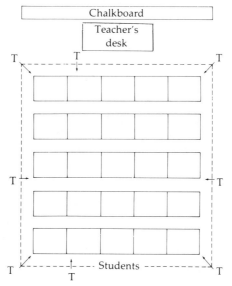

Key: - - - = route for quick tour (inital 1-2 minute maximum)
     T → = direction T faces when helping individuals

Fig. 1.5 Positioning of teacher during supervised practice.

and they are not all like thee or me. The tour should be quick and complete. So try not to interrupt the tour to spend time with a single student. If you haven't guessed why, the next chapter offers some reasons.

4. Systematically move into the room to check the work of individual students. But five hands are up! Use verbal and nonverbal signals to let students know you see their hands and will be with them in order. In the meantime, they could try another easier problem or be directed to share their question with another student.

5. Be aware of the entire class even while helping one student. Turn to face most of the class. Bend at the knees, rather than the waist. (It's good for posture, too!) Give a cue, but insist on student responsibility to try. Students soon learn that some teachers will do the work for them if asked.

   Supervised practice is such a critical mode that more attention is paid to it in later chapters. For now, we leave you with questions. When should a teacher end a supervised practice session? Do honor-level twelfth-graders need supervised practice?

Homework

Three examples of nonroutine homework assignments were described in Section 1.1. Refer back to these examples and consider how the teacher would make use of the products of the students' efforts during the subsequent day's lesson. You should be able to think of several good possibilities. However, actually making use of the homework is based upon the assumption that nearly all students have done the assigned task. How can the teacher ensure that such will be the case? One often-overlooked technique is to inform students how data from an assignment will be used. This technique encourages students to view homework as an important part of the course rather than simply as "busy work." However, in spite of your best efforts to head-off the problem, you must be prepared to cope with the reality that one or two students will come to class unprepared. What alternatives exist to handle this kind of problem? Shouting, screaming, and idle threats will do nothing to salvage the situation nor will they prevent its recurrence. Positive action, which demonstrates the consequences of students' failure to prepare, is needed. For example, if your plan calls for a question/answer session based on the collected data, then you should refuse to allow unprepared students to participate in that portion of the lesson and emphasize to them the importance of the assignment in a private teacher/student conference after class. However, perhaps your plan calls for students to share and analyze data in small groups. In the case of older students, peer pressure from the unprepared students is often the most effective remedy, along with evidence that the teacher is alert to the problem. Suppose unprepared students begin to disrupt the work of the group? Then, you must step in so that prepared students are not penalized. One alternative is to direct the offenders to read relevant material in other texts instead of participating with their classmates. Notice that the teacher must have alternate class assignments ready to use, as needed.

Does the typical paper-and-pencil homework have a place in instruction? Yes. In fact, the most obvious use of this mode is to provide *relevant* practice on skills introduced in the day's lesson. Notice the emphasis on the word *relevant*. Recall the statement in Section 1.1 on the danger inherent in routine selection of the even-numbered problems that leads students to perceive homework as mindless practice. But caution is advised! There is considerable evidence that practice has no effect—or even negative effects—beyond a certain point. When students perceive homework as a way to keep them busy, they tune out. The key to this is to err on the side of too little, rather than too much, of this kind of homework. Choose only a few exercises or activities, and make sure the ones you choose make sense to the students.

Another sure way to turn off the class is to use homework as a punishment. If your class has already learned to associate homework with punishment, you will need to be particularly thoughtful about your use of this mode. Resource books are filled with appropriate possibilities: open-ended questions, practice in coded or puzzle form, take-home labs. See Chapter 11 for specific references.

A less often used, but effective, approach to get the most out of relevant paper-and-pencil exercises is to build the foundation of tomorrow's lesson into today's homework. For example, a carefully structured sequence of series and parallel circuit problems could be assigned to give practice in applying $I = E/R$

to these situations. Then a combination circuit problem could be posed as a challenge for students to find a way to apply the same basic rule to the novel situation. The teacher now has an entrée to the topic of complex combination circuit problems. A teacher who comprehends and analyzes subject matter is at a distinct advantage in designing such assignments.

The "what" of homework is crucial; the "how" is equally important. When possible, let students begin work on exercises in class, and *don't* call it *homework!* The alert student often has his or her own definition of homework, and will tell you that it is to be done at home. There are a variety of reasons for allowing students to start such work in class. One of these has to do with feedback. By now you probably have some idea what that is. Think of some other advantages of an early start.

"How" also refers to the post-mortem procedure (the day after). Will you collect the homework every day in every class? Why? When? Will you take class time to check on the results of the class work? How? When? The answers depend to an extent on your need to get and give immediate feedback to the class. There are some specific post-mortem procedures suggested in Chapter 2, but two rules of thumb are basic. First, don't do the homework for the students. Second, don't ignore the homework. If it can be ignored, it wasn't worth doing.

You've heard the expression "Different strokes for different folks." Can you think of any implications of this saying for use of the homework mode? If not, you are typical of most people with long careers as students who have seldom, if ever, experienced differentiated assignments. Do those students who whiz through five typical application problems at the end of today's lesson need to do more of the same for homework? Then, too, consider that small group of students who could solve none of the problems by the end of the lesson. Diverse feedback of this kind is a clue that different homework assignments need to be designed and matched to various student needs. Think of other situations where it makes maximum instructional sense to ask that different students pursue varied tasks as homework.

As is the case with all instructional modes, effective and efficient use of homework requires careful consideration of alternatives and thoughtful planning by the teacher. *Effective* and *efficient* are key ideas you will find emphasized throughout this text. One of the greatest rewards of teaching is evidence of student learning as a result of teacher attention to these ideas.

1.4 SUMMARY AND SELF-CHECK

Where have we been and where are we going? We began with the consideration of a model of instruction and devoted our initial attention to that part to which novices typically bring the greatest range of personal experience. We asked you to reflect on the component labeled "Instructional Strategies" and to begin identifying the ways teachers promote student learning—modes. These are important parts but *only parts* of what is meant by the term *strategy* (overall plans targeting on the achievement of an objective). Nine typical modes were identified and defined operationally. Common uses and abuses of each were explained, and you were introduced to the feedback-getting and -giving potential of each of these modes. More questions were raised than were fully answered; and that was by design rather than by accident. Some of the answers depend on the exploration of other components of the model in later chapters.

Right now, however, you should be able to:

1. Name and operationally define nine common instructional modes.

2. Identify modes being employed during either a "live" or recorded lesson.

3. List at least two uses and two abuses of each mode and provide reasoned justification for your choices.

The exercises in the next section are designed to test your understanding of some of these modes as they relate to your role as a teacher of science. Your understanding of the content of your subject matter discipline will be put to the test, as well as your ability to move from the role of a student to that of a teacher. These situations are based on actual classroom happenings, and the content analysis exercises have been used by classroom teachers to improve instruction. Give all of them your best efforts. Then go back and check your responses against your experience and your learning as you progress through other sections of the text.

1.5 SIMULATION/PRACTICE ACTIVITIES

A. Each of the following questions is defective in its potential for eliciting unambiguous evidence of student learning. Identify the defect and construct a more effective question.

1. How about flowering plants?

2. Is a rock the same thing as a mineral?

3. Can you write the equation for the electrolysis of water?

4. Does everybody understand Newton's three laws of motion?

5. "Where do you want me to put the decimal point?" (Hint: While we were observing a class, a student teacher asked this question. A response by students, inaudible to the student teacher, was rather specific in terms of an anatomical reference.)

B. As soon as the teacher started a demonstration, several students began to stretch to the right and the left in their seats; three students in the last row stood up. This teacher probably ignored the need to have demonstrations visible to the class. Suggest two or three ways of overcoming this problem if the physical object is small or cannot be moved.

C. Select one of the following topics: chemical change, eclipse, magnetic force, plant. Describe a demonstration that would help teach the central idea. Be specific about the material(s) you would use, how you would manipulate them, and other modes you would use in connection with the demonstration. Limit this teaching segment to a five- to ten-minute portion of the class period.

D. During successive periods you observed the same laboratory taught to comparable groups by two different teachers. Teacher A's class paired off quietly, got their materials quickly, returned to their desks, and immediately began to work along the lines directed by the teacher. In Teacher B's class, students jammed up at the front of the room and began jostling and making extraneous noise. The students returned to their desks with needed materials only after a period of several minutes, during which there were frequent loud reprimands by the teacher. Next there was a rapid series of requests for the teacher's help from various parts of the room and sporadic verbal commands by the teacher to "follow directions," "get to work," "stop wasting time."

List at least three variables in teacher behavior that could account for the differences in the students' performance in the classes. Defend your selections.

E. Choose any topic in your principal field (such as biology, physics, chemistry, or earth science) and design a homework assignment to serve two purposes: (1) It should provide relevant practice of some skill. Identify the skill. (2) It should be structured to allow you to elicit a subsequent idea or skill.

Provide answers to the exercises, and write a brief justification of the ways in which your assignment meets both of the above purposes.

SUGGESTIONS FOR FURTHER STUDY

Carin, A., & Sund, R. (1971). *Developing questioning techniques: A concept approach.* Columbus, Ohio: Charles E. Merrill.

The aim of this book is to help classroom teachers select and use questioning techniques not only to promote cognitive development, but also as a way of building student self-esteem. This goal is realized to a high degree. The taxonomies of the cognitive and affective domains (Bloom and Krathwohl) are used throughout, and numerous examples are provided to illustrate the ideas presented. The relevance of the work of well-known cognitive psychologists (Bruner, Gagné and Piaget) is shown and Budd-Rowe's research on the effects of "wait-time" is used effectively. The chapters on creativity and the construction of guided discovery lessons are highlights of this book.

Harper, D. O., & Stewart, J. H. (Eds.). (1986). *Run: Computer education* (2nd ed.). Monterey, CA.: Brooks/Cole.

This collection of short essays contains a wealth of practical information, as well as presentations of issues related to computer education. We recommend the selection by Andrew Yeaman, "Put Your Computers in the Most Efficient Environment" (pp. 130–131), for hints on the ergonomic arrangement of computer furniture and computers, with attention to alleviating fatigue, eye strain and stress. Equity issues related to computer-access are also affected by arrangement and location of computers, as well as by scheduling of computer time. See Marlaine Lockheed and Steven Frakt's article, " Sex Equity: Increasing Girls' Use of Computers" (pp. 237–240), for valuable information on this issue and ways the teacher can help to provide equal access to boys and girls.

Hunkins, F. P. (1972). *Questioning strategies and techniques.* Boston, MA: Allyn and Bacon.

This very useful paperback assumes no previous knowledge of techniques and attempts to deal with all aspects of the subject in a clear but concise way. For the most part, the author has accomplished these goals quite well. The entire presentation is made within the frame of reference of curriculum study groups in science. Sufficient examples are included to illustrate the major points, and frequent ties are made to Bloom's Taxonomy. Novice teachers would do well to skip over the detailed treatment of various categorizing schemes (such as those of Taba, Suchman, and Hunkins) and to concentrate their attention on the other parts of the book.

CHAPTER TWO

FEEDBACK

The Heart of Instruction

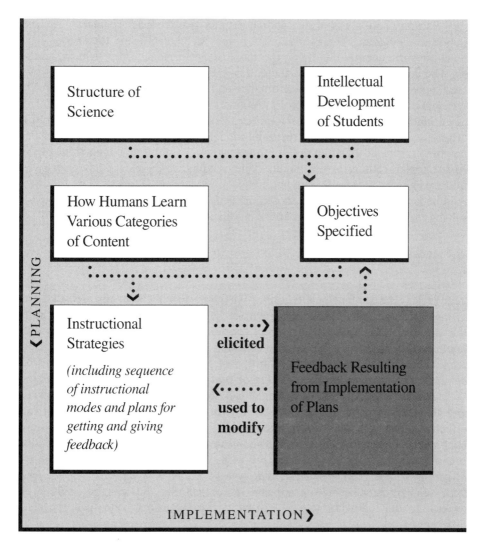

Many teachers assess their effectiveness in the classroom in terms of student reaction. Some teachers do this sporadically; some, naively; a few, regularly and systematically. Yet this kind of assessment, the *getting of feedback*, is the basis of all learning theories and the core of all attempts to communicate with others.

Some college instructors are notorious ignorers of feedback procedures, according to students who sit through lectures where no questions are asked or answered and no recognition of student attention or confusion occurs. In these cases, students learn to psyche out the instructor on the basis of feedback unknowingly given them. In contrast, when instructors consciously and systematically provide feedback, students learn whether their performance is correct, nearly correct, or totally incorrect both from the feedback provided by the instructor and from the built-in feedback components of the content.

In nonschool areas of life, people get and give feedback regularly. The mechanic who diagnoses a car's malfunction does so by testing and then observing a reaction, subsequently modifying the test and performance on that basis, and so on. The doctor, the lawyer, and the golfer—all with varying degrees of success—use feedback to modify their performance so that they may reach some goal. The systematic approach exemplified by computer work and characteristic of analysis of all kinds of complex systems requires the feedback loop. Notice the position of the feedback box in the instructional model on the chapter opening page. Follow the arrowheads, and analyze the reasons for the multiple connections of this component to others in the model. Your reading in Chapter 1 has already introduced you to the connecting link between modes and feedback. The following reading and activities spell out those connections and engage you in the problem-solving task of interpreting and analyzing feedback.

2.1 DEFINITIONS

Feedback   The student gets feedback when the teacher says "incorrect" in response to a student's answer; the teacher gets feedback when he or she notes that a student has written the correct solution to a problem posed by the textbook; a student gets feedback while checking the results of a solution to a problem. Therefore, an operational definition of *feedback* is *any information, verbal or nonverbal, communicated to teacher or student, on the results of instruction.*

Notice that the definition of feedback makes it clear that both the teacher and the student need to *get* feedback if instruction is to be both efficient and effective. From the teacher's point of view, plans must be made to *get* feedback and to *give* feedback. Now you've guessed it; we've spiraled back to modes. *When the teacher uses a sequence of two or more modes with the planned intention of getting and/or giving feedback, that type of sequence is referred to as a feedback strategy.* Feedback often appears in subtle forms and can be easily overlooked. In the following activity you will be introduced to one such aspect of feedback.

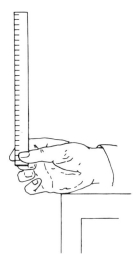

Fig. 2.1

Results for P₁

Trial #	1	2	3	4	5	6	7	8	9	10
Ruler mark										

Fig. 2.2

2.2 INTRODUCTORY ACTIVITY

A two-person team is needed for this activity. One person, P_1, rests one arm on a table so that the heel of the hand is on the edge of the table. P_1 should turn that hand sideways and prepare to catch an object between the thumb and the index finger. The other partner, P_2, holds the object, a 30-cm ruler, at the 30-cm mark between the thumb and index finger of one hand. P_2 then positions the ruler so that it is almost entirely above P_1's hand— actually with the 1-cm mark at the level of P_1's thumb (see Figure 2.1). When P_2 drops the ruler, P_1 tries to catch it. The measurement at which P_1 caught it is recorded.

A. Repeat the procedure ten times, and record P_1's results in a table such as the one shown in Figure 2.2.

B. Switch roles and record P_2's results in a similar table.

C. Identify the various kinds of feedback that were observed throughout the entire activity. Describe the changing nature of the feedback. Who got feedback? Who (what) gave feedback? Account for any improved performance on the basis of feedback received by the "catcher." What other variables may have interfered with an improvement in performance?

Activities such as the ruler activity are specifically designed to teach students the nature of feedback in tasks involving motor reflexes, such as braking a car suddenly. The popular computer video games, such as the PACMAN series, are certainly teaching players about the use of feedback and its relation to hand-eye coordination, as well as about certain types of problem-solving strategies.

2.3 FEEDBACK: GETTING, USING, AND GIVING

Assumptions

The major assumption that forms the theme of this chapter is that feedback is a key part of all instruction. The byproducts of this general assumption are four specific assumptions:

1. Feedback should be given to, and elicited from, the widest possible sampling of students.
2. Feedback strategies should be implemented frequently and at key points during *each* instructional period.
3. Feedback should be interpreted and used to pace instruction and/or to alter the sequence of instruction.
4. Feedback should also be used to assess the feasibility of the stated objectives.

Getting Feedback

Throughout the previous chapter, you were urged to consider each mode's feedback potential. Check your understanding of this against Figure 2.3. If you do not agree, it may be due to the fact that you are thinking about various forms of nonverbal feedback while we are considering only verbal feedback at the moment. On the other hand, disagreement might indicate a need to review operational definitions of the various instructional modes. In any case, try to resolve this matter in your mind before reading any further.

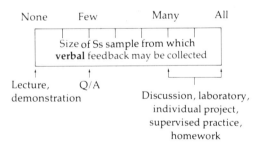

Fig. 2.3 Verbal feedback potential for various instructional modes.

Since each mode does have unique purposes in instruction, modes with zero verbal feedback-getting potential need to be followed by and interspersed with positively valued feedback strategies in order to assess the effects of instruction and modify it when necessary. For example, a short lecture can be followed by questions specifically designed to assess the listener's grasp of the lecture. Questions can range all the way from the "What did I say" type to the more meaningful "How" or "Why" types. At all costs the lecturer should avoid the "Any questions" habit unless the typical silence from the class response is quickly followed by a specific question from the teacher. Most students have learned to shrug off "Any questions?" as merely rhetorical. Further, sometimes the student who is confused and knows that the teacher is willing to field questions just can't phrase a sensible question and doesn't want to admit it! Such a student profits from class reactions to thoughtful teacher-constructed questions on the content of the lecture. The teacher might ask students to write the answers to appropriate questions then and there. Feedback from many students can then be obtained as the teacher quickly tours the room. Such a procedure might be followed by a *straw vote* (poll).

The straw vote is one of the most useful techniques for efficiently obtaining feedback. The teacher asks to see the hands of those who agree, who disagree, who aren't sure (or any analogous classification). The procedure takes less than a minute and provides information to the teacher on the diversity of class views. However, the teacher who immediately begins to reteach the topic or to quickly move on to the next topic on the sole basis of a straw vote may be in for a shock. Why? Suppose that one-third of the class disagreed with the expected answer, but that all of these students had simply misinterpreted one minor aspect of the question!

You can probably imagine many other possible reasons for diverse feedback. Therefore, straw votes should frequently be followed by a more sophisticated kind of feedback strategy—for example, a series of questions to members of each faction probing the reason(s) behind their response, or a quick tour around the room sampling papers of members of each group, or a student demonstration in defense of a response. The alternatives are many, but the teacher must plan these alternatives based on the likely stumbling blocks in the lesson and the teacher's knowledge of the needed prerequisites for subsequent phases of the lesson.

All of the preceding suggestions could be adapted easily for use during or after the other modes that have little or no feedback potential. It is particularly important to intersperse higher-rated modes to get feedback *after* a sequence of developmental questions has been used. There is a serious caution to be observed here. Suppose your class was being led through a careful sequence of developmental questions that was interspersed with straw votes at every third question. You've got it! Many students would stop voting and would probably stop thinking—about the lesson. Developmental questions must flow as smoothly as possible with members of the class learning from one another's answers as well as from the teacher's cues. With the modes rated high in feedback potential, the teacher can get a broad sampling of specific feedback if the modes are being used in appropriate ways.

Two of these higher-rated modes, laboratory and supervised practice, are critical in feedback getting. However, most novices and some experienced teachers frequently overlook the enormous potential these modes possess for improving instruction. The two illustrations that follow include elements of feedback getting, using, and giving.

Supervised practice sample

T has just completed a lecture and Q/A sequence on drawing atomic diagrams of elements #1 through #20 with the table given. A straw vote on a single practice example showed most Ss with the correct answer. Therefore, T directs the Ss to begin working on examples 4, 8, 9, 15 and 24. Before T moves from the front, T checks to make sure that all Ss have started, reminds two Ss of the location of the table in the text, and tells a S whose hand is raised for help to reread notes until T has had a chance to check on others' progress. All others are now at work. T tours the room (as suggested in Chapter 1) and sees that only a few Ss are having difficulty with examples 4 and 8. T praises individual Ss quietly, indicates in a clear voice that many Ss are making good progress, quietly gives a cue to one S in difficulty, then moves to a second S and notices that some Ss have almost finished all five examples. T sends selected Ss to the board, asks one S to serve as tutor for any S needing help, assists another S, and checks progress of class. (T has to decide if enough Ss are far enough along to stop the practice and look at the models of correct performance on the board. T must also decide if progress was sporadic or substantial. Do the Ss need additional practice on the same kind of examples or on a more complex set, or should T move into another mode to introduce a new rule?) T calls the class to attention, tells them to compare their work with the board work and to be prepared to identify areas of difficulty. T stands in the rear quietly while this occurs and then takes straw votes on the number of Ss who agree or disagree with board work and seeks corrections where needed. Ss are frequently asked to respond to Q from other Ss.

Notice that the teacher refused to immediately move to the first student who raised a hand. Why? Suppose the quick tour had uncovered a far different story? If most students were blithely working away on the basis of a misconception, the delay caused by the teacher's conversation with an individual could lead to, at least, wasted time and, at worst, chaos. The same kind of rationale can be advanced for not interrupting the tour. (Remember the question asked of you in Chapter 1?) This teacher was also alert to differential progress and tried to use positive feedback in more than one way. Students were used as individual tutors and were asked to display their work on the board so that all other students could get feedback on the nature of the completed work. The other instances of feedback getting and giving in this sample are numerous. After you read the next section on feedback giving, check this illustration again for specific examples.

Laboratory sample

T begins with a ten-minute lecture with demo related to finding the ideal mechanical advantage (IMA) of simple machines. A three-minute Q/A session, in which T sampled eight students, provided positive feedback on Ss understanding of (1) techniques of measuring effort and resistance distances of the types of machines to be used, (2) the location of supplies and equipment, (3) the methods of recording data and calculating results, (4) safety precautions, and (5) the roles of each lab partner.

T then gives the signal to begin work and takes a position in the room from which the Ss collection of materials and equipment can be observed. All Ss gather materials quickly and quietly, then return to their assigned laboratory places. At this point, T begins to move quickly and systematically from group to group. T notes that the first four groups visited are proceeding exactly as directed but just as T reached the fifth group, loud voices were heard coming from the opposite corner of the room.

T moves quickly to the loud group, touches one S on the shoulder, and uses the finger-across-the-lips signal when the S looks up. Both partners quiet immediately and T asks if they are having a problem with the exercise. Both partners start to talk at once, each complaining that the other is measuring the effort distance of the egg beater incorrectly. "Herman is measuring the distance between the beaters," complains Yvonne. T holds up one hand in a "stop" gesture; the Ss quiet down; and T uses Q/A with each in turn to clarify the procedure. The partners return to work; T observes they are now working amiably, and T moves on to other groups that are all proceeding in an orderly fashion.

As T continues to move from group to group, observations indicate that all Ss are now measuring the IMA correctly in the case of the egg beater, pliers, pulley, and can opener. However, the first three groups to progress as far as the screwdriver require T's assistance on what to measure. T turns off the lights for three seconds. All the Ss quickly stop whatever they're doing and look at T, who then turns the lights back on and gives a lecture-demo on this particular technique. All groups then return to work at T's signal, and T's subsequent observations while touring groups indicate all are now measuring correctly.

With about five minutes of work time left in the class period, T overheard the following conversation among one pair of partners:

Saul: *"We calculated the IMA of the screwdriver as 4.3 and that of the screw as 8. If we used them both together, we would have a combined IMA of 34.4."*

Alice: *"No, we wouldn't! We would just be adding the screwdriver to the screw so we would really be just adding the IMAs and that would be 12.3 total."*

Saul: *"Look, think of it this way. The screwdriver multiplies our effort by 4.3 and that feeds into the screw which multiplies that effort by 8."*

T praises Saul and Alice privately for thinking ahead and gives each credit for having a certain amount of logic. T then points out to them that science is often confronted with exactly this same type of situation where reasons can be cited to support two conflicting predictions. A short Q/A sequence by T gets Saul and Alice to recall that experimentation is the acid test of thinking in science. T asks both to think of how to design a simple test to reconcile the disagreement. Then T goes to the chalkboard, writes a brief statement of the problem posed by Saul and Alice, and for the evening's assignment asks each student to write a brief experimental design to be carried out in class the next day to resolve the issue. A brief flickering of the lights signals "clean-up," which progresses smoothly and quickly. T calls attention to the assignment, publicly gives credit to Saul and Alice for thinking ahead, and praises all for their very good work during the period. The bell rings, the Ss leave, and T checks to see that all is in readiness for the next class, which is to begin in four minutes.

Note the highly positive feedback the teacher received on the effectiveness of the introduction to this laboratory exercise. Identify all the things the teacher did to ensure that all students would begin the laboratory work effectively and efficiently. Also note how the teacher found out that only one group was encountering difficulty with the egg beater and how this problem was handled without interrupting the other students who were proceeding without problems. Nonverbal feedback giving, as well as feedback getting, is highly effective for all who learn how to use it.

Apparently the teacher was quick to read the negative feedback collected on the screwdriver and made use of it to reorient the entire class. If the teacher had failed to interpret this as a widespread problem, no doubt it would have been necessary to treat the same problem over and over in successive individual visits to nearly all the groups.

The student-to-student discussion between Alice and Saul not only provided the teacher with valuable feedback, but also presented a golden opportunity to reinforce prior learning on the nature of the scientific enterprise and to provide for an in-context extension of that learning by means of a creative homework assignment.

Most of us are quick to criticize and slow to praise. Note that the teacher in this instance did find numerous opportunities and ways to give well-deserved praise to individuals as well as to the entire class. In the long run, this approach yields big dividends for all and helps put in proper perspective those occasions when a teacher must offer constructive criticism as part of instruction. It will be well worth the effort to reread the entire description of this laboratory class and recount the occasions and techniques of praise-giving that occurred.

In addition to the specific modes referred to in this section thus far, there are two other common instructional situations that are frequently mismanaged because the teacher ignores available feedback. The two situations are labeled homework post-mortem (HWPM) and test or quiz post-mortem (T/QPM). In the former case, post-mortem refers to what the teacher plans to do about yesterday's homework. In the latter case, post-mortem refers to the return of a test or quiz and the teacher's plans for "going over it." Unfortunately, "going over it" is literally what happens in many classrooms. In the case of a test or quiz that has been corrected and analyzed, there is no excuse for boring the class by requiring everyone to sit through a rehash of each answer regardless of class performance. The teacher already has specific feedback from every student. Feedback so general that the teacher is still not sure where the students' learning problems are signifies a defect in test construction (more on that in Chapter 8).

Homework post-mortems are a somewhat different kind of beast. The teacher who let the students start the homework in yesterday's class may have some feedback on the initial success of the students, but many teachers are misled by this and assume far too much. At other times, teachers can receive useful feedback from students who come in for extra help after class. But once again, it would be a mistake not to check out the generalizability of the data before acting on it. So Mary, Jim, and Abby had trouble with example 5! So what?! Why should the teacher assume that the other 23 students need to sit through a lecture on the ins and outs of this question? What can you do to avoid these pitfalls and others like these?

Several illustrations of feedback strategies used in both homework post-mortem and test or quiz post-mortem are detailed next. Identify the ways in which the teacher gets, gives, and uses feedback not only at the start of the post-mortem, but during it.

Homework post-mortem   If a teacher wishes to ascertain the extent of student mastery of homework tasks, both of the following illustrations have proved useful.

1. In a class of 24, T sends 6 Ss to the board (at or prior to the opening bell) to put answers to 6 questions on the board *without* taking homework papers with them. T instructs Ss at seats to check their solutions against work as it is being put on board. T then tells the seated Ss that they will be required to talk through one of the examples, agree and tell why, correct errors and give reasons, or explain alternative correct solutions as soon as Ss at the

board finish. Meanwhile, T walks around, makes a quick check of homework papers, identifies (a) those papers that are complete, (b) those on which various problems have been left out, and (c) types of errors made. Then T sends 6 *other* Ss to the board to critique the earlier work. Next, a third set of 6 students may be used to settle disagreements among the previous 2 Ss who worked at a problem.

or

2. T distributes copies with answers, or solutions and answers (overhead may be substituted for individual copies) *as Ss enter* the room. Ss are directed to check their work against the standard displayed by the copy or on the overhead while T walks around to check as in example 1 above. Then T selects Ss to explain typical errors T has detected from papers.

If the teacher is satisfied that most students have achieved mastery of the task but wishes to provide feedback in an efficient way on details of the procedure, the teacher may:

1. Check papers as Ss walk in, identify correct answers, and instruct Ss with correct models to put work on board. Then, direct Ss to stay there to explain and to answer questions from other Ss.

or

2. Give selected Ss acetate sheets to take home. Then tell them to do the assigned problem on acetate for projection the next day. Also, inform them that they will be expected to explain and answer the questions of other Ss.

Test or quiz post-mortem   After a full-period test has been given and graded, the teacher does an item analysis (see Chapter 8) *prior* to handing back papers and uses the results to:

1. Identify those problems that will be treated in class. Procedures similar to those detailed in the section on homework post-mortem might be followed.

or

2. Make an instructional decision to completely reteach selected parts of the content.

or

3. Divide class into groups of five Ss whose grades were distributed over the range. Instruct Ss to work cooperatively until all students in the group can do each problem. Walk around and act as a resource person.

After giving a short quiz and collecting papers, the teacher may display answers on overhead immediately if major disagreement is not expected; materials tested are prerequisite to next topic; and/or little time remains in the instructional period.

Perhaps at no other time in the classroom is the teacher's identification of positive and negative feedback and use of both so crucial to attention keeping and to promoting time-on-task. In the interest of calling on everyone, teachers sometimes ask students to read answers to homework or test questions. If this can be done quickly and efficiently, the practice has some merit. But read the conversational sequence that follows.

T: "Question 5. Rachel."
Rachel: "I didn't get it."
T: "Why?"
Rachel: "I just didn't try."
T: "Jack? 5?"
Jack: "3057?"
T: "Is that what all of you got?"
Ss (mixed chorus of shouts): "No," "Yes," "I don't know," "Who cares?"

Variations of the above conversation have occurred with disturbing frequency in some of the classes we've observed. However, effective teachers try to avoid this kind of time wasting. They provide the feedback needed by the students who tried to do the homework in one or more of the following ways:

1. T reads all answers and tells Ss to record them and check their responses.

2. T projects a prepared acetate with answers and proceeds as in 1 above.

3. T has answers posted on the bulletin board for Ss to check during supervised practice time.

As soon as the class has seen or heard the correct answers, it then makes sense for the teacher to take a straw vote on the total number of correct answers or on examples most often missed. Here you must be alert to both positive and negative feedback.

When should the class wait for one or two students to be helped? If all but three students got examples 5 and 7 correct, how can the teacher differentiate subsequent instruction? If many students missed all of the examples, what factors might cause the teacher to decide to reconsider only one example? These questions and others like these are representative of the need for intelligent decisions by the teacher during ongoing instruction.

Take another look at the instructional model that appears at the beginning of this and every other chapter. Notice the arrows leading *from* the Instructional Strategies box *to* the Feedback box. As a result of planned feedback strategies, the teacher gets feedback on the effectiveness of the instruction thus far. Now the teacher must use that feedback and may need to alter the planned instructional strategies—the arrows leading *to* the Instructional Strategies box *from* the Feedback box. The loop continues as long as instruction continues and will be used effectively to the extent that the teacher gets feedback, can interpret feedback, and can draw on background knowledge to generate immediate modifications of planned strategies.

These are some aspects of feedback use that depend on an analysis of the subject being taught, or the intended objectives, or the intent of the planned strategies. You should be prepared to make more sophisticated decisions on these aspects after working through Chapters 4, 5, 6, and 7. However, even at this point in the text, you have read enough about modes and feedback to make some tentative hypotheses about next steps. See if your conjectures are included in the next section.

Using Feedback

Sometimes the best immediate use of feedback is to get more feedback. More feedback may imply a larger or broader sampling of students, or it may refer to the nature of the responses and the need to obtain more specific or more extensive responses. More extensive feedback getting is essential if instructional strategies are to be implemented.

Some of the more common uses of feedback are listed below.

1. After obtaining feedback on the number of students who possess the prerequisite learning for the next topic, T may:

    a) Reteach the prerequisite material if all or most Ss have given negative feedback to T. If T has received positive feedback from a few Ss, they may be encouraged to help T in the instruction by demonstrating, justifying correct answers, analyzing the reasons behind the misconceptions. In any case, T should reteach the topic in some novel way. The original set of strategies obviously failed!

    b) Ask Ss to try a practice example (while T makes a quick tour of the room) if there seems to be ambiguous feedback.

    c) Use appropriate recall Q/A and lecture to weave specific instances of the prerequisites into the ongoing lesson if only a few Ss give negative feedback on the prerequisites. Tell the Ss that you will be doing this, and reinforce the "old" when it occurs.

2. When beginning HWPM, T displays or reads the answers and then gets feedback (in one of the ways suggested earlier) on the extent of the students' problems with homework.

    a) If only a few Ss give T negative feedback, T may:

        (1) Use Q/A with members of the rest of the class assisting *if* the analysis can be accomplished in a short period of time and *if* it can be made meaningful to the rest of the class.

        (2) Work with the small group of Ss while putting the large group to work on other materials.

        (3) Tell the small group of Ss that they will be helped later in the class when supervised practice occurs, or after class in a remedial period.

    b) If a diverse number of examples were missed by varying numbers of Ss, T may:

(1) Tell Ss only example 5 will be treated at this time, since all other examples are simply variations of example 5. T can then follow the reconsideration of example 5 by supervised practice of one or more of the other examples.

(2) Group Ss by cluster of examples missed *if* there are some Ss who got most or all of the examples correct. These latter Ss will serve as teachers of the small groups.

(3) Reteach the basic idea underlying the homework *if* the nature of the feedback suggests serious learning problems. T may use one of the homework examples in this set of teaching strategies and should include a supervised practice session on one or more of the remaining examples.

(4) Tell Ss to hand in the papers so that T can locate the sources of the errors *if* T has noticed that diverse, careless errors seem to be common. T should return the papers the next day and may add some general oral comments to the individual written comments.

Many of the suggestions given on the preceding pages could be used in other instructional situations—after a sequence of developmental questions, during a lab, or during the use of an ATA, for example. Notice the recurrence of "ifs" in almost every statement. There is no recipe for perfect teaching. In each case you must consider the consequences of your actions and make those moves that seem most promising in relation to your objectives.

One of the important characteristics of any of the preceding suggestions is letting the students know what to expect. Suggestion 2a(3) spells this out, but you should add similar notes to each of the suggestions. Students can get the impression that their successes and failures are being ignored or dismissed as unimportant if you don't *give* explicit feedback on your expectations. You should have noticed many examples of feedback giving in earlier sections. In the following paragraphs, specific attention is paid to this important topic.

Giving Feedback

If the reading thus far has seemed to de-emphasize nonverbal feedback, you might ask yourself why. Are there modes where nonverbal feedback may be especially misleading and others where it provides information not otherwise available to the teacher? Check out your ideas on this with classmates, then reread the introductory section of this chapter and the sample practice and lab situations in Section 2.3.

However, if nonverbal feedback is sometimes misleading when the teacher gets it and tries to interpret it, it is often doubly misleading when the teacher *unconsciously* gives such feedback. For this reason, it is often asserted that we teach students many things in addition to those we intend. Teachers give students feedback on the importance they attach to a topic by verbal emphasis, projected seriousness of purpose, and time spent in instruction or in correcting students' misconceptions. Teachers convey to students that they are progressing toward the intended objectives by smiling, giving a "thumbs up" signal, or patting a student on the back during supervised practice. It is important that the nonverbal feedback given by teachers parallels the verbal feedback. How would you feel if an employer verbally praised your work but *looked* disgusted at the same time? Imagine the confusion of a toddler who has just said a four-letter word and been scolded verbally by chuckling parents. No wonder the tot repeats the word for more laughs!

Feedback giving needs to be incorporated in all instructional strategies. If we follow the events of instruction in a typical lesson, we can pinpoint places where the teacher must *plan* to give feedback.

The events of instruction* and feedback giving

1. *Gaining and controlling attention.* T gives Ss feedback on what to observe, its relevance to past work, and so on.

2. *Informing the student of expected outcomes.* T tells Ss whether they will be expected to reproduce a derivation, apply a rule to typical problems, or write down observations made during a film.

3. *Stimulating recall of prerequisites.* T may tell Ss the relevant aspects of prerequisites needed today.

4. *Presenting the new material.*

5. *Guiding the new material.*

6. *Providing feedback.* T praises correct responses, modifies partially correct ones, and clarifies in case of errors. T has Ss copy a sample problem with its solution.

7. *Appraising performance.* As the Ss check out their learning in supervised practice, Q/A, or discussion, T gives feedback as in event 6.

Two categories of feedback giving that are especially important are: (1) providing a model of correct performance and (2) praise. As noted in the events of instruction, one time when the teacher must provide a model of correct performance is in the teaching of type problems (see event 6). The teacher does this when he or she puts type problems on the board (overhead), shows correct procedure step-by-step *after* appropriate rule teaching has occurred, and emphasizes format or labeling that is acceptable. Now the students have a model against which they can compare their efforts on similar-problems. The teacher should give praise to individual students for correct alternative solutions, for fast as well as correct work, for good questions about the procedures, or for improvement toward a solution even if the solution has not yet been obtained. Some teachers have learned to effectively use nonverbal as well as verbal signals to give feedback

---

*The "events of instruction" used here are an adaptation of Gagné's (1970, p. 304) description of the events of instruction.

to students on their efforts. Feedback often needs to be provided by immediate reinforcement for correct verbal and nonverbal responses from an individual student, from small groups of students, or from the entire class. This kind of positive feedback (or praise) should occur during supervised practice, when Ss ask good questions, for S responses that show connections, after quizzes or tests, and during homework review.

There are also times when the teacher must give feedback in response to an incorrect answer. A mistaken interpretation of discovery teaching leaves some teachers with the impression that they should never give students this kind of information. As a result, students try to guess what is in the instructor's mind. Experienced teachers learn to give this kind of feedback by means of contingency questions or by using analogy, a physical model, or a numerical illustration. In these ways students "read" the indirect feedback and conclude for themselves that their original response was in error.

A similar kind of feedback is inherent in a design or puzzle based on the coding of the correct answers to a set of exercises. The students note the existence of an error when the design is lopsided and most, if not all, students will then attempt to eliminate the error. Such built-in feedback systems are a tremendous aid to both the teacher and the student. Connect-the-dot pictures, used in children's coloring books, have often been adapted for this kind of science practice. If your students have access to microcomputers, they will surely be interacting with computer programs designed to give feedback on correct and incorrect results, to praise efforts and even to provide cues or remediation in the case of errors. Thus, computers, as well as interactive videodiscs, can be powerful aids to the teacher in giving immediate feedback to individual students. The teacher should be on the alert for courseware that also collects feedback for later analysis—perhaps in the form of the amount of time that particular students worked at problems, or in the form of a record of all strategies used by each student. You will find some sources of all of these built-in feedback systems in Chapter 11, and many more in the experienced teacher's files. Finally, teachers provide feedback on written work by writing comments on test papers, homework papers, projects, and so on.

From our point of view, it would be hard to overemphasize the importance of feedback. We're willing to bet that you, as we, have sat in classes where the ineffective and the inefficient use of feedback was a central problem. Without the collection, interpretation, and use of feedback, the assessment of classroom activities must fall back on unreliable factors such as the desires of a supervisor, the gut feelings of the teacher next door, or the words of wisdom of some quasi-expert enshrined in a textbook.

2.4 SUMMARY AND SELF-CHECK

In the present chapter, we elaborated on the concept of feedback and considered specific strategies for getting, using, and giving both verbal and nonverbal feedback. Several illustrations of instructional situations were described and analyzed in detail to focus attention on the crucial importance of feedback. A host of specific recommendations for getting, using, and giving feedback were incorporated throughout. Novices would be well advised to heed these carefully, since many of our former students have confided that they reread this material several times with increasing profit as they progressed through student teaching and even after they had taught for one or more years. We consider this to be excellent evidence that feedback is indeed the heart of instruction.

Right now you should be able to:

1. Operationally define feedback, feedback getting, feedback using, and feedback giving and describe several classroom illustrations of each.

2. Identify instances of effective versus ineffective feedback getting, using, and giving occurring during either a "live" or taped lesson and state reasons for your judgments.

3. Design effective feedback strategies that can be incorporated into actual lessons that you will present to students.

The exercises that follow are designed to test your comprehension of feedback as it relates to your role as a teacher of science. These situations are based on actual secondary school classroom situations typical of those we have regularly observed. Give them your best efforts. Then compare your proposed solutions with those of your colleagues, instructor, college supervisor of student teaching, cooperating public school teacher, and/or other experienced teachers. Discuss all differences in proposed solutions thoroughly, and reconsider and amend your responses where this seems appropriate. However, defend your ideas vigorously wherever evidence and reason support your views and resist the temptation to react only on the basis of gut feelings and established tradition.

2.5 SIMULATION/PRACTICE ACTIVITIES

A. T follows homework strategy of checking all papers at seats while Ss work on a review problem. T collects the following feedback:

1. Four Ss have perfect papers in every respect.

2. Six Ss either have no papers or papers with little work done on the assignment. (Two of these Ss rarely bother to do homework.)

3. Ten Ss have most of the assignment correct. There is no common pattern in types of errors made and no common pattern of missed problems.

   Design a promising strategy that makes use of the positive and negative feedback described.

B. T has just taught a rule and received some feedback that a variety of Ss could apply the formula in stereotype situations. Now T gives Ss three or four examples to do in an eight-minute supervised practice session. T begins the supervised practice in the fashion outlined in Chapter 1. When T collects initial feedback, T finds that 8 Ss can't even begin the work while the other 17 Ss seem to be progressing very well.

Design a promising strategy for using this positive and negative feedback.

C. T administered a ten-minute surprise quiz at the beginning of the period. T observed from the rear of the classroom and noticed that several Ss just sat and stared for the last three minutes while others seemed to finish during the last minute. T collected papers systematically. Some Ss complained that the quiz was too long. Some asked: "How much is this going to count?" and "Can I take a makeup?"

Interpret the feedback and outline the T's immediate strategy for handling the situation.

D. T planned to introduce a complex rule by a carefully designed sequence of developmental questions. Some Ss moved quickly from correct responses, to the early easy questions, to a correct generalization before T had asked all of the planned intermediate questions. T asked a sample of other Ss questions designed to diagnose whether they also accepted the generalization. This feedback and a straw vote gave T feedback that the class had moved faster than expected.

The next step in T's plan for the day called for several short practice sessions with problem sets of gradually increasing difficulty. Use the feedback described above as the basis for suggesting an appropriate change in the pacing of T's planned practice sessions.

SUGGESTIONS FOR FURTHER STUDY

Abbey, D. S. (1973). *Now see hear! Applying communications to teaching.* Toronto, Ontario: The Ontario Institute for Studies in Education.

This little paperback is filled with practical ways to improve feedback giving and getting. Abbey included sections on body language, listening skills, uses of media, and ways to provide positive reinforcement.

Gagné, R. M. (1975). *Essentials of learning for instruction.* Hinsdale, IL: Dryden Press.

This brief paperback incorporates a presentation of Gagné's views on the place and importance of feedback in human learning. His model of the act of learning phases depicts feedback (reinforcement) as the final phase in any act of learning, and the author explains its interrelationship with other components of the model. The need to involve a large sampling of students in both feedback getting and giving is stressed, and some specific techniques for achieving this end are included.

CHAPTER THREE

THE INTELLECTUAL DEVELOPMENT OF STUDENTS

Adolescent Reasoning Patterns

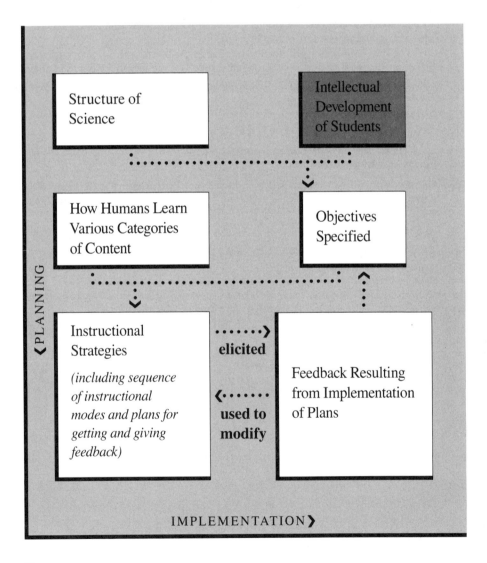

At the turn of the century, magazine pictures of children depicted them as them as shrunken adults. The pictures were a fairly accurate representation of the belief that children reason in the same way as adolescents and adults. Although some early psychologists, such as G. Stanley Hall (1883), were interested in the development of children, the emphasis was primarily on *quantitative* rather than *qualitative* differences in intellectual development. As a result of this view of mind, many teachers approached all age groups the same way—lecture and then set all students to work copying and practicing. Differentiate instruction between younger and older students by giving younger students smaller doses of ideas. Unfortunately, some teachers still behave this way. Even teachers of honors classes unwittingly imitate this teaching behavior when they equate *differentiation* of instruction with giving these more capable students "more of the same." If you had the latter experience, you know that this approach placed a new burden on the memory, but didn't help you understand.

How do secondary school students reason? What preconceptions do they bring to the classroom? When they think about science, what do they think it involves? The most promising source of help on all of these questions begins with the work of the Swiss genetic epistemologist, Jean Piaget. His massive collection of data puts to eternal rest the myth that children are intellectually shrunken adults. A four-year-old boy asks "Why do the clouds move?" or "Why is the grass green?" A tenth-grader cannot estimate the capacity of an irregular container. How is each of them thinking? What factors will alter the four-year-old's approach to his world? What obstacle is confusing the tenth-grader? Piaget directed our attention to the active nature of the human intellect. The key to both cognitive development and to apparent stumbling blocks in reasoning seems to be in the nature of the *interaction* between the individual and the environment.

Piaget's rejection of the mind as a blank paper on which the teacher writes was not new. Others writing about science education from Jackman in 1904 to Samples in 1932, as well as prominent educational philosophers, such as John Dewey, as early as his Pedagogic Creed of 1897, had argued that meaningful knowledge is *constructed* by the student. More recently, Sipe and Farmer (1982), in their review of science education research, found that interaction was fundamental in the teaching of problem solving or process skills in science, while White (1988) emphasized the need for teaching that focuses on the active nature of the learner of science. We're getting ahead of our story. What exactly did Piaget find out? How did he explain his findings? What additional analyses of adolescent reasoning have been completed by more recent researchers? What is the relevance of all of these findings to the teaching of science to middle and high school students? These are the questions we address in this chapter.

3.1 INTRODUCTORY ACTIVITY

I hear and I forget; I see and I remember;
I do and I understand.

A. Although this activity can be completed by one person, it will be more effective if it is completed by several students who can then discuss the analysis questions. It is appropriate for either novice or more experienced teachers of science.

B. Each person needs a piece of plain paper and a piece of cardboard the same size as the paper, a ruler, masking tape, a plane mirror in a wooden stand, and a large pin with a head (such as a dissecting pin). Draw a straight line across the middle of the paper and place a dot about 7 cm from one side of the line. Use the cardboard as a backing for the paper and tape the corners of the two layers of paper and cardboard to the top of the desk or table for stability. Stand the pin on the dot by inserting it through the paper and cardboard layers. Finally, stand the mirror's base on the straight line (the line will now be called the *mirror-line*), so that the pin is reflected in the mirror (Figure 3.1).

With your eye at the edge of the table and at the right side of the pin, sight along the ruler until you locate the pin's image in the mirror. Carefully draw that line of sight. Continue this process from both left and right sides of the pin and look for a pattern in the lines that you are drawing (Figure 3.2).

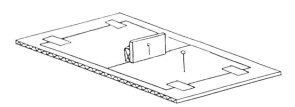

Fig. 3.1 Mirror set up.

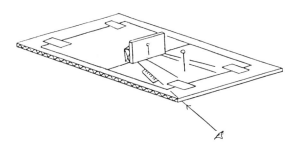

Fig. 3.2 Lines of sight.

C. Respond to the questions in this section individually and then talk about your answers with others doing the activity.

    1. As you located the pin's image in the mirror from different positions, what changes seemed to occur in the drawings of the lines of sight? Were you eventually able to predict the angle at which a line of sight would meet the mirror-line? If all the drawn lines of sight were extended beyond the mirror-line, how would they look? Check your idea by removing the mirror and extending the lines across the mirror-line. If you were working carefully, the lines will intersect in one point.

2. Reflect on your thinking as you drew two, three, four, ... lines. When did you connect (and possibly, use) the concepts of angle of incidence and angle of reflection with the activity? What is the significance of the point of intersection of the drawn lines of sight? How is it related to the pin and the various images of the pin in the mirror? If you haven't already done so, measure the distance from the point of intersection of the lines along any line to the mirror-line; then measure the distance from that point of the mirror-line to the pin. Repeat this for several drawn lines of sight.

    In what ways does this entire activity help make visual, various properties of a plane mirror? You've studied and used mirrors before. If this activity was a novel experience for you, in what way(s) did it clarify or strengthen your understanding of the principles of reflection of light rays in a plane mirror? (Refer to Chapter 10 for related examples on the paths of light rays.)

D. In this activity, you were constructing representations of rays of light that were being reflected from the pin to the mirror to your eye. If you were following the directions in B mechanically, you were only interacting with materials. If you were thinking about the emerging pattern, making tentative conjectures and testing them, you were mentally active and there was a dynamic interplay between your mind and the activity. Then, when you were asked to reflect on your earlier thoughts, you were mentally active at another level, one that researchers call the "metacognitive" level—thinking about your own thinking.

3.2 COGNITIVE DEVELOPMENT FROM A PIAGETIAN PERSPECTIVE

While doing some routine intelligence testing in Alfred Binet's laboratory school in Paris around 1920, Piaget became curious about the answers children gave—especially the wrong answers. This stimulated him to study cognitive development by systematically observing the responses of his own children to various real-world stimuli and to tasks that he contrived. As soon as the children were able to respond to questions, he used the semi-clinical interview method he had learned while serving a brief internship at Bleuler's psychiatric clinic in Zurich. He reported the results of his studies in books such as *The Origins of Intelligence in Children, The Reconstruction of Reality in the Child*, and *Play, Dreams and Imitation in Childhood*. The interviews were replicated with other children by collaborators of Piaget. Eventually he and his collaborators added tasks involving manipulation of physical materials or equipment to the semi-clinical interview in order to assess reasoning, not only by what the youngsters said, but also by observing what the youngsters did with the equipment. Piaget's written reports of the data collected in the interviews, the reasoning patterns revealed by the data and his analysis of patterns of cognitive development eventually resulted in over thirty books and hundreds of articles. During the 20 years between the two world wars, Piaget's colleagues, along with psychologists in France, Russia and

Great Britain, replicated and extended Piaget's research efforts with hundreds of people from birth to ages 16 or 17. After World War II, American psychologists became more aware of, and more interested in, Piaget's work. Behaviorists and, later, neo-behaviorists were critical of his qualitative methodology and skeptical about the generalizibility of his results. Logicians and some mathematics educators questioned the closeness of fit of the mathematical models he chose to explain his data. Over the decades, however, one major result was confirmed. When the Piagetian tasks were replicated faithfully, youngsters in diverse cultures and social strata responded with predictable reasoning patterns and provided justifications in almost the same words.

What patterns did Piaget claim existed? What qualitative differences did he find as children moved from primary to secondary school age? Inhelder and Piaget (1958) described responses to fifteen tasks that illustrated the changes in reasoning patterns for youngsters ranging in age from five years to seventeen years. An excellent illustration comes from a task that involves the law of floating bodies. Recall that concepts of volume (liquid and solid), weight, and specific gravity and density are involved. Students are given various objects to place in a container of water and asked to predict whether the objects will float or not, and why. After some preliminary tests, the youngest children incorrectly predict that a coin will float because it is "little" or that a wooden plank will sink because it is "heavy." Individual perceptual characteristics of the objects are cited as causal factors. The next stage in reasoning is shown by the more advanced youngsters who take into account the level of the water, the volume of the object, or even the weight of the object, all of which are quantifiable variables. Still this group of youngsters cannot solve the problem because they seem to be limited to reasoning about observables. Finally, the next stage of reasoning is characterized by responses in which the students hypothesize about a situation that is not directly observable, such as the comparison of the weight of the object with the weight of an equal volume of water. For although the entire volume of water in the container can be observed, the volume of water equal to that of the object in question has no observable shape. Thus it is necessary that an abstraction be conceptualized. This last illustration is an example of the kind of reasoning in the most sophisticated stage of reasoning, labeled the "formal" stage by Piaget. The label, "formal," suggests freedom from the constraints of the concrete world as well as the ability to reason about the form apart from the substance that the form might represent. It is the kind of reasoning we regularly need in many areas of science, such as probability theory, homeostasis, or particle theory.

Piaget and his colleagues devised and administered multiple tasks across domains such as space, movement and speed, and probability. The data they collected formed clusters of similar reasoning responses to these tasks; and their analysis of all of these clusters of responses resulted in a more general set of reasoning patterns. These more general reasoning patterns always appeared in an *invariant sequence* that Piaget conceptualized as consisting of four major stages. Because Piaget asserted that even our earliest abilities are not eradicated but serve as a basis for later abilities, teachers at all levels need to be aware of the major characteristics of all of the stages of cognitive development.

The Stages of Cognitive Development

The first stage (usually birth to about 2 years) is characterized by the gradual refinement of motor reflexes as the child begins to "know" the world by using the five senses. Infants touch, taste, smell, listen to, and look at everything within range. Piaget called this stage *sensori-motor*.

In the second stage, language development increases children's ability to represent things in a variety of ways. Pots and pans become cars and trucks and a child may become upset if one of his or her "cars" is put in the microwave. Labels, to this reasoner, are literally what they name. Perception develops further and notions of large, small, wide, hot, cold and so on are refined. However, it is perception that sometimes leads youngsters of this stage of cognitive development to make decisions that seem unreasonable to the adult. The response of six-year-old Mary to one of the Piagetian tasks graphically illustrates this dependence on perception. Mary was shown two jars of identical capacity and shape (Figure 3.3) and allowed to fill each with limeade. She agreed that both jars contained the same amount of limeade. However, when the limeade from container B was poured into container C—a taller, thinner jar with the same capacity as the other two jars—Mary no longer agreed that the amount of limeade remained the same (*i.e.* was *conserved*). Her justification was that jar C has more limeade because it's taller. (Another child distracted by a different perceptual change might have said jar C is thinner and, thus, holds less limeade.) Mary's inability to divorce her thinking from a perceptual change, to consider the two compensating perceptual changes simultaneously, or to mentally reverse the action of pouring limeade from one jar to another are all characteristics peculiar to this second stage, which Piaget called *pre-operational*. The label he chose comes from the meaning he gave to the term "operation"—an action that is mentally internalized, reversible and organized in a complex system.

The third and fourth stages are both characterized by operational thinking but are differentiated from one another by the nature of the reality about which youngsters are able to reason, as well as by the form of their reasoning. Piaget called the third stage *concrete operational*. By using the term "concrete" he emphasized these youngsters' dependence on reality concrete to themselves, for example, a familiar experience or a hands-on activity. In contrast, in the fourth stage, the formal operational stage, the more advanced reasoners are relatively free from the restrictions of their senses. These youngsters can imagine the possible as containing the real so hypotheses may be based on non-observed and non-experienced phenomena, as they were in the floating bodies task outlined earlier. For the formal students, the real is a subset of the possible.

Reasoning patterns of the concrete and formal stages   The major contrasting reasoning patterns of the concrete and formal stages are outlined in Table 3.1.

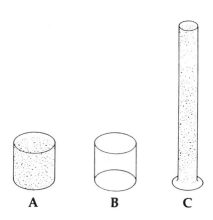

Fig. 3.3   Conservation of liquid capacity.

Table 3.1
Reasoning Patterns of Concrete and Formal Operational Students

Concrete	Formal
Needs reference to concrete experiences, familiar objects or events.	Also reasons with concepts and indirect relationships, assumptions and theories.
Is restricted to reasoning inductively (generalizes on the basis of data).	Also uses hypothetico-deductive reasoning.
Needs step-by-step instructions in a lengthy procedure.	Plans a lengthy procedure and tends to use systematic approaches in recording data and in deciding next steps.
Does not attempt to check conclusions; seems unaware of inconsistencies in own reasoning.	Reflects on own reasoning and tries to resolve inconsistencies; seeks necessary, as well as sufficient, conditions for a conclusion.

The reasoning patterns of the formal reasoner, listed in Table 3.1, correspond to the four characteristics of the formal operational stage: (1) the treatment of the real as a subset of the possible; (2) the ability to use hypothetico-deductive reasoning; (3) the ability to use combinatorial reasoning; and (4) second-level or propositional thinking (Inhelder & Piaget, 1958). The abilities of the concrete operational student include important building blocks for the subsequent stage. For example, the ability to generalize is a very powerful intellectual skill. However, if many adolescents are still limited to the reasoning patterns of the concrete operational stage (and we will see later that a substantial number do exhibit, at most, concrete reasoning skills), it is not surprising that many students find experiment-designing skills difficult to attain. These skills require the ability to think in the hypothetico-deductive mode—"*If* this solvent *were* similar to water, then ...." Students who are restricted to deductions based solely on experience ("If it rains tomorrow, then the ground will be wet.") are puzzled and frustrated by the kind of "If, then" reasoning required in designing an experiment. As you continue to study the relationships between cognitive development and prerequisite science reasoning skills, watch for instances of hypothetico-deductive reasoning, problems in which both a general and a necessary conclusion is required. Ask yourself why so many science students have difficulty understanding the difference between necessary conditions and sufficient conditions. Study the following statements.

1. A sufficient condition for matter to be homogeneous is that it is a compound.

2. A necessary condition for matter to be homogeneous is that it is a compound.

Which of these statements is true? Why? Teachers sometimes resort to Venn diagrams showing compounds as a subset of homogeneous materials to help students understand that statement 1 is true and statement 2 is false. Reflect on your own cognitive processing when you compared statements 1 and 2. Now consider the comparative difficulty of verifying a rule by finding one instance that works versus attempting to show that this rule is true for all instances. We think you'll agree that the reasoning involved in verifying for one case is much easier than that involved in deducing that the rule makes sense for all cases of the variables.

There are also specific reasoning patterns, intellectual skills or, more properly, schemata that develop in either the concrete or formal stage. Some of these are summarized in Table 3.2 along with descriptive comments about the nature of these schemata.

The single asterisk (*) in Table 3.2 indicates that there is a developmental lag between understanding conservation of area itself and understanding how area is measured. Why should there be a lag? Isn't this a fairly obvious formula? The science teacher expects that rectangular area will be taught in the mathematics class and that the formula will be ready for application in the science class. Let's reflect on a typical developmental approach to the teaching of the formula and see if that sheds any light on the conceptual difficulty. Area measure is often introduced by drawing a rectangular shape on a grid, counting the squares in the grid and calling that result the area. Then the students are shown that the total number of squares can also be obtained by multiplying the number of squares on the width by the number of squares on the length. All too often, the teacher immediately sets the students at work practicing examples where they are given lengths and widths of rectangles and asked to compute areas. What's wrong with this sequence of events? Here is a typical set of practice examples:

1. $l = 5$ cm and $w = 4$ cm   4. $l = 4.5$ cm and $w = 2.5$ cm

2. $l = 12$ cm and $w = 3$ cm   5. $l = 7/2$ cm and $w = 2$ cm

3. $l = 14$ cm and $w = 10$ cm

Notice that there are at least two conceptual leaps from the counting of squares lesson to these examples. One is the fact that the number of squares on

Table 3.2
Selected Schemata of the Concrete and Formal Stages

Concrete Stage	
Schemata	**Description**
Classification simple	Distinguishes between familiar objects (*e.g.* flowers and fruits).
Classification hierarchical	Applies class-inclusion concept when constructing classification trees (*e.g.* tree of homogeneous matter).
Seriation or Ordering simple	Arranges a collection of ordered objects (*e.g.* Solution A is more acidic than solution B and solution B is more acidic than solution C).
Seriation or Ordering complex	Solves ordered relationship problems in concrete way (*e.g.* Solves problems where the elements are asymmetrically related in more than one way (*e.g.* Jenny is taller and heavier than Philip and Melissa is shorter and lighter than Jenny. What can be said about Philip's height and weight in relation to Jenny's and Melissa's?).
Conservation of number, weight, length, mass, area*, volume**	Knows that measure (*e.g.* weight) does not change even if the form of that being measured is perceptually altered.
*Determination of area by use of length and width multiplication	Knows why the area formula results in an estimate of "covering"

Formal Stage	
Schemata	**Description**
Combinatorial operations	Considers and acts on all possible combinations, given 4 or more variables (already noted in Table 3.1)
Proportional reasoning	Solves ratio and simple direct proportion problems. By the end of this stage, the ability to solve inverse proportion problems develops.
Probability	Concepts of randomness and of compound probability develop late in the stage.
Correlational reasoning	Understands correlation statements and the distinction between these and causal statements.
Multiplicative compensations determination of volume** by multiplication of length, width and height.	Understands why the formula results in an estimate of capacity and that a change in one dimension requires a compensating multiplicative change in one or both of the other dimensions in order to maintain a constant volume.

the length and width are no longer mentioned; instead the continuous measure of each of those dimensions is given. Can you find the other conceptual leap? If you identified the difficulty of thinking about parts of squares as represented in the last two examples, you're beginning to think about the learner's problems. Suppose that most students *succeed* (get the correct numerical answer) on these practice exercises. Does this positive feedback mean that the use of the area formula has been understood by these students so that they can apply this formula to related science problems? An example like the one that follows is one way to get more specific feedback on their level of understanding.

> Mr. Allsop, the life science teacher, planned a unit on water loss from the leaves of trees. He decided to have each pair of students estimate the "covering" of a leaf by placing it inside a rectangular frame and covering it with dice. Each face of a die is shaped like a square, and each edge of the ones he had in stock is 1 cm. Describe the steps Mr. Allsop might take to find out how many dice would need to be on hand so that each pair of students could "cover" the largest leaf in the collection. What are some of the problems he might face?

Notice that this problem requires that the students reverse the developmental lesson and actually come up with a count of the dice. In a class question/answer session, the teacher can find out whether the students realize that measuring the length and width of the rectangular frame of the leaf in cm and computing the area will also provide a count of the number of dice. Dimensions for the leaf frame were deliberately omitted from the problem statement to avoid blind application of a rule. By suggesting different possible measures for the length and width of the largest leaf frame, the teacher can also find out whether the students realize that the results might point to a need to envision splitting dice to fit in the frame properly.

Mrs. Newell, a junior high science teacher, knew that in the past her students hadn't seemed to understand the area estimates they obtained when they outlined leaves on a grid, subdivided the leaf region into rectangles and applied the area formula repeatedly. She decided to develop a leaf surface area lesson as part of her unit on respiration. She had her students estimate the surface area of a leaf by using different congruent real-world objects, from pennies to bananas; they expressed the area as p pennies or b bananas. Then they used some of the more interesting Escher pattern cutouts, perhaps like those in Figure 3.4 (Ranucci & Teeters, 1977). They worked in groups and discussed the advantages and disadvantages of the different shapes as area unit figures. Eventually, they worked with grids, triangular and parallelogram, as well as square grids and came to an understanding of the usefulness of square grids. Then when Mrs. Newell helped them divide a leaf shape drawn on a square grid into a series of rectangular (including square) regions (Figure 3.5), she found that these ninth graders had a new appreciation for the relationship of the area formula to the area concept.

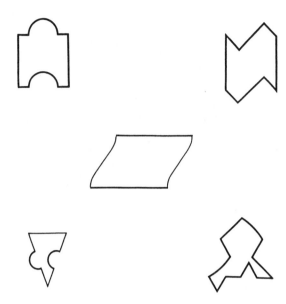

Fig. 3.4

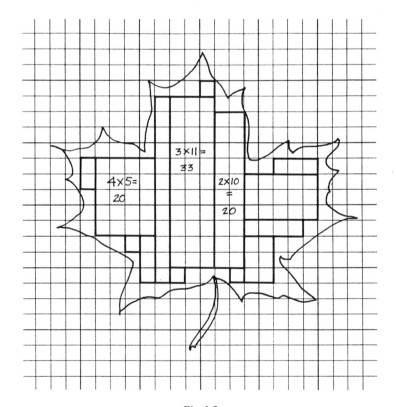

Fig. 3.5

They now possessed the concrete prerequisites to suggest transformations of the figures to get equivalent areas and were imaginative about subdividing the leaf's region in different ways. In fact, when Mrs. Newell tested their understanding by suggesting that they use even smaller unit squares to estimate the remaining regions of the leaf, the students argued that that would be like using pennies for part of the covering and dimes for the rest. Now Mrs. Newell's students were ready to collect data on the amount of transpiration from the leaves of a tree on the school grounds. (For details on the rest of this lesson, see School Mathematics Study Group, *Mathematics and living things*, 1965).

Look back at Table 3.2 and notice that there is a double asterisk (**) in two places, indicating a similar difficulty with the concept of rectangular volume and the related volume formula. Try to work out for yourself the developmental issues represented here. Think about the additional complications that occur in science classes when a teacher demonstration depends on an understanding of occupied volume or of displacement volume. Until a student understands interior volume, the basic concept referred to in Table 3.2, these other aspects of volume are not understood fully (Lovell & Ogilvie, 1968).

The nested stages and the secondary school student   Throughout all of Piaget's work, the concept of developmental stages includes the notion that early intellectual abilities are built upon, modified and extended by later ones, rather than eradicated by them. The diagram that follows is an attempt to illustrate this relationship, as well as the complex one of individual differences within stages and across stages (Figure 3.6). The *nesting* illustrates the formal operational student's ability to use intellectual skills of an earlier stage when needed, while the crevices in the schema illustrate that same student's inability to reason formally about tasks for which he or she lacks concrete prerequisite experiences. College students who were talented and highly abstract reasoners in the field of literature have reported their frustration and anxiety when faced with a symbolic approach to a mathematics topic (Buerk, 1982). For these students, past experiences in mathematics classrooms had convinced them that mathematics is a collection of rules to be memorized. Similarly, the main reason given by students for not liking science is that there are too many terms to memorize (Center for Educational Research and Evaluation, 1981). These students need a concrete basis to help them make sense of particular topics, and their instructors did not provide that basis. Some college science majors have had a similar experience when taught thermodynamics without any reference to a developmental, concrete basis. Perhaps you were one of them. How did you overcome the problem? Are there some aspects of chemistry that are still semi-mysterious to you?

The nested stages model is suggestive of considerable diversity in reasoning ability among students of the same age group. It is clear that much depends on the prior experiences, both in and out of school, with which the students in-

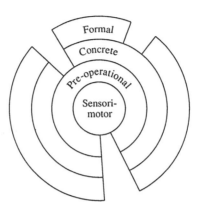

Fig. 3.6   The nested stages model.

teracted. Furthermore, there is a substantial body of evidence that even students who are capable of formal reasoning in a particular topic area may choose not to operate at a formal level (Neimark, DeLisi, & Newman, 1985). Some of these differences between competence and behavior may be due to preferred learning style, a topic we'll consider in the section on individual differences. Some of the differences may be a response to the kind of questions asked in school. For example, if the problems are simple, if students are never asked to predict or if the teacher always demonstrates the solution, then students need not use formal operational reasoning. The unintentional discouragement of formal operational thinking in those who are capable of it may be the most disastrous result of this kind of teaching. Teachers who intentionally attack this problem use some or all of the following: "What if" questions; tree diagrams to encourage a systematic approach to many combinations; a "Predict, explain your prediction, now verify, modify predictions" sequence; or classwork on a problem for which the teacher has no answer.

How does the teacher decide whether the students in a particular course are likely to be primarily concrete operational or formal operational reasoners? From the many studies of reasoning, especially those related to mathematics and science (e.g. Farrell & Farmer, 1985; Rumsey, 1986; Shayer & Wylam, 1978), we can conclude that even among the "college-bound" students from middle school through college, there will be a mix of concrete and formal reasoners in *all* classes. In group tests of college-bound tenth graders, from 30 to 40 percent have reasoned at the concrete level. Another approximately 30 percent showed some evidence of formal reasoning, but were not consistent, even in the same topic area. These reasoners, called "transitional thinkers," are of special interest because classroom experiences may inhibit or enhance their progress to formal reasoning. Even among the seniors in advanced science classes, there are students who do not exhibit formal reasoning in areas such as proportions, a major conceptual strand throughout secondary school science classes. Thus, the teacher must analyze the subject matter for clues as to the kind of reasoning it implies and be cognizant of the reasoning abilities of the students who are expected to learn the subject matter. Piaget (1971) warned that science classes in which students are primarily watching demonstrations or repeating past experiments whose results are known are particularly deficient. They do not help students gain the concrete background they need to understand experimentation and to recognize the necessity for checking and verification.

Thus, a senior high teacher might plan a laboratory, such as the activity using M & M's, found in Simulation Activity E, before presenting concepts of theoretical probability. Even if the students have had previous experience calculating the probability for various rolls of the dice in middle school classes, it is unlikely that this concrete activity was a sufficient basis for the transition to the concepts of theoretical probability.

Well-structured concrete activities, even for less formal content, are not wasted on formal reasoners. Ms. Royce, a biology student teacher, tried to do just that when introducing the hydra. She constructed a model that consisted of two paper bags, one inside the other, with several rolled-up paper tentacles attached to the open end of the bag. Each tentacle had several unwound paper clips inserted in it. When Ms. Royce demonstrated the motions of the hydra, showed the operation of the stinging cells (the paper clips), and compared the two paper bag layers to the dual cell layers of the hydra, she not only got and kept everyone's attention but also found that the concrete model clarified what students had read, and served to be an immediate assist to comprehension.

These illustrations are samples of the many ways in which instructional modes may be used to help adolescent reasoners at various levels of cognitive development. Reconsider the potential of these teaching ideas for enhancing interaction after studying the next section.

Process of Cognitive Development

How did Piaget explain the transition from one stage to another? Piaget identified four factors, all of which were assumed to affect cognitive development. These are: (1) maturation, (2) experience, (3) social interaction, and (4) equilibration (Piaget & Inhelder, 1969, pp. 154–157). According to the first two factors, a person's genetic makeup as well as the environmental stimuli with which he or she is faced are important mediators of development. Equilibration, the fourth factor, and the most controversial of Piaget's constructs, might be thought of as the tendency of a complex cybernetic system, the human mind, to adjust and restructure in response to apparent aberrations. We've left consideration of the factor of social interaction for last because this factor deserves particular attention in terms of instructional implications.

Cognitive and social interaction   Piaget insisted that knowledge is active: that to *know* an idea or an object required that the person manipulate it physically and mentally and thereby transform it. At different developmental stages, the activity of transformation takes on different forms. Nine-month-old Marcy shakes a toy, tastes it, looks at it, and listens to it. In her own way, through her senses she transforms the object and so "knows" it to the extent that these actions transform it for her.

In the Introductory Activity, you performed a reflection task and were asked to respond to questions about it and to reflect on your thinking. You physically transformed the paper and, it is assumed, mentally transformed (perhaps enhanced?) your prior knowledge about the properties of a plane mirror as well as your ideas about the nature of knowledge. Notice that "to transform" doesn't necessarily mean to radically change; it may mean to become more sure of concepts and principles. The **cognitive interaction** occurred when you were *mentally* active.

Social interaction occurred when you discussed your ideas about the reflection lab with other students. For Piaget, this aspect of working out ideas by talking them over with others is a major mediator of development. Think about your own strategies when you have to solve real-world problems. If you're working on a computer program, trying to master advanced techniques on the ski slope, or muddling through a personal dilemma, you will spontaneously and actively think about those characteristics of the real situation that you perceive as relevant to your problem.

For example, Tony, a ski instructor, can easily identify the external characteristics of your interaction as he watches you systematically trying to weight and unweight your skis across a steep slope in response to slides and skids. If you are unable to correct your parallel turns, Tony will try to create a new mental model for you to reflect on. Whether Tony knows the theory or not, he instinctively recognizes the necessity of cognitive interaction managing the physical interaction on the slope. There is also bound to be social interaction in the ski school as you and Tony, and perhaps you and other skiers, talk about the lesson, translate Tony's instructions in different ways, and praise and encourage each other.

On the other hand, you may solve your computer programming problem by yourself. There does not need to be social interaction in all cases for development to proceed. Without it, according to Piaget, development is hindered; and with social interaction, development is enhanced. Perhaps discussion of the computer programming problem would have led to deeper insights, not just a solution for the specific case.

Think through your own school instruction and consider when interaction seemed to be enhanced. Which teaching/learning modes were used often, seldom, or not at all? The answer we often are given is that listening to lecture was emphasized; small-group discussions were minimized and laboratory, outside of science class, was never used after the elementary grades. Moreover, even in science, the lab lesson all-too-often had little to do with the lesson in the *regular* science class. Might there be some connection between the mode used and failure to retain the ideas in any meaningful way for very long? Are there times when listening is an appropriate way to introduce ideas? Are there times when reading can be said to encourage interaction? You can answer that last question now. Do you recall reading an article throughout which you were struggling with the ideas being communicated? You may have even felt impelled to argue with the author. Have you also had the experience of reading an article and not being able to recall its major theme a few hours later? What were the characteristics of each article, the differences in the knowledge you brought to the task, the differences in your desire to "know"?

In many of your college classes, listening is expected to be the student's major role. What do you find are essential prerequisites for you, the listener, if listening is to result in knowledge, not just memorized bits and pieces? Suppose you, the listener, have all the needed prerequisites. What is required of the lecturer? Must the lecturer also write on the board (overhead acetate) or provide handout notes? If you haven't already done so, compare your answers to these questions with those of two other readers of this section. Try to come to some consensus on major points. In a later section, we'll reconsider the questions raised here.

Adaptation   Piaget provided us with other constructs to explain the functioning of cognitive interaction. Consider your own mental activity as you read these paragraphs. Each reader comes to the reading with different experiences, differing degrees of understanding of Piaget, and different retention of past school learning. You read the same words. Some of the words may be familiar, but may be used in a slightly novel way. Some of the ideas may be, for you, old friends; for another reader, the same ideas might present a totally new notion. If you were to talk out your mental activity as you read for understanding (we all know that it's possible to read just to finish an assignment and then wind up with a cognitive residue of zero!), you might describe it as a *matching-patching* task. You may try to *match* the inferred ideas to ones you possess that seem to be similar, or you may *patch* previous cognitive knowledge on the basis of a new twist. It is important to realize that 30 readers may conclude the same reading with 30 different shades of meaning. It must be obvious that if you possess no conceptual glue with which to do the matching-patching, then no meaningful knowledge will be added to your cognitive structure.

Piaget had specific labels for the match-patch function described here. He labeled the process where an individual interacts with an experience (a real object, a situation, inferred ideas through reading, listening, or seeing) *adaptation*. He described adaptation in terms of two concurrent functions: *assimilation* and *accommodation*. In the illustration we used, the reader *assimilates* (matches) the ideas inferred from the paragraphs as he or she simultaneously *accommodates* (patches) prior cognitive structures to the new input. Notice that when adaptation (matching-patching) occurs, the individual is changed in a cognitive sense while he or she changes the experience.

There are some clear signals to the teacher in the functioning of adaptation. First, if assimilation-accommodation is to occur, the gap between the new experience and past knowledge cannot be too large. How large? There is no easy answer, but there are hints. If you analyze the nature of the content and search for prerequisites, some obvious prior needs will be identified. Then you can informally diagnose through homework assignments, or a short question/answer period or any number of other modes.

Warning: We've already seen that what students were exposed to is not necessarily what they've learned! What's between the covers of a syllabus or text may or may not have been included in instruction. Even if it were, you now know enough about the variable potential on the receiving end of instruction to question the probable retention of that base. What are we proposing here? Assume ignorance? Reteach everything needed? Certainly not! If you do, you'll bore a great many capable students. However, we are back to the necessity of getting feedback on the nature and extent of prerequisite knowledge. Diagnosis!

Now we're ready to respond to the earlier questions as to the roles of the lecturer and the listener in an effective college class. The lecturer has to know his or her "stuff." Equally important, though, the listener has to have enough background knowledge so that the spoken words trigger meaningful associations. Also the lecturer has to capture the listener's attention at the start and keep it throughout. Is the listener expected to recall data and to dig into the lecture for deeper meanings? If so, the listener will probably need to take notes and the lecturer may need to facilitate the note taking with a written aid and possibly, a demonstration, e.g. a dissectable solid or a computer simulation. Notice how much more is demanded of the lecturer if listening is to be active. Regardless of the lecturer's oratorical charms, notice how difficult it is to keep the atmosphere right for interaction on the part of the listener! Perhaps this is why most college students take notes during a lecture. That physical activity may be a stimulus to mental activity, although sometimes note taking can be done automatically with the more complex areas of the brain tuned out.

3.3 RESEARCH ON REASONING ABOUT SCIENCE TOPICS

Much of the research on cognitive development completed by Piaget and his colleagues is related to reasoning about science concepts. More recent research by science educators interested primarily in school learning complements the Piagetian research and provides the science teacher with more insights into adolescent reasoning. In this section, we have included selected studies relevant to middle and high school science.

An expanding area of research in science education has been the identification of students' misconceptions of science content (Clough & Wood-Robinson, 1985; Driver & Erickson, 1983; Posner, Strike, Hewson, & Gertzog, 1982; Trowbridge & Mintzes, 1985).

Lawson and Thompson (1988) examined the misconceptions of seventh graders on genetics and natural selection topics after students received classroom instruction on the topics. Using a series of three open-ended essay questions, they found that the most common misconception was the belief that parents' environmentally acquired characteristics would be passed on to their offspring. For example, in response to a situation where a female with an amputated finger married a male with an amputated finger, several students thought that each of the couple's children would be born with a missing finger. The number of misconceptions on the three problems was significantly related to the reasoning ability of the students. In particular, 33% of the students identified as formal, 58% of those identified as transitional, and 93% of those identified as concrete thinkers had at least one misconception. Lawson and Thompson surmised that many of the students did not fully integrate the genetics and natural selection concepts and principles with their prior conceptions about inherited traits. The researchers suggested that while concrete students may have understood the theory of natural selection after the month-long instructional unit, they failed to consistently apply it when making predictions. Instead they often reverted to naive conceptions.

These results, along with others from research on misconceptions, are evidence that students often have naive conceptions of natural phenomena that instruction may not change. One possible reason why students are reluctant to change their naive beliefs is their inability to use hypothetico-deductive reasoning to evaluate competing conceptions—i.e. naive versus scientific conceptions—of natural phenomena. Thus, science teachers must attempt to identify student naive conceptions and help them evaluate the inconsistencies between these prior conceptions and scientific data.

The concept of ratio and proportion has been the subject of intensive study by researchers in both mathematics education and science education (Fajemidagba,1983; Farrell & Farmer, 1985; Hart, 1978; Karplus & Karplus, 1972; Karplus, Pulos, & Stage, 1983; Rumsey, 1986). Early concrete thinkers have shown little understanding of either ratio or proportion. They sometimes succeed on proportion problems involving doubling, but they use an additive strategy to get the answer. Late concrete or early formal reasoners (a group often called "transitional" reasoners) have some success in solving problems involving first-order direct proportions if the word problems are about familiar experiences and if pictorial representations or some kind of concrete references are included.

Farrell and Farmer (1985) in a study involving over 900 tenth-, eleventh- and twelfth-grade students in college-bound mathematics and/or science classes found that approximately 47% of the students could not solve a puzzle problem involving a simple direct proportion, where the variables were related in a 2:3 ratio. The puzzle problem, which was called Mr. Tall and Mr. Short (see Figure 3.7), was developed by Robert Karplus and used both in multiple research studies, some of which have been cited earlier, and in inservice workshop materials (Karplus, Lawson, Wollman, Appel, Bernoff, Howe, Rusch, & Sullivan, 1977, pp. 1–6). The common erroneous strategy was an additive one. Such students

Mr. Tall and Mr. Short

The figure at the left is called Mr. Short. We used large round buttons laid side-by-side to measure Mr. Short's height, starting from the floor between his feet and going to the top of his head. His height was *four* buttons. Then we took a similar figure called Mr. Tall and measured it in the same way with the same buttons. Mr. Tall was *six* buttons high.

Now please do these things:

1. Measure the height of Mr. Short using paper clips in a chain provided. The height is ____

2. Predict the height of Mr. Tall if he were measured with the same paper clips. _____

3. Explain how you figured out your prediction. (You may use diagrams, words, or calculations. Please explain your steps carefully.)

_____

_____

_____

_____

_____

Fig. 3.7

said that because Mr. Tall was two buttons taller than Mr. Short, he should be two paper clips taller. When a random sample of the successful students was interviewed on a hands-on proportionality task involving direct as well as inverse proportions (Inhelder & Piaget's [1958] projection of shadows task), only 24% were able to correctly apply inverse proportional reasoning. The evidence supports Piaget's contention that proportional reasoning is a late acquisition of the formal stage of reasoning. That explains the difficulty teachers report with the teaching of percentage composition, conversion from one system of measurement to another and other topics requiring the understanding of proportions. In fact, McBride and Chiapetta (1978), who studied ninth graders' understanding of equivalent fractions, concluded that ability to use that concept improved as proportional reasoning developed. Karplus et al. (1983) suggested that teaching that stresses "cross-multiplication" actually inhibits the development of the understanding of proportion. Students seize on this easily memorized strategy and misapply it throughout their secondary school mathematics and science courses. Instead, it is recommended that tables of data be examined; that students get practice constructing equal ratios in different forms; and that problem contexts include concrete referents and real-world examples.

Another area of concern to secondary science teachers is the development of science process skills (Padilla, Okey, & Garrard, 1984). These skills consist of basic processes, such as observing, and the more complex, integrated processes, such as experimenting (American Association for the Advancement of Science, 1965). As you re-examine the reasoning patterns of the concrete and the formal reasoners in Table 3.1, you'll notice that the ability to design an experiment requires the reasoning of the formal operational student. Specific process skills (all of which are a necessary part of the more complex skill of designing an experiment) that have been investigated by researchers include identifying variables (Allen, 1973), controlling variables (Kuhn & Phelps, 1979), generating hypotheses (Pouler & Wright, 1980), and interpreting data (Weber & Renner, 1972). Padilla, Okey, and Garrard found that middle school students benefitted more from process skill instruction when the processes were integrated with science content throughout the semester, than when process skills, themselves, were taught as separate and distinct topics.

Recent research on process skill development has focused on the use of technology (Mokros & Tinker, 1987; Rivers & Vockell, 1987). Mokros and Tinker found that middle school students using microcomputer-based laboratory (MBL) materials significantly improved their ability to interpret and use graphs. One possible explanation of these results posited by the authors was the computer's ability to link a concrete experience by the student (activity) to the abstract representation (graph) of the experience.

These are only a few of the sample topics being studied by science education researchers. One important message is that science teachers must realize that mistakes, especially consistent ones, need to be analyzed carefully rather than dismissed as evidence of failure to listen or failure to study. Very often the developmental differences among the students are the underlying sources of inability to understand a teacher's explanation.

3.4 INDIVIDUAL DIFFERENCES

We have already talked about the individual differences in cognitive development in a typical middle school or high school class. However, there are factors other than cognitive development that result in individual differences in reasoning performance. One such factor is called "cognitive style."

Cognitive Style

Cognitive style is usually described in terms of the two opposite ends of a continuum. Does a student seem to respond to problems quickly with the first idea associated with the problem (an example of impulsivity) or does he or she think about the problem and consider it from several angles before responding (an example of reflection)? Teachers have to be aware of these differences that adolescents may have developed over time and that affect how they respond to questions and thought activities in the classroom. If you pose a complex, thought question, you may have to provide special cues for students on the impulsivity end of the continuum—("This is a question that I want everyone to have a chance to consider. No responses until I give a signal.").

Another way of considering cognitive style is in terms of a continuum with poles of field independence and field dependence. Field independent students are more flexible, are aware of the parts of a problem and tend to be analytical, while field dependent students attend to the global picture or the total environment. This aspect of cognitive style may explain why some students refuse to give up a problem-solving strategy even when it is not working. Ronning and McCurdy (1982) found that the field independent students were more likely than field dependent students to restate problems in hypothesis-testing ways.

Processing Information

There are also differences in how students process and store information—the way they put ideas together mentally to help them recall the information or the application process. High performing students seem to seek efficient ways to *chunk* information. They seem to store organized structures, in which rules and concepts are linked together. McDonald (1982) found that formal operational tenth graders had concept maps (ways of interrelating concepts and principles) very similar to those of experts in geometry and significantly different from those of the concrete operational students.

Differences in processing information may also be affected by differences in the ways students represent problems mentally. For example, a problem situation might be represented in a physical or visual way, an informal linguistic way, or an algebraic manner. Secondary school students vary in their ability to use all three ways effectively. Middle school students are just learning the connection between ordinary language and the language of symbols, whereas, senior high students who are skilled symbol-manipulators have difficulty understanding the relationship between a symbolic statement and the real-world situation modeled by it. From a developmental perspective, secondary students need visual and hands-on experiences to help them form the mental representations most likely to be retained in long-term memory. More generally, classroom experience with all three kinds of representation is needed to help students move gradually from one kind of representation to another (Resnick & Ford, 1981, p. 217).

Gender Differences

Gender differences in science achievement and participation have been studied by a number of science educators (DeBoer, 1984; Kahle & Lakes, 1983; Linn, DeBenedictis, Delucchi, Harris, & Stage, 1987; Tobin & Garnett, 1987; Vetter, 1986; Vockell & Lobonc, 1981). Gender-related differences have been found for achievement, attitudes, career choice, and teacher interaction. Female achievement is below that of their male counterparts at the secondary level, especially in the physical sciences. This area, chemistry and physics, is often viewed by students as a *male* domain with fewer girls than boys electing these courses. Within science classrooms, females tend to rate themselves lower than males in scientific competence and to avoid tasks labeled difficult ("learned helplessness"). It has also been found that science teachers interact more with males than with females during instruction. It is perhaps no surprise that fewer women than men enroll in postsecondary science courses, and that women are underrepresented in scientific occupations.

Thus, performance, participation, and eventual career choice can be affected by learned attitudes related to gender-stereotyping. Performance in science may also be related to prior experiences of males and females outside of school in developing abilities needed to learn science. For example, some girls have been found to outperform most boys in linguistic tasks and some boys, to outperform most girls in spatial tasks. These differences may result from the mass of experiences typically built up by boys in games, hobbies and out-of-school work experiences that use spatial abilities, and from the contrasting experiences of girls with verbal tasks. Whatever the causes, science teachers need to be conscious of the need to reverse this trend, which is already quite advanced by secondary school. Introduction of female and male role models in science careers and reports on female and male scientists (see sources in Chapter 4) are two specific ways to begin to show that science is a subject area open to women and men. It is important to monitor laboratory work and computer area use to ensure that males and females get equal access and are equally involved. Most important, the teacher has to demonstrate equal expectations for males and females in the class. There is a growing set of resources in this entire area. See Chapter 11 for some of these resource books for teachers.

Slow Learners and Academically Talented Students

These two groups of students have been the subject of many articles and research studies. As a result, we have learned about some of the most common reasoning and learning patterns of each group.

The slow learner   The "reluctant learner," the "underachiever"—these are some of the labels used to designate students who achieve below some minimum standard. When these labels are used to designate students at the **lowest** range of achievement they refer to students who tend to have poor study habits and learning difficulties. Their reasoning patterns are, at best, concrete operational, and, even then, restricted to the simplest reasoning of the concrete operational student. On tests of reading, listening and speaking, they score far below grade level. These adolescent students typically score below criterion on retention tests. They try to represent information exactly as presented and, therefore, memory overload occurs very quickly. It is no surprise that these lowest achievers do not persevere in tasks, are motivated by short-range rather than long-range goals and have little self-confidence in their ability to learn.

Typical classroom instruction seems to fly in the face of these characteristics. Repetitious drill on arrays of meaningless (to the student) information is bound to fail with students whose memory skills are poor. What they do need is a variety of concrete, everyday activities presented in a meaningful manner to help them make sense out of schoolwork. They need many experiences with hands-on materials, careful step-by-step directions, intermittent reinforcement for progress, and praise at each completed stage of the learning. Notice that there's little difference between this suggestion and those given for the concrete operational reasoner at any age. The chief difference is the need for strategies to combat the failure syndrome these learners have acquired. There must be built-in opportunities for deserved praise and positive reinforcement; the rate of presentation needs to be matched to the attention span and reading/listening levels of the students and problem situations must be in terms of real-world experiences relevant to this age group. These adolescents may read at the second grade level and reason like fifth or sixth graders, but their interests are those of sixteen or seventeen year olds. The illustrations that follow illustrate some of the adaptations the teacher might use.

Omit the reading in a creatively designed worksheet and audiotape the directions, being careful to speak slowly, to repeat and to avoid complicated words. Arrange individual projects cooperatively with the industrial arts teacher or the English teacher. For example, give as much help as necessary in a model-constructing project. Help the student draw up the specifications. The completed model can be submitted jointly for industrial arts and science credit. Instead of a written explanation of project design, an oral report can be audiotaped and again serve two subject areas—science and English. In the ideal mechanical advantage laboratory described in Chapter 2, additional demonstrations by the teacher may be needed before getting the students into laboratory groups. Then allow these students to measure more examples of the most obvious machines before proceeding to work with screwdrivers and screws. Also, provide them with more guidance in how to measure the less obvious and more complicated machines such as the egg beater and automobile jack. Teach the students to use calculators to obtain the IMA to the nearest tenth and, thus, remove one of their excuses for failure (*"I never could divide!"*). Students are more willing to seek help in the measuring skills or the division process as part of a laboratory with an immediate goal than they would be to attend to separate division and measuring lessons. Common sense is needed so that the task does not become impossible. You must decide on the modification that takes the student gradually from familiar territory to new learnings.

It should be clear that we believe that these students can learn if taught in a meaningful way with many concrete experiences. What's all-important is that the teacher demonstrate the same belief. You do slow learners no service by passing them on despite inability to meet standards. However, reasonable standards, interesting and challenging activities, and the atmosphere promoted by a thoughtful teacher will help give the slow learner confidence and an appreciation of the accessibility of science.

The academically talented   These students are not always those with the highest grades, nor even those who speed through exercise material. As a school boy, Newton showed no particular aptitude for science, mathematics, or, indeed, any other school subject. However, outside of school he constructed a host of working mechanical devices, including sundials, clocks, waterwheels, and a mill that ground wheat (complete with a greedy mouse that devoured most of the flour). He also read extensively and kept a notebook, which he filled with atypical observations and mysterious recipes. History is replete with similar tales of intellectual giants who in their youth were considered stupid, recalcitrant, and unmotivated. Yet even in their youth, a discerning teacher would have been able to collect clues as to their capability.

What are the characteristics of this group of students? Their reasoning patterns develop more quickly than those of their age group and they process information in very efficient ways (Renzulli, 1979). Thus, they have well-developed memory skills. In fact, their excellent memory sometimes misleads teachers into assuming that they understand everything they can memorize.

Farmer (1983) tested a group of thirty academically talented middle school youngsters involved in a summer mathematics and science program who demonstrated superb memory skills and insightful responses to problems. It was tempting to assume that they would reason formally. In fact, their reasoning ranged from concrete to transitional and formal. Twenty-six out of the thirty students succeeded on the Tall-Short task depicted in Figure 3.7, but only eight were able to respond at the formal level to an inverse proportional reasoning task (the projection of shadows task).

While repetitious drill is wasted on the slow learner for one reason, it is an anathema to the academically talented for another reason. Bright students need less practice than the average student. However, bright students are able to go deeper and further into a problem situation than others in their age group. These academically talented students generalize after fewer hands-on activities. Notice that we aren't saying that the concrete basis can be omitted. (Think back to the nested stages model.) Given their capabilities, these academically talented students have more self-confidence and will persist in a task interesting to them over long periods of time. Thus, teachers can make excellent use of individualized projects.

In a twelfth-grade science class, three gifted students had capabilities far beyond the rest of the class. By group consent, a special Friday class was designed. The three students read and studied a topic external to the course in the room or the library, while the rest of the students worked with the teacher on trouble spots identified during the week. Occasional teacher conferences with the talented students gave them a chance to report on progress.

Freedom to explore an interest, to use different methods of solution, and to seek answers to atypical questions are what the talented student needs (Sacco, Melville, Copes, Sloyer, & Morningstar, 1983). That doesn't mean that the teacher isn't needed, or that anything goes, or that the rest of the class can be ignored. Students who are working at an individual project while the rest of the class is pursuing a lesson should have clearly defined responsibilities. A teacher may "contract" with such students as to both the quality and the amount of work to be completed by a deadline. If talented students enjoy helping other students, they can, under careful supervision, become teacher aides. Some students find this role an exciting way of increasing their own depth in science, but don't assume that all do. Diversity is the norm among humans.

3.5 SUMMARY AND SELF-CHECK

The subtitle of this chapter, "Adolescent Reasoning Patterns," was selected to emphasize the intellectual gap between you and your students. You presumably, have learned the subject matter you will be teaching. However, you have transformed it so completely from your initial experience with it that your resulting knowledge is now in a form inappropriate for the initial learning of your students. Somehow you have to retrieve that initial experience and help your students to transform knowledge successfully. To do this, you must first learn all you can about the adolescent intellect, their particular reasoning patterns in areas of science, and the individual differences that affect the development of their reasoning. How do your students learn? What has been their history of knowing? What do their questions and errors tell you? What differences can you expect in a typical classroom? These and related questions have been the subject matter of this chapter.

In this chapter, secondary students' reasoning was described as an active, constructive process. The development of reasoning from sensori-motor to preoperational to concrete and, then, formal reasoning was outlined, with special emphasis on the reasoning of the concrete and formal operational thinkers. The importance of interaction, in particular social interaction, in cognitive development was described. The way in which all of us develop our reasoning abilities by interacting with environmental stimuli was pictured as a matching-patching analogy (adaptation). Recent research results related to reasoning problems in particular secondary science areas were described. Individual cognitive differences that have an effect on the reasoning of adolescents about science were presented and special attention was given to low achievers and academically talented students. Throughout the chapter, specific implications for science instruction were provided.

The title of this chapter is repeated in the shaded component of the instructional model on the title page of the chapter. Notice the connecting link between that box and the "Structure of Science" component. Although there have been continuous references to student reasoning about science in this chapter, the emphasis has been on the student. It is now important to highlight science itself—the subject of the next chapter.

Now you should be able to:

1. Operationally define cognitive interaction, social interaction, adaptation, accommodation, and assimilation.

2. Contrast the abilities of the concrete operational reasoner with those of the formal operational reasoner.

3. Explain the significance of the nested stages model.

4. Give at least two types of individual differences that could have an effect on reasoning.

5. Rank instructional modes from most to least promising in terms of research on the cognitive development of adolescents, given a specific set of modes and a description of the students.

6. Classify student behavior in terms of research on adolescent reasoning after viewing a "live" or video-taped lesson in which students were involved in a laboratory problem-solving activity.

7. Suggest at least three different methods that could be used to obtain some initial clues as to your students' cognitive development.

The exercises that follow include some additional ways to deepen your understanding of the theory and research on adolescents' reasoning and help you apply that understanding to issues of instruction in science.

3.6 SIMULATION/PRACTICE ACTIVITIES

A. Ms. Pringle was feeling very pleased with herself and with her ninth-grade physical science class. Every student had demonstrated the ability to calculate density when given mass and volume data. Then she posed this question: "Water has a density less than sulfuric acid. Which would have the greater volume, 100 grams of water or 100 grams of sulfuric acid?" A straw poll showed nine for water, ten for the acid, three for no difference, and two who confessed to having no idea. The now-troubled Ms. Pringle became even more disturbed when follow-up questions to proponents of various views revealed that even several students selecting the correct answer did so through faulty reasoning.

1. Analyze the nature of the reasoning task inherent in Ms. Pringle's question.

2. Explain the results of the straw poll and follow-up questions in terms of Piagetian theory.

B. Obtain a copy of one of the pieces of problem solving software described in the article that follows. Review its use, study the documentation, and be prepared to talk about the reasoning needed to succeed on the various activities.

Krajcik, J., & Berg, C. (1987). "Exemplary software for the science classroom," *School Science and Mathematics*, **87** (6), 494–500.

C. Make copies of the TALL-SHORT puzzle (Figure 3.7) and prepare chains of ten #1 paper clips. Then try out the puzzle on a sample of volunteer junior high and senior high students. Be prepared to talk about the data.

D. Read:

Rice, K., & Feher, L. (1987). "Pinholes and images: Children's conceptions of light and vision I." *Science Education*, 71 (4), 629–639.

Then construct the light source and aperture cards and replicate Rice and Feher's study with adolescents and/or adults. Be sure to have respondents predict and then explain the images that they see on the screen. What is the relationship between their predictions and explanations, and the reasoning patterns presented in this chapter?

E. The lab described in this exercise was used by a junior high teacher. After reading about the lab, identify the ways in which the lesson incorporates aspects of research and theory on the reasoning of junior high students.

LAB: The teacher divided the class into pairs and gave each pair a small bag of M & M's (20 brown, 8 yellow, 8 orange and 4 green in each bag). The students were to predict how many M and M's of each color were in the bag without looking. After demonstrating how to carefully shake the bag and how to draw without looking, the teacher told the groups to draw one candy, record its color, return it to the bag, draw, record and return that candy to the bag, and so on until each pair had completed 40 draws. Each pair's totals were recorded on the board and a class set of totals was obtained. The ensuing discussion included a consideration of empirical probability, the comparison of the results with the actual contents of the bags, and a consideration of theoretical probability (Farmer & Farrell, 1989).

SUGGESTIONS FOR FURTHER STUDY

Adler, I. (1966). "Mental growth and the art of teaching." *Mathematics Teacher*, 59, 706–715.

Adler's article has become a classic introduction to Piaget's theory. It has the advantage of focusing on highlights, identifying and disposing of major misconceptions about the theory, and specifically pinpointing implications for all teachers in both the choice of strategy and of content. Since all the examples are from mathematics or science, the article can be read with most profit by teachers of those disciplines. The reader will do well to obtain a basic understanding of Piagetian theory from *other* sources and to read Adler for his interpretation of Piagetian contributions to the "Art of Teaching." They are excellent!

Good, R. (1977). *How children learn science; Conceptual development and implications for learning.* New York: Macmillan.

The author takes a practical approach in an attempt to help readers understand research findings of studies on cognitive development. Although the interview data is primarily from work with elementary school children, the secondary science teacher will find helpful descriptions of teacher roles based on a consideration of developmental theory and the nature of science.

Gorman, R. M. (1972). *Discovering Piaget: A guide for teachers.* Columbus, Ohio: Charles E. Merrill.

This small paperback is still the best introduction to Piaget on the market. The author intends that the book will promote a guided discovery approach and so encourage that interaction at the core of Piaget's theory. For this reason, much of the material is read with ease. The exception is the section on the INRC group (pages 44–57), which is highly technical and could well be omitted in favor of concentration on other sections.

Karplus, R., Lawson, A. E., Wollman, W., Appel, M., Bernoff, R., Howe, A., Rusch, J. J., & Sullivan, F. (1977). *Science teaching and the development of reasoning* (Volumes for Biology, Chemistry, Earth Science, General Science and Physics). Berkeley, CA: The University of California.

Each of these five guides contains common instructional modules based on the developmental psychology of Piaget with specific applications to the secondary science curricular area in the title. Laboratory kits and a motion picture film were developed to accompany the printed materials.

The guides are especially valuable for helping science teachers diagnose the types of reasoning students display in typical science learning situations. Considerable attention is also given to analyzing the types of reasoning demanded by a variety of science learning tasks. The materials may be read with profit and adapted for classroom use by the experienced teacher, as well as by the beginning teacher.

Oxenhorn, J. M. (1972). *Teaching science to underachievers in secondary schools.* New York: Globe Book.

This practical, method-type book includes sections on the philosophical basis for good science teaching based on the ideas of Ausubel, Bloom, Bruner, and others. Science teachers will find chapter 3, *A Profile of Underachievers*, of special interest.

Romey, W. D., & Hibert, M. (1987). *Teaching the gifted and talented in the science classroom.* Washington, D.C.: National Education Association.

This 64 page book is part of the NEA's series *Teaching the Gifted and the Talented in the Content Area.* Topics include *on being gifted and talented, characteristics of gifted, teaching science,* and *science activities for the gifted.*

CHAPTER FOUR

THE STRUCTURE OF SCIENCE

Products and Processes

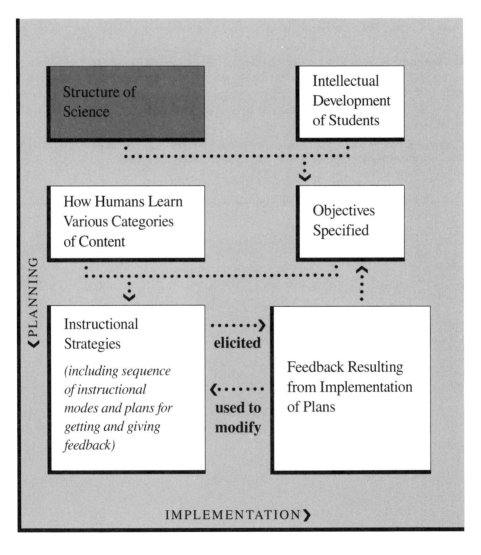

It is a truism that we learn more about a subject when we teach it. Every tutor, swimming coach, and scout leader knows the experience. So be prepared for some rude shocks to your scientific belief system. Such shocks are part of teaching and can be learned from and capitalized on. In this chapter we'll pose a range of questions designed to help you learn (and relearn) science from views other than that of a student.

Why is a thorough analysis of subject matter content and structure so important? Why pursue this matter at this particular point in our study of teaching? Let's see if you can begin to formulate answers to these questions by looking back at the opening page of this chapter. Note that the shaded box "Structure of Science" couples with the previously treated "Intellectual Development of Students" portion of the instructional model to form the bases for specifying objectives. In any thoughtful approach to instruction it is vital to formulate clear objectives that closely match both the students they are presumed to affect and the subject matter content they are claimed to represent. Why vital? As the rest of the model depicts, these objectives will be used to design instructional strategies, guide the collection of feedback, and then be reassessed in light of resultant learning. Thus the teacher's comprehension of the subject matter of science will have profound effects on all aspects of instruction. Now is the time to face the issues. College students typically have spent nearly all of their time in three to four years of science courses committing to memory the mechanics of the subject, dutifully completing exercises in how to obtain the correct answers and learning how to prepare for final examinations. A few college students have experienced courses in the history, philosophy, or structure of the discipline of science where the focus has been on the analysis of various subcategories of knowledge within the subject matter and the interdependence of the processes used to generate knowledge within this specialized field. If you are one of the fortunate few with this type of background, a quick reading of the early sections of this chapter should suffice to check the completeness of your own comprehension. If you are one of the great majority who have not yet concerned yourself with the structure of scientific knowledge and the processes used to generate it, you will need to give immediate and concentrated attention to this chapter.

We begin by asking you to take a stand on an issue that intrigued scholars for centuries. The issue is phrased as an either/or, but not both statement.

Science was invented

or

Science was discovered

You must choose a stance now. So stop and consider the implications of each statement. Let's be clear about the meaning assigned to the key words. *Invented* is to be thought of as it is used in a sentence such as "Alexander Graham Bell invented the telephone," while *discovered* is to be used in the sense of "Mary discovered her diamond ring under the counter." Notice that in both cases the person may have had an insightful idea, but in Mary's search the product—a ring—was not altered or brought into being by her activity. Take a few minutes of thinking time to decide on your position before reading any further.

Did you choose "invented"? Then how do you explain the scientific knowledge generated by entomologists who collect, study, and classfy specimens of insects? Didn't those insects already exist and couldn't they be seen, touched, heard, smelled, and measured? Were the insect specimens altered by being measured or classified? Similarly, consider Mendelyeev's periodic charting of the elements. Wasn't this schema based upon observable properties of the elements?

Or did you opt for "discovered"? Then how do you explain Newton's formulation of the concept of "gravity"? Did he see it, touch it, smell it, measure it (gravity itself), or hear it? Ask yourself similar questions about Neils Bohr's thought model for atomic structure and Watson and Crick's thought model for DNA.

If you are a bit confused trying to respond with certainty to the dichotomy posed by our question, just imagine the plight of secondary school youngsters facing the task of comprehending what may appear to be a two-headed monster named *Science*. To be sure, science does have both an empirical and a theoretical aspect, and post-Newtonian science has been concerned with obtaining the closest possible match of the two aspects.

In contrast, pre-Newtonian science was characterized by two distinct and nonconnected roots. The artisans and craftsmen, typically unable to read or write, were the empiricists who learned to manipulate natural objects/phenomena by "cut-and-try" methods. Their knowledge and techniques were passed on through an apprenticeship system by word of mouth and supervised practice. Most contemporary dog breeders continue this tradition by a similar approach to their art. Consequently, very little theoretical knowledge of canine genetics is available at the present time.

The other root of science was that of the theorists and scholars. These were typically men with considerable book knowledge and with access to the wealth it took to pursue an activity that itself produced little or no income. Steeped in the knowledge of ideas generated and recorded by others, these scholars had the time and training to debate old ideas about the universe and how it works, contrive their own notions, and persuasively argue the logic of their positions with colleagues. Once a notion was firmly accepted on the basis of both logic and authority, it was slow to die. For example, consider all those years when scholars agreed that a ball of iron would fall faster than a ball of wood because both "logic" and Aristotle so dictated.

Since the time of the Newtonian synthesis, these two roots have become joined inseparably together into the main trunk of modern science (Figure 4.1). The inventive ideas of theory must face the acid test of empirical verification—the experiment. Creative theories are valued to the extent that their logical deductions match phenomena manipulated under controlled conditions. In a complementary fashion, the observations and data patterns of the empirical root of science stimulate further creative thinking in a constant search for theoretical

Fig. 4.1 Tree of science.

mechanisms that can provide scientific explanations for phenomena of the natural world.

Thus, the tree of science has roots in both the idea world and the physical world. Does this mean that science is partly invented and partly discovered? If you've decided that your answer depends on what science is, not solely on how it was generated, you're on the right track. What is science? Is its structure hierarchical? What do scientists do when they are "sciencing"? These and other relevant questions are considered in detail throughout this chapter as we begin to analyze the nature of science and the implications of that nature for you as a science teacher.

We start in the next section with an activity designed to help you begin to construct a valid view of contemporary science.

4.1 INTRODUCTORY ACTIVITY

Science is a verb, as well as a noun.

What kinds of things do we do when we are sciencing? What do we obtain as a result of sciencing? In this activity you are asked to identify as many processes and products of science as you can, and to record them in a chart like the one portrayed by Figure 4.2. Write the "ing" form of verbs in the "processes" column and nouns in the "products" column. Think in terms of any actual science activities you may have personally done as well as about accounts of activities you have read or been told about by teachers. We have included a few ideas to help you get started. We recommend that you match products with the process(es) that generate each as the list lengthens.

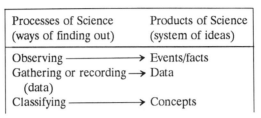

Processes of Science (ways of finding out)	Products of Science (system of ideas)
Observing ──────────→	Events/facts
Gathering or recording ──→ (data)	Data
Classifying ──────────→	Concepts

Fig. 4.2

A. Compare your chart with those of at least two other classmates. Make modifications as a result of discussing each other's ideas.

B. Which of the listed processes are employed primarily by the user of established science? Which are used primarily by the person who needs to develop novel science?

C. Try to rank, or to classify, both the products and the processes in the order in which they might occur in the development of science. (Did you remember to include deducing and inducing?)

D. Which of the processes are likely to be emphasized in junior high science? Which in senior high science, or in elementary school science?

As you read through this chapter, you may want to revise your original chart. In this and later chapters we'll consider ways of teaching these aspects of the subject matter.

4.2 PRODUCT ASPECTS OF SCIENCE

Facts was one of the terms we supplied to help you begin your chart. Most people think of this category as soon as the topic of science content is mentioned. Obviously, facts are vital parts of the system of ideas of science, but you should be alert to some related problems in comprehension. If you ask a secondary school student or an adult layperson for an operational definition of the word *fact*, you are likely to get either a period of silence coupled with a blank stare, or a statement like "things that are true." Few understand that a *fact is an event that has occurred and been recorded with no disagreement among the observers.* This widespread lack of understanding of the term's meaning is at least partially responsible for the misguided and oversimplified definition "Science is an organized body of facts." Unfortunately, you must expect to encounter students who believe this. Some junior high science texts previously on the market actually included such statements. The science curriculum revolution of the 1960s, led by scientists rebelling against such gross distortions of their discipline, has corrected the language in texts to a large extent, but students still tend to misinterpret more accurate statements such as "Science is based on facts." To these students, this statement means that science *equals* facts. Watch and listen for evidence of this misconception when you observe science classes, and begin thinking how you will deal with this problem when you step into the role of science teacher.

Data is another of the terms supplied to help you begin your chart; its meaning, like that of *facts*, is often partially misunderstood. *Data* refers to *information, often quantified, that is judged relevant to an investigation and that is collected under conditions that are specified.* We hear and read the phrase *objective data.* How does this match the accepted definition that includes the phrase *judged relevant*? Then, too, we must remain alert to the other criterion stated in the definition. Some commonly used curriculum materials fail to focus on the need to decide upon and record the specific conditions under which data are collected. It should be becoming clear to you that data are selected facts/events gathered in specific ways for certain purposes according to someone's best judgment. If so, you have another reason to object to the "science equals facts" misconception.

The third term we supplied was *concepts.* Be alert to the potential abuse of this term, both in your own thinking about its meaning and in your use of published materials with your students. Designers of some texts, audiovisual and technological aids, or curriculum guides all-too-often treat this term as a magic word, which characterizes the entire set of materials as good, wholesome, true, or useful. Are we exaggerating? Check out the number of science texts with titles such as *Fundamental Concepts of* _____, film series advertising coverage of the *Basic Concepts of* _____, and curriculum guides with columns labeled "Fundamental Concepts and Understandings." Try to find where the authors and/or ad writers have defined their use of the term *concept.* Good luck with your search! What is a working definition of this all-important term? We have synthesized the following definition as one that seems to be consistent with the psychology of learning usage and at the same time applicable to science content. *A concept is a classification of ideas, objects, or events into a set by mentally abstracting the common essential characteristics/attributes that define that set.* The concept itself exists in the mind as an abstraction and is not to be confused with its *label*, which is usually either one symbol (such as g, I, or π) or a single word (such as animal, atom, mineral). For example, consider the person who has attained the concept of "insect." When confronted with a conglomeration of unfamiliar, small, winged creatures with legs, he or she can correctly sort out the ones that meet the essential criteria for that classification from those that exhibit none or only some of the essential criteria. Some further examples of science concepts are space, time, energy, element, mammal, chromosome, magnetism, and growth.

You may be a little disturbed by the fact that the examples of concepts cited thus far seem to fall into two subcategories. Some, such as "animal," refer to things that can be observed by direct sensory experience while others, such as "magnetism," refer to ideas that are not subject to direct observation. Yes, we have been dealing with *two* kinds of concepts thus far. *Concepts by inspection* and *theoretical concepts* (also called *theoretical constructs* or *concepts by definition*) are commonly accepted labels for these two related, but different, types of concepts. A third type of concept is also important. Just think how often such terms as *less, more,* and *equal* are used to express relationships among concepts of the other two types. Logically enough, these ideas are called *relational concepts*. Try to think of some further examples of relational concepts borrowed from mathematics and used all the time in science. If ideas such as *inverse, proportional*, and *congruence* come to mind, you are getting the idea. But wait. Giving additional correct examples is insufficient evidence of concept attainment. The only way to insure that you now have the concept of a concept is to determine whether you can sort out correct examples from related and potentially confusing nonexamples.

Consider the statement "The electric current in a circuit is directly proportional to the electromotive force and inversely proportional to the resistance." Does this statement describe a concept? Obviously it contains concept labels, but note that its meaning goes beyond the operational definition of a concept in a number of ways. This time the "label" is a sentence instead of a single word or short phrase. The idea is composed of a *chain* of several individual concepts (such as electric, current, circuit, and proportional) and it *predicts* what will happen in an interaction among these concepts. If this description sounds like *rule* would be a good label for this category of idea, your thinking is in accord with accepted usage. On the other hand, you may have learned that the label for this statement is Ohm's *law*. It is true that the terms *rule, law*, and *principle* are frequently used interchangeably in the literature of science. However, we prefer not to use the term *law* with students because it tends to convey the notions of "invariably true" and "accepted because people have debated its merits and voted in favor of it." Both of these are false impressions within the context of contemporary science and there is no reason to further complicate the problem of communicating with students. We urge you to use either *rule* or *principle* as the more appropriate label for this category of idea.

Now let's consider another example of a rule/principle. "At all temperatures other than absolute zero, the motion of gas molecules is random with respect to both rate and direction." It is probably obvious to you that this statement meets the same criteria as the example dealing with electric current. Now take a second look and note that it also provides part of an *explanation* for the observable phenomena that gases fill containers uniformly. That explanation derives from the kinetic molecular theory along with its accompanying thought model and includes reference to theoretical concepts (molecules). Thus, this type of principle has far more power than the type exemplified by Ohm's principle. These more powerful statements are characterized by their explanatory power couched in terms of theory, in addition to their ability to predict. Thus, the name *theoretical rule/principle* is an apt one. In contrast, the type that predicts but does not explain is derived from sense experience and has, therefore, been labeled *empirical rule/principle*. Electrical meters, which are extensions of the human senses, can measure the effect on current (I) as electromotive force (E) and resistance (R) are varied in turn. The pattern of $I = E/R$ emerges from the collected data pool. From this uniform pattern, the scientist predicts future related events, but the pattern provides no reference to the body of matching theory that gives an explanation for the prediction. Of course there are theoretical principles that closely match this empirical principle and that are *verified, not proved*, by the established empirical pattern. We'll talk more about this later, but now let's state three operational definitions. *A scientific rule (principle) is a statement predicting interrelationships among concepts. An empirical principle is one that refers only to concepts by inspection and that does not provide explanation for the predicted relationship*, while *a theoretical principle refers to theoretical concepts and provides explanation in addition to prediction.*

Test your ability to apply these operational definitions by analyzing the principles/rules of dominance, segregation, and independent assortment as stated by Mendel. Identify each concept included in each of these three principles as either a concept by inspection or a theoretical concept. Next, decide whether each statement only predicts, or both predicts and explains in terms of matching theory. It should then be clear to you why Mendel's principles are considered excellent examples of empirical rules/principles. Now go to the content of modern genetic theory and find matching principles/rules of the theoretical type and subject them to similar analysis. Note the goodness of fit of the empirical to the theoretical—typical of a maturing branch of science.

Be forewarned! Many of your secondary school students will react negatively to ideas either you or their texts label as *theory*. Be prepared for comments such as "But that is *only* theory," "Why don't you just teach us the facts," and "If no one has ever seen one, I don't believe in them." Yes, you can count on having to work hard to overcome some students' distorted meaning of the term *theory*. To many of them, it means only someone's blind guess rather than *a carefully constructed system of logical reasoning derived from well-founded assumptions regarding the basic nature of the physical world.* Of course, these doubting students *do* believe in things they have never seen and can never hope to see, but they fail to realize this. Help them by asking if they believe in wind, magnetism, or electricity. Then question them on why they believe in these notions. They may begin to realize it is the *effects* of wind, magnetism, and electricity on observable objects that cause them to believe.

We frequently share with students our own reason for believing in the idea that all matter is composed of molecules. The reason is simple. We can explain more things by thinking in terms of molecules than we can by holding to any of several competing notions about the nature of matter. Explaining length changes of a copper bar as it is heated and cooled makes a simple but appropriate example, as does that of magnetizing and demagnetizing a soft iron rod. A friendly challenge to students to come up with a more adequate explanation based on alternative notions is usually both interesting and productive. A timely follow-up to this type of question/answer or discussion is to present a brief historical account of the development of some related theory such as the kinetic-molecular theory. Succinct summaries of the related contributions of Dalton, Boyle, Charles, Gay-Lussac, and Avogadro could well be followed by a description of Clausius' work of gathering together their ideas and providing the unified interpretation that resulted in the kinetic-molecular theory of gases. Examples of assumptions, such as the assumption that gases are composed of molecules and space and the pictorial mental model of tiny, perfectly elastic spheres uniformly distributed in a confined space, can be illustrated. Similarly, rules for the operation of this model (for example, molecules travel in a straight line until they collide either with another molecule or with the sides of the container) can be demonstrated. Also, the tight logical system formed by these assumptions, model, and accompanying rules make an excellent example of a theory that has proved to be extremely useful both in explaining related phenomena and in generating new hypotheses. Fortunately, each branch of science has a number of well-developed theories with similar potential for illustrating the nature and value of the theoretical aspects of science. It makes a great deal of sense to include a careful examination of several theories in any science course where there is a serious intent to achieve these types of objectives. For example, advanced theories often have a quantified mathematical model, such as an equation, which accompanies or supplements mental models of the pictorial type. At least some of these theories should be included to give an accurate view of contemporary science.

While stressing the role of theoretical science and examining its goodness of fit to empirical science, there are many opportunities to teach other product (system of ideas) aspects. The cumulative, tentative, probabilistic, and revisionary nature of scientific knowledge can be pointed out by numerous examples. Further, the central role of the creative human mind at work inventing more adequate theories can be amply demonstrated. Similarly, the strong preference for the simplest of adequate explanations should become clear. Many consider physics to be the most advanced branch of science because it has the clearest and most internally consistent theoretical framework resting upon the smallest number of assumptions. According to this mode of thinking, chemistry is assigned to the second highest ranking, followed in turn by biology and then by the earth and atmospheric sciences. Recent secondary school science curriculum movements have also echoed this regard for simplicity coupled with internal consistency.

Authors of several of the major curriculum projects of the 1960s attempted to structure courses around unifying themes or schemes inherent in a particular branch of science. These curriculum writers were concerned as we must be lest students get lost in the branches and subbranches that have developed from the main trunk of science. But biology, chemistry, earth/atmospheric science, and physics—as well as their many subspecializations—are all part and parcel of *one main* enterprise, in spite of a host of detailed distinctions that confuse novices. One example of a unifying theme fundamental to all branches of science is that all matter is composed of fundamental particles that can be transformed into energy and vice versa.

Unifying themes, theories, thought models, principles/rules, concepts, data, and facts are all integral parts of the products aspect of science. Look back at the chart you started as the introductory activity of this chapter. Which of these kinds of products did you include in your original list? If you included most of them and can now justify adding the others, you are off to a fine start. Now try to go further and impose a hierarchical relationship among these categories of products. For a start in this direction, reflect back on the stated connections among concepts and rules/principles. Then analyze all other categories for analogous relationships. You will have the opportunity to check your thoughts with ours in a later part of this chapter.

However, the products aspect is only one part of the structure of science, and that is why you were also asked to list accompanying processes. If you found it necessary to modify your original list of products, you will now have to make parallel alterations in the processes section of your list. Take a few minutes to make these changes now before you interact with the reading material that follows.

4.3 PROCESS ASPECTS OF SCIENCE

Having just referred back to the chart we asked you to begin as an introductory activity (Figure 4.2), you probably recall that "observing" was listed as a process by which facts are gathered. Many additional processes using the best efforts of creative human minds are also involved, as must now be evident from the previous considerations of the products aspect of science. But first, let's be clear on an operational definition of *observing*. This term is generally agreed to mean *the use of all human senses and extensions thereof to obtain information about the natural world.* Beginning students are predictably prone to equate the term with the sense of sight. They will need your help in identifying numerous examples of the use of the other four senses.

Ms. Roberts found that a "black box" type laboratory activity worked well with her eighth-grade classes. She obtained three shoeboxes, painted them black, and labeled each with a numeral. Before class she placed a sharpened pencil in box 1, a small rubber ball in box 2, and an iron "keeper" from a horseshoe magnet in box 3. She closed the boxes and placed them in a drawer of the demonstration desk. With ten minutes remaining in the class period, she praised all for their good work on learning to observe and said a challenging game was now in order. Ms. Roberts placed the boxes on the demonstration table and explained that each row would constitute a team and be given five minutes to *observe* one of the boxes and its contents.

"Each row should choose a captain who will speak for the row when time is called," she said. "The row producing the most complete and accurate description will be declared the winning team. There's just one little catch. You *cannot* open the boxes! You will have to observe with the other four senses—a predicament often faced by scientists in their work on real-world problems." Ms. Roberts then handed each captain a box and gave the signal to begin.

As the students studied the box assigned to their row, Ms. Roberts toured and noted the various observing approaches being used. She was pleased to note students tilting, hefting, smelling, and listening as they manipulated the boxes,

Fig. 4.3   Human senses versus thermometer demonstration.

and she was delighted when Jack asked for a magnet to use in connection with box 3. The student-to-student discussions among team members were going well when Ms. Roberts announced that one minute remained before she would call on captains to summarize each team's observations. When time was up, each captain reported excellent observations and described how these were obtained. Teacher-led question/answer (1) identified the few inferences that had crept into some observations, (2) emphasized the number of human senses that had been used, (3) pointed out that one group used an extension of the human senses (magnet), and (4) invited each captain to guess the actual object in the assigned box. The half-minute remaining in the period provided just enough time for well-deserved praise by Ms. Roberts and for the students to open the boxes and get direct visual feedback on their efforts. Students still chatted excitedly about the activity after dismissal while Ms. Roberts began thinking of various follow-up activities appropriate to subsequent lessons.

Whenever we deal with observing, we typically find opportunities to include illustrations of instrumentation and techniques that are extensions of the human senses. It is a rare secondary school student who thinks about the microscope as an extension of sight or who considers the thermometer and beam balance as extensions of the sense of touch. Knowing this, Mr. Cain decided to illustrate the point to his biology class by using the demonstration setup depicted in Figure 4.3.

He called for a volunteer to assist in an "easy" demonstration. Sally came forward and placed her right hand in the hot water and her left hand in the ice water as directed by Mr. Cain. After 30 seconds she reported the sensations reaching her brain from each hand. Next, she placed both hands into the room-temperature water and reported the disparate information reaching her brain from each hand. Mr. Cain thanked Sally, had her dry her hands, and asked her to measure the actual temperatures of all three containers. A question/answer session followed, and the use of thermometers to refine and extend human sense information became clear, as evidenced by many student-initiated illustrations from everyday life. However, Mr. Cain was not content to rest on these laurels. Experience had taught him that the success of this lesson would not ensure that his students would make similar connections to chemical testing and differential staining techniques. He would have to seek out opportunities to call attention to these matters throughout the course and he would also have to teach accompanying manipulative skills if his students were to develop a valid view of science.

Although data gathering depends upon observing as the basic process for collecting events/facts about the natural world, data gathering is not equal to observing. Judgments must be made as to *which* facts are relevant and how and when observing should occur, *before* the process of data gathering can begin. Descriptive data are typically gathered in the form of written words or other symbols recorded systematically in note form, in pictorial form on lap computers, on audiotape or other suitable device if the data consist of sounds, or by means of other technological aids appropriate to the data being collected. However, contemporary science prizes quantitative data; thus, whenever possible, measurements are gathered in a form consistent with the nature of the data and its projected use.

Ms. Hafiz tried to work on these ideas with her ninth-grade science class during the unit on plant growth. Each student was given a set of seeds (three bean and three corn) and two milk cartons full of potting soil plus instructions to (1) germinate the seeds, (2) grow the plants for two months, and (3) keep a daily record of plant height. A demonstration with lecture was given on planting, germinating, and measuring techniques. Ms. Hafiz concluded with a short lecture on the importance of recording all data that would be likely to affect the outcome of the activity. The students took their materials home and began the activity. A month later Ms. Hafiz instructed all the students to bring their data sheets to class so she could see how things were progressing. Almost every student brought in some sort of record that showed a serious attempt to follow instructions. However, Ms. Hafiz was shocked at what she saw on the papers and learned by questioning. Some students had thinned out seedlings and had retained one seedling per carton, while others kept two or three. A number of students had dutifully recorded measurements for several plants each day, but had no idea which plants were corn and which were beans. A few admitted they forgot to water the plants "for a while," but that they "made it up by watering twice as much during the next week." Some had recorded "day 1" data for the day the first seedling emerged from the soil; others kept a separate "day 1 "for each seedling as it sprouted; others counted "day 1" as the time when the seeds were planted; and a few couldn't remember how they decided when to begin recording data.

Yes, teachers *do* have to teach students how to decide on the relevance of data, the importance of keeping accurate records, how to set up appropriate tabular forms, and all the related considerations that are "old hat" to teachers but novel to students. Hence, *data gathering* refers to a *variety of processes and techniques for systematically collecting and recording relevant events and the conditions under which they were gathered.*

Careful observing plus thoughtful data-gathering procedures are necessary, but not sufficient prerequisites for finding meaning in the events of the natural world. Patterns are often not obvious by inspection of raw data in relatively unorganized forms. Thus, *data reducing* is needed and *consists of the application of mathematical/statistical techniques designed to reveal patterns in raw data.*

It is at this point in the processes of science that the importance of the science/mathematics interface first becomes obvious to most secondary school students. Various types of graphic representation are great assists to the human mind in detecting patterns in the data. Care must be taken, however, to help students choose appropriate types of representation. For instance, histograms are a useful way to depict continuous data, but discrete events call for another form of representation (such as a bar graph). Line graphs (seldom straight) are the type most often used in secondary school science courses. Some students typically connect plotted points and extend the line beyond the range of data collected with little thought as to what they are doing. *Interpolating (estimating intermediate values between known points)* and *extrapolating (estimating values beyond the range of available data)* are both viable ways of seeking patterns. However, students must be taught to use these processes with care and caution. Remember that "Two points determine a line" is true *only* if you know in advance that the pattern is a straight line—hardly the case when you are trying to find out if a relationship does exist and, if so, what kind of dependency is exhibited.

Closely related to the process of extrapolating is the process of *classifying* by means of which *objects, events, and ideas are grouped in terms of selected criteria thought to be most relevant for specific purposes.* Think back to the operational definition of concepts and check this definition against that one. Do the two operational definitions fit together? They should, because the process of classifying is what generated the products known as concepts. Also recall the earlier question we raised about the collection of insects. The relationship between classifying and concept referred to here should be convincing evidence that the categorizations of these animals were *inventions* of the human mind, even though the creatures themselves existed previously and hence were subject to being *discovered* by humans. If you believe that the mere awareness of the existence of various forms of matter and energy constitutes science, then you're in the "discovered" corner of the discovered versus invented question. However, if you believe that science is more than this (for example, grouping data by means of the relationship known as classifying), then you're leaning heavily toward the "invented" corner.

Relationships of an even more pervasive type are embedded in those products we have labeled as principles (rules). How are these patterns identified? The scientist uses the process of *experimenting—planning, carrying out, and analyzing series of data-gathering operations under controlled conditions.* The design may be aimed at either (1) finding among concepts a patterned interrelationship that predicts only or (2) testing the reasonableness of a hypothesis (derived from theory) that both predicts and explains interrelationships.

In the first case, the reasoning used is *induction—from many specific instances to general patterns.* The resulting principles (empirical) are of varying degrees of certainty or probability, but always less than 100 percent. As the number of specific instances involved in establishing the pattern increases, the degree of probability that the pattern will predict related events in the future also increases.

However, since not all possible cases (present and future) can be tested, certainty is always impossible. In the second case, the reasoning involves *deduction—from one or more general propositions to their specific logical consequences.* In science these generalities are an integral part of theory and the test of their reasonableness lies in goodness of fit to the specific observable events predicted. Why reasonableness instead of correctness? Is that also because every possible present and future case cannot be tested? Partly, but there is also another reason.

Before we consider this matter further, let's be sure that the difference between inductive and deductive reasoning is clear. You will find that many of your students have problems with this distinction—a problem exacerbated by misuse of the terms in the popular press and stories they read. Induction or deduction—which kind of thinking did Sherlock Holmes use? From the clues he found, he arrived at conclusions as to the killer, motive, and method. When Watson asked Holmes how he reached his conclusions, Holmes would reply, "Deduction, Watson, pure deduction." Was it pure *deduction*, or did Holmes actually use *induction*? Inductive reasoning must be in operation when we generalize (arrive at conclusions) from specific instances. So Sherlock Holmes often used inductive reasoning. He behaved very much like the researcher who collects data, orders and classifies it, and then mentally "jumps from" the data to a conclusion. *Deductive reasoning*, on the other hand, *occurs when we move from an accepted generalization to specific instances.* If you're recalling some of Holmes' conversations with Watson as Holmes explained his reasoning, you're probably remembering that he also used the "If A were true, Watson, then B would follow" argument. Thus, Holmes also used deductive, more properly *hypothetico-deductive*, reasoning. Sir Arthur Conan Doyle invented a detective who was surely reasoning in a formal operational way. Thus, Sherlock Holmes used a combination of inductive and deductive reasoning—never *pure deduction.* You'll be helping your students learn these distinctions through illustrations of both kinds of reasoning.

As we said, when scientists use deductive reasoning, they always have to consider the reasonableness, rather than the correctness, of the generalities that are part of the theory they are using. To understand why reasonableness is the criterion used, let's consider an example of hypothesis testing. By now it should be clear that a *hypothesis is a predictive statement in "If–then" form that accounts for events in terms of relationships to theory.* Assume that a given theory postulates visual stimuli as the mechanism for bird navigation. A hypothesis derived from this theory might be:

> *If species X employs only visual stimuli to find the way back to the nesting area, then blindfolded individuals of species X will not find their way to the nesting area.*

This hypothesis would be *disproved* if blindfolded individuals do find their way back. If it turns out that blindfolded creatures do not return, the notion in question is merely supported or verified. It is *not proved*. Why not? The blindfolds may have effects in addition to removing contact with visual stimuli. An incorrect "if" part of a hypothesis may lead to a correct "then" (prediction) part.

Thus, it is evident that science, unlike its sister discipline of mathematics, characterizes its relationships as probable, rather than certain. Alert science teachers are aware of the fact that truth tables and truth values of logical statements are topics often included in mathematics curricula in grades 10 through 12. They learn to use mathematics teachers as resource persons and to question students about the similarities and differences between terms such as *theory* versus *theorem* and *verify* versus *prove*. Such tactics help to head off student confusion and to promote increased understanding of both disciplines. We will return to this topic in a later section in order to clarify further aspects of the structure of science.

Experimenting is certainly one of the most crucial aspects of the ways of finding out, for it is the acid test of ideas drawn from the theoretical root of science. The "truths" (proximate, not ultimate) that emerge are then used as springboards to others. These, in turn, are thought to be true because of believed connections to the first set. This process of *inferring—concluding from given data or premises to other instances*—is very much a part of science processes. Further experimentation either lends increased credibility to these mental leaps or reveals weaknesses in the principles/rules so espoused. No wonder all experiments must be repeatable by any qualified scientist before being accepted as valid!

Do scientists ever make assumptions? Yes, every theory is based on one or more assumptions regarding the nature of our physical world. Indeed, all of science rests on one basic assumption that is so obvious that we are prone to forget it —"The universe is *not* capricious." A prediction that works on Monday ought to work the same way on Saturday (provided the conditions remain constant) and $s = (1/2)at^2$ ought to hold in Russia as well as in the United States. Thus, *assuming—tentatively accepting a proposition without firm evidence to support it*—is also an important process of science. Of course, science is restricted to assumptions that seem reasonable in the light of available evidence. Otherwise, a host of nonproductive theories and thought models would be produced by using logical thinking processes on faulty assumptions.

What kinds of logical thought processes are used in science? All of them are used, including assuming, inferring, and hypothesizing (which have been defined earlier). Another key thought process inherent in inventing thought models is *reasoning by analogy—proposing a resemblance of principle between objects, ideas, and situations, superficially unalike*. The fruitfulness of this thinking mode has been demonstrated repeatedly throughout the history of science. Just think of the advances made possible by conceiving of the universe as a gigantic clocklike mechanism. However, like any other productive thinking process, this one involves some risk. This is particularly dangerous if the proposed resemblance is only superficial. For instance, the tendency to think about machines (*e.g.*, levers) as if they were humans leads to misconceptions if one overlooks purpose in humans versus the nonpurposefulness of machines. We must remain alert to the fact that *every* analogy limps.

This train of thought leads us to consider two types of thinking that *have no place* in scientific reasoning. *Anthropomorphic reasoning is the process of ascribing human characteristics to nonhuman creatures or things.* The machine/human analogy is one example. Others are statements such as "Roots seek water," "Nature *abhors* a vacuum," and "A negative ion *wants* to lose electrons." A similar, often overlapping, type of thinking is known as *teleological reasoning—explaining an end state by simply asserting it as a given in the beginning premise.* This puts the future into the past and reverses the cause (antecedent) and effect (consequent) sequence insisted upon in scientific thinking. The statement "Eggs have yolk *so that* they can provide food for embryonic development" implies that eggs can both (1) foresee the future nutritional problem and (2) as a result, of their own volition, proceed to develop structures that will satisfy the need. The same type of reasoning has led some people to conclude that the whole purpose of the evolution of living things was to produce the human species as its final and most magnificent product. Certainly anyone who is aware of the hordes of parasites that cannot live anywhere but inside the human body would have a hard time accepting that reasoning.

Both anthropomorphic and teleological reasoning are rooted in the philosophy of vitalism, which is based on the notion that every natural object is autonomous with a vital, internal force. Vitalistic doctrines, and reasoning emanating from them, may have their place in other modes of human inquiry. However, they have no place in science because they do not lead to hypotheses that can be either falsified or verified by empirical testing. Questions regarding the purposes of the universe lie outside the province of science. Rather science is limited to the investigation of those questions answerable in terms of *scientific explanations—the description of antecedent conditions and specification of their influences on subsequent observable phenomena.* The recognition of this insistence on hypotheses testable in terms of one-to-one correspondence with observables brings us full cycle to where we started at the beginning of this section. Observing is truly the alpha and omega of all scientific exploration.

4.4 A MODEL OF THE NATURE OF SCIENCE

Doubtless you are impressed, as we are, that science is a complex enterprise. You've also been repeatedly directed to study the instructional model that appears at the beginning of every chapter. Of course, the actual model doesn't appear on paper, but its representation does. The thought model, which we call an instructional model, exists in the mind and cannot be accurately captured by any representation. However, we've found that the selected representation stimulates an understanding of the complex processes of instruction. Every representation, or physical model, of a thought model has a similar reason for its construction— to clarify, to simplify, and to suggest novel relationships. The *thought model,* itself, *is a mental likeness that seems to correspond to observed structures, systems, and processes and that has explanatory value.* It should subsume a host of relevant details and make relationships clear, thus reducing the load on the human mind that attempts to use it. The schematic thought model shown in Figure 4.4 is a synthesis of the process/product views of science in relation to the physical world and the idea world. Study it carefully.

First consider some of the more obvious aspects of the schema. The terms included under each of the two headings of PROCESSES and PRODUCTS are arranged in a vertical sequence starting with the most specific and concrete at the bottom and progressing upward to the more general and abstract. This arrangement should make sense to you in terms of the operational definitions proposed earlier. Also note that most process terms are lined up horizontally with a product term, just as we asked you to do in the introductory activity. Did you come up with essentially the same matches in your attempt? What differences exist? Consider your rationale and compare it with ours. Now think about the two words in solid caps whose letters are arranged vertically between the two columns. What in the world is NOITCUDNI? Check the arrow for a clue if the answer is not obvious. We placed its initial letter at the bottom of this vertical column and spelled out the word in an upward direction to emphasize the "from specific to general" aspect of its meaning. Similarly the "from general to specific" essence of deduction is stressed by its opposite arrangement on the page.

Next, think about some of the less obvious features of Figure 4.4. Why did we place a dotted line between the top and bottom halves of the diagram? Try to think of some descriptive words that would categorize the terms above the line, and then contrast these with descriptors for those appearing below the line. Did you choose words such as *theoretical, ideal,* and *abstract* versus *empirical, real* (in a physical sense), and *phenomena* (observables)? If so, you have grasped our reasoning. If not, rethink the operational definitions presented earlier in this chapter and re-examine the model of science. Why not use a solid line? We did not wish to imply the notion of watertight compartments for these two worlds of science. Also notice the circle of verification part of the schema. Here is where the end products of theorizing meet the acid test of sciencing—the results of experimenting. A close match of theoretical principle with its empirical twin means verification and thus acceptance as a viable idea of science. On the other hand, when deductive logic yields notions that are in disharmony with empirical findings, it is the theory and logical reasoning that must be repaired or discarded, provided both the design and execution of experimentation check out. Valid and repeatable data can never be disregarded.

Just as every analogy limps, so every model has its limitations. Ours is no exception. One obvious limitation is that not all possible processes and products are included. Another imperfection is the lack of an exact one-to-one match of product to process in several places. A third is that the hierarchical organization of science is not well depicted by the schema. We hold to this model, however, for the same reasons we accept and use any other model. It seems to correspond

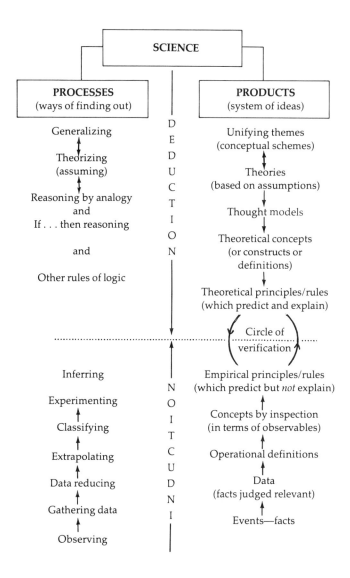

Fig. 4.4 A model of science processes and products.
Developed in collaboration with Dr. H. Craig Sipe, SUNY-Albany.

to observations, has explanatory value and is simple enough to be useful in our work.

One way of studying both the thought model and the related schema is by contrast with the sister discipline of science, mathematics. Recall the fascinating tale of Kepler's struggles to mathematically ascertain the orbit of Mars. His eventual success depended on the earlier work of Napier, who had invented logarithms, and Tycho Brahe, who had collected an enormous amount of planetary observational data. The genius of Kepler was to use both of these tools in the pursuit of a best-fit mathematical model and to reject previously held sacrosanct notions—*i.e.*, that the planets moved in circular orbits with uniform motion. Kepler chose to assume the existence of a different mathematical model for the orbit of Mars, that of an ellipse. His use of the circle of verification showed that the existing data fit that model like a glove (Polya, 1963). Thus, inventions of mathematics have been used to communicate scientific knowledge, to represent data, and to pave the way to scientific development by simplifying, clarifying, and, in particular, inspiring new hypotheses.

However, there are some aspects of this model of science that differ sharply from any model of mathematics. Two, in particular, are worth critical consideration for you as a science teacher—theory and concept. The label *theory* appears in the model of science. A similar-sounding but vastly different label, *theorem*, appears in any model of mathematics. Whereas theories are tested by returning to the physical world and checking their correspondence with real-world data, theorems are proved in the idea world by deductive logic. Theories are *not* proved; they are tentatively verified. What happens to the idea-world and physical-world notions in a model of science? What processes in the model of science might not appear in a model of mathematics? If these questions disturb your confidence, then join the crowd. There are college graduates who think that mathematical results must correspond to real-world data. Next, consider the second aspect of the model of science that was identified as being worthy of further study—scientific concepts.

Are mathematical concepts different from scientific concepts? Well, unlike other kinds of concepts such as cow, dog, glass, ant, and the like, you cannot see or subject to the other senses exemplars of triangles, points, pi, or congruence. We write numbers, don't we? No, we write symbols, which some prefer to call *numerals* (names for numbers). Now you have the key to another difference between mathematics and science. Scientific concepts include *both* those whose exemplars can be perceived by the senses, such as insect and flower (concepts by inspection), and those whose exemplars cannot be perceived by the senses, such as atom and gravity (theoretical concepts). As in the case of mathematics, these latter concepts are taught by using physical models or representations of the concepts. Now you should be a little closer to an understanding of some of the differences and some of the similarities between mathematics and science. You should also be starting to sense the enormous possibilities for helping students learn science through the vehicle of mathematics.

4.5 INSTRUCTION AND THE DYNAMIC NATURE OF SCIENCE

Data from recent reports on science teaching reveal that the textbook is the curriculum, the lecture is the major mode of instruction, and most students do not conduct any experiments with an unknown solution (Yager, Aldrich, & Penick, 1983). Yager (1987) has emphasized the need for students to understand and experience science processes and the interrelationships of these to the invention of scientific products to reflect the dynamic nature of science. Other researchers (Lederman & Zeidler, 1987) have been studying the relationship between science teachers' beliefs about the nature of science and their instruction in the classroom. If you were taught to look for patterns, to examine strategies, or to engage in different approaches to a problem, you were being taught something about the dynamic nature of science. Your teachers were, in all probability, designing lessons that illustrated *their* beliefs about science. In the introductory section of this chapter, we asked you to reflect on your beliefs. Subsequent sections of this chapter have included illustrations from the history of science and from the classrooms of reflective teachers against which to test those beliefs. You'll need to continue to reflect on your beliefs about the discipline of science as you engage in the life-long study of teaching. In this section, we consider some further illustrative strategies and principles that highlight the dynamic nature of science.

If many of the important objectives of contemporary curricula are to be achieved, there must be a *continuous interweaving* of attention to the process and product aspects of science. Consider the following description of instruction in a tenth-grade biology class.

Mr. Werter had noted that beginning biology students typically showed considerable interest in animals but regarded plants as simple, almost inanimate objects and thus dull subjects for investigation. Convinced that the topic of plant physiology merited attention and committed to the value of teaching the process aspects of science, Mr. Werter worked out a long-range demonstration-experiment to teach these problems.

The students were asked to list the essential conditions for germination while the teacher acted as a secretary at the chalkboard. They usually listed "dirt," sunlight, heat, moisture, and air, and sometimes volunteered a variety of other factors. Further probing questions posed by the teacher resulted in refinement of these conditions so that the revised list contained items such as "good, rich garden soil" and "enough water so that the seeds stay wet at all times." The students were then asked to design experimental set-ups to test each of these ideas. The statement of the hypotheses, isolation of control and variable factors, and design of the experiments proceeded concurrently with the actual setting-up, since needed materials had been brought in ahead of time and kept in a drawer of the demonstration desk. Petri dishes, soil, paper towels, seeds and thermometers were among the widely available and fairly obvious materials used to test all factors except the 'air" or oxygen requirement. Students were usually at a loss to think of effective ways to test this variable.

At this point, a library assignment was given to all as homework. The time remaining in the period was then devoted to making predictions of the outcomes, which the students were often willing to do with great finality. Friday was selected for this period of activity so that observations could be started on Monday or Tuesday.

Often the students would suggest placing one germination set-up in a refrigerator, but almost never did they specify the location within the refrigerator or attach any significance to the kind of seed used. After the students left, the teacher produced some additional set-ups. Several different kinds of seeds were used, including radish and maple; and one dish of each kind was placed on each shelf of the refrigerator. The temperature control was turned to its lowest setting.

On Monday or Tuesday the predictions previously made by the students were reviewed immediately prior to observing the results of each part of the experiment. The results both surprised and interested the students. Some students simply could not believe their eyes. Seeds were germinating in sand, sawdust, and paper towels as well as in "good, rich garden soil." Seeds were germinating in the dark as well as in sunlight, and some were even germinating in the refrigerator! An attempt to write tentative conclusions followed. This led to increased sensitivity regarding the need to restrict conclusions to the actual data collected. Students then usually suggested many other sub-experiments that should be tried. These suggestions, coupled with the results of the library or homework assignment on how the air or oxygen factor could be tested, were used as a basis for the week's laboratory work. Some leading questions by the teacher developed interest in "why" some conditions are essential in terms of function.

At this point, the teacher set up a puzzling demonstration to supply continuing motivation for the related topics that were to follow. A bean seed that had germinated to the point where secondary roots had started to develop was selected. One of its cotyledons was impaled on the point of a pin over a shallow dish of water so that the ends of the developing roots were in contact with the water. Soft wood was used to make a supporting base for the head end of the pin. A small tumbler was used to cover the entire set-up (see Figure 4.5). This was shown to the class and they were asked to predict what would happen. The range of these predictions was always quite revealing! Placed in a conspicuous spot in the classroom, this demonstration always continued to attract a good deal of attention during the next week or two. Frequent and heated debates among students were not uncommon, since the text provided no ready answers to their dilemma and the teacher parried each question with another question.

After the plant outgrew larger and larger beakers, it was suspended inside a hydrometer jar containing an inch of water by means of a string tied loosely around its cotyledons (see Figure 4.6). Since many of the class now had some understanding of the function of cotyledons, many class members predicted a speedy death as soon as these structures were absorbed or fell off. When the plant continued to flourish after the cotyledons were gone, most students formed definite ideas about the future fate of the plant. Some thought that essential minerals, which they now knew something about, were present in the water. Others argued that these must get into the system via the air. Yet others insisted that there were enough stored minerals in the cotyledons to last the plant a long time.

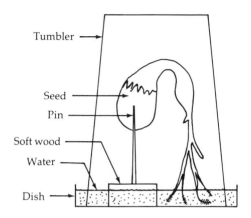

Fig. 4.5   Germinating seed on a pin.

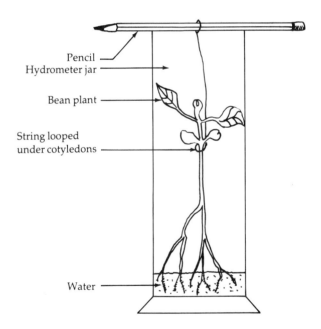

Fig. 4.6   Seedling in a hydrometer jar.

Many similar set-ups were always suggested and produced. They included some with sealed tops to prevent the entrance of air from outside the system, one or more using distilled water, and several containing different kinds of developing plants. Some individual student projects and library reading usually followed, and many questions about plant physiology were raised. Beans almost always survived to the point of flowering and starting to form fruit. (We have never seen one survive beyond this point with either tap water or distilled water as the growing medium.) An interesting homework assignment was to have the students attempt to explain the observations they had been making throughout the entire length of time from germination until the death of the plant. This demonstration also provided quiz and test questions throughout the progress of the demonstration.

Now go back and analyze this use of a long-term demonstration-experiment to teach the structure of science. Which parts of our model of science processes and products were explicitly included in the description? What other processes or products, not explicitly included, can you identify? Think of examples from other science content areas that could form the basis for lessons that emphasize the structure of science. See Chapters 9, 10, and 11 for additional classroom illustrations and sources of related teaching ideas.

Further opportunities to get at the underlying structure of the subject matter are present *every time* a physical model is used in instruction. Point to the dissectible human model, the plaster flower, and the wooden spheres connected by sticks and ask, "Is this an actual person, or flower, or molecule?" "In what ways is each an accurate representation of the object or idea represented?" "In what respects is each a less than perfect representation?" "What are the differences between a thought model and a physical model?" "Why does science use thought models?" "How do we decide which thought models to use and which to discard?"

For other types of lessons, it is sometimes appropriate to bring in quotations from famous figures of either the present or the past. For instance, one of the most famous Renaissance men, Leonardo da Vinci (1452–1519), said: "He who loves practice without theory is like a sailor who boards a ship without a rudder and compass and never knows where he may be cast" (Kline, 1972). Students can be asked to evaluate the relevance of da Vinci's statement to the historical development of a science idea traced by the text or by their teacher.

The history of science also abounds with interesting examples that you can interweave in lessons with other important understandings about the nature of science. One case in point is the fact that ancients believed that the sun orbits the earth. Acceptance of this assumption leads to the prediction that the sun will appear to rise, cross the sky, and then set behind the opposite horizon—a *true* prediction based on a *false* assumption. You can call this to students' attention and then ask them how it came to be that this geocentric model of the solar system was later rejected by scientists. (See the Polya source in the Suggestions for Further Study for some teaching ideas on this area.) Developmental questioning about *other* predictions based on the same erroneous assumption can lead to increased insight about the processes of verification/falsification.

Demonstrations and laboratory exercises are loaded with potential for teaching numerous aspects of science processes as well as products. Questions such as the following can be used in conjunction with demonstrations or laboratory exercises: "What assumptions have we made by agreeing to collect data on time and the height and length of the inclined plane but to ignore other factors such as room temperature and relative humidity?" "What are three probable sources of error in the specific heat of metals laboratory exercise we just completed?" "Why is it unjustifiable to infer a linear relationship from these three plotted points that could be connected by a straight line?" "How can we design an experiment to test the notion that sunlight inhibits stem growth of green plants?" These questions direct students' attention to important parts of the scientific enterprise that are all too often overlooked.

Similarly, the many radio, television, magazine, and newspaper advertisements that attempt to project a scientific aura can be analyzed by posing thoughtful questions. Consider the following examples: "Under what conditions were the experiments conducted that prompted an independent testing laboratory to conclude that brand A is 30 percent more effective than the other leading brands?" "How was the survey structured that prompted three out of four dentists to recommend the product, Fourtooth, to patients who chew gum?" "Are there any known side effects to overdoses of Stomachease tablets, which laypersons are encouraged to self-prescribe?" "With so many guaranteed ways to lose X pounds painlessly in Y days, why are there still so many overweight people around?" "What is the meaning of the phrase,'medically proven ingredients'?" Interesting homework assignments can be structured around the collection and preliminary analysis of current advertising. Follow-up classwork might well involve a combination of other modes ranging from developmental question/answer through individual student projects designed to contrast science and pseudoscience.

Old sayings are also grist for the science teacher's mill. Is there any theoretical or empirical base for "Red in the morning, sailors take warning; red at night, sailors delight"? Does it generally hold that "It is always calm just before a storm"? These and other similar sayings are productive points of departure because they do summarize observations made by people under uncontrolled conditions. They do contain an element of truth and that is why they have endured for so many years. It is both possible and profitable to explore the accuracy of these predictions *without* poking fun at students (or their parents) who have come to believe in them. After all, the present stage of science owes a great debt to its earlier natural history stage of development. In any case, ridicule has never proved to be an effective approach to changing people's belief systems, and generally does irreparable harm to the teacher/student relationship.

These same cautions hold for dealing with anthropomorphic and teleological "explanations." Competent science teachers cannot ignore student statements to the effect that "Hot air *rises*," "Water *seeks* its own level," or "The heart is muscular *so that* it can pump blood around the body." However, sternly lecturing about the magic and twisted cause-and-effect relationships of such statements is not the only alternative to letting them pass unnoticed. Again, a series of developmental questions focusing on relative densities, gravitational force, or structure-to-function relationships is a more promising approach.

As you search professional journals and other sources you will find many additional ideas that can be used by teachers to help students understand more fully the nature of science. How do you decide when to use each of these ideas? That depends on the objectives you set for each lesson. It should now be clear that setting these objectives must depend both on the intellectual development of your students and on the nature of science. As you interact with the material in the next chapter, keep checking your ideas with the theory and research on adolescent reasoning and the model of science presented in this chapter.

4.6 SUMMARY AND SELF-CHECK

In this chapter we opened with a question: Science—Invented or Discovered? We asked you to make an initial response and to test that response against ideas presented in later sections. Selected processes and products of science were first illustrated and operationally defined and then synthesized into a simplified model of science.

Throughout this chapter you were presented with illustrations of classroom teachers attending to some part of this model. The power and weaknesses of the use of analogy and the need to be alert to anthropomorphic and teleological reasoning were emphasized. You were provided with several ways to begin helping non-formal reasoners learn about the complex processes involved in designing an experiment.

Now you should be able to:

1. Operationally define each of the process and product aspects of science included in the model.

2. Explain the interrelationships among the product aspects and the processes that generate each.

3. Explain the hierarchical relationships inherent in the model.

4. Explain the circle of verification depicted in the model.

5. Identify errors, by both omission and commission, in communicating the nature of science during either "live" or "taped" lessons and give reasons for your judgments.

6. Analyze instructional materials in terms of their potential for teaching the structure of science.

4.7 SIMULATION/PRACTICE ACTIVITIES

A. Obtain a copy of a syllabus or course guide for one course you are preparing to teach. Select one unit for which you think your own subject matter preparation has been particularly strong (e.g., genetics, acids and bases, weather, or radioactivity). Prepare a sheet of paper with headings and columns corresponding to each category under the "System of Ideas" (Products Aspects) part of the Model of Science presented in this chapter (Fig. 4.2). Then analyze the content of the selected unit and write words, formulas, and so on, in the appropriate columns as you categorize each idea to be taught. Check your results against those obtained by one or more other students who selected the same unit and attempt to resolve any differences by discussion. Submit your final results to your instructor for critique.

B. Read one of the following accounts of a scientific breakthrough and keep a running tally of the various categories of science processes that came into play and examples of the tentative, cumulative, and self-correcting nature of science.

Seaborg, G. T., & Valens, E. G. (1958). *Elements of the universe*. New York, NY: E. P. Dutton & Co.

Watson, J. D. (1968). *The double helix: A personal account of the discovery of the structure of DNA*. New York, NY: Atheneum.

Wilson, J. (Ed.). (1975). *All in our time: The reminiscences of twelve nuclear pioneers*. Chicago, IL: The Bulletin of Atomic Scientists.

C. Locate an article in the popular press (newspaper or magazine) that reports some recent scientific breakthrough. Keep a running tally on the reported process and product aspects. Then make a list of those aspects not included that you think should be added in order to present a more adequate account.

D. Consult one of the sources on the history of science and look up the scientific contribution and the personal history of one or more of the following: Joseph Black, Camerius, Lady Anne Conway, Chester More Hall, Caroline Herschel, Marcello Malpighi, Rosalyn Yalow.

E. Refer to the Resource File modular assigment in the Appendix. This is an excellent time to begin collecting ideas in one area of that assignment. As you read, or hear of, ways to include in your instruction illustrations communicating the processes/products of science, excerpt the key features (sketches, historical notes, instructional ties) and begin filing these on individual sheets or 5 × 8 cards in the appropriate file folder. Ask your instructor to check your classification scheme and your use of it. Extend your file gradually to each subject you will teach. Continue collecting ideas from experienced teachers, as well as from professional journals and texts (see Chapters 9, 10, and 11 for other recommended sources).

F. Miss Take told her seventh-grade science class that she was going to demonstrate some experiments to prove how to test for some nutrients. She showed a piece of brown paper bag, then rubbed a shelled peanut on it and passed the paper around so all could see the resulting grease spot. Next she called attention to the blue color of Benedict's solution as it was poured into a clean test tube, dissolved some glucose in the solution, and then heated the mixture. After the heated mixture turned red-orange, she carried it around for all to observe. During the follow-up question/answer session, she elicited conclusions from the students that she had proved that the test for fat-oil is the appearance of a grease spot when the unknown is rubbed on a piece of brown paper bag and that the test for sugar is a red-orange color produced when the unknown is heated in Benedict's solution. Make a list of the specific science content violations committed by Miss Take and briefly describe corrective measures needed to protect content validity.

G. Complete the checklist (as adapted from a version in Sagness, 1970) provided here and share your results with those of other preservice or inservice teachers of science.

Profile of a Science Teacher

This checklist has been designed to help you reflect on the beliefs you hold as a prospective or present teacher of science. For each statement, indicate whether you strongly agree (SA), agree (A), disagree (D), or strongly disagree (SD).

1. Science classes should provide for some discussion of the problem facing scientists in the discovery of a scientific principle.
2. It is important that students discuss the evidence behind a scientist's conclusion.
3. Students should be told step-by-step what they are to do in the laboratory.
4. Tests should often require the figuring out of new problems.
5. The textbook is based on scientific fact and as such should not be questioned by students.
6. It is important that students frequently write out definitions of word lists.
7. A majority of class time should be spent lecturing about science.
8. Classroom laboratory activities, such as experiments and demonstrations, should usually be performed by students rather than by the teacher.
9. Students should often read in sources of science information (books, magazines, etc.) other than their textbook.
10. Tests should seldom contain problems that involve the use of mathematics in their solution.
11. Science laboratories should meet on a regularly scheduled basis (such as every Tuesday or Friday).
12. Science should be presented as having almost all of the answers to questions about the natural world.

SUGGESTIONS FOR FURTHER STUDY

Abbott, E. A. (1952). *Flatland* (6th ed., rev.). New York, NY: Dover Publications.

The subtitle of this book is a *A Romance of Many Dimensions*. The reader is first taken on a journey into a world of two dimensions where all of the inhabitants are some sort of geometric shape. However, these inhabitants move, communicate and seem to have feelings. The adventurer is then transported to Lineland and finally, to Spaceland. This book has been enjoyed by mathematics and science students and all interested in science fiction. It is an excellent way for students and teachers to explore concepts of relativity and hyperspace, as well as Euclidean and non-Euclidean geometry.

Alic, Margaret (1986). *Hypatia's heritage: A history of women in science from antiquity to the late nineteenth century*. London, England: The Women's Press, Ltd.

Although American women in science are not included in this book, Alic provides a wealth of information on the contributions of women in the physical sciences, natural sciences, and mathematics from antiquity to the last decade of the nineteenth century.

Asimov, I. (1982). *Asimov's biographical encyclopedia of science and technology*. New York, NY: Doubleday.

Asimov provides 1195 biographies, each describing both scientific and personal information about the scientist. The use of cross-referencing allows the reader to see how scientists extended the work of others. The nature of science is further illuminated by the listing of mistakes that were later corrected by others.

Bronowski, J. (1965). *Science and human values*. New York, NY: Harper and Row.

This small, but potent, paperback was written by a man who has the rare distinction of being both a respected professional scientist and an inspiring humanist. The contents, in the form of four related essays, focus on the creative mind, the habit of truth, human dignity, and the science versus literary arts dilemma popularized by C. P. Snow's *The Two Cultures*. The central theme of the author is that the practice of science compels the practitioner to form a personal fundamental set of universal values. The ideas presented are powerful and readers must pause and reflect on the contents in order to abstract the full value of Bronowski's work.

Dampier, W. C. (1966). *A history of sciences*. New York, NY: Cambridge Univ. Press.

The author traces the development of the structure of modern science from the ancient world to the middle ages to the twentieth century. Notable topics include the nature of science, contributions by scientists, nineteenth-century physics, and nineteenth-century biology.

National Science Teachers Association. (1984). *Career oriented modules to explore topics in science (COMETS)*. Washington, DC: National Science Teachers Association.

In Volume II, COMETS Science provides 24 sets of supplemental lesson plans for grades 5–9 to enable teachers to use community resource people. Each module also describes the historical, scientific contribution made by women on the topic.

Polya, G. (1963). *Mathematical methods in science* (Studies in Mathematics, Vol. 11). Stanford, CA: School Mathematics Study Group.

This little book was written for teachers of mathematics and science, in terms that could be understood by their students. Historical details of developments in science and mathematics are cleverly presented so that secondary students can follow complex results. Here the reader will find sections that sound as if they have been cross-referenced to this chapter—*e.g.*, Heavier bodies fall faster? How do heavy bodies fall? and Scientific Attitude: Verification. Newton, Tycho Brahe, Galileo, Stevinus, and Kepler are major stars in these chapters. This is an excellent teaching resource.

Shepherd, W. (1968). *Outline history of science*. New York, NY: Philosophical Library, Inc.

In this small paperback, the author provides a brief summary of notable events in science from 500 B.C. to 1965. The organization of the material makes it very easy for the reader to see which scientists were contemporaries. A bibliography is provided for those seeking additional details.

CHAPTER FIVE

INSTRUCTIONAL OBJECTIVES

Targets of Instruction

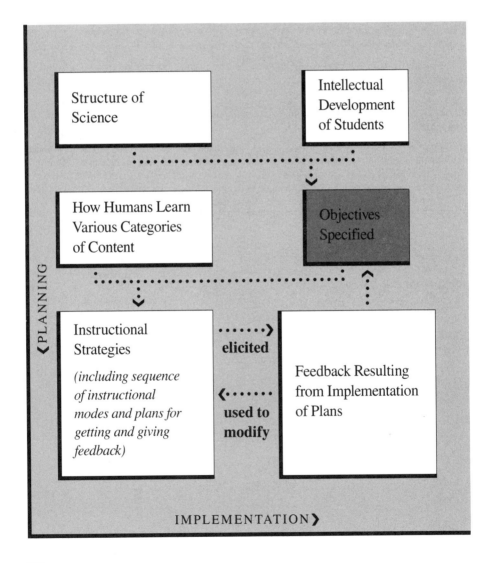

The comedian leaves the stage as the guffaws and cheers finally die down. Will he be asked back? Was he effective? The surgeon slowly and grimly leaves the operating theater. She must find a way to tell Mr. Mack that his wife died on the table. Will the surgeon be sued for malpractice? Was she incompetent? Professor Seedwell lectures to over two hundred students on Mendelian genetics. His voice is clear and his articulation good. Printed notes that accompany the lecture are well organized and easily adapted to incorporating additional material from the lecture. As the class ends, some students can be heard griping about his cold, impersonal style. "He never even looks at us." Does this necessarily mean that Professor Seedwell is incompetent?

By now you should be wary, for all these situations are characterized by a hidden agenda. Effectiveness seems to be tied to some result or outcome, but what outcome? If Professor Seedwell had lectured in such a fashion that many students left with smiles on their faces, would his lecture have necessarily been effective? If Mrs. Mack had lived after the operation, would that be firm evidence that the surgeon had been skillful? If the audience had been quiet after the last joke, should the comedian have been fired? You're right if you tended to avoid straightforward "yes" or "no" answers and found yourself responding in terms of, "It would depend ...." If the lecturer's intention was to get students to smile, then he and the comedian have both been effective to the extent that their audiences were left with happy grins on their faces. However, we all expect more of Professor Seedwell. His students are supposed to learn something about genetics. Let's look, in some detail, at Professor Seedwell's approach to teaching this topic.

Professor Seedwell had decided to spend two weeks on Mendelian genetics. He directed his graduate assistants to continue lecturing in the small-group sections so that more types of crosses could be worked out on the chalkboard. No questions were to be directed at the students, and no time was to be provided for questioning by them. Is this choice of modes appropriate? If your response is no, then you agree with our assessment of this situation.

Next Professor Seedwell asked each of his graduate assistants to propose test questions based on the content material of this unit. Joe Martin formulated questions in which the students would have to predict the results of crosses similar to, but not the same as, those presented in any of the classes. Art Cary thought that was unfair and instead proposed questions that required the reproduction of a sample of the crosses presented by one of the instructors. Sally Beers's questions were of an entirely different kind. She proposed that the students be given partially completed family tree diagrams and that they be asked to find the missing genotypes of progeny and parents. Which set of questions would provide better evidence of the effectiveness of the instruction? If you lean toward Sally's test but you wouldn't want to take it under the described circumstances, you'll have lots of company.

There ought to be a connection between instruction and testing. That connection might be characterized as "knowing where you're going." If Professor

Seedwell had decided what he expected of his students with relation to genetic crosses, he might have proposed different uses of small-group time and then he should have been able to be quite clear about the kinds of evidence needed from a test.

Where are we going? How will we know when and if we get there? What are the objectives? The position of the shaded "Objectives Specified" box as an output based on analysis of the content of science and analysis of the intellectual development of the students is a reminder that these two aspects of planning are precursors to defining "where we are going." In the activity that follows, be alert to the effects on choice of objective, of the type of science content being studied and the probable intellectual developmental level of the students.

5.1 INTRODUCTORY ACTIVITY

Where are we going, and how will we
know when we get there?

In order to perform this activity, you need to observe a junior high or senior high science class.

A. Before the class, ask the teacher *only* the topic(s) to be developed in the class. While observing the class, take notes on specifics in the following areas:

    1. What do you infer that the students are expected to be able to *do* as a result of instruction? Cite evidence, verbal and nonverbal observables, on which you base your inferences.

    2. At what point in the lesson did you become aware of these possible objectives?

    3. What did the students say and/or do that seemed to illustrate that they knew what was expected of them?

    4. When and how did the teacher get feedback as to the extent to which the inferred objectives were met?

    5. Cite any verbal and/or nonverbal cues that might indicate student confusion about the objectives.

B. After the observation, ask the teacher to tell you the intended objectives. Share your observations and attempt to clarify areas of confusion.

C. Compare the results of your observation with results of at least two other classmates who observed different classes in your subject field. In classes where objectives seemed to be clear to both you and the students, which of the following characteristics were present?

    1. The teacher verbally related past learning to today's lesson.

    2. The teacher specifically told and/or showed students what they were expected to recall, how they were to apply a rule/principle, for what specific problem types they would be responsible.

    3. The teacher introduced each new concept and successive skill by tying these to earlier concepts and skills.

4. At times in the lesson the teacher attempted to get specific feedback on student achievement thus far, and the teacher gave oral feedback to the class relating to progress.

5. Instead of telling students only that they must "understand," the teacher followed up with expressions like "be able to give new examples of this concept" or "be able to use a formula to solve type problems."

If you were able to find examples of observables supporting each of the preceding, you have identified a class where teacher and students know where they are going and when they have arrived. If, on the other hand, the students began asking questions such as "What are we doing?" "What good is this anyway?" or "Why do I have to write all this?" then these are cues that the students were not tuned in on the objectives and, as a result, may have missed important developments in the lesson.

Your observations in this activity should be convincing evidence of the importance of having clear objectives and communicating these objectives to the students. Before you work through the next section of this chapter, try writing what seem to be suitable objectives for the class you observed. Be sure they are expressed clearly enough to communicate to students exactly what is expected of them after the lesson. As you interact with the reading in Section 5.2, modify your objectives as needed to make them consistent with the criteria you will learn to apply to such statements.

5.2 INSTRUCTIONAL OBJECTIVES VERSUS OTHER KINDS OF GOAL STATEMENTS

What are instructional objectives? In Chapter 2, you learned about diverse feedback strategies—ways to get and give feedback on progress toward objectives. In all those illustrations, who were the subjects of the teacher's feedback strategies? The students. Then the instructional objectives must be phrased in terms of *student* performance, not in terms of *teacher* performance. Remember Professor Seedwell? If he intended to lecture in an organized fashion, he apparently accomplished that goal. But he could have accomplished that goal in an empty lecture hall! There is no way to use that kind of teacher performance as a measure of *student* learning. But Professor Seedwell's graduate assistants were concerned about student learning and were still at odds over the nature of the test they should give. Suppose they had been told that the students were expected to "understand Mendelian genetics." Would that have helped? You're on the right track if you're still dissatisfied with this statement of an "objective." The verb *understand* is too broad in its scope to be helpful to either the students in the class or the instructors as a clue to what the test should demand. On the other hand, if the students were expected to be able to "write the genotypes of all progeny predicted in a dihybrid cross where the genotypes of both parents are given," then the character of the test questions becomes much clearer. Notice that student performance in this case is described in terms of *observable behavior*.

Stop and check your understanding by studying the four statements of possible "objectives" below. Which of these represent clear statements of instructional objectives that could be used as a guide toward planning of instructional and feedback strategies? Which are defective, and why?

1. The teacher will illustrate the use of computer software for the construction of graphs from laboratory data.
2. The students will observe a teacher demonstration of the use of computer software for graph generation.
3. The students will understand how to generate graphs using computer software.
4. The students will generate graphs from laboratory data for any pair of variables, given the use of computer software.

If you characterized the first statement as defective because it describes *teacher* behavior rather than *student* behavior, you have correctly focused on the first critical feature of instructional objectives. The last three statements are all written in terms of the student, so these seem to pass that test. Did you quickly reject statement 3 for its use of the word *understand* as a description of performance? Just as in the illustrative example, *understand* has too broad a range of meanings to be useful as an indicator of performance. Statements 2 and 4 should look good by comparison. Now put each of them to the dual test of feedback and content. How could a teacher get feedback on whether the students were able to perform the described task, and is performance of each task evidence that the students have learned computer-graphing skills? Now statement 2 should seem less promising. On the one hand, there is some obvious difficulty in assessing whether students are "observing." If all students are looking at the teacher during the demonstration, are they "observing"? On the other hand, even if we could agree on specific feedback cues that would assess observing, there is a lack of match between observing in this case, and appropriate outcomes of a computer demonstration. Observing is not one of the important terminal outcomes of a computer-graphing lesson. Can you think of content areas where specific observing skills *would* be important terminal outcomes? If you can't, it's time to refer back to the "Process" section of Chapter 4. For now, let's examine the fourth statement more closely. It is *specific*, is in terms of *student performance*, and does include *necessary conditions* under which the student must perform. Does the word "any" disturb you? It needn't. The teacher can sample the student's ability by selecting a variety of examples. If the sample is small or ill-conceived (such as using two variables measured with an interval scale), the teacher may infer erroneously that the student has met this objective. Effective sampling procedures are an important aspect of feedback collection and evaluation. You've already been alerted to sampling problems with respect to feedback collection and use in Chapter 2. You'll be reading an approach to sampling for evaluation purposes in Chapter 8.

By now you should be able to write your own operational definition of an instructional objective. Take a minute and try it. Check your definition against the nonexamples represented by the first three statements of "objectives" as well as the example illustrated by the final computer-graphing statement. Now match your definition against the one we have devised. An *instructional objective is a statement that describes a desired student outcome of instruction in terms of observable performance under given conditions.* If your definition contained most of the above features, then you're off to a fine start. Why did we include the modifier *observable* before *performance?* The answer resides in the need to get feedback. You've got it. Feedback can only be obtained by observing what students do, write, or say.

As a first check on your understanding of the definition, react to each of the following statements that Mr. Jackson included among his objectives for a seventh-grade ecology unit.

1. The student will be able to write operational definitions of the terms *producer* and *consumer*.

2. The student will discover that the sun is the basic source of all energy used by living things by viewing a motion picture that traces a wide variety of food/energy chains back to their ultimate source.

3. Given a list of the names of common local animals, the student will be able to label primary versus secondary consumers.

4. The student will be able to state two reasons why all animal life depends upon green plants.

5. The student will appreciate the role of bacteria of decay in our biotic world.

6. The student will understand that all living things are interdependent in a web-like relationship.

7. Given a soil thermometer, the student will be able to record soil temperatures accurate to within ±0.5° C.

Which of Mr. Jackson's objectives satisfy all the criteria specified in the operational definition? You should have listed statements 1, 3, 4, and 7. If you rejected statements 5 and 6 on the basis of the nonobservable verbs *(appreciate* and *understand),* you were absolutely correct. Statement 2 may have seemed less of a problem since the students will be viewing a motion picture. But how will Mr. Jackson know they have "discovered" anything? Statement 2 fails to meet the criterion of observable performance, but it does describe a desirable teaching mode aimed at meaningful learning of an important concept. If you are somewhat uncomfortable about eliminating statements 2, 5, and 6, you agree with Mr. Jackson and the authors that attention to underlying concepts (as in 2 and 6) and to attitudes toward science (as in 5) are vitally important overall goals of instruction. Try rewriting those three statements so that they do satisfy the definition. Then check your efforts against ours as we consider various classes of objectives in the next section.

5.3 DOMAINS OF INSTRUCTIONAL OBJECTIVES

A cursory examination of Mr. Jackson's "objectives" makes it clear that he was concerned about learning in distinct areas of emphasis and at various levels of

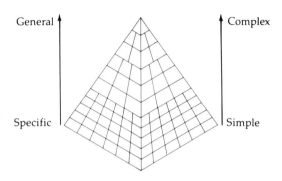

Fig. 5.1 Model of a hierarchy.

significance within some of those areas. The name given to the three major areas of emphasis into which all instructional objectives may be classified is *domain*. The *cognitive domain deals with recall or recognition of knowledge and the development of intellectual abilities and skills*. Most of Mr. Jackson's statements dealt with this domain, as will most of your objectives. However, remember that Mr. Jackson *did* try to write an objective aimed at attitude. *Changes in interest, attitudes, values and the development of appreciation belong to the affective domain*. The third domain, the *psychomotor domain, refers to the manipulative or motor-skill areas*. Did Mr. Jackson's objectives include any in this domain? Yes, statement 7 was an objective from the psychomotor domain. All of these domains should be considered sources of potential objectives.

Within each of these domains, there have been attempts to devise categorization systems called taxonomies. The purposes of such taxonomies are to make more explicit the varied levels of instructional objectives, to improve testing and research efforts, and to clarify communication among professionals in education. Why was the term *taxonomy* selected as the label for these systems of classification? You probably remember the biological taxonomy used in junior and senior high science classes wherein all living things are classified into categories such as kingdom, phylum, class, order, family, genus, and species. So a taxonomy is a set of standard classifications, and these categories are related in a hierarchical fashion. Figure 5.1 depicts a thought model of a hierarchy. At the base of the pyramid are the simple bits of knowledge. As one proceeds upward, ideas become increasingly complex. Similarly, one might think of the base as representative of the specifics of a field while the apex represents the generalizations. Since generalizations are built from specifics and since complex knowledge depends on simple units related in various ways, each layer of the hierarchy subsumes lower layers. Does the concept of hierarchy remind you of the nested stages model of Piagetian theory? You should be alert for correspondences between Piagetian theory and kinds of objectives as we build our taxonomies of instructional objectives.

Although all three domains are sources of potential objectives, taxonomies in two of the domains, the cognitive and the affective, are particularly useful tools for the secondary school science teacher. Since most of your work will deal with cognition, we will start with a classification of objectives in this domain.

The Cognitive Domain

The most widely used taxonomy of cognitive objectives is that devised by Benjamin Bloom and colleagues (1956). Bloom's taxonomy contains six major levels, or classes. We will use a version of Bloom's taxonomy as illustrated in Table 5.1.

Table 5.1
Cognitive Taxonomy

Level	Descriptive label	Description of level
Above III	Evaluation	Judgments about the *value* of material and methods for given purposes.
	Synthesis	Putting together parts so as to form a whole pattern or structure of ideas not clearly there before.
	Analysis	Breaking down of material into its parts so that the relationships among ideas are made explicit.
III	Novel application	The selection and use of a learned rule, concept, method in a situation *novel* to the student.
II	Comprehension	The use of a specific rule, concept, method in a situation *typical* to those used in class.
I	Knowledge	The recall of material with little or no alteration required.

It is important to keep in mind that a taxonomy is a hierarchy. Therefore, a level II objective implies that command of related level I behaviors is assumed. For example, if a student is expected to be able to use Ohm's *law* to find the current when given the resistance and electromotive force in a series circuit, that student is implicitly expected to be able to recall the formula for Ohm's *law*. However, the reverse does not hold. If a teacher plans lessons only on level I, then luck alone will be responsible for student learning of the level II *use* of recalled material.

Before we get too involved with all this background, let's look at some specific examples. If Mr. Jackson had written at least one objective at each level of the taxonomy, his list might have included some of the following.

The student will be able to:

Level I	List the names of three local animals classified as predators.
Level II	Compute the net change in a population, given the natality and mortality rates.

Level III	Propose a biological reason to account for the fact that an unfamiliar antarctic species of animal is larger than a very similar species that inhabits a more temperate zone.
Levels above III (Analysis)	Prepare lists of (1) facts cited, (2) data collected, and (3) inferences made, given unfamiliar paragraphs describing an ecological experiment.
(Synthesis)	Design an experiment to test the idea that increased crowding leads to increased aggressive behavior on the part of laboratory mice.
(Evaluation)	Discriminate the most effective from the least effective population management practices and justify these decisions, given an article describing the history of a project aimed at increasing the deer population on a certain island.

Study each of the preceding objectives and the descriptions of the corresponding taxonomic levels. Why is the third objective considered a *novel* application? Note that the final three objectives also contain elements of *novelty*. When you are attempting to identify the level of a particular objective, this element of *novelty to the learner* is a crucial characteristic that separates levels I and II from all other levels. The first question to ask of yourself then, is "Is the student expected to perform a task that has some element of novelty?" A negative response leads you to the next question: "Can the objective be satisfied by recall alone?" An affirmative response leads to the identification of level I as the correct one for the objective (see Figure 5.2). For most classroom purposes, it is sufficient for beginning teachers to be able to distinguish among levels I, II, III, and above III. Table 5.1 gives descriptions of the subdivisions above III for clarification only.

Sometimes the idea of novelty is mistakenly equated with the notion of complexity. The ability to use a long series of rules in a complicated chemistry problem is still level II behavior *if* the problem is a typical one, whereas the ability to select the correct rule, however simple, in a situation new to the student is level III behavior. An example of such a situation is illustrated here.

Find the smallest area of square filter paper stock that could be used to produce the circular piece shown in the diagram.

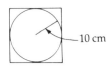

Notice that the student must realize that the radius is one-half the length of a side of the square—a step that requires a mental restructuring of the diagram!

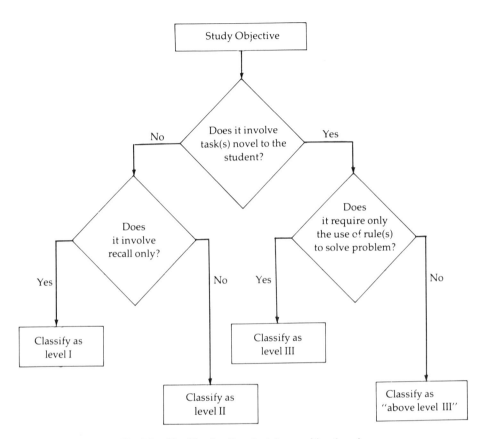

Fig. 5.2 Classification flowchart for cognitive domain.

This is a level III task. A second flow chart (Figure 5.3) schematizes this aspect of problem solving that distinguishes level III and above tasks from the lower levels of the taxonomy.

The "search" component of the flowchart may cause a person to think for a matter of seconds, minutes, or days. In any case, the objective represented by the problem is at or above level III. On the other hand, even though students cannot solve a type problem because they have forgotten needed formulas or are applying rules in an incorrect manner, the objective that is represented by the type problem is still a level II objective.

Examples and explanations are important ingredients in developing understanding, but there's no substitute for experience. Now it's time for you to check your own ability to classify objectives. Study each of the following objectives written by Ms. Bonner for her eleventh-grade chemistry class and classify each at one of the *four major* taxonomic levels described in Table 5.1.

The student will be able to:

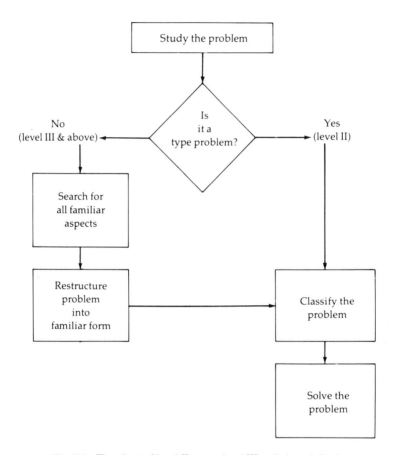

Fig. 5.3   Flowchart of level II versus level III and above behavior.

1. Draw electron dot models for any element, given access to a periodic chart.
2. Write the combined gas law in symbolic form.
3. Balance chemical equations, given the formulas for both reactants and products.
4. Complete and balance chemical equations for double replacement reactions, given only the formulas for the reactants.
5. Identify and explain the fallacy contained in any article purporting to describe a perpetual motion device run by a rechargeable battery.
6. Solve mass-volume problems, given the quantity of one of the relevant substances.

   Notice that Ms. Bonner took the same shortcut Mr. Jackson used in the last set of objectives. Since all objectives are in terms of student performance, both teachers wrote, "The student will be able to:" only once before the entire set of objectives. As a matter of fact, some teachers omit that phrase entirely since it is understood to be present. Did you perhaps want to reject some of Ms. Bonner's statements as instructional objectives because verbs such as *complete, balance, solve,* or *identify* suggest mental activity rather than observable performance? If so, you've been interacting carefully with the reading thus far. But we also slipped in some others like these earlier. Go back to Mr. Jackson's second set and note that some of his statements *seem* to be characterized by the same defect. If you're thinking that these objectives are perfectly clear and that to say otherwise is to make mountains out of molehills, we agree with you. Some instructors and curriculum writers would prefer to insert "in writing" or "orally" in each of the above statements. Whenever there is any ambiguity, we recommend this. However, as a general rule of thumb, highly specific, content-related verbs that are typically understood to imply observable performance may be used without any additional modifying phrase.

Be sure that you have written down your classification of each of Ms. Bonner's objectives before you read further. We classified objective 2 as the only objective at level I. It is the only one of the six statements where recall *alone* is sufficient to meet the objective. Granted, some students may forget the combined law formula and, recalling the separate gas laws, may combine them to obtain the desired formula. Although these students might be performing at level II, Ms. Bonner, as most eleventh-grade teachers, desired the eventual memorization of these formulas and intended this as a level I objective. If you classified most of her other objectives as level II, you are catching the idea. We classified objectives 1, 3, 4, and 6 as level II objectives and objective 5 as above level III. As written, each of the four level II objectives refers to the solution of *typical* problems for this unit. Ms. Bonner should have taught a series of strategies which the student is expected to use in each of these type problems. If you classified objective 5 as level III, rather than above III, don't be overly concerned. You correctly identified the element of novelty. However, we see that objective as requiring *more than* the application of rules to a novel task. It also entails breaking down material into its parts and making relationships explicit. Thus, we would more specifically classify this objective as at the analysis level. For further practice on this kind of task, see the Simulation/Practice Activities in Section 5.5.

Now you're ready to start on the first written component of each lesson plan—the stated instructional objectives. We asked you to test yourself on this earlier by rewriting Mr. Jackson's defective statements from Section 5.2. Two of these statements, 2 and 6, were cognitive, so it's appropriate to consider those now. Compare your versions with those of the authors.

Substitute 2. *The student will diagram all examples of food/energy chains in a manner that indicates the sun's energy as the starting point.*

Substitute 6. *The student will predict at least one probable effect in a food/energy chain other than the one most directly affected by any proposed change.*

Table 5.2
A Sample List of Performance Verbs

calculate	describe	hypothesize	label	solve
cite	design	identify	list	state
contrast	diagram	induce	plan	translate
criticize	evaluate	infer	plot	verify
deduce	explain	interpret	predict	write
defend	extrapolate	interpolate	propose	
derive	graph	justify	select	

Table 5.3
Affective Taxonomy

Level	Descriptive label	Description of level
III	Valuing	Commitment to a value shown by consistent and stable response to objects, people, phenomena, etc.
II	Responding	Voluntary participation in activities, or selection of one activity out of several.
I	Complying	Passive acceptance of role assigned by teacher. No overt avoidance of activity.

If your versions differ substantially from ours and you are not clear as to their suitability, check with other classmates and/or your instructor. Like most beginners, you may encounter initial difficulty in selecting performance verbs that accurately convey your intentions. Thus we have prepared a sample list of those verbs that have proved particularly useful in your subject matter field (see Table 5.2). Use it to the extent it proves helpful, but don't assume that including one verb from this list *guarantees* a well-structured objective.

The Affective Domain

Remember Mr. Jackson's defective objective that was rejected because it included the nonobservable verb *appreciate?* Mr. Jackson attempted to include an objective in the affective domain (feelings, attitudes, and values) that would help students to relate scientific concepts to physical world applications. He was struggling to communicate in a domain studied and classified by Krathwohl, Bloom and Masia (1964) who constructed a taxonomy of five levels—commonly called "Krathwohl's taxonomy." We use a version of this taxonomy that includes a modification of the second and third levels of Krathwohl's taxonomy. See Table 5.3 for a description of these three levels.

As in the taxonomy of cognitive objectives, this taxonomy is also a hierarchy. At the lowest level, the student may, for example, merely sit quietly in a condition of apparent listening during a lecture, rather than chatting with neighbors, doing homework, or reading *Popular Mechanics.* When question/answer begins, those students who volunteer are exhibiting behavior beyond level I. But the teacher must refrain from the immediate assumption that these students are interested in the subject. They may only be interested in being "on stage" momentarily. As you may have guessed, it is relatively easy to write objectives at levels I and II and far more difficult both to write a level III objective and to have it attained by many students. Yet there is little point in being a science teacher, in the opinion of the authors, if you do not work toward motivation based on the acceptance of some of the values inherent in or related to the subject matter. Let's see what Mr. Jackson might have written if he had wanted at least one objective at each of the three levels of this taxonomy. Recall he was teaching seventh-graders a unit on ecology.

Level I	Participates in the lab-group role assigned by the teacher.
Level II	Attempts an optional challenge problem on food pyramids.
Level III	Volunteers illustrative examples from nonassigned outside sources during a class discussion on the application of ecology principles to a local pollution problem.

As you compare each of the above objectives with the description of the matching taxonomic level, you will probably realize that levels II and III cannot be attained with any certainty if the teacher "motivates" tasks by either the threat or promise of a grade. In these cases, students may merely be complying with instructions—thus behaving at level I. The students may, in fact, be interested in the lab activity, but obedient participation gives the teacher no feedback as to this interest. The word "voluntarily" or a synonymous word or phrase will be found in a level II objective. However, a major distinction between level II and level III is that in a level II objective the teacher has defined the choice(s) to which the student can *respond*. Notice that in Mr. Jackson's level II objective, he will have to devise a challenge problem and state the free choice aspect of completing it. However, in his level III objective, the reference to "nonassigned outside sources" suggests that students would have to voluntarily do some investigating and have formed some judgment as to the value of applications, rather than responding to a specific task posed by Mr. Jackson. Over the course of the entire two-week unit, Mr. Jackson would be looking for repeated instances of similar commitment before he could feel any confidence in the attainment of level III objectives by any one student.

This simplied affective taxonomy should be represented by some objectives in the total set written by each teacher as a new unit is planned. Ms. Bonner included these in the set she wrote for her chemistry class. Study each statement carefully and classify each at one of the three taxonomic levels of the affective domain.

1. Perform optional laboratory exercises.

2. Select science-related books for report material when given a "free" reading assignment in English class.

3. Consistently wear safety goggles when working in the vicinity of hot liquids or caustic substances.

4. Hand in assigned homework papers on time.

5. Use science data, concepts, and theories in structuring arguments during social studies class debates/discussions on contemporary issues.

6. Raise questions about the content of TV commercials that overtly claim that "Scientific findings have established … "

We classified objectives 3 and 4 as level I, objectives 1 and 2 as level II, and objectives 5 and 6 as level III. The major difference between the level II and level III objectives seems to be evidence of student-initiated interest over time. It is surely true that objectives at level III have little chance of success unless the teacher has consistently worked toward this level of performance. It is also true that objectives in this domain necessitate matching assessment forms. We will be developing this area in Chapter 8.

You're almost ready to begin writing your own affective objectives. Check your first attempt, the revision of Mr. Jackson's defective objective 5, with our version.

Substitute 5. *The student will elect to do an outside project on the importance of bacteria of decay.*

Have you observed the intrinsic connections between the cognitive and the affective domain? For instance, the student who is able to meet the above objective will, at the same time, be exhibiting behavior at level II in the cognitive domain. You will observe similar overlap in other objectives in both of these domains. However, where the intended emphasis is on the development of feelings, attitudes, or values rather than on recalling, comprehending, or applying intellectual skills, the objective is classified as affective.

In the not-so-distant past, affective objectives were rarely included in curriculum materials. It was hoped that the intrinsic overlap of cognitive with affective domains would somehow become actualized. Now it is clear that even students who successfully complete science courses often perceive science as uninteresting and lacking in meaning for them (Yager, 1989). This may be one reason why so many students do not select science courses beyond those designated as satisfying minimum requirements (Gardner & Yager, 1983). If your students show a tendency toward such attitudes because of their previous experiences in science classes, you will have to incorporate many activities that capture student interest and demonstrate real-world connections. In addition to the ideas in Chapter 4, see especially the illustrations and sources in Chapters 9, 10 and 11 for specific activities to use in this way.

"All right," we hear you say, "attitudes are important; and I do want my students to like science, or at least not to dislike it. But I can't see any need to emphasize psychomotor objectives." Unfortunately, even some experienced science teachers feel the same way. Why "unfortunately"? Read on, and see.

The Psychomotor Domain

Check out the label given to this third major category of human learning capabilities. Note that *psycho* conveys the notion that motor (muscle) learning is intertwined with mind, soul, and spirit. Earlier we called attention to the interconnections between the cognitive and affective aspects of learning and stressed that it was largely a matter of the major emphasis of a given objective that allowed classification into one domain versus another. So it is with targeting instruction on manipulative skills important to science. These kinds of objectives *do* require specific and intentional efforts on the part of teachers. Teachers must choose to select those to be included as important goals of the course and must then design special strategies to promote their attainment. Novice teachers are prone to assume that psychomotor skills will develop naturally since laboratory facilities are usually provided for science classes, and high school science courses typically are assigned one or more extra periods for laboratory exercises. Rid yourself of this notion quickly by observing a second-semester biology laboratory exercise where students are supposed to be applying microscope-use skills learned during six to ten previous laboratory periods. Walk around and tabulate the number of students viewing poorly focused slides, observing inadequately illuminated specimens, diagramming air bubbles, and demonstrating other evidence of the *absence* of psychomotor skills. Then believe the evidence instead of the pious hopes of teachers and curriculum guides, and take the first step toward heading off such disasters in groups you will teach. That first step is specifying objectives in the psychomotor domain. The time to begin is now.

We have constructed a few sample objectives—some with deficiencies—to help you get started. Read each carefully. Then decide whether or not each (1) contains a specific performance verb, (2) communicates clearly, (3) places primary emphasis on coordinated muscle movements, and (4) makes obvious the materials and equipment that would be made available to the learner. (It is our experience that one could write "given access to all required equipment and materials" after almost every objective in this domain. This seems senseless to us so we *assume* that phrase is understood to be part of each objective *unless* there is some good reason to state more specific limitations on these conditions for performance.)

1. Mass solid objects on an analytical balance to within ±.005 gram.

2. Dissect a preserved frog so as to expose intact all parts of the digestive and uro-genital systems.

3. Pipette liquids to within ±.1 ml.

4. Describe how to (1) light a Bunsen burner and (2) adjust it to produce the hottest possible flame.

5. Prepare a whole wet-mount slide containing no air bubbles, given a prepared specimen section and all other required materials.

Now let's see how closely your analysis of these sample objectives agrees with ours. We consider massing objects, dissecting specimens, pipetting liquids, describing procedures, and preparing microscope slides to be specific performances and we think that each of the five statements communicates clearly. However, did you pick out the fact that *describe* in objective 4 emphasizes the cognitive aspects of learning and does *not* call for a demonstration of the indicated motor skills? We certainly hope so, for there is a world of difference between talking about manipulative skills and actually performing them, though comprehension is often a helpful prerequisite to motor learning. Perhaps this very thought occurred to you when you considered objective 2. It did to us when we wrote it. Why did we state conditions for objective 5 and not the others? We simply wanted to delimit the expectations by ruling out dehydrating, staining, paraffin imbedding, and microtome techniques as being part of this particular objective.

You should now be ready to try constructing a few objectives on your own. Think in terms of the manipulative skills associated with the use of devices such as balances, burettes, graduated cylinders, meter sticks, micrometers, and microscopes. Then write at least three objectives relevant to a subject you expect to teach and submit them to a critique by your instructor or a classmate.

In the cases of the cognitive and affective domains we concerned ourselves with classifying objectives at a variety of levels within each domain. However, we will *not* deal with a taxonomy within the psychomotor domain. Why? Isn't there any such thing? Yes, there is a taxonomy for this domain, but it appears much more relevant to the elementary school age group or physical education content than to secondary school science instruction.

This is *not* to say, however, that we should, or can, ignore varying complexities of objectives aimed at motor skill development. Consider some practicalities of planning instruction. Nearly all biology teachers want students to learn how to use the compound microscope at both low- and high-power settings to examine a wide variety of types of specimens. This complex aim incorporates a large number of more specific psychomotor objectives, some of which depend upon the prior achievement of others. Thus, the probability of the major goal being attained will depend, in large part, on the teacher's ability to identify and correctly sequence the learning of component skills. A number of other similar examples ought to become obvious as you gain experience as an observer, planner, and director of learning activities.

5.4 SUMMARY AND SELF-CHECK

Instructional objectives can be considered analogous to route directions written on a road map. Without these the teacher can easily fall into the trap of jousting at every windmill sighted along the way. The route map must be well designed so that an equally trained professional, another teacher of the same subject, would agree on the nature of specific behaviors represented by the objectives. We emphasized the need for clear communication of ideas without excessive verbiage. Recall how the later objectives did not contain the commonly assumed phrase "The student will be able to:" nor conditions that ought to be obvious to any other trained teacher. You may find it difficult to write both clearly and succinctly. If it comes to a choice, there is no argument. Clarity should win out.

Throughout this chapter, you were provided illustrations of objectives in each of three domains—the cognitive, the affective, and the psychomotor. Three criteria to be used in writing instructional objectives of any kind were stressed and categorizations within the cognitive and affective domains were described and illustrated.

At this time, you should be able to:

1. Operationally define instructional objective, cognitive domain, affective domain, and psychomotor domain.

2. Operationally define each of the levels in the cognitive and affective domains.

3. Identify given statements as either meeting or failing to meet all criteria for an instructional objective and give reasons for your decisions.

4. Classify given instructional objectives according to domain and according to level for those in the cognitive and affective categories.

5. Write instructional objectives for each level of the cognitive and affective domains.

6. Write instructional objectives in the psychomotor domain.

The exercises in the next section are designed to provide you with some further experience in identifying, classifying, and writing instructional objectives. Skills developed in these areas will give you a head start in designing lesson plans and in constructing appropriate assessment measures—both everyday tasks of the classroom teacher.

5.5 SIMULATION/PRACTICE ACTIVITIES

A. Below are ten statements purported to be instructional objectives. Assume that each is of educational value to its subject matter area. React to each *only* in terms of whether or not it satisfies all three criteria for instructional objectives. Use an X to indicate your judgment.

	No	*Uncertain*	*Yes*
1. Draw labeled Bohr diagrams of elements #1–#20, given access to a periodic chart.	_____	_____	_____
2. Solve Ohm's *law* problems.	_____	_____	_____

3. Distinguish reptiles from amphibians _____   _____   _____
   when given three common live
   specimens of each.
4. Understand the importance of   _____   _____   _____
   geological knowledge to solving the
   energy crisis.
5. State the criteria used to   _____   _____   _____
   discriminate mammals from birds.
6. Become keenly aware of the dangers _____   _____   _____
   of using data collected in an
   uncontrolled experiment.
7. Label the eyepiece, mirror,   _____   _____   _____
   high-power objective, low-power
   objective, coarse adjustment, fine
   adjustment, and stage on an
   unlabeled diagram of the instrument.
8. Use the *Handbook of Physics and*   _____   _____   _____
   Chemistry.
9. Appreciate the importance of safety _____   _____   _____
   precautions in all laboratory work.
10. Solder wires to circuit board   _____   _____   _____
    connectors.

If you checked any of the above "no," revise those statements so that you would check each "yes." Then compare all your responses with those of two other students. Discuss differences in judgment, attempt to arrive at a consensus, and then ask your instructor for feedback on your efforts.

B. The statements below are instructional objectives based on junior/senior high school science content. Classify *each* according to domain (cognitive, affective, or psychomotor) and then by level for those within the cognitive and affective domains.

1. Measure lengths with a meter stick to within ±0.5 mm (General Science).
2. State Ohm's *law* in symbolic form (General Science).
3. Write at least two inferences based upon the line graph of a set of data (General Science).
4. Solve volume-volume problems, given the quantity of one of the relevant substances (Chemistry).
5. Keep a live organism within the low-power field of view of a compound microscope (Biology).
6. Predict the effect of a given environmental factor on the population growth of a species (Biology).
7. Voluntarily bring in magazine photos illustrating the use of triangular shapes in the construction of rigid structures such as automobiles, buildings, and bridges (Physical Science).
8. Describe the use of a streak plate in mineral identification (Earth Science).
9. For a given salt solution, explain whether or not it would be wise to store the solution in various metal-lined containers (Chemistry).

10. Calculate the ideal and actual mechanical advantage for a machine, given effort and resistance data (Physics).

C. Choose a topic from the subject matter of junior/senior high science. Check textbooks and syllabi to ensure that the selected topic would be one developed over at least a two-week period. Study student exercises and resource materials related to the topic. Then write *ten* instructional objectives in the cognitive domain that would be appropriate for this topic and the anticipated students. At least *five* of the objectives should be at level II. Include at least 1 at level III and at least 1 above level III.

D. Use the topic selected by you in exercise C to write at least *five* instructional objectives in the affective domain. Include some at level II and at least one at level III.

E. Use the topic selected by you in exercise C or choose another topic and write at least *three* instructional objectives in the psychomotor domain.

SUGGESTIONS FOR FURTHER STUDY

Mager, R. F. (1968). *Developing attitude toward learning*. Belmont, CA: Fearon Publishers.

In chapters 1–5 Mager emphasizes the importance of the affective domain for learning any school subject. Mager uses an easy-to-read interactive style to illustrate what he calls "approach behaviors" indicative of positive attitudes. Attention is also given to interrelationships with the cognitive domain, and readers are directed to reflect upon the development of their own system of values.

Mager, R. F. (1962). *Preparing instructional objectives*. Belmont, CA: Fearon Publishers.

This brief paperback provides a simple introduction to writing objectives. Written in programmed format, most novice teachers can complete the book in a little over an hour's time. The explanations are brief; the examples, clear. Feedback is immediate and those who catch on quickly are directed to skip repetitive materials.

Sund, R., & Picard, A. (1972). *Behavioral objectives and evaluational measures: Science and mathematics*. Columbus, OH: Charles E. Merrill.

Behavioral objectives and their use in designing evaluation measures are viewed within the framework of a systems analysis approach to instruction. The authors include a rationale for the use of behavioral objectives, provide clear instructions for writing such objectives (including numerous examples from both mathematics and science), and relate these to the taxonomies of both the cognitive and affective domains. The use of objectives in curriculum design comes in for some attention but much more emphasis is placed on their use in developing evaluation measures.

CHAPTER SIX

THE LEARNING OF SCIENCE

Stepping Stones to Planning

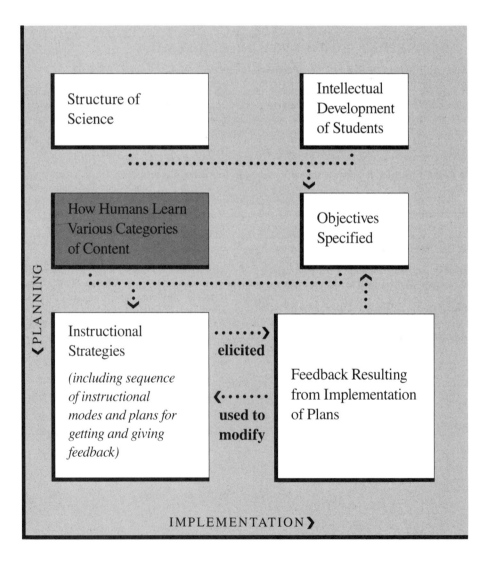

We have come a long way in our study of systematic instruction. Together we explored the modes used by teachers and the feedback strategies associated with those modes. We sought an answer to the question: "What are the intellectual capabilities of the typical junior/senior high student?" and to the equally important query: "What is science?" Armed with this background, we considered the nature of instructional objectives. Now we have mapped out where we are going, with whom, and for what purpose. But how do we get there? Instructional modes surely are part of that answer, but modes need to be chosen, sequenced, and implemented on a dual basis—the choice of specified objectives and the evidence illuminating the ways learning takes place.

How do humans learn various categories of science content? That question should look familiar. Of course, you've been in a position to see it each time you begin a new chapter of this text. Notice the place of this component in the instructional model and be alert to the interconnections to lesson planning that will be foreshadowed in this chapter. Wait a minute. Haven't we already studied learning? Didn't the work of cognitive developmental psychologists, particularly Piaget, provide us with all the evidence we need as to how learning takes place? You're making a common mistake if these are your thoughts, but you're not completely out in left field. Piaget studied the ways in which intellectual structures develop—the spontaneous development of knowledge as opposed to learning attributed to instruction. We have already stressed that his data and his theoretical constructs are invaluable inputs in our choice of objectives and in the eventual design of instructional strategies. We have also learned about the common reasoning strategies of students in certain areas of science, as well as something about individual difference characteristics affecting reasoning. The focus was on the students in Chapter 3—what they bring to the science classroom. Now we need to examine the content again, from the perspective of research on learning that results from intentional attempts to change behavior.

Let's be sure we're on the same wavelength when we use the term *learning*. We concur with the definition used by most contemporary psychologists that *learning is a change in human attitudes, cognitions, or psychomotor skills that is not due simply to the process of growth*. The definition excludes a change in human capabilities, such as increase in the size of the muscles, but includes specific eye-hand coordination abilities. Moreover, if learning is a *change*, then it is necessary for teachers to get feedback on the student's capability *before* instruction as well as *after* instruction. Have you had the experience of sitting through a college science course where at times you were bored by the repetition of concepts you had learned in high school? Were there perhaps other times in the same course when you were lost by an all-too-brief treatment of a content idea to which you had been exposed in high school but which you had never really learned? What accounts for such selective learning and remembering? Why is it that we seem to learn some ideas so thoroughly that they are easily recalled while there are others that we never could understand? Even stranger, why are there ideas we thought we had indelibly learned but can no longer recall? Remembering, like learning, becomes a mental process of more than passing interest.

Memorizing is the bane of most students. Yet probably every teacher of yours emphasized memory to some degree. (Too much, perhaps?) "King Philip Came Over From German Soil," chorused the class. Was this one of your memory crutches?

King	Kingdom
Philip	Phylum
Came	Class
Over	Order
From	Family
German	Genus
Soil	Species

This is an example of a mnemonic, a mental trigger to assist the memorizer. The student who successfully applies the mnemonic is able to list the seven categories in order—an essential prerequisite to use of these categories. Any human capable of imitating the verbalisms in the above statements and able to recall statements of this length can be taught the mnemonic and the related words. Animal learning is limited in this respect. The use of symbols of all kinds to represent ideas makes human learning far more complex than some psychologists once believed.

Experiments with pigeons, laboratory rats, and even higher animals have intrigued psychologists for years. Early attempts to equate human learning with animal learning led Thorndike, a psychologist, to write a methodology text (1921), in which he promoted the teaching of 100 addition facts as separate bits of unrelated material. Teachers were warned that $3 + 2 = 5$ and $2 + 3 = 5$ were separate bonds, each of which needed distinct instruction and practice. Although Thorndike was interested in relevance and problem solving, his followers applied his approach to instruction in extreme ways and drill and practice became the only instructional event in many classrooms. Little wonder that educational psychology left a bad taste in the mouths of some teachers. Where was the meaning? Were there not relationships among parts? Which terms needed to be memorized? Which might be deduced, or even reconstructed when and as needed? Names and labels must surely be learned differently from concepts, principles, problem solving, and the like. What are those differences? These are some of the questions we address in this chapter. We begin by engaging you in an activity that further explores the intricacies of memory and its relationship to understanding.

6.1 INTRODUCTORY ACTIVITY

You will need to enlist the aid of two or three acquaintances to serve as subjects for this activity. Seek out science majors who are *not* presently in this course and have not taken it previously.

A. Provide each volunteer with a quiet place to study a typed copy of the list of words below. At the end of one minute ask the subject to look up from the list and recite the words *in order.* Stop the person at the first error and provide another minute of study time. Allow five such study periods of one minute duration each and record the number of correct words (in sequence) achieved by the student at the end of each study period.

List of words

cleaver	child's	the	on
he	typical	until	name
only	by	was	a
IMA	Weaver	finding	levers
solve	faced	could	Sam
student	play	a	of
was	problems	with	

B. Using the same volunteer(s), substitute for the list of words a typed copy of the limerick below. Repeat five similar trials and keep comparable records of the results.

Limerick

A student by the name of Sam Weaver
could solve typical problems on levers.
Finding IMA
was only child's play,
until he was faced with a cleaver.

C. Compare the data you collected with that of at least five to seven of your classmates. Does a clear pattern emerge? If so, how do you account for the fact that one ordering (sequencing) of the same words was easier to learn than the other? Was there any factor other than sequencing that could also have made a difference in the ease of initial learning? Discuss your thoughts on these matters with classmates and your instructor and remain alert to further inputs in the sections that follow.

D. Design a simple way to check up on comparative retention of the list versus the limerick. We suggest allowing at least seven days to elapse between the initial learning and the remembering (retention) trials.

6.2 MEANINGFUL LEARNING

What made the limerick easier to learn than the same words in scrambled order? Doubtless your discussions generated ideas such as meaning, rhyme, and rhythm as likely causes of the observed results. If you further proposed that *meaning* was the most important factor, then your thinking is attuned to what has been clearly demonstrated both by researchers (Ausubel, 1979; Bruner, 1960; Mayer, 1983; White, 1988) and effective teachers (see the many articles authored by teachers in journals published by the National Science Teachers Association, the American Chemical Society, the National Association of Biology Teachers, and the American Association of Physics Teachers). Further, meaning of the material has been shown to be the prime factor associated with retention (remembering)

Rote ←————————————————————————————————→ Meaningful

Fig. 6.1   Rote/meaningful learning continuum.

of subject matter over time. Even the most cursory reflection on the nature and extent of the subject matter you are preparing to teach underscores the need to give careful attention to the central task of ensuring meaningful learning. Unlike computers, the human intellect is *not* capable of storing or retrieving large amounts of discrete bits of information.

Although meaningful learning and instructional strategies that promote the meaningful learning of science have been the subject of writings and studies by many science educators and psychologists (*e.g.*, Ausubel, 1979; Bruner, 1960; Dewey, 1910; Holliday, 1975; Wertheimer, 1945/1959; White, 1988; Winne, 1982), David Ausubel is known for making a substantial contribution to our understanding of the psychological character of meaningful learning. Writing in an era when many science and mathematics curricula projects were designed to reflect the structure of their disciplines, Ausubel clarified loose notions of what might make science content meaningful to students. In the paragraphs that follow, we adapt Ausubel's ideas to the teaching of secondary school science.

The term *learning* has already been defined in the introductory section and we urge you to review that definition at this point. Now let's see if we can nail down the key components of that all-important idea of *meaningful*. Meaningful to whom? The learner, of course. Recall that the directions for the Introductory Activity specified the use of science majors. The words *levers* and *IMA* have special meanings to one trained in this subject field and these in turn facilitate comprehension of the whole idea of the poem. Persons who do not attach subject-specific meanings to these key words might learn to recite the limerick perfectly given sufficient time, but would respond differently to in-depth questioning about the student's plight as described in this poem. Thus, new content becomes *meaningful* to the extent that it is *substantively (nonarbitrarily) related to ideas already existing in the cognitive structure of the learner* (Ausubel, 1968). This definition stands in clear contrast to that of *rote* learning wherein the *new content is arbitrarily (nonsubstantively) related to the existing cognitive structure of the learner.* If we imagine a continuum ranging from pure rote to highly meaningful learning, the task of memorizing the scrambled word list would be placed near, but not at, the rote (no-sense or nonsense) pole (see Figure 6.1).

As an independent information bit, each *familiar* word did relate to existing cognitive structure. However, the list did not represent a meaningful whole. Had the scrambled list consisted of nonsense syllables (XTU, KLMA, DTTIZ), then we would clearly place the task *at* the rote pole. On the other hand, a competent science teacher learning the limerick would be performing a task near the highly meaningful end of the continuum.

Consider a very real learning problem that occurs in all too many tenth-grade biology classes each fall. Students are confronted with the task of learning a host of structural formulas, the complicated names of numerous chemicals, and the results of many reactions occurring in living things. Do these constitute *potentially meaningful* content? Of course they do. No one would argue against the importance of the biochemical basis of contemporary biological knowledge. Recall, however, that the crucial point is to make new content meaningful *to the learner.* What already exists in these tenth-grade students' cognitive structures, to which the new material can be substantively related? Are concepts such as atom, bond, energy, and reaction already there in a stable form? If not, and time isn't taken to establish such prerequisites, students face a horrendous task of rote learning in this unit. Yes, much depends on what was meaningfully learned and retained as a result of junior high science courses.

By this time you have undoubtedly surmised that we believe that meaningful learning and retention depend primarily upon the *way* the learning occurs. Our constant reminders to you to interact with the material, to compare answers with those of other classmates, and to hypothesize and then check out your hypotheses are all specific learning strategies that are supportive of meaningful learning.

In the post-Sputnik era of curriculum reform, some teachers and some curriculum writers behaved as if all learning processes could be categorized as one of two types: reception learning or discovery learning. Indeed, some went one step further and equated reception learning with rote learning and discovery learning with meaningful learning. We've already explored the difference between meaningful and rote learning. But to what do reception and discovery learning refer? The term *reception* might remind you of a telephone receiver, a receptionist, a receipt. Thus, *reception learning* occurs when *the entire content of the intended learning is presented to the learner in its final form and the learner incorporates the content into his or her cognitive structure.* If the new content becomes substantively related to ideas already present in the individual's cognitive structure, then meaningful reception learning has occurred. If this condition is not met, then *rote reception learning* would be the appropriate descriptor.

Which modes would you identify as potentially promising ways of promoting reception learning? If you chose lecture as a potential way to promote reception learning, your judgment is in accord with ours. However, if you believe that lecture could not be employed to promote discovery learning, you doubtless have an erroneous concept of discovery learning. In contrast to reception learning, in *discovery learning the learner must generate the desired content end-product or construct a missing interrelationship.* As in the case of reception learning, discovery learning may be *either* meaningful or rote, depending upon the kind of relationship (arbitrary or substantive) established between the new and previously learned content.

It is true that a lecture aimed at student discovery would be carefully structured to pose a problem or highlight conjecture and would not fill in all the gaps for the student. If you've already decided that a mixture of lecture with question/answer, laboratory, or some other mode would be even more successful in promoting meaningful learning of either type than lecture alone, you're absolutely correct. Furthermore, while lecture might be used to promote either reception or discovery learning, the use of the laboratory mode is not a guarantee of the co-existence of discovery learning, although it should be. A frequent abuse of the laboratory mode in junior/senior high science classes is to tell the students what results they will obtain *before* they have begun to perform any of the manipulations. Imagine how that kind of teacher behavior affects meaningful learning. How are those students likely to view the process aspects of the nature of science? Does that mean that the teacher stands back and lets the students fumble away at their own pace? Not likely. *Pure* discovery learning is almost never a viable approach. We agree with Ausubel that there simply isn't enough time to have students rediscover all they need to learn.

Furthermore, secondary school science students do not yet possess the background knowledge, intellectual skills, and sometimes even the laboratory techniques required to learn without guidance from teacher and text. In fact, the discovery learning recommended by many teachers and scholars is more correctly called *guided* discovery learning. The teacher sets the scene, cues judiciously, and carefully structures the sequence of events so that the students need not reinvent the wheel. This kind of guided discovery has received much attention from Jerome S. Bruner (1960, 1966), a Harvard psychologist, whose research in school learning has resulted in both scholarly treatises on the nature of learning and essays to teachers on the nature of "going beyond the given."

However, ensuring that learning will be meaningful is not as easy as it sounds. Remember all those *potentially* meaningful concepts we mentioned earlier? Making content meaningful to the learner is a two-edged sword. The teacher must consider characteristics of the content as well as the match between the new content and the student's existing mental structure. We already learned that science content could be classified in diverse ways—by process and product; by concept, principle, and theory. To what extent do these differences in content affect learning? What ways exist for categorizing various types of learning tasks and what conditions facilitate the learning of each type of task? These are the considerations to which we next direct our attention.

6.3 CATEGORIES OF HUMAN LEARNING

Unlike the early twentieth-century learning theorists, Robert Gagné rejected the notion of classifying all learning into a single category. Instead he added to and modified the theories of Thorndike and Skinner and selected aspects of the theory proposed by the Gestalt school of psychology. Moreover, he did all this in the context of school learning. Not only did he continuously conduct experiments with human subjects, but much of his data were collected in existing classrooms as opposed to the carefully controlled and contrived environment of a pseudo-class in a college laboratory. As a result, his inferences make practical instructional sense and are translatable into instructional strategies. In the following sections, we summarize two of Gagné's major contributions on which we base instructional strategy design to be considered in Chapter 7.

Learning Types

Gagné (1970) classified all human learning into eight major types, which are related in hierarchical fashion (Figure 6.2). In Gagné's later writings (Gagné, 1977, 1979; Gagné & Briggs, 1979), he collapsed the eight types into four larger categories and added a fifth human capability, attitudes. We have chosen to retain eight categories but in slightly modified form, since our experience and that of our students is that this hierarchy provides a helpful analysis of learning related to the cognitive and psychomotor domains. We will need to look elsewhere for background on learning in the affective domain. The hierarchy depicted in Figure 6.2, like the others you have studied, contains categories ranging from simple to complex, with each successive layer depending upon and subsuming those directly under it. However, unlike either the nested stages model or the taxonomies of instructional objectives, Gagné's hierarchy of learning types contains a branch midway up. This indicates that type 5 learning may depend just on related type 2 and type 1 learning. Branching of diverse kinds is prevalent throughout the learning of any subject. For example, learning to compute the IMA may depend on first learning to measure distances moved by effort and resistance *or* on first learning to measure the effort and resistance arms. This concept of prerequisites *necessary* to future learning is the second of Gagné's contributions which we will study and relate to science learning.

For the time being, we need to pay closer attention to the levels in Gagné's hierarchy. What does he mean by "concept"? Does his meaning agree with what we learned in Chapter 4? Would rule include such ideas as the principle of independent assortment and $s = (1/2)at^2$? The answer to these last two questions is a resounding yes. And although you will be primarily concerned with the learning of discriminations and the types dependent on these, the hierarchical nature of learning makes it imperative to have at least an acquaintance with all eight types of learning.

Signal learning   Gagné was not the first to distinguish between signal learning and stimulus-response learning. Probably the most commonly known experiments in signal learning are those of Pavlov, whose dog learned to salivate in response to the signal of a buzzer. The shell-shock symptoms demonstrated by war-weary soldiers on hearing a car backfire or firecrackers explode is another example of signal learning. The buzzer or the noise of the backfire serve as signals (conditioned stimuli) in these illustrations and the response of the learner—salivating in the case of the dog and fear symptoms in the case of the soldier—are conditioned responses of a reflexive, emotional nature. Notice that a general attitude, in this case fear related to a stimulus, is learned as the result of conditioning.

Stimulus-response learning   In stimulus-response learning we move toward more differentiated responses. Now the signal, or stimulus, must be connected with the response and the response itself is a *specific* terminal behavior that provides satisfaction to the learner. The training of animals and, indeed, the shaping

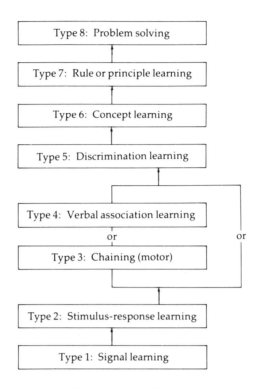

Fig. 6.2   Hierarchy of learning types.

of human behavior to respond in specific ways to verbal or nonverbal cues are good examples of these $S \rightarrow R$ (stimulus-response) connections. Some aspects of classroom management (for example, lab groups being taught to cease talking when the lights momentarily are switched off-then-on) are applications of stimulus-response learning. There have been entire texts written on the subject of behavior modification that deal with this kind of learning. Suffice it to say that (1) the correct response must result in some reinforcement—perhaps praise, a reward, or a success experience; (2) the reinforcement must occur fairly close in time to the response; and (3) the stimulus must be repeated often with partially correct responses being identified and positively treated. As you interact with Chapter 12, look for cues such as "use Grandma's Rule" and "be consistent." These are specific applications of $S \rightarrow R$ learning to classroom control. "You mean learning theory is practical?" You bet it is.

Chaining   Learning to swim requires a whole series of coordinated responses— each subunit being a $S \rightarrow R$ connection. The movement of arms and legs and the breathing behavior must all be appropriately linked, or *chained* together. So chaining is the name given to the type of learning represented by these nonverbal sequences.

Think back to the behavior described by the sample instructional objectives in Chapter 5. In which cases did the objectives clearly refer to the learning type Gagné has called "chaining"? If you fumbled over the answer to that question, you'd better go back and reread Section 5.3 with special attention to the psychomotor domain. Yes, psychomotor objectives all require that the student chain together individual $S \rightarrow R$ units. (1) These units must be well learned and (2) then integrated in the correct sequence. (3) Again, immediate reinforcement of the final response and repetition of the entire chain and pieces of it in close time succession are conditions required in order that chaining may occur. In the example given, learning to swim, the reinforcement for most people is success, an example of an intrinsic or internal reward. Some novices mistakenly believe that only extrinsic rewards (such as prizes, verbal praise, or grades) are satisfying to the learner. Initially, it is true that the struggling student may need the satisfaction of an external reward. However, if some internal reward does not gradually replace the external one, the learning has less chance of permanence.

Verbal association learning   Gagné's type 4 learning encompasses much the same bonding of stimulus and response as that described by chaining. However, in this case, the response is a verbalism. Naming minerals, labeling constants such as g, and even the memorizing of verbal information such as the order of the names of mitotic stages are instances of the learning called verbal association. All the conditions required to assure the learning of motor chains are also required here. Of course, the stimulus situation now includes a drawing, an object, or a printed expression and an initial repetition of the desired response by the teacher. The teacher may also include cues, such as the mnemonic "King Philip Came Over From German Soil," that must be learned and then recalled to assist the learner in obtaining the desired verbal response. As you remember from the Introductory Activity, long verbal chains are easily forgotten unless they are learned in a meaningful context. Verbal association learning in science includes fewer long verbal chains than social studies or even English, but like mathematics, it is complicated by a written and spoken language of symbols and groups of symbols.

Discrimination learning   Closely related to this last illustration of verbal association learning is the learning of discriminations, Gagné's type 5. The ability to perceive the differences in shape between ♂ and ♀ may follow the learning of the respective verbalisms "male" and "female," but is a prerequisite if the student is to correctly distinguish one printed mark from the other. Similarly, the ability to perceive the *distinctive* features of objects observed, sounds heard, materials touched, foods tasted, and odors smelled are all examples of discrimination learning. Even intelligent adults are sometimes tricked by ignoring one perceptual change or overemphasizing another. How many smart chefs know this and slice all sandwiches on the diagonal? The sandwiches look bigger. The importance of discrimination learning to the learning of concepts cannot be underestimated. Some students never learn the *essential* features of a class of objects and are at a loss when novel examples are proposed. Biology teachers have experienced this phenomenon when students who have learned to identify the typical horizontal sections of mitotic stages are puzzled by polar views of the same structures. Thus, the most important condition needed to promote discrimination learning is the presentation of diverse exemplars of the feature to be learned. Perceptual problems are often the source of difficulty at this level of learning—a difficulty that blocks progress at the levels above.

Concept learning   Concept learning is the basic coin of the realm in areas usually described by words such as *thinking, understanding,* and *problem solving.* In Chapter 4 several kinds of concepts were used as examples—animal, a concept by inspection; force, a theoretical (defined) concept; greater than, a relational concept. An operational definition of *concept* was provided. Do you remember the use of the term, *classification* in the definition of concept? Classification, as used by Piaget, by logicians, and by all scientists, is the key to the conditions under which a concept is learned.

Suppose Mr. Mapes had written a definition of an atom on the board, had placed next to it several diagrams of atoms, and had drilled on the oral recitation of the label and definition? Would his sixth-grade students be likely to have learned the concept of atom? If not, what could they be credited with learning? If you said they probably learned the *name of the concept* and a verbal association describing that name, you're in agreement with what experience has taught us. Suppose the students had been tenth-graders? Would it have made a difference? Yes, *if* they had already had concrete referents to attach to the presented verbalisms; otherwise, no. In general, the conditions for concept learning include (1) the availability of prior prerequisite discrimination and/or verbal association learning and (2) the presentation of gradually differentiated examples and nonexamples. In the case of those concepts of science that exist in the idea world (such as bond, ion, atom, gravity, and magnetism), the examples and nonexamples take the form of physical models and/or demonstrations of the effects of such concepts on observable objects (such as holding a series of magnetic and nonmagnetic materials near a magnet). Sometimes an analogy is used to exemplify a science concept: "Gas molecules behave as if they were perfectly elastic spheres traveling in straight lines until they hit something."

Whatever method the teacher uses to establish the conditions for learning, the evidence that a concept has been learned is *not* the recitation of a definition, nor is it any other feedback that might signify nothing more than accurate recall, such as responding correctly to examples used by the teacher during instruction. However, if the student responds correctly to examples not used in instruction and can produce novel examples when asked, then the teacher has obtained positive feedback on concept learning. *Concept learning,* then, is demonstrated by *the ability to generalize beyond the instances used in the learning situation and beyond the physical similarities present in some instances.* For example, a student who has learned the concept *bird* will not be misled by the apparent earthbound nature of the ostrich and the penguin *nor* trapped into classifying the bat as a bird because of its flying ability. Thus, learning of concepts frees the student from total reliance on the physical world and makes it possible for rules and principles to be meaningfully learned.

Rule/principle learning   Rules and principles, the heart of science, depend on concept learning. Why? Let's look at an example of a principle. "A pure dominant crossed with a pure recessive yields 100 percent hybrids" might be memorized without any prior concept learning. However, this sequence of words is only a *statement of a principle* just as the label "dominant" is the *name of a concept.* What is the principle? To answer this question, identify the learning you would desire with respect to the statement of the given principle. If you'd expect the ability to *use* the statement in a variety of appropriate situations, you've captured the essence of principle/rule learning. To use the principle, Esther (one of your tenth-grade students) would need to have learned the concepts of pure, dominant, crossed, recessive, yields, 100 percent, and hybrid. She would also have to know how to use other related concepts, such as gamete, and finally would have to use all these in the proper sequence and manner. *Rule learning*, then, is *the capability to respond to a class of situations with a class of performances where the situations and performances are related by a chain of concepts.* The rule itself is a chain of concepts. In this instance, Esther would be expected to predict hybrid offspring as the result of a cross of parents possessing contrasting genotypes for a given trait. Furthermore, she should also be able to supply the genotypes of both parents when given F_1 genotypes that indicate all offspring are hybrid. The ability to rule out the possibility of one pure dominant and one pure recessive parent for a generation of offspring that are *not* all hybrids would be another indicator of the learning of the principle. In all of these cases, it is impossible to tell what Esther might be thinking, but if the final performance results in the solution of the problems, then it is inferred that the principle has been learned.

Notice that her ability to state the principle is not even mentioned. However, you would probably want Esther to be able to state the verbal principle to avoid prolonged searching for this repeatedly used intellectual tool. That's fine, but that's a verbal association that must be learned differently and tested separately. Just don't make the mistake of assuming that instant recall of the statement of the principle guarantees the ability to use that rule. Are you getting the idea? Your instructional objectives with regard to any principle may range from low-level and restricted use to complex and widely generalizable use. If, however, there is to be any subsequent problem solving (type 8), the rule that has been learned must be of the latter class.

What conditions must be present so that widely generalizable rule learning may take place? As in the example given: (1) The concepts that are to be chained must be separately mastered first. (2) The teacher must clearly let the students know what kind of terminal performance is expected. (Esther should be told that she'll be asked to both predict offspring and to work back from known offspring to unknown parent types, *if* that is what her teacher has decided.) (3) Verbal cues, concrete examples, or a carefully structured exercise can be used to (a) help students recall essential concepts and to (b) encapsulate the structure or main idea of the rule. (4) The use of the rule should be demonstrated in the format desired by the teacher. (5) Finally, the students must be asked to demonstrate the rule in *diverse* situations. If they can demonstrate its use successfully, they have learned the rule. Retaining it is another matter. In a later section in this chapter, we consider retention and transfer of learning.

Problem solving   Rules, no matter how complex the situation they encompass, are useful only if the problem can be characterized as belonging to a particular kind. However, throughout much of our in- and out-of-school life, the questions that intrigue us most are not typical problems. They belong instead to Gagné's type 8 learning, problem solving. Gagné is referring here to the moves toward the solution of *novel* problems—that is, problems *novel* to the student. (You should be reminded of the cognitive taxonomy.) Since the student cannot classify the problem as a typical one, search behavior continues until the problem is solved or at least restructured. Search behavior includes defining the problem, formulating hypotheses, verifying these, or altering hypotheses and then verifying the modifications. At this point we part company with Gagné, for he seems to imply that learning does not take place if the problem is not solved. We assert that thoughtful strategies engaged in by a student faced with problems like the mindboggler below are behaviors characteristic of type 8, whether or not the problem is solved.

The town planning board has already committed itself to approve the subdivision of a 200-acre parcel of land bordering Clear River. It is to be divided into equal areas for use by a plywood factory and a year-round trailer park and day-use picnic area with public fishing access. Study the accompanying package of maps and environmental impact data that have been gathered and propose a subdivision that best protects the environment of the parcel and surrounding area. Give reasons to support your plan.

The modifier *thoughtful* eliminates erratic trial and error attempts or blind algorithmic tactics. The student who has engaged in problem solving may have been successful in intermediate stages. Some approaches may have been rejected after testing them. Additional data may have been deduced. The problem is definitely restructured, even if it has not yet been solved.

Emphasis on problem-solving strategies for all students has been identified as a major goal by the National Science Teachers Association in reports, such as *Criteria for Excellence* (1987). The characteristics of successful problem solvers have been studied extensively (Gabel & Sherwood, 1982; Larkin, 1983; Smith & Good, 1984), but interest in how problem-solving is learned is not new. Gestalt psychologists, such as Duncker (1945), gave examples of the restructuring done by successful problem-solvers.

The illustrative problem on environmental issues and town planning is a good example of the kinds of content that students must be engaged in if they are to learn problem-solving strategies. Students who persist in trying different approaches on each problem, even when these do not result in final solution of the problem, are learning about problem-solving processes. What conditions enhance the occurrence of this kind of learning?

(1) The problem must be a problem to the learner—that is, the learner must conceive of the problem as posing a difficulty, an obstacle. Many so-called problems posed by teachers are considered simplistic questions by the students.

(2) The student must have a clearly defined goal whose attainment is desired. Unless the student understands the nature of the problem and is motivated to try to solve it, there will be no learning of problem-solving processes.

(3) The relevant prerequisite rules and concepts must be recalled by the learner. If these were learned previously in meaningful ways and retained in long-term memory, then the student already possesses the knowledge needed to work on the problem. Suppose the student just hasn't been instructed in one or more relevant rules? Isn't it a hopeless task to expect that student to work toward solution of the problem? Although it may seem that the obvious answer to that question is yes, some educators (e.g., John Dewey, 1910; Suchman, 1977) have found that this can be the best time to have a student stop and learn some of the needed prerequisites. If the problem or project is of great interest to the student, an impasse could motivate that student to stop and learn the needed, relevant rules. The key aspect of such problems is that students are highly motivated to solve them. Think of real-world examples where such behavior is not at all surprising. Contemporary renovators of old homes sometimes have to stop and learn fundamentals of nineteenth-century plumbing before they can continue with the design of a colonial kitchen. You should be able to think of many more examples of this kind of behavior.

(4) Cues to help the learner recall appropriate rules and to suggest approaches to the hypothesizing, testing, and modifying processes are assets to problem solving. However, if the cues become a step-by-step exposition of a solution, then the student is off the mental hook and has lost out on this most important aspect of science teaching. The student must be given time to fumble, to explore unpromising paths, to make mistakes. Indeed, in the final condition we emphasize this aspect of student performance.

(5) The instructor must stress the nature of the task and carefully distinguish expectations here from those in rule learning. It is *not* the case that a short-cut, algorithm, or principle is the important output. The objectives here are to seek sensible strategies, to develop systematic ways of checking conjectures, to be open-minded about both possible solutions and potential routes to a

solution. Subsequent to work on the problem, an examination of the profitable and unprofitable approaches is in order to further clarify the potential of this new strategy.

Terms like *hypothesizing* and *systematic approaches* were used in this text in an earlier chapter. Remember the floating bodies problem and the approaches of the formal versus the concrete operational student in Chapter 3? Piaget's data clearly illustrate the effect of intellectual development on the nature of problem-solving abilities. In particular, more guidance and cues would be required if the concrete operational student were facing a problem having multiple potential factors. What are some other possible differences? Compare your ideas with those of a classmate.

Attitudes   Attitudes were given prominence in Chapter 5 when we considered objectives in the Affective Domain. It should be fairly clear that behaviors associated with Level I of that domain may represent nothing more than compliance with classroom regulations. When we think of attitudes specifically related to science, we are talking about objectives that correspond to Levels II, III, or III+ of the Affective Domain. Each of those domains is associated with a degree of student choice and actions based on that choice. Thus, our definition of attitude is taken from Gagné and Briggs (1979). An attitude is *an internal state which affects an individual's choice of action toward some object, person, or event.* Attitudes are usually described in terms of positive or negative tendencies.

In the previous sections, we have alluded to attitudes or dispositions sometimes being learned along with a reflex action or a chain of responses. Some researchers, notably Skinner (1968), have suggested that attitudes of liking for a topic area might be learned by following the work in that topic area by some rewarding activity. The theory is based on the idea that the student who likes the subsequent activity (the reinforcer) will eventually acquire a liking for the prior activity, work in the topic area. Some classroom teachers have tried to apply this theory with rewards of candy for completion of remedial exercises in science. They reported that although the students wanted to complete the exercises in order to receive the candy that subsequent measures of student attitudes toward science were not more positive. It seems that the reinforcer (the external reward) must be connected to the prior content work in some substantive scientific way. In general, it is assumed that success in completing science work, especially problems that have been characterized as challenging, might lead to a positive attitude toward similar problem work. In this case, success acts as an internal reward and thus, is intimately connected to the science activity. If you know an exception to this principle, you are beginning to identify the tenuous nature of research on the learning of attitudes. What is success? When are certain science activities perceived as challenging, but not frustratingly difficult? Is the student more concerned about gaining a certain grade than reaching the goal of completing the science activity? These are just some of the questions related to the learning of attitudes.

Bandura's work on human modeling (1969) provides some hope for being more specific about the conditions that foster the learning of attitudes. The importance of role models or *significant others* has already been mentioned in Chapter 3 with respect to forces affecting gender-differences in achievement or persistence in science coursework. Many of these same issues are relevant to the participation of various ethnic groups in elective science courses or science-related careers (see Kahle, 1982). According to Gagné and Briggs (1979), the essential conditions for learning attitudes, using human modeling, include the following. (1) The learner must already identify with, or respect, the human model and (2) the learner must already have learned any cognitive skills related to the attitude being fostered. For example, it is difficult to learn a positive attitude toward experiment-designing activities if the learner doesn't possess the prerequisite rules and concepts for designing an experiment and has not learned what is meant by controls. The next set of conditions all refer to actions by the human model. (3) The model must demonstrate (or describe) the desirable behavior and (4) show some overt sign of satisfaction with some outcome of the behavior. In the case of experiment-designing, if the teacher had already gained respect from the students, she or he could demonstrate the hypothetico-deductive nature of experiment-designing by proposing alternative designs, identifying strengths and limitations in each, and showing pleasure at new ideas and the prospect of implementing one of the designs. Students regularly identify the importance of this kind of role model in their decision to take another science course and in the emergence of their positive attitudes toward the subject (CASDA, 1985–1986).

Study the section on problem solving again for cues to the connections between the affective domain and this aspect of the cognitive domain. In fact, the importance of cultivating a positive attitude, or disposition toward problem solving has been repeatedly stressed by those who study and write about problem solving in science (Mills & Dean, 1960; Rubinstein, 1980). Throughout the description of the conditions necessary for learning problem solving are suggestions and warnings about the importance of the milieu of the classroom. One way of describing that milieu is in terms of four freedoms (1) freedom to make a mistake, (2) freedom to think for oneself, (3) freedom to ask a question and (4) freedom to choose methods of solution (Fremont, 1969).

6.4 TASK ANALYSIS

One of the most striking characteristics of the subject matter of science is its hierarchical nature. Small wonder that Gagné's emphasis on prerequisites has been found to be especially useful in science instruction. An outgrowth of Gagné's analysis of learning types led to the development of a technique called *task analysis*. Very simply, Gagné recognized the fact that instructional objectives at the concept, rule, and problem-solving levels depend upon the attainment of subbehaviors and then the integration of these. He devised a method by which complex objectives can be analyzed for instructional purposes—a method which consists of asking the following question: "What *must* the student be able to do in order

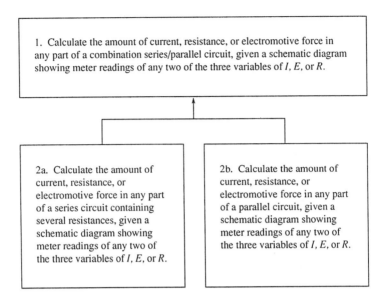

Fig. 6.3   A partial learning hierarchy.

to meet the terminal objective?" Suppose the terminal, or major, objective is the following:

Calculate the amount of current, resistance, or electromotive force in any part of a combination series/parallel circuit, given a schematic diagram, showing meter readings of any two of the three variables of I, E, or R.

A task analysis might result in the partial learning hierarchy depicted in Figure 6.3. Such hierarchies must be read from the top down. Each of the prerequisite objectives (2a and 2b) must be mastered by the student if the terminal objective is to be met. Since both are *necessary* prerequisites, they are joined by a two-way branch. These must be integrated in some fashion before objective 1 can be met so a single arrow connects the branch to the terminal objective. Why are these two prerequisites on the same level? Surely a student might meet objective 2a before meeting objective 2b? That's true, but the task analysis is intended to illustrate *necessary dependence* and neither of these two prerequisites depend on one another. Thus, task analysis helps the teacher identify the range of choices open for the sequencing of instruction. However, a task analysis does not depict the sequence in which a student must *use* these two skills in order to master the terminal objective.

Let's see if you have the idea. Below we've listed five additional objectives that are prerequisite to those in Figure 6.3. Read each carefully and sketch out the extended learning hierarchy by asking of each upper-level objective the task analysis question: "What *must* the student be able to do in order to perform this complex task?"

1. State Ohm's *law* in words or in symbolic form.
2. Label the standard symbols (including switches, resistance, cell, battery, generator, connecting wires, and meters) given a schematic diagram of an electric circuit.
3. Match current, resistance, and electromotive force with the units by which they are measured.
4. Solve Ohm's *law* type problems, given the values of any two of *I*, *E*, *R*.
5. Apply the relationship between total current (total voltage, total resistance) and current (voltage, resistance) in the parts of a parallel or series circuit to find the value of the total when corresponding values of the parts are known.

We recommend the writing of all eight objectives on cards and arranging them on a flat surface, such as the floor. Then test each one by asking the task analysis question and checking carefully the lower objectives. Our response to this exercise can be found in the Simulation/Practice Activities, where we ask you to go one step further with this partial hierarchy.

Our student teachers have found that task analysis of the objectives in a unit they are to teach is an excellent way for them to identify the prerequisites for each objective, the content links among objectives, and appropriate ways to assess learning.

6.5 CONCEPT MAPPING

Most learners don't think about subject matter in tight, sequential chains, such as that portrayed by learning hierarchies. They more often associate concepts with one another or link them in terms of some relationship. For example, after instruction on the nature of matter in eighth-grade physical science, a student's representation of the concepts that are associated might take the form shown in Figure 6.4. Concept-terms that are connected are associated by some relationship. The fact that one curved arrow has no stated relationship simply indicates that the student couldn't verbalize the association. Notice the problem this student had with the concept MOLECULE. Figure 6.4 is one example of a concept map, a diagram that students construct to try to picture how they mentally link concepts. Although several researchers (Ault, 1985; O'Connell, 1984; Shavelson, 1974) have used forms of concept maps, the work of Novak and Gowin (1984) is particularly helpful. Novak and Gowin used concept maps to help identify student misconceptions. One way of proceeding is to give a class a group of concept labels, 8–10 at most. Then ask them to choose the concept they think is most important and write that term in a balloon in the center of their paper. Then, tell them to select other concepts that seem to be associated with the first one, enclose them in balloons and connect the ones they relate together. The first two or three might be done together. After all labels have been considered, help the students to go back and decide what the relationship is that led them to connect pairs of concepts. The emphasis is on the relationship constructed by the *students*

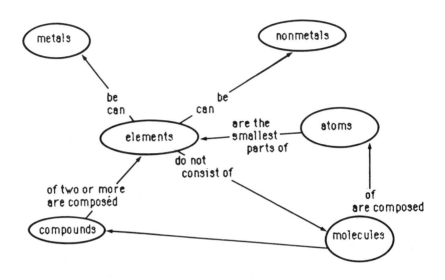

Fig. 6.4

between pairs of concepts, rather than on some ideal relationship the teacher has constructed. Concept maps constructed in this way can be an important graph of the students' mental representations of the content. Misconceptions or absence of important associations can be identified. O'Connell (1984) used this technique with sixth-grade science students. The sixth-grade science teachers found that the concept maps created at the end of instruction corresponded to the results of the individual students on classroom achievement tests. It's probably no surprise to learn that the concept maps of formal students differ significantly from those of concrete students (McDonald, 1982).

We've found that concept mapping is another excellent way for teachers to analyze the scientific structure of a unit—this time focusing on concepts and the associations between them. In Chapter 7, concept maps are referred to as an approach to long-range planning.

6.6 ADVANCE ORGANIZERS

It should be obvious from the word *advance* that an advance organizer comes prior to something else and from the word *organizer* that it is designed to facilitate putting things together in a meaningful way. Thus the term itself tells when an advance organizer occurs in an instructional sequence and sheds light on its overall purpose. David Ausubel (1963, 1968), the cognitive psychologist who originated this idea, has identified the attributes essential to this concept. First, *the advance organizer must present relevant content ideas that are of a higher order of abstraction, generality, and inclusiveness than the new material to follow.* Advance organizers typically take the form of broad concepts, rules/principles, thought models, theories, or conceptual schemes (themes) which subsume the more detailed knowledge to be learned next. Thus it becomes clear that teachers must have command of the structure of the subject matter, as presented in Chapter 4, if advance organizers are to be used in instruction. For example, the thought model of "food web" could be taught as an advance organizer for related subsumed concepts/rules such as consumer, primary consumer, secondary consumer, producer, decomposer, food, energy, and nutrient.

Second, *the advance organizer must be presented in terms of what is already known by the learner.* In other words, the teacher must find out what relevant knowledge the learners possess and then use it to teach the generalization(s) that will serve as the advance organizer. For example, assume that the teacher finds out that the students already know (either from life experience or from previous instruction) that the diets of particular animals may consist of either plant or animal material or both, and that green plants manufacture food while non-green plants depend on dead organisms for sustenance. The teacher can then use these ideas as prerequisites to build comprehension of the desired generalization (food web), which in turn will subsume the related facts, operational definitions, concepts, and rules/principles to be learned in the new work.

You should be starting to get the idea of what an advance organizer is. Now let's consider a few potentially confusing nonexamples—that is, what an advance organizer *is not.* Many science texts begin each chapter with a short introductory or overview section that consists of anywhere from one paragraph to several pages of writing. Often the one- or two-paragraph variety is really a summary of the main ideas to be treated in the chapter. These overviews almost always fail to meet *either* of the essential criteria for an advance organizer since (1) the ideas presented in capsule form are at the same level of abstraction as the content to follow and (2) little or no provision has been made to use the existing knowledge of the reader to teach the ideas summarized in such an introductory section. Similarly, several pages of introductory material tracing the historical development of a major science idea may stimulate the interest of some students but fail to qualify as an advance organizer on the basis of one or both essential criteria. However, introductions consisting of long excerpts from original papers written by famous scientists of years gone by not only fail to qualify as advance organizers, but also often serve to kill student interest. This is not to say that anything using a historical frame of reference is necessarily ineffective. Both the history of science, as well as the conceptual themes of science, can be used to structure advance organizers. See the Biological Sciences Curriculum Study Green Version text for some good examples of this and then contrast these against the introductory sections of chapters in the Blue and Yellow Versions of the same curriculum study.

How did we tackle the problem of providing you with advance organizers? We elected to use our model of instruction as a unifying (conceptual) theme throughout this text, beginning with the "To The Student" section. Our plan was to use this overarching idea to subsume all the main ideas and information in this book. Thus, both the diagrammatic representation of this thought model, and relevant written material appear at the start of each chapter. Then common background of the reader (both from real-life experiences and from preceding chapters) was used to teach meaningfully a new aspect of the model which in turn would constitute ideational scaffolding for the contents of subsequent chapter sections. To the extent that we were successful, each introductory section should have provided you with anchoring ideas and bridged the gap between what you already knew and what you needed to know in order to learn the tasks at hand. Did our attempts work in your case? Feedback from past students has been very encouraging and therefore we continue to use this technique.

Why are advance organizers important? One of their major functions is to facilitate the initial learning of new material so that it is of the meaningful variety (as opposed to rote). There is a growing body of research evidence that the degree of meaningfulness of newly learned material correlates positively with both remembering and the ability to use that material in applicable situations. Since both remembering (retention) and future applied use (transfer) are major goals of education, any device with potential for promoting their achievement merits our careful attention and best efforts.

Think back to previously learned material that might help you structure effective advance organizers. We have already called your attention to the contributions of Gagné as they apply to this task. Now consider the research of Piaget summarized in Chapter 3. What comes to mind first? Most people think of the nature of the concrete operational student and cite the need to include many concrete referents in an advance organizer. This is good thinking, as far as it goes, but it does not go far enough. Can you identify yet another application of Piaget's work to making effective use of advance organizers? If not, turn back to the nested stages model in Chapter 3 (Figure 3.6) and focus your attention on the thought modes available to formal operational students when they are working with content for which they do not have a base of concrete experiences. Always remember that in the long run all is lost if the initial learning is meaningless (rote) to the learner.

6.7 RETENTION, TRANSFER AND PRACTICE

We have already seen that humans are ill-equipped to behave like walking computers. People are just not capable of storing huge numbers of isolated information bits to be retrieved instantly upon demand. It is also true that much of what our students will need to know in their adult life 10 to 50 years hence is not now in the storehouse of human knowledge. Thus, formal schooling must educate the young to *transfer* learning—to develop both the *ability to perform new tasks at about the same level of difficulty as previously learned ones (lateral transfer) and also perform those of more complex difficulty by using the base of past learnings (vertical transfer).* Students who have learned that salt and water are products of the reaction of HCL and NaOH should give evidence of lateral transfer by making similar predictions for the reactions of other inorganic acids with bases. Further, we look for evidence of vertical transfer from students who, having mastered monohybrid cross predictions, later encounter dihybrid cross problems in class. Vertical transfer would also be illustrated by these same students' ability to account for the many variations seen in a neighbor's litter of kittens. How can we as teachers ensure that the maximum amount of transfer takes place? We can make certain that those factors known to promote transfer are accounted for in planning and implementing lessons.

Transfer, going beyond present learning, obviously depends upon a student's ability to *remember* or *recall previous learning (retention)*. As noted earlier, there is firm evidence to support the assertion that the most important factor in promoting retention is the degree of meaningfulness of the initial learning to the student.

The work of Gagné and Ausubel, as well as that of Bruner, White, and the Gestalt psychologists, have helped us to understand the importance of meaningfulness. More recently, information-processing psychologists have concentrated on the way learners encode knowledge, the nature and capacity of memory and the ways knowledge is retrieved from memory.

Retention

According to information-processing theorists (Resnick & Ford, 1981), when we pay attention to environmental stimuli (*e.g.*, music, teacher's questions and explanations, a silent movie), sensory input is registered and will be lost within one second unless we make an attempt to encode the information (perhaps in symbolic, pictorial, or verbal form). The encoded information is temporarily stored in short term, or working, memory which has a limited capacity. If we now have some reason to reflect on the encoded information and can relate it to other information in our attempts to remember it, the knowledge will be transferred to long term memory, where it will be retained until there is a need to retrieve it (Figure 6.5).

The process schematized in Figure 6.5 is often compared to the workings of a computer. Working memory is thought of as one memory storage area where all processes and data essential for the completion of a task are stored. Another storage area, but one of vast capacity, is labeled long term memory. Computer-users are often frustrated when the message "Out of Memory. Cannot Undo this Procedure" flashes on the screen. Like working memory, certain amounts of memory are reserved so that procedures can be completed. The "Load" command is analogous to a mental search in long term memory and the attempt to retrieve needed information for use in working memory. Unless some meaningful clusters have been generated by the learner, the search may be fruitless, as it might be if a data file were scrambled.

Larkin (1977) used the construct of "chunking" to explain how learners seem to process information. For example, a better chemistry student might

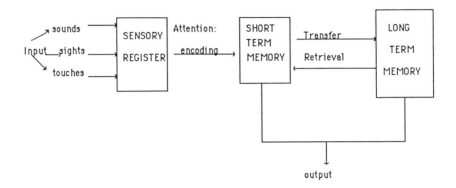

Fig. 6.5   Information processing model.

chunk a cluster of information about elements, such as atomic number, atomic size, or electron configuration, and recall and use this related set of concepts when predicting reactivity trends for elements (Lehman, Koran, & Koran, 1984). Information-processing theorists suggest that retention depends on the ability to invent chunks that can subsume, or be subsumed, by new chunks.

It is important to realize that this view of memory means that all learners chunk somehow. However, some learners do so in ways that are not efficient and sometimes not directly related to the structure of the subject. These chunks often represent superficial patterns invented by students. Refer back to Chapter 3 for specific examples of error patterns or trivial generalizations that some students construct. Unfortunately, some teachers mistakenly offer students superficial patterns (*e.g.*, OH in a formula will indicate a base) to help them remember a science generalization. In the short run, this strategy is successful. In the long run, it is not only unsuccessful, but can lead to a learned error pattern on the part of the students. Figure 6.6 graphically illustrates how long term retention of such material might be affected when teaching promotes nonsense learning. Frightening, isn't it? Yet, the research findings related to adolescent reasoning and learning and the analysis of the structure of science should guide you in designing instructional strategies that will help to avoid the situation depicted in Figure 6.6.

There are also other measures you can take to promote retention. The hierarchical structure of the subject matter makes it possible to help students think in ways that will facilitate retention and retrieval. Students who have learned the kinetic-molecular theory and accompanying thought model can be taught the value of recalling this set of abstractions first whenever a problem involving the pressure, temperature, or volume of gases is encountered. A few experiences are usually sufficient to convince students that one can use the pictorial model to reconstruct or retrieve any particular gas "law" as needed. Demonstrating this degree of utility of the model also helps establish both the intent to remember and the students' confidence that they will be able to remember, two additional

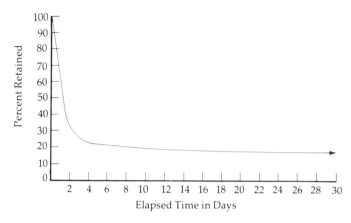

Percent Retained

Elapsed Time in Days

Fig. 6.6   Retention of nonsense learning.

factors that promote retention. Skillful teachers have learned to stress the relatively small number of thought models that need to be mastered in order to give one command over the many principles and in turn, the even more numerous concepts, that constitute the product aspect of science. Of course, such instruction must be coupled with strategies aimed at getting and using feedback if it is to produce the desired effect.

Practice

What is the role of practice (drill) in promoting the retention so essential to transfer? Surely the time-honored tradition of drilling students on newly learned content must contribute heavily to later recall? Not necessarily. In fact, there is good evidence (Resnick & Ford, 1981) that practice *per se* has little effect on retention! The desired positive effects of practice can be enhanced by attending to four factors.

First, drill sessions should be kept short and spaced out over time. Massed sessions in which students "plug in" numbers for *I*, *E*, or *R* in a dozen or more Ohm's *law* type problems are neither efficient nor effective. The equivalent amount of time divided into five- or ten-minute practice sessions distributed throughout a two-week period would yield higher returns for the time invested.

Second, practice should be provided on both the parts and the whole in the case of complex tasks. This has been found to be true for both cognitive and psychomotor learning. For example, it is important to devote some portions of practice to each of the separate subtasks of figuring out possible gamete combinations, setting up Punnet squares, finding the genotypes for each square, interpreting phenotypes from the genotypes, and expressing results as ratios. It is also necessary to allow sufficient time to practice performing all of these parts within the total problem complex. Similarly, students need practice in manipulating the parts of the microscope separately and in performing each manipulation as part of the total integrated technique. One caution! In the case of motor skills, the sequence of part-whole practice needs particular attention. Motor skill learning is enhanced when the whole skill is practiced first, followed by practice on each subskill and, finally, by practice on the subskills as part of an integrated whole (known as the whole → part → whole approach). Remember that Ms. Jetty taught the overall skills of low- and high-power focusing *prior* to slide preparation. Subsequent examination of the homemade slides provided practice of subskills within the context of the whole skill being learned.

Even in the cognitive domain, it has been found effective to begin with practice on a simplified whole, then practice on gradually more complex applications of the parts, and finally practice on the integrated whole. Thus, the teacher might introduce balancing equations by providing students with the chemical formula for each reactant and each product. After sufficient practice balancing such equations, the students have the ideational scaffolding on which to hang the learning associated with parts (writing formulas for compounds and predicting products from reactants) in the usual writing and balancing of chemical equations. Sound like an advance organizer? It is.

Third, practice is more effective when it is structured within a framework that the student would consider meaningful—such as real-world applications. For instance, students who have demonstrated success in finding the *IMA* of basic types of machines can be shown a ten-speed bicycle and asked to find the *IMA* of each shift position. It is clear that while the initial instruction may emphasize the solution of type problems (level II—cognitive taxonomy), retention depends partly on practice that places the student in a novel situation (level III—cognitive taxonomy).

Last, but perhaps so logically obvious that we tend to forget it, practice must *actively* involve the learners. This does not imply that students must be engaged in some sort of obvious and vigorous physical activity. It does mean that repetitious and boring drill that encourages students to take a mental vacation must be avoided. How can anyone profit from a cognitive learning activity if the mind is not attending to the task at hand and if there is little effort or intent to learn? Because of past unpleasant experiences, just the use of the label *drill* is enough to turn off many students. Thus, we have learned not to use the word with junior/senior high school students. Remember the example of using the ten-speed bicycle to extend practice so as to include applications in context? Doesn't it at the same time include drill on the use of the formula IMA = ED/RD, and also drill to measure ED and RD in various types of simple machines? It certainly does, and students do become mentally active in working out these solutions.

Transfer

If we are able to design instruction to maximize retention, the task of promoting transfer is 90 percent accomplished! What constitutes the final 10 percent? One of the most important conditions for promoting transfer is to make sure students know that they will be expected to apply their learning to novel situations. Equally important is that the students have learning experiences related to that objective. Such learning experiences should include ways to help students *verbalize the methods* of problem solution, in the case of the cognitive domain, or *comprehend the theory* that underlies each motor skill to be learned, in the case of the psychomotor domain. Yes, understanding the reasons for performing a manipulation in a certain way does promote transfer of that skill to other relevant situations—another reminder that the three domains of human learning are not like watertight compartments.

Above all, *never* think or behave as if transfer is automatic. Prior to the beginning of the twentieth century the human brain was commonly considered analogous to a muscle. One could certainly develop the biceps by repeated lifting of a blacksmith's hammer, and this increased the capability of that set of muscles to move any other heavy object. Thus, it seemed logical that exercising the memory portion of the brain by memorizing lengthy Latin poems ought to facilitate the memorization of physics formulas. However, countless research studies performed from 1890 (see Shulman, 1970 for summary) through the present day (Tomera, 1974; Doran & Ngoi, 1979) continue to provide evidence that refutes this notion. Muscle tissue does *not* equal nerve tissue! Analyzing the standard proofs in geometry does not automatically help students cope with data analysis in physics or vice versa. Transfer must be specifically taught if it is to be caught.

6.8 SUMMARY AND SELF-CHECK

Learning is an activity we engage in throughout our lives, but we seldom stop to reflect on how we learn. However, successful teaching depends on thoughtful reflection and study. So we chose to begin with the learning of a jumble of words and then a limerick as a way to clarify some characteristics of meaningful learning. Discovery learning, learning hierarchies, learning types, concept maps, and the role of an advance organizer were described and applied to the learning of science. The pervasive threads of retention, drill (practice), and transfer were treated by considering an information processing model.

You should be able to:

1. Operationally define learning, meaningful learning, rote learning, discovery learning, reception learning, Gagné's learning types, task analysis, learning hierarchy, advance organizer, and concept maps.

2. State the conditions for learning *each* of the types of learning.

3. Construct a learning hierarchy in your subject field.

4. Identify concepts (by inspection, theoretical, relational) and rules/principles by an analysis of syllabi, course outlines, or textbooks in your teaching field.

5. Evaluate the extent to which textbook presentations use advance organizers and justify your decision.

6. Construct a concept map for a unit in your subject field.

7. Assess the extent to which feedback in a "live," "canned," or simulated classroom scene would justify inferences that a concept or a rule had been learned.

8. Given a "live" or video lesson, cite episodes where the teacher appears to be aiming at retention and transfer. Justify your choices.

9. Given a "live" or video lesson in which practice is occurring, characterize the practice as either rote or meaningful and justify your decision.

10. Design practice sets for a specific rule/principle that have potential for retention or transfer.

The exercises that follow are designed to test your ability to meet the preceding objectives and to extend your acquaintance with related writings in this area. We encourage thoughtful consideration of as many of these activities as possible.

6.9 SIMULATION/PRACTICE ACTIVITIES

A. Obtain a state or local syllabus or course outline for a subject you are likely to teach. Read through the first two major units and make separate lists of concepts (by inspection, theoretical, and relational) and rules/principles that are referred to as learning outcomes. Be sure to include those concepts prerequisite to each rule you list whether or not these were specifically identified in the syllabus. Compare your results with those of another classmate.

B. Obtain a copy of two contemporary texts that are used in secondary science classes. Read the first few pages of several chapters and decide on the extent to which the authors have written advance organizers. Justify your decisions.

C. In each of the articles below, the authors have focused on problems associated with the learning of science. Choose any *two* of these and prepare a written review of two or three paragraphs. Include in your review a summary of the writer's chief ideas and a consideration of the match among those ideas and the positions taken by the authors of this text.

   1. Ausubel, D. P. (1964). "Some psychological and educational limitations of learning by discovery." *Arithmetic Teacher*, **11** (5), 290–302.

   2. Kuhn, D. J. (1972). "Models, memory, and meaningful learning in the sciences." *The Science Teacher*, **39** (5), 44–47.

   3. Novak, J. D. (1979). "Applying psychology and philosophy to the improvement of laboratory teaching." *American Biology Teacher*, **41** (8), 466–470.

   4. Shulman, L. S. (1968). "Psychological controversies in the teaching of science and mathematics." *The Science Teacher*, **35**, 34–38, 89–90.

D. The solution to the learning hierarchy question posed in Section 6.4 is illustrated in Figure 6.7. Compare your version with the authors' solution and check out differences with your instructor. Then task analyze objective 3a and construct a learning hierarchy of prerequisites to that objective alone.

E. Read through a chapter in a contemporary secondary school science text and list 8–10 concepts found in that chapter. Then construct a concept map using the labels

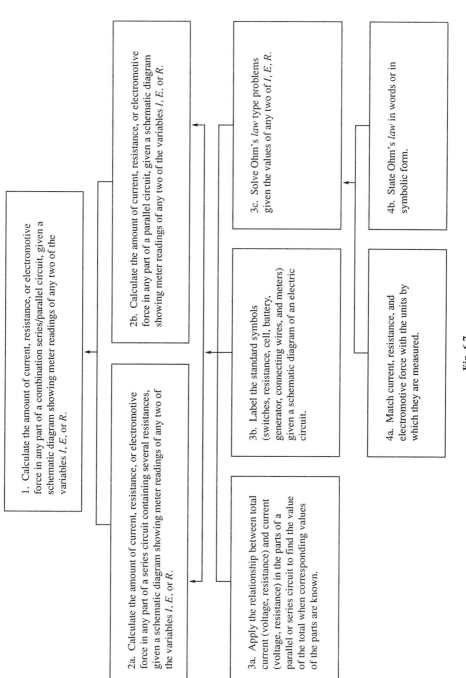

Fig. 6.7

for the concepts. Try to describe the way the concepts are related by phrases on the connecting linkages.

F. Refer to the Learning Hierarchy modular assignment in the Appendix. The careful completion of this assignment will give you a "leg up" when it comes to the writing of well-sequenced lesson plans. Proceed as indicated in the directions, or as modified by your instructor.

G. Choose a rule from the content of secondary school science. Assume it has been introduced meaningfully. Now, a week later, you plan to assign spaced practice. Design a practice worksheet that has potential for optimizing retention and transfer.

H. Column 1 contains concepts or rules which are usually learned in junior/senior high science classes. Column 2 contains feedback the teacher might obtain from the students. In each case, decide whether the feedback is *sufficient* to assure the teacher that the matching concept or rule has been learned. What else would you require in each instance of inadequate or inappropriate feedback?

Column 1 Concepts and Rules	Column 2 Feedback Obtained
1. Mineral	1. Uses the terms "rock" and "mineral" interchangeably.
2. Cell	2. Identifies all microscopic plant and animal sections and protozoans provided as examples of cells; identifies air bubbles, dust particles, and cork slices as nonexamples.
3. Flowering plant	3. Cites rose, apple, and dandelion as examples; gives lawn grass, maple, mushroom, and elodea as nonexamples.
4. IMA=ED/RD	4. Computes IMA of inclined plane, wheel and axle, lever and screw, based on measurements; adds separate IMAs of screw driver and screw to get combined IMA of screw driver-screw system.
5. Bond	5. States that sticks in the sphere and models are not bonds, but that they only represent force fields.
6. Mendelian principles	6. Predicts genotypic and phenotypic ratios of offspring when given genotypes and phenotypes of parents.

SUGGESTIONS FOR FURTHER STUDY

Bruner, J. S. (1960). *The process of education*. Cambridge, MA: Harvard University Press.

This little book has become a classic reference on the curriculum reform movement of the 1950s and 1960s. Bruner illustrates the ways in which the teaching of the structure of the subject matter will facilitate retention and transfer. The examples are often from secondary school science and mathematics and Bruner's style of presentation makes the text highly readable.

LeFrancois, G. R. (1976). *Psychological theories and human learning: Kongor's report*. Monterey, CA: Brooks/Cole.

This lively text is written from the point of view of Kongor, a being from another planet. We especially recommend Chapter 10, in which Kongor introduces the reader to aspects of the cognitive theories of Bruner and Ausubel.

Fehr, H. (Ed.). (1953). *The learning of mathematics* (21st Yearbook). Washington, DC: National Council of Teachers of Mathematics.

Although this yearbook is a sourcebook for mathematics teachers, we recommend a section of Chapter 8—pages 228–247—to all science education students. In Chapter 8, Henderson and Pingry analyze the learning called problem solving. The accounts of flashes of insight recorded by famous mathematicians and scientists and the illustrations of several students' differing conceptions of the nature of a problem are not only fascinating reading, but help to clarify the way this kind of learning occurs.

White, R. T. (1988). *Learning science*. New York: Basil Blackwell.

The theme of this book is that each individual constructs his or her own meaning from stimuli. Drawing on the work of Gagne, Ausubel, Wittrock and others, White provides a model for the learning of science, both in and out of formal school settings. We especially direct science teachers' attention to Chapter 9, which focuses on information processing and constructivist theories of learning.

Yager, R. E. (Ed.). (1982). *What research says to the science teacher* (Vol. 4). Washington, DC: National Science Teachers Association.

Several papers in this volume relate to topics presented in Chapter 6. We encourage science teachers to examine Larkin's paper, *How People Think*, and Ronning and McCurdy's paper, *Problem Solving in Science*.

Wertheimer, M. (1959). *Productive thinking* (Enl. ed.). New York, NY: Harper & Row. (Original work published in 1945).

In this classic written by the father of Gestalt psychology, Wertheimer traced the possible mental restructurations of Galileo as he studied the speed of moving bodies. In another chapter, Einstein reflects on the thinking processes that led to the theory of relativity. In Chapter 5, a physics experiment is used to explore students' reactions to a puzzling situation.

CHAPTER SEVEN

DESIGN OF INSTRUCTIONAL STRATEGIES

The Game Plan

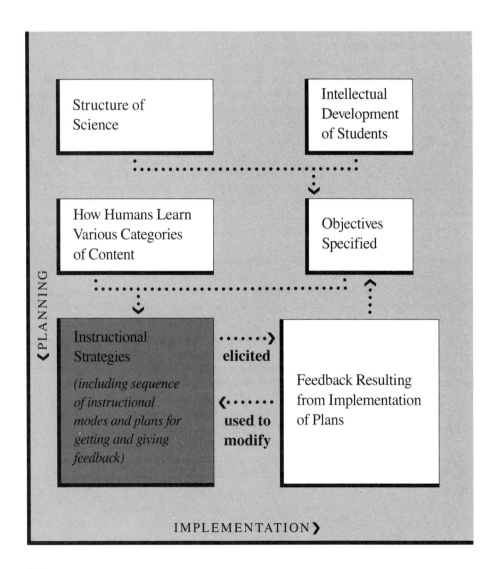

"Tom, I'm really glad you were assigned to do your student teaching with me this semester. You have asked many meaningful questions during your first few days of observing my classes. I have noticed you assisting individuals during class and working with students who come in after school for extra help. I know you are anxious to start teaching a class section on your own, and I have decided that the second-period biology class would be best for your initial assignment. They are a typical sort of group, and biology is your strongest area. Let's see. Today is Thursday and we'll be finishing the enzyme topic tomorrow. Monday would be a good day for you to take over. Bring me a proposed lesson plan tomorrow; we'll look it over together; and I'll see what suggestions I can make. Then you will have the weekend to polish things up and be ready for a solid start on Monday."

You are Tom (or Thomasina). Being an excellent student, you have thoroughly learned the material presented in the first six chapters of this text. You have learned to analyze the nature of science and couple this with knowledge of the intellectual development of students in order to specify objectives that are clearly stated, accurately representative of the content, and attainable by the intended learners. You understand some of the major findings of cognitive psychologists with respect to human learning and can identify uses and abuses of nine main teaching modes. And not only are you alert to the need to give and get feedback during lessons, but you also can design a variety of ways to provide for this all-important aspect of instruction. What else could you possibly need in order to whip that first lesson plan into good shape?

Note the shaded box in the instructional model on the opening page of this chapter and recall that this is the same box we directed attention to at the start of Chapter 1. At that time we concentrated on commonly employed instructional modes and said very little about the design of instructional strategies—the overall theme of that part of the model. At that point in time we had developed neither the prerequisites nor the need for detailed attention to the task of strategy design. Now you have *both* background and need. Efforts to plan effective lessons will be stymied until you are able to synthesize instructional strategies based on all you have learned thus far.

But what is an instructional strategy? We define an *instructional strategy as a sequence of instructional modes designed to promote the attainment of a particular type of objective.* Think in terms of the notion of *patterns.* It is neither necessary nor productive to think of teaching each bit of subject matter as an entirely novel task. Just as we can categorize many items of content as concepts, we can also construct an overall instructional strategy pattern to teach concepts. Likewise, we can design appropriate overall strategies for teaching other kinds of outcomes such as principles/rules. The introductory activity that follows is intended to provide some initial experience in the critical matter of strategy design.

7.1 INTRODUCTORY ACTIVITY

Planning is a Bloom level III–VI activity.

This activity is based on the use of the ruler lab described in Section 2.2 of Chapter 2. If you've forgotten the details, take time to refresh your memory now. The activity refers to a quiz situation faced by science education majors who, like you, had studied the ideas incorporated in Chapters 1–6. The students participated in the ruler lab and then wrote their responses to a follow-up quiz question. The question and one student's response are reproduced below.

> Assume you are teaching a lesson incorporating the ruler lab to a ninth-grade science class in which most of the students have been assessed as concrete operational. Write two objectives that would be appropriate for this class. Then list a sequence of modes that would be likely to achieve your stated objectives and that would incorporate the ruler lab.
>
> **Mary's answer**
>
> *Objectives:*
>
> 1. Choose a graphic way to display the data and justify the decision.
> 2. Extrapolate the coordinates of the next three points on the basis of the graph.
>
> *Modes used in sequence:*
>
> 1. Divide Ss into groups and have them perform the ruler lab.
> 2. With total group watching, T has small groups record cumulative data on the board.
> 3. T lectures on feedback T observed.
> 4. T lectures on "best" way to graph this data and Q/A Ss as to reason it is "best" way.

After studying the above response, react to:

1. the aspects of Mary's answer that were consistent with what you have studied thus far,
2. the match between the strategy and the stated objectives,
3. the match between the type of Ss and the modes, and
4. the sequence of modes and choice of modes.
   a) Look for omissions.
   b) Identify places where students, rather than the teacher, should be at the focal point.

Check Simulation/Practice Activity A for a response we judged more adequate, *after* you have interacted with the preceding exercise.

7.2 DAILY PLANNING BASED ON THE INSTRUCTIONAL MODEL

How can plans be designed so as to attend to all aspects of the instructional model? How much should be written? What written format is helpful to the beginner? We have found that detailed written plans organized to correspond to key components of the model are invariably excellent bases for the beginning teacher. Such plans do not guarantee success, but their absence correlates highly with failure. In other words, they are necessary, but not sufficient, conditions for teaching effective lessons.

Topic _____   Date _____
Class/Period _____

Instructional Objectives:			Routines:		

1 CONTENT ITEM	2 SPECIAL MATERIAL, EQUIPMENT	3 INSTRUCTIONAL STRATEGIES	4 FEEDBACK STRATEGIES		5 TIME EST.
			GET	GIVE	

Fig. 7.1   Daily plan format.

What format is amenable to the organized planning we have been emphasizing? We have found that the one depicted in Figure 7.1 not only accounts
for all aspects of the model, but also has proved workable in the hands of both
novices and experienced teachers. Analyze the lesson plan format in Figure 7.1
and note the categories explicitly represented in the outline. Some items, such
as date, topic, and class period, are simply identifiers for the teacher or visitors.
The routine box is included so that announcements, attendance notes, and other
such items might be recorded. However, the remainder of the headings should
make sense as a synthesis of modes, feedback, objectives, and characteristics of
students and of content. Most novices find that the spacing in Figure 7.1 is inadequate in certain areas. You should adjust the spacing to fit your needs. Under
content item are listed the labels of the concepts, the rule statements, the rule
use ideas, and so on, in the sequence in which you expect to introduce these.
Across from each content item in column 3 would be a description of the sequence of modes designed to achieve the stated objective(s) with respect to that
content item. If materials other than standard chalk and chalkboard are to be
used, these are listed opposite the related strategy in column 2. In addition, we
added two columns labeled *feedback strategies* to give particular emphasis to the
need to plan ways to *get* feedback as well as ways to *give* feedback. Be careful.
These columns are not meant to be diaries of what happened, nor fond hopes as
to what students might say. They should contain the strategies you have chosen in
order to elicit feedback at critical times and to give certain kinds of feedback during the lesson. Finally, column 5 should contain your time estimates for a strategy

aimed at a particular objective. After the lesson has been taught, these estimates should be checked against actual times to assure more realistic planning of time use in the future.

Skeletons may provide helpful clues to the trained archeologist, but beginners need to study the human body in the flesh before graduating to the inference-making of the science of archeology. In like manner, the teacher-to-be needs to analyze completed lesson plans before attempting to construct plans. In the subsections that follow, we have included some sample plans that deal with differing kinds of content. Study each of these plans carefully and look for patterns.

Planning to Teach Concepts and Vocabulary

The plan that follows (Figure 7.2) was designed for a seventh-grade class that had previously been taught an introductory lesson on reproduction in higher plants and completed a set of related laboratory exercises.

We recommend that you study the plan before continuing with the reading in this section. In your first reading of the plan, read the objectives and just the first three columns so that you can get a sense of the sequence and emphasis of the instructional strategies. Stop now and turn to Figure 7.2.

You should assume that this plan is, at least, a second draft attempt on the part of a student teacher. The cooperating teacher would have checked objectives, the match of strategies to objectives, the sequence, and the time estimates. Notice the time ranges indicated at several points in the plan. If the maximum times are used throughout, 44 minutes will be consumed. But the class is scheduled for 40 minutes and you can't keep students beyond the assigned class time. What could you plan to do? If the instructions and format for working with the ads were placed on a handout, along with directions for the assignment (homework), then the final 5 to 8 minutes of the plan could be compressed to 1 to 4 minutes if the need should arise. Suppose that the minimum times are used. You should have obtained a sum less than 40 and, if this were your plan, you should be worried about what might happen in that leftover time. If you don't plan an activity for all parts of the class period, you can be sure that students will innovatively use the time in ways you might prefer to consign to oblivion. This plan badly needs an *elastic clause*—an instructional strategy that can be inserted into the lesson at the teacher's discretion as a response to feedback. The nature of the elastic clause will determine its position in the plan, but we recommend that it be inserted somewhere in the plan rather than "tacked on" at the end. Do you see why? The old reward and punishment aura rears its ugly head if the elastic clause comes over as "You've done so well, you can do some more of these."

Suppose a few color slides showing close-ups of the flowers and fruits of local shade trees were shown prior to distributing the ad sheets. This elastic clause

Topic: Concepts of Flower, Fruit, and Vegetable   Date: May 1 (Tuesday)

Class/Period: Life Science 7, Period 4

Instructional Objectives:

1. Operationally define the terms *flower, fruit,* and *vegetable.*
2. Name and classify plant parts as either roots, stems, leaves, flowers, fruits, or seeds when given either specimens or photos of common vascular plants.
3. Justify classifications made in 2 on the basis of structure and function.
4. Use the terms *flower, fruit,* and *vegetable* correctly in written and oral work.

Routines:

1. Take attendance via seating chart as Ss enter.
2. Collect overdue field trip permission slips from Mary T. and Pete K. as they enter.

Fig. 7.2 Sample concept and vocabulary plan.

CONTENT ITEM	SPECIAL MATERIAL OR EQUIPMENT	INSTRUCTIONAL STRATEGIES	FEEDBACK STRATEGIES		TIME EST.
			GET	GIVE	
Recall of concepts of reproduction in higher plants.	Demo setup of labs previously completed (various asexual means of reproduction in plants vs. seed germination and growth)	T demos and conducts recall Q/A for operational definitions. T has Ss point out ex. and non-ex. of concepts. "Name the parts of each plant as I point to them." "How can we tell where the root stops and the stem begins? Stem stops and leaf begins?" "I cut a branch off here and this new branch grew out of the stem. Is that reproduction or growth? Why?" "What colors can leaves be? Roots? Stems? Seeds?"	T spreads Qs. T takes some straw polls followed by Q/A for reasons.	T confirms some ans.; asks another S to confirm others; T praises thoughtful responses.	4-5 min.
Importance of both asexual and sexual reproduction in plants.	2 oranges (one seeded and one seedless)	T holds up oranges and asks name of items, name of part of plant represented, whether associated with asexual or sexual reproduction, and why. T opens each and shows one is seedless. Q/A on origin and means of reproducing; or lecture if feedback from Q/A is − or 0. Lecture on advantages and disadvantages of sexual vs. asexual reproduction to (1) species and (2) man's interests. Verbal reminder to take notes from Bd.	T spreads Qs. T asks "why," "how" Q; has varied Ss defend or expand. Tour Ss and ck. on note-taking.	Write "FRUIT" on Bd. Praise correct reasons. Write main ideas on Bd. in columns.	5-7 min.

CONTENT ITEM	SPECIAL MATERIAL OR EQUIPMENT	INSTRUCTIONAL STRATEGIES	FEEDBACK STRATEGIES		TIME EST.
			GET	GIVE	
Concepts of flower and fruit.	6 apples (1/4 sections) 6 grapefruit (1/4 sections) 6 tulip flowers 6 rose flowers	"Which plant organ develops into fruit?" "What life function does fruit serve for the plant?" Write ans. on Bd. as elicited. "How can you tell a flower from a root, stem, or leaf? From a fruit?"		Write "FLOWER," "FRUIT," "SEXUAL REPRO-DUCTION" on Bd.	
		Tell Ss to examine object to be passed to them and decide if it is flower or fruit and why. Warn Ss not to put any into mouths and why. Pass tulip and rose flowers plus longitudinal sections of apple and grapefruit so each S gets one specimen.			
		Q/A on which is which, why, and parts of each.	Tour and spread Q/A.		
	Overhead (OH), acetate-labeled diagrams of "typical" (1) flower and (2) fruit plus handouts of same diagrams, *but* un-labeled	OH off and handouts passed by rows as specimens passed back to T.			
		T tells Ss to label diagrams as to flower or fruit.		Put on OH when Ss begin to fumble for names of parts. Tell Ss to ck. OH.	
	Crabapple flowers in various stages of development into fruit	T distributes crabapple specimens by rows as Ss complete handout.			
		T tells each row to arrange their crabapple specimens into a time sequence and then ck. quietly for agreement of neighboring row. Ss told to use correct names of parts in talking to T and other Ss.	Tour, Q/A on reasons and names of parts.	Slice open speci-mens to ans. Ss questions. Praise good questions, use of correct names and pronunciation.	
Discrimination of plant organs.	1 carrot (whole plant) 1 celery (whole plant) 1 lettuce (whole plant)	T holds up each, Q/A on which part(s) humans typically eat; name of plant organ, whether fruit, flower, or vegetable and reasons. Elicit operational def. of. vegetable.	T selectively polls, asks indiv. Ss why.		10-12 min.

Fig. 7.2   (Continued)

Concept of vegetable vs. fruit, seed, and flower.	1 pod of peas, unopened	Elicit operational def. of fruit, seed, and flower. Write on Bd. REPRODUCTION [Root Stem Leaf] [Flower Seed Fruit] Q/A for which boxes to write in "Sexual" and "Asexual."	Tour Ss and ck. on note-taking. Call on Ss who have not yet answered today. Take straw poll and Q/A for reasons.	Write op'al def. on Bd. as obtained and remind Ss to take notes. Write ans. in boxes and tell Ss to copy Bd. work.	10-12 min.
Generalizing to other cases.	24 copies of various supermarket display ads from newspapers	Pass out ads via row as Ss copy notes. Tell Ss to make lists of plant material (1) correctly classified, (2) incorrectly classified, and (3) not sure whether correctly classified, by the ad.	T supervises this practice session and cks. for errors by types.		4-6 min.
Look ahead.		T tells Ss: (1) If not finished, complete lists at home and bring to class Wed. so we can ck. for agreements and disagreements. (2) Bring in one specimen of plant material used for human food. Be sure your ex. is not one treated in today's class so we can classify it tomorrow. (3) Bring in one specimen of plant material put to nonfood use by humans.		Cue Ss to write assignment in notes.	1-2 min.

Fig. 7.2   (Continued)

would help students further generalize the concepts to other interesting and often overlooked examples within the range of everyone's day-to-day experience. Also note the time of year selected for this lesson. It was timed so that local spring flowers would be available to supplement "over-the-hill" specimens liberated from the neighborhood florist shop and grocery store. However, one should plan on starting seeds well ahead of time to insure availability of whole plants where these are needed. Another practical concern must always be safety. Students need to be alerted to the dangers of tasting old and much-handled food items and must be informed that certain parts of common food plants are toxic to humans (such as rhubarb leaves).

This sample plan deals with the concepts of flower, fruit and vegetable, and their concept labels (*i.e.*, vocabulary). Which objectives are related to the concepts? Which objectives are related to the vocabulary? Analyze the instructional strategies column for strategies matching the conditions for concept learning outlined in Section 6.3 of Chapter 6. Where are the examples and the non-examples? Why did the teacher choose to use oranges, apples, grapefruit, tulip, and rose flowers early in the new work instead of starting with tomatoes, cucumber, eggplant, maple tree flowers, and rye grass flowers? These more difficult exemplars are better saved until after operational definitions for fruit and flower have been established. Notice the analysis of newspaper ads at the end of this lesson plan. Some of these commonly mislabeled exemplars will surely come to attention at that time. Others should be introduced by the teacher in a subsequent lesson to extend the concept to the total range desired. Note also how examples of various new and review concepts are made to serve as potentially confusing non-examples of each other. The subject matter of this lesson lends itself to this approach. Such is not always the case and then the teacher must take care to include contrasting but potentially confusing non-examples to help students sort out essential versus non-essential attributes of the target concept(s). For this reason, introductory lessons on magnetic effects often include some attention to electrostatic phenomena.

If you followed our instructions and didn't read the feedback strategies columns, now is the time to return to Figure 7.2 and analyze those strategies in terms of the instructional strategies opposite them. When and how does the teacher plan to get feedback on the extent to which students' thinking is starting to focus on the essential attributes of the concepts? Developmental Q/A, used in conjunction with demo and lab modes, certainly is the key to this crucial aspect. Will it work? Yes, *if* the teacher implements it well. That's why novices are well advised to write out the exact wording of key questions, check them out with the cooperating teacher in advance, and prepare contingency questions in case responses to the first planned questions are not along the desired lines. Many beginners have found it useful to prepare three-by-five-inch cards listing key questions and to carry these into class as a supplement to the lesson plan sheet(s). Experience will gradually reduce the need for specific written teacher cues, but, as a beginner, use as much detail as needed to make the plan work for you in your classroom.

When does the teacher plan to get feedback on whether today's objectives for these concepts have been met? That's right! The best evidence of this would be the tour during the generalizing to other cases part of the plan. At this time, the teacher has a chance to observe individual students practice typical use of the concepts and attempt to extend their use in novel (to the student) situations.

You should have been able to identify connections among the conditions for learning a concept and the instructional strategies outlined in this plan. However, the specific instructional strategies in this plan can readily be generalized to an instructional strategy pattern common to all plans designed to teach concepts. Study the pattern outlined below; note its relationship to Gagné's conditions for learning a concept; and identify the specific strategies in the flower/fruit/vegetable plan that illustrate the generalizations in the pattern.

Instructional Strategy Pattern for Concepts

Provide differentiated examples and non-examples in sequence; sometimes model by analogy; get essential and non-essential characteristics identified; elicit operational definition; elicit generalization of the concept to a variety of specific instances not previously used.

If some of the strategies in the sample plan seem to be "extra," you may have correctly excluded those that are aimed at the teaching of vocabulary. Objective 4 referred to the learning of verbal associations, important goals of science instruction that are often interwoven with the teaching of concepts. It is important to notice that these labels were used as the need arose to "give it a name." As a matter of fact, the vocabulary problem in the sample plan was not one of introducing terms unfamiliar to most students, but rather one of correcting inappropriate use of some labels. However, you will encounter many lessons in which vocabulary totally new to the students must be taught. In these cases the old adage "Don't name the baby before it's born" is worth applying to most concept and vocabulary lessons. An unfamiliar label for which the student has no concrete referents is meaningless if introduced early and can sometimes lead to a negative attitude on the part of the students. Announcing that today's lab will be on "erethyroblastosis" or that the next topic is "plate tectonics" will not exactly create a thirst for knowledge in many students. Reactions such as "More big-word biology" or "Who cares!" are likely to result.

An alternative approach is illustrated by the physical science teacher who suspended a powerful magnet on a ring stand and then silently demonstrated its influence at varying distances and in different directions. A paper clip tied to a piece of string held in the hand was used to probe the limits of the magnet's observable effects prior to introduction of the term *field*. The new label was then written on the board as was the operational definition elicited from the students. Next the teacher inserted sheets of various materials into the space between clip and magnet after asking students to predict the effect of each. Straw votes were taken on each prediction. Then each material was inserted and students asked to describe and explain observations avoiding the use of the word *it* and using the term *field* correctly in context. Likewise this teacher insisted that students continue to use the term appropriately during subsequent demo and Q/A sequences designed both to delimit the concept and generalize it to other relevant phenomena (such as electrostatics).

Meaningful and effective vocabulary learning constitutes a larger part of science than most novices realize. You are not convinced? Go through a commonly used high school text and make a list of important words that are either (1) not used in everyday language or (2) used to connote specifically different meanings within a science context. If your list contains *less than* 250 entries, you had better take another look at the textbook! This number of new science words is very close to the length of a basic vocabulary list for first-year foreign language courses taught in secondary school. Thus, it is important to pay close attention to the generalized instructional strategy pattern for vocabulary that follows and match it against the specific illustrations provided thus far.

Instructional Strategy Pattern for Vocabulary

Show object (or exemplify idea); then pronounce name and spell or write it on board; have students do likewise; repeat (practice); give name and elicit statement of idea or description of object; have students use in context.

The two instructional strategy patterns outlined in this section are standards against which concept and/or vocabulary plans can be checked. They are also guidelines both novices and experienced teachers have found useful in constructing their own concept and vocabulary plans. However, important as the strategy patterns are, they are ineffective unless used in conjunction with the other components of the instructional model. Note that the choice of modes, laboratory and demonstration in particular, was heavily concrete, and even the exercise based on newspaper ads dealt with real phenomena. That kind of choice agrees with the Piagetian implications you studied earlier, just as the particular set of objectives reflects both the kind and degree of content detail suitable for seventh graders. If the students had been an able and interested group of tenth graders, they might have been expected to consider the details of pollen tube growth and double fertilization and to be able to classify various types of fruits.

What else is contained in the sample plan? There is an attempt to produce an overall mix of guided discovery with reception learning, and *if* the teacher implements this plan effectively, the result promises to be meaningful learning. Check for the existence of an advance organizer. The recall of the higher order concepts of reproduction (sexual and asexual) and the related concepts at the same level of abstraction (root, stem, leaf, and seed) should serve this function well. Also, the attention given to the importance of asexual and sexual reproduction provides further opportunity to develop ideational scaffolding. Notice how the board work by the teacher was carefully planned to emphasize the interrelationships among the "old" and the "new" ideas.

Have you wondered why dashed lines are used to separate strategies from one another? Lines are useful at the planning stage to help us check our own thinking and are very helpful during actual implementation as an assist to keeping track of where we are in the lesson. However, solid lines would tend to convey more separation among lesson segments than is intended. Dashed lines are meant to imply the need for the kind of connections that will enable the lesson to flow smoothly. Are such connections provided in the sample plan? Go back and read the end of each strategy and the beginning of the next and identify the connections. Are they explicit? What could the teacher say or do so that students will comprehend the connections? Be sure to satisfy yourself on this important concern before continuing. Perhaps you are thinking that sequencing decisions can either enhance the building of connections or make the task all but impossible. We agree! Try mentally rearranging the strategies on any lesson plan and then analyze the resulting effects. Sometimes you will find equally (or perhaps more) productive ways to structure the lesson. In other cases bizarre results will show up fast.

There certainly is a lot more to this business of planning lessons than is obvious to the casual observer. And just think—we have considered only concept and vocabulary instruction thus far. Does the task seem overwhelming when you realize that coping with plans aimed at principles, novel problem solving, process aspects of science, and psychomotor skills lie ahead, and that many lessons will involve combinations of these? Don't let yourself be discouraged. The situation is not nearly as momentous as it may seem at this point. What you learn about concept and vocabulary plans will serve as the base for all these other types of plans. Thus, the next task is to apply that and add some new ideas that have special relevance to various other types of target outcomes. Since science is said to be a rule-governed subject, we consider planning for principle (rule) learning in the next section.

Planning for Rules/Principles

There are two major types of rules/principles that are found repeatedly in science lessons: formulas and type problems solved by algebraic methods. Both have the common characteristics found in rule-learning, but each possesses unique characteristics that must be considered by the science teacher in planning a lesson.

Formulas   The ninth-grade lesson outlined in the next sample plan (Figure 7.3) focused on the principle of mechanical efficiency, a principle that involves related principles learned in previous lessons. Study the plan carefully for the earmarks of rule learning from Section 6.3 of Chapter 6. Once again, we recommend that you interrupt your reading of the text material to study the rule plan. Then check out your ideas with the comments and questions that follow in the text.

The length of a full class period in this particular school is 45 minutes. Did you notice that the elastic clause was placed near the end of the lesson? In this case, the elastic clause applies to those more able students who have completed the application examples and now are asked to extend their understanding by generating a list of additional mechanical devices. If the maximum time estimates are used, there will still be enough time for the teacher to insure that all students are able to begin the assignment. Attached to this plan is a copy of the problem set. This was completed in response to advice given by the cooperating teacher when preliminary ideas for the plan were discussed two days earlier. Check its contents for such features as graded order of difficulty, match to objectives, and "real-world" contexts of potential interest to ninth graders. The cooperating teacher thought it was quite good, and had only a few minor suggestions for improvement prior to the duplication of copies for class use. The cooperating teacher also asked to see the prepared acetate sheets so that they could be carefully scrutinized prior to use to determine whether the data were organized so as to facilitate the desired comparisons. (These have not been included here.)

You may wonder why so many teacher questions are written out on this particular plan. The answer is just what you might guess if we first told you to look at the date on the plan. This student teacher had only taught a few days and, like many beginners, was having trouble phrasing questions under fire. Thus, both college supervisor and cooperating teacher had urged that this approach be used until further experience made the practice unnecessary.

However, the central issue here concerns the rule-learning objectives and the strategies that are related to the conditions for rule learning. You should have identified specific strategies which conform to the pattern that follows.

Instructional Strategy Pattern for Rules/Principles

Get students to recall/review prerequisites; indicate nature of expected terminal performance; cue (via questions, lab work, applications) students to find the pattern by chaining concepts; get the rule stated (by students, if possible); provide a model of correct performance; have students demonstrate instances of the rule in a variety of situations. *Fix and maintain skills by spaced and varied drill.

The key elements in the rule strategy pattern are prominent features in this or any other well-designed rule/principle plan. However, "prominent" does not mean disjointed. Note how well this novice has provided for a natural flow among the elements of the plan. If implemented well, the lesson should result in smooth transitions that enhance learning by making connections clear to

Topic: Principle of Mechanical Efficiency

Class/Period: Physical Science 9, Period 1

Date: September 15 (Thurs)

Instructional Objectives:
1. State in symbols and in words that E = work out/work in and $E = AMA/IMA$.
2. Compute any unknown in the efficiency formulas when given values for the other two terms.
3. Explain why E must always be a decimal or a fraction less than 1.0 or a percentage less that 100.

Routines:
Take attendance via seating chart as Ss enter.

CONTENT ITEM	SPECIAL MATERIAL OR EQUIPMENT	INSTRUCTIONAL STRATEGIES	FEEDBACK STRATEGIES		TIME EST.
			GET	GIVE	
Recall of concepts force (F) effort (E) resistance (R) effort distance (ED) resistance distance (RD)	Demo setups of labs previously completed on 1st, 2nd, and 3rd class lever.	T demos and conducts Q/A for op. definitions, names, and symbols using setup of 1st class lever. T has Ss point out ex. and non-ex. of concepts. "Name each part as I point to it." "Come up and show us where to measure ED and RD" on model setup and on crowbar and can opener.	T spreads Qs. T takes some straw polls followed by Q/A for reasons.	T confirms some ans.; asks another S to confirm others; T praises correct ans. to Qs on 2nd and 3rd class levers and application to practical examples.	
Recall of rules (principles) work = $F \times D$ work in = work out $AMA = R/E$ $IMA = ED/RD$	— and —	Repeats above for 2nd class lever and practical exs.			
	Practical ex. of various levers (crowbar, punch-type can opener, fishing rod, baseball bat, nutcracker).	Repeat above for 3rd class lever and practical exs.			
		T asks S volunteer to demo at front and describe how to find "work in," "work out," AMA and IMA of 1st class levers.	Ss at seats to raise hands if they spot error.		
		T has other S volunteers do the same for 2nd and 3rd class levers.			8–10 min.

Where we're headed.	Overhead projector	T shows composite data of past two days' labs using meter stick and weights model of levers. Q/A on comparisons of (1) "work in" vs. "work out" and (2) AMA vs. IMA for each case. "Why was 'work in' not *exactly* the same as 'work out' in all cases?" "Why was AMA not *exactly* equal to IMA in all cases?"	Spread Q/A.	Write on Bd. "MEASUREMENT ERRORS"	5-7 min.
Comparison of AMA and IMA.	Rusty hedge clippers and bolt cutters	T walks around rm. showing devices while conducting Q/A. "Assuming we could eliminate *all* errors of measurement, would 'work in' = 'work out' in these? IMA = AMA? Why?" "Which would be larger and why?" "Would removing all rust make the quantities equal and why not?" "What else would make them *closer* to equal and why?" "Could we ever eliminate all friction? If not, why not?" "In the case of *more complex* machines would you expect Ideal and Actual figures to be closer or further apart than in the case of simple levers and why?"	Call on Ss who have not yet answered.	Write on Bd. "FRICTION" Write on Bd. "WORK IN > WORK OUT" "IMA > AMA" Verbal praise for correct generalizations.	
Importance and use of rule.		T lectures on importance of designing machines where Actual approaches Ideal figures. Cite Efficiency figures (in terms of ranges) for steam engines, gasoline engines, bicycles, and electric motors. (Write on Bd.)			3-4 min.

Fig. 7.3 (Continued)

CONTENT ITEM	SPECIAL MATERIAL OR EQUIPMENT	INSTRUCTIONAL STRATEGIES	FEEDBACK STRATEGIES		TIME EST.
			GET	GIVE	
Rules E = work out/work in and $E = AMA/IMA$		T sets Ss to work at seats to try to work out one or more formulas that could be used to obtain such efficiency figures. T reminds Ss to use ideas and symbols developed in class. T directs Ss to work alone and raise hands when ready to explain result.	Tour and observe Ss progress.	Cue Ss who need help to get started. Praise Ss who are on right track.	
		After 3–4 min. send selected Ss to Bd. to put work on and explain to class. Pick 1 with correct AMA/IMA approach and 1 with correct "work out/work in" approach.	Tour; spread Qs. Take straw votes on reasons.		
		T tells all other Ss to watch/listen and prepare to agree/disagree and give reasons.		Tell Ss to write correct formulas in notes.	7-8 min.
Model Problem 1 Model Problem 2	Handouts of type problem sets (see attached)	T tells Ss to take one problem sheet and pass the rest back by rows as T erases formulas from board. T: Q/A steps and writes correct ans. on Bd. as Ss write on sheets. "Which of the two formulas should we use in this case?" "Why?" "What is the next step?" etc. Repeat for problem 2.	Spread Q/A. Call on other Ss to confirm each step and give reasons.	Write correct ans. on Bd. and Verbal praise.	5-7 min.

Fig. 7.3 (Continued)

Applying formulas to a variety of problems (inc. elastic clause).	T sets Ss to work on remaining ex., emphasizes showing all steps, reminds Ss to work alone quietly. If any S finishes early, T suggests that S compose a list of mechanical devices T might include in future work on unit.	Tour and look for any pattern errors.	Stop work and Q/A with Bd. work if pattern error is evident; otherwise, cue individuals.	6-8 min.
Assignment and Look ahead.	About 1 minute before the end of class, T directs Ss to complete whatever remains by tomorrow's class. T indicates that *after* all problems with these ex. are cleared up, tomorrow's lab with more complex and interesting devices from everyday life will be "a piece of cake."		T shares group progress with all. Compliment class on good work of today (to extent this proves true).	1 min.

PLAN ATTACHMENT: PROBLEM SET ON EFFICIENCY

1. A boy using an iron pipe as a first-class lever found that he had to push with a force of 20 lbs at a distance of 8 ft from the fulcrum in order to lift a 100 lb rock from his mother's garden. The rock was 1 ft from the fulcrum. Compute the efficiency of the lever and express it both as a percent and as a fraction.

2. A can opener with an *IMA* of 4 was found to produce an *AMA* of 3. Compute its efficiency in terms of both a decimal and a percent.

3. A fishing rod requires 23 ft lbs of work be expended in order to provide 21 ft lbs of thrust to the lure being cast. Compute the efficiency of this rod.

4. A nutcracker was found to have an efficiency of .80 and an *IMA* of 2.0. Find its *AMA*.

5. A consumer testing agency found that its top-rated auto jack was 73% efficient and delivered an *AMA* of 67. Find its *IMA*.

6. A 103 lb girl bet her boyfriend that she could lift the engine out of his car by using her father's block and tackle. The engine weighed 475 lbs. The block and tackle was so designed that 8.5 ft of chain pulled through would result in the engine being lifted 1 ft. What is the minimum efficiency figure for this device that would be required if the girl were to win the bet?

Fig. 7.3   (Continued)

students. Also pay attention to the timing and treatment given to informing students of expected terminal performance. Although the explicit consideration of goals should be present in every type of plan, it is particularly important to attend to this matter early in the development of a rule lesson. Then the students' outlook during the eliciting of the rule is not cluttered by musings such as where we're headed, what I'll need to remember, whether two questions in a sequence are related or not. They know what to listen for and concentrate on. When the teacher later "provides a model of correct performance" as this designer of the sample plan proposed to do with model problems 1 and 2, the details of the teacher's expectations for the student should be crystal clear. Finally, no rule instruction is complete if a lesson does not contain a well-structured strategy aimed at *student* demonstration of learning. Too many novice teachers are trapped by lazy or confused students into doing "one more problem together" and thus demonstrating that the *teacher* has learned the rule. You were warned about this abuse of feedback in Chapter 2. Sometimes, it's true, the students are honestly confused because the teacher didn't initially clarify the expected student outcomes, and/or has in the past immediately given practice examples far more complex than the model problem. Once again, we emphasize the need for gradually differentiated practice examples and for in-class decisions as to the number and kind of problems to be assigned, based on feedback. We hope you noticed that this plan included more than one written practice sequence as well as oral practice. That final six to eight minutes of written practice is a *must*. Unless the teacher obtains positive feedback on a substantial part of these mixed exercises, there is no solid evidence of student capability on such tasks.

Why did we star the last sentence in the instructional strategy pattern? The star is meant to identify the long-range nature of this aspect of the strategy pattern. Intellectual skills, however effectively introduced, are maintained only by means of selective practice in later lessons. Look back at some of the suggestions in Chapter 6.

Type problems solved by algebraic methods Many secondary school science textbooks contain long lists of "problem" exercises. Even a cursory look at these sample exercises will convince the reader that nearly all of them are examples of rule/principle learning. Very, very few are illustrations of what we call novel problem solving (Gagné's type 8 learning). Thus, instruction for such lessons should be patterned after the rule/principle strategy pattern we have just been considering. However, these problems cast in the context of a situation seem to cause particular problems for learners and all-too-often are viewed by students as one of the more disagreeable aspects of science class. Why?

One of the major causes of negative attitudes and ineffective rule learning resides in the very nature of some of the problem contexts. Mathematics teachers face this problem when students complain about the unreality and uselessness of age, digit, and coin problems. Your students may already have negative attitudes about this kind of problem material if interesting and relevant problems have not been used in their mathematics classes. As a result, science teachers must take extra care to couch verbal problems in terms of actual and potentially interesting situations.

Moreover, even when interesting type problems are used, some teachers behave initially as though the students should be engaging in novel problem-solving strategies. Yet, at the end of the lesson the students of these teachers learn that there is *one* strategy they should have "discovered" and *one* procedure they are expected to use with similar problems from now on. Even more unfortunate, the teacher has lost the opportunity to help students see the importance of classifying important groups of problems that may then be treated in an algorithmic way. Thus, as with all instruction in rule learning, it is vital that the teacher let the students know the nature of the expected outcomes. In this case, the outcome is for the students to identify a problem as belonging to a certain type, a type of sufficient interest and usefulness that it recurs frequently in the real world.

It is equally important that the lesson begin with an interesting problem. Fortunately, the nature of the subject matter of science lends itself to this approach. Unfortunately, we must often look beyond the standard text to find suitable materials. For example, most students understand that motion relationships are important in many areas of life from the Olympics record-breakers to the car manufacturer. Thus, an attention-getter like the pigeon problem can create a positive mind-set toward the new topic.

> *Pigeon racing, a development of the use of homing pigeons in the ancient Olympic Games (776 B.C.–393 A.D.), originated in Belgium. The longest recorded flight was estimated to be 7000 miles flown in 55 days by a pigeon owned by the Duke of Wellington. The flight ended when the exhausted pigeon dropped dead one mile from its home loft in London, England, on June 1, 1845. What average velocity in mph was attained by this record breaking pigeon? (McWhirter & McWhirter, 1976)*

The pigeon problem contains a characteristic even more important than that of simply provoking curiosity. It makes sense. It is a *bona fide* motion problem to which even we non-pigeon-fanciers can relate. And that latter characteristic, the meaningfulness of the situation *to the student*, is the one most frequently ignored by textbook writers and thus by those teachers who rely solely on textbook problems.

Even though the pigeon problem contains extraneous information in terms of the question asked, the information is not extraneous in terms of real-world events. As long as the students have learned the prerequisite relationships among distance, rate and time and know the conversion from days to hours, the final question can be solved by applying the distance formula. Students who follow the progress of their school track team, the results of the Indianapolis 500 or any of the other multiple real-world distance/time events will quickly see this problem as one of an important type. Notice that we haven't advised that a chart be set up. Although some teachers find charts indispensable, we recommend that charts be used sparingly, if at all. Too often, they are presented before the students have had the opportunity to study the problem, talk about its meaning and try their hand at solution strategies.

Problems that can be represented in terms of known formulas are situation problems in which the problem of translation is relatively simple. The student must first recognize that the problem situation is modeling some known formula and then study the problem for the quantities corresponding to the concepts in the formula. One important aid in studying the problem is the use of a diagram. For example, with motion problems, labeled arrow diagrams form a pictorial representation of the problem. Two important questions, What changed? and What remained the same?, should then be asked. The answer to the second question points the way to the equation—perhaps "time going equals time returning." Then the distance formula is used as a tool to represent time going and time returning, rather than being directly used as in the pigeon problem.

Some type problems cannot be represented by a common formula. Even the most skilled translator of verbal problems often is stumped by a problem such as this:

> A bottle containing 40 cc of tincture of iodine (iodine crystals dissolved in alcohol) is labeled as having 2% concentration of iodine. However, each time the cap is removed some alcohol evaporates, and thus the concentration of iodine is altered from the medically prescribed percentage. How much alcohol would have to be evaporated in order to double the recommended concentration? To triple it?

In order to solve such a problem, the student must be able to apply translation skills at two levels of complexity. In the following paragraphs, we outline the idea concocted by Mrs. Armstrong, who was beginning to plan a lesson on an introduction to solution problems. Mrs. Armstrong kept in mind the two important characteristics of situation type problems pointed out earlier.

1. The situation must be meaningful *to the student* and

2. The student must be alerted to the need for an initial strategy other than translation.

The first characteristic is the key to what should occur in the construction of the advance organizer and the follow-up development of this kind of rule. The situation must be made meaningful in a concrete way. The plan itself is not included, but you should be able to expand the development described below into an appropriate sequence of instructional and feedback strategies.

> I'll start with a demonstration that can be matched to a specific problem. I'd better start with a situation in which water is added; evaporating may befuddle their thinking," Mrs Armstrong mused.
>
> She got out two 100 cc graduated beakers, two 10 cc graduated beakers, and a bottle of fluorescein dye. Then, she added drops of the dye to the 90 cc of

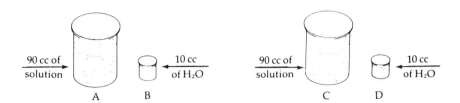

Fig. 7.4   Beakers set up for solutions demo.

water in one of the beakers until an intense color was present. She recorded the number of drops used and then observed the effect of adding 10 cc of water on the color. There was a perceptible change.

Mrs. Armstrong decided to do the final step of the demo in exactly the same way at the beginning of class and then question the students as to their observations. As a result of a last-minute brainstorm she decided to use all four beakers with the two 100 cc kind already containing identical amounts and intensity of the fluorescein solution, while the two 10 cc beakers would each contain 10 cc of water. When the students entered class, they would see the apparatus set up as in Figure 7.4.

The students in the front rows would be able to read aloud the total number of cc of liquid in each of the four beakers, but it would be up to the instructor to reveal the nature of the ingredients and the concentration of the solution in beakers A and C.

Mrs. Armstrong intended to pour the water in beaker B into the solution in beaker A but leave the other two beakers as is, so that students might have a ready reference as to the "before" situation. She knew she must obtain answers to two major questions: (1) What changed? and (2) What remained the same? She would have to use contingency questions to elicit the hidden constant—that is, the constant volume of the fluorescein dye in beaker A both before and after the demonstration. Then she would help the students compose a list of varied practical situations where mixing of this kind might occur, but where the desired final concentration would be known (in order to clarify where the class was headed).

If Mrs. Armstrong implements the above idea successfully, she should next provide students with a model problem. The model problem should be matched to the action illustrated by the demo (that is, one ingredient should be added to a mixture) although the unknown might differ. Then she will need to move gradually from the demo to the mathematical model in at least three steps (pictorial, English sentence, mathematical sentence). Mrs. Armstrong would probably cue students to help complete:

1. A labeled sketch of the situation in the case of the model problem with perhaps a "before" and "after" version.

2. An English sentence that describes what stays the same (for example, the cc of fluorescein dye "before" is the same as the cc of fluorescein dye "after").
3. The corresponding mathematical sentence with the appropriate designation of the unknown.

Notice the levels of translation that are provided for in this lesson outline. The situation and its dynamics are pictured and labeled. The importance of this kind of iconic representation of the problem is unparalleled in helping students identify the changing and unchanging quantities in the problem. Now the students must create an English sentence based on their analysis of the iconic representation. This step transforms the problem into a statement that can be translated from left to right with the first level of translation skills.

Although the new rule has been obtained at the equation-stating step, the students should still be asked to complete the problem and check the result in the statement of the problem as well as in the original equation. Moreover, as in all problem-solving instruction, it is vital that the teacher and the students review the process which led to this rule. Next comes student practice of the new rule, right? Yes, but it takes a relatively long time to completely work through even a small number of these problems. And leaving the bulk of them for homework is never a sound substitute for supervised practice. The answer is to assign several problems, direct the students to label the variable(s) and set up the equation for all examples, but to completely work through only one or two designated examples.

Mrs. Armstrong's approach might seem time-consuming and unnecessarily elaborate unless you've read the results of the National Assessment of Educational Progress administered in 1986. According to Mullis and Jenkins (1988), the tested students' knowledge of science content and the ability of students to use this knowledge were very limited. The authors emphasized the need for students to have many opportunities to apply knowledge to solve problems.

Our own classroom experience has convinced us that the rote application of a standard tabular arrangement can be presented quickly and will yield fairly high scores on a quiz given the next day on exactly the same kind of problems. However, if the teacher slips in mixture problems, such as feed mixtures, medicinal dosages, fuel mixtures, fertilizer or pesticide mixtures, (all possessing the same structure as solution problems), the students will be lost and must be taught to memorize still more procedures for each of these "types." Mrs. Armstrong's initial investment of time will pay off dividends in meaningful learning and make her later attempts to transfer learning of this rule to all problems in the same family far more successful. For now we suggest that you begin to search out and add to your Resource File a wide variety of relevant and interesting problems.

Planning for Novel Problem Solving

Problem solving of the nontypical variety is really where it's at if you believe, as we do, that the ideal of education is to teach the students to think for themselves.

One aspect of the Search for Excellence project in science education has been the identification of criteria for excellence in science programs (National Science Teachers Association, 1987). A commonly identified criterion for excellence in secondary school science programs is providing students with opportunities to solve real-world problems (sometimes with the use of a computer), many of which have no "set or pat" answer.

Like any other educationally significant objective, this one must be the target of instruction specifically designed to achieve that kind of outcome. Unlike other types of outcomes, this kind is more difficult to attain and more time-consuming to pursue. But isn't that what we should expect if it really is of the most worth?

Having been forewarned about both the difficulty and the desirability of fostering problem solving, let's now turn our attention to the "hows" of the matter. A second look at the conditions for learning novel problem solving found in Chapter 6 is definitely in order at this point. Notice that novel problem solving is at the top of the hierarchy of cognitive learning and thus is dependent upon prior attainment of relevant principles/rules, which are in turn dependent upon attainment of relevant concepts. The wise teacher will keep this relationship in mind during the initial instruction in concept and principle learning and work to head off future problems. How? An extensive number of key concepts, as well as potentially confusing non-examples, will gradually be elicited *from* the students. Then, during the initial learning of important principles, the teacher will incorporate such behaviors as (1) describing the ways scientists originally progressed toward formulation of the same pattern(s) (including fumblings and trips up blind alleys), (2) weighing advantages and disadvantages of various modes of attack, and (3) cuing on ways to get feedback on proposed solutions without resorting to the authority of teacher or text. These and similar teacher moves will gradually shift the responsibility of thinking from teacher to student.

Mr. Potter had been gradually moving his eleventh-grade science class toward problem solving. He included all the above behaviors and, in addition, encouraged students to work in groups and to defend their work to one another. Then, one day he began class this way:

Last night you read descriptions of four theories/models invented to account for the origin of the universe [He points to board where big-bang, oscillating, steady-state, and Snoopy's theory are written]. Today I want you to behave like working scientists and decide which of the four best accounts for known phenomena. Rank them 1 for the most adequate through 4 for the least adequate theory. Be sure to include attention to the age of the earth, moon rocks, quasars, pulsars, and black holes, plus any other phenomena you consider to be very important [writes these on board]. However, keep in mind that you will be required to defend your decisions with both logic and evidence. You may use the handout describing the four theories and the other references you see on the side table. I have divided you into five teams and appointed a leader for each. When I give the signal, each group is to move to its assigned location quietly and begin work. Each group leader must see that the directions are followed, ensure that everyone has a chance to participate, appoint one person to obtain and return reference books as needed, and report the team's findings orally when I signal the end of the group work. Let me see the hands of any who are not clear as to what we are going to do or how we are going to do it. Fine, now look at the overhead projection screen [turns on the overhead] to find the location of your team and the starred name of your leader. Remember there is no one "pat" answer, and a number of approaches may prove equally good in trying to solve the problem. I'll be moving from group to group so raise your hand if you require my help. Let's set 25 minutes as the time limit for group work so we will have 10 to 15 minutes left for oral reports of our findings. You may begin now.

Mr. Potter's success today will depend partly on his prior developmental work and partly on his students' previous knowledge. Mr. Potter's quoted preamble would constitute only the introduction to the activity. You should be able to identify the next instructional strategy he would list in his plan and the associated feedback strategies. That's right. Next would come small-group discussions with Mr. Potter touring, listening for attention to relevant data and the kind of reasoning used, trying to get students to help one another, praising an insightful idea, and so on. Take a few minutes now and sketch out the rest of the plan with appropriate time estimates. Don't forget to write the instructional objectives. After you have produced an outline, check it for correspondence with the instructional strategy pattern presented next.

Instructional Strategy Pattern for Novel Problem Solving

Present problem; may question students to elicit alternative approaches and will emphasize the desirability of a variety of search strategies; arrange for individual work or small-group discussion (in the collection of data, the analysis of data, the making and testing of conjectures); reassemble class; ask students to weigh the advantages and disadvantages of the proposals (including processes) that resulted from the group discussions or individual work.

This instructional strategy pattern included references to individual or group work. In fact, recent research on both problem solving and adolescent reasoning is supportive of *both* individual and group work, but for different purposes. One of the characteristics of the successful problem solver is persistence. Thus, it is important that the teacher structure some long-term project work dealing with problem solving so that students realize that many atypical problems require thinking time, time away from the problem and time reconsidering the problem from a different point of view. Here is where the individual project becomes a useful instructional mode. However, it is also clear from researchers in problem solving (Whimbey & Lochhead, 1982) and cooperative learning (Slavin, 1980) that carefully structured small group (or pairs) discussions add another dimension to the learning of problem solving. The requirement to share tentative ideas and to talk out a sequence of strategies has great potential in generating a problem-solving attitude. We remind you that small group work often follows a period of individual work on a problem or situation. Notice once again the importance of modes that are likely to enhance cognitive interaction, often through social interaction.

We've already emphasized the need for a gradual move toward instruction in problem solving. These prior teacher-led explanations of "thinking through a problem" need to be continued and expanded during problem-solving lessons. Reread the final step in the strategy pattern. That step includes class consideration of the *processes* used by small groups or individuals during work on the problem. It is analogous to the summarizing step prior to practice in lessons on type word problems, but the difference resides in the focus of the summary. In type problem work, the teacher's aim is to clarify the structure that is reflected in all similar problems and, therefore, the typical steps to solution. However, in novel problem-solving lessons, the aim of this summarizing step is to clarify the tactic(s) used in this case and to consider the pros and cons of a more general use for these specific processes. Over time, the teacher should help the class attain a list of such tactics that *may* illuminate a problem but are not guaranteed to produce a solution. Such tactics are labeled *heuristic strategies* or simply *heuristics*. *Heuristic* is a word derived from the Greek *heuriskein*, which translates roughly "to find out." Of course, sometimes you *find out* that the particular heuristic you tried is of no help. We've compiled a list of potentially useful heuristics with some examples from the literature and our classroom experience. We recommend that you begin collecting additional examples of heuristics.

Heuristics

1. Use analogy or contrast. ("This phenomenon seems to be behaving like ..., so let's try ... ")

2. Plot the data on a graph.

3. Change the scale (or frame of reference). (Try different types of graphs; plot on log-log paper.)

4. Use successive approximation; exploit errors (guess, try, correct, guess again.)

5. Ask "What if such and such were *not* true?"

6. Change the problem to a closely related one that you can solve.

7. Focus attention on one part of the problem at a time.

8. Look at the extremes. (In the case of quantitative data, let the numbers get very small and very large.)

9. Ask another student.

Fig. 7.5 Collection of shapes to be classified.

It's clear that some of these heuristics may not be useful tactics in the case of certain problems and students will need to be reminded that none of them guarantees success. A "guaranteed successful" stamp on a tactic is a sign that the tactic is really an algorithm and the problem, a type problem.

Are novel problems difficult to find? Not at all. There are numerous sources of novel problems, including professional journals, some curriculum projects, and texts devoted solely to them. But you do have to know what to look for. Then, there is your own creative imagination. Here is a sampling of a few different kinds of novel problems to get you started.

1. Design a way to test the idea that snow covered with soot melts faster than "clean" snow.

2. How can one get the greatest number of cars into a parking lot, permitting access and egress? If one needs to put in still more cars, how can we do it so as to minimize shuffling? (A real-world problem from *Goals for the Correlation of Elementary Science and Mathematics*, 1969)

3. Invent a taxonomic scheme for classifying these shapes. Codify the scheme in the form of a dichotomous key and validate its usefulness by having five classmates use it to classify the shapes (see Figure 7.5).

4. Given this block of balsa wood, cut pieces and glue them together in the form of a bridge at least 50 cm long and 5 cm wide which will support a 500 gram mass suspended from its midpoint.

5. Farmer Brown wishes to obtain an environmental grant for managing his 250 acre farm for the maximum production of deer, pheasants, and cottontail rabbits consistent with maintaining a 90% level of production of each of his current farm products—corn, hay, milk, apples and firewood. Attached is a map* of his farm showing contours, existing vegetation, cultivated fields, planting/harvesting dates, buildings, and roads. Produce a detailed plan (map and descriptive materials) which would qualify his farm for the grant.

6. Contemporary types of dogs have evolved by selective breeding processes. Note the differences between the original Airedale breed as a "poacher's dog" in England many years ago and the present AKC standards for that breed (see attached sheet*). Assume that you have one male and one female Airedale each closely matching current AKC standards and wish to eventually produce the original Airedale type. Design a detailed plan which would achieve that goal.

Novel problems, then, may belong to advanced science (more complex problems on the topic being studied) or applied science (problems from mathematics or the social sciences). There is a time when each of these kinds of problems serves an instructional purpose. We encourage you to begin collecting such problems in appropriate folders of your resource file. Be sure to organize *within* folders so that novel problems are separated from relevant type problems. You will find selected references to use as a starting point at the end of this chapter and additional references in Chapters 9, 10, and 11.

Process aspects   Notice the integration of the product and process aspects of science that seems to occur so naturally in most of the examples of novel problems just cited. This is a frequent bonus when novel problem solving is included in science instruction. Moreover, in our judgment, it is the most appropriate approach to teaching the dual nature of the subject matter. If you engage students in novel problem solving (at level III and above), they will invariably have to use some combination of processes such as observing, inferring, data gathering, data reducing, hypothesizing, designing experiments, inducing, deducing, assuming, and model building. Similarly, it is difficult to imagine how students could be meaningfully engaged in using various science processes in a context devoid of the phenomena and ideas of the subject. This is not to say that prerequisite initial learning of processes (at levels I and II) can be omitted. Previous lessons and/or lesson segments focused on initial learning of science processes and designed along the lines of the strategy patterns for concept and rule learning are essential prerequisites.

Planning for Psychomotor Learning

Introspection is always a difficult and uncertain proposition. For you to recall from many years past exactly what it was like to learn to use a burette, mass

*Note: These attachments can be developed from standard sources and are not included here.

objects, or prepare whole wet-mounts is all but impossible. However, you can increase your own understanding of the task your students face by doing three things.

First, write down each of the separate motor chain connections and the sequence in which they must occur in order to perform the selected task. If you have never done this before, we guarantee some surprises. There is more to lighting and adjusting a Bunsen burner, pipetting liquids, and focusing a microscope than appears to the casual observer!

Second, make note of previous experiences the students already have had that are likely to either help or hinder the new learning. All too often previous everyday experience hinders rather than helps. For example, the "twist and pull" conditioning in response to doorknobs has negative transfer value in response to microscope adjustment knobs and burette stopcocks!

Third, consider the limited value of verbal instructions in guiding learning of the specific motor skills we teach in science. For instance, the instruction "turn the knobs slowly" with regard to focusing a microscope is intended to convey a barely perceptible rotation on the order of a fraction of a millimeter over seconds. However, novice teachers are repeatedly appalled by the response to that verbal direction. Could it be that what goes through the hearer's mind is the gross motion associated with the turning of the steering wheel of a car? Thoughtful attention to these three aspects when analyzing the task will help lay the groundwork for designing plans that will work.

Refer back to Section 5.3 for a sample of the kinds of psychomotor objectives that are typically sought in science instruction. Note that each is limited, rather than global, in scope. You do not see statements such as "Use the compound microscope." Such a global objective implies inclusion of techniques such as the use of oil immersion, mechanical stage, condensing lenses, and light filtering—a set of skills whose mastery requires months or even years of training and experience. You would do well to begin with basic skills of limited scope and ensure that these are effectively and efficiently learned. Then related skills building upon basic prerequisites can be added over time.

A word of caution is in order here. Is it justifiable to spend 40 to 80 minutes of laboratory time to teach a skill that will be used only once for 10 or 20 minutes? We think not. Instead we suggest a teacher-performed demonstration with lecture as an equally effective and more efficient way to gather data in such cases. During student teaching you will need the help of your cooperating teacher in identifying those manipulative skills that will be used in subsequent units.

Now let's turn our attention to one psychomotor skill that is typically used frequently throughout a life science course. Ms. Jetty, a life science teacher, had devoted several laboratory sessions to instruction and practice in which the microscope (low and high power) was used to examine prepared slides. Feedback on those objectives was positive. Therefore, she set as her next objective:

Prepare a whole wet-mount slide containing no air bubbles, given a prepared specimen section and all other required materials.

Ms. Jetty did not want to complicate the learning of basic microscope skills by including slide preparation earlier. You might also surmise that she wanted to wait until students attempting slide production could get accurate feedback (via microscope viewing). So far, so good.

Next, Ms. Jetty made several basic instructional decisions that would serve as a frame of reference for developing details of strategy design. Study each carefully and check your understanding of the reasons for them.

1. The specimens used will be fairly large, be resistant to tearing, and contain a minimum of imperfections.

2. The tissues represented will consist of those obtained from people, pets, and familiar plants.

3. All students will have identical sets of material at their laboratory benches (microscope, lamp, lens paper, paper towels, plane slide, *new plastic* cover slip, sharpened pencil, dropper bottle full of water, and labeled dishes of specimen sections).

4. The teacher will demonstrate using the same materials available to the students.

5. The demonstration will be performed on the lighted stage of the overhead projector.

6. The demonstration will include a modeling of both correct and incorrect performance.

Decision 1 is clearly designed to "load the dice" in favor of students achieving success on their first attempts, as is the specification for *new* (not scratched) *plastic* cover slips. The time to complicate matters with delicate specimens and fragile glass cover slips is *after* the basic technique has been learned. Decision 2 is aimed at attention getting/keeping and at integrating this manipulative skill with the cognitive objectives of the present topic. The implementation of decisions 3 and 4 ought to help students find close correspondence between the teacher's showing and their own attempts to do the same thing in the same way. Obviously each student must see details of the demonstration. In this case, no giant-sized versions of student laboratory materials are available. Thus, a shadow projection making use of the overhead projector was selected as the best alternative. Ms. Jetty might also consider asking the students in the rear rows to stand at each side of the overhead as she demonstrates how and how not to manipulate. What should this teacher do if she accidentally gets an air bubble or two when trying to show the correct technique? Students respect honesty. Ms. Jetty might say: "Anyone can make a mistake with this technique regardless of how many times it has been practiced. Thus, don't be discouraged if you get air bubbles on your first few attempts. Simply start over again, as I am doing now, and try to lower the cover slip more steadily and slowly next time. We'll all become more skilled by the end of today's lesson; perfection may take some of us a bit longer." A little empathy coupled with assurance of realistic expectation levels is always in order.

With the above decisions in mind and your knowledge about the conditions for learning motor chains (check Section 6.3 as needed), you are ready to draft a lesson plan based on Ms. Jetty's objective on slide preparation. Remember to analyze the task into each sequential step required, figure out how to make best use of students' previous experiences, and plan the execution of the demonstration so that it clarifies the verbal instructions. When you have completed your rough draft, compare your instructional strategies with the pattern outline that follows.

Instructional Strategy Pattern for Psychomotor Skills

Demonstrate (show how) one step at a time; have students perform each step immediately after the teacher shows each; watch students perform each step and get and give feedback; then show several steps put together; have students do several steps put together; have students practice to get closer approximations of correct performance; then have them practice to increase speed.

How did your draft compare? Did you include steps such as cleaning and drying the slide, getting the specimen flat, positioning it in the center of the slide, and adding the correct amount of water as well as lowering the cover slip slowly and steadily with the point of a pencil? Did you incorporate strategies for getting and giving feedback as the students tried each step? Some of our student teachers, who became convinced that feedback provisions can make or break a lesson of this type, found ways to use audiotape presentations to free them to more completely observe student progress. An experienced teacher made a home videotape of the complete demonstration which he was able to show while he gave directions and toured systematically. Segments of the videotape were repeated whenever he observed a common error. What did you use as a tieback to previous lessons and how did you elect to present a rationale for learning this skill? You should now understand the need for yet *another* kind of material to add to your resource file.

Planning for Attitudes

Reread the definitions of levels I and II of the affective domain and take a second look at the two sample plans in this chapter. If all the planner was after were level I objectives (compliance), the careful instructions before small group work and the tours during supervised practice should help to promote this level of affective objective. In addition, both plans indicate places where students may volunteer, perhaps to answer a question or to assist with a demonstration. However, these are only first steps toward level II objectives. Both level II and level III affective objectives require attention over time and might not show up in isolated plans. However, over a period of several days, the teacher can include strategies likely to promote positive attitudes towards science. For example, after the lesson on flower, fruit, and vegetable, the teacher might suggest that interested students use their library time to find some further information on the composition and nutritional value of a specific fruit or vegetable. The teacher might show one or two sources that could be borrowed at the end of class, like Salunkhe's (1974) *Storage, Processing, and Quality of Fruits and Vegetables*. Students could share with the class both the information and a sample of the fruit or vegetable. Other students might enjoy the challenge of planning and growing a "class garden."

In any case, it is important that the teacher follow up the suggestions, behave as if some Ss will have chosen to find out more or to try the gardening project, provide a way for them to share their work with the class, and demonstrate the teacher's own enthusiasm for their work. At the same time, if this is to be a real choice, the teacher must not demonstrate negative attitudes toward those who did not choose to go further. Notice how these teacher behaviors and plans match the instructional strategy pattern given next.

Instructional Strategy Pattern for Attitudes

Provide opportunities for voluntary extension activities; facilitate by making initial activities relatively easy to choose; follow up soon after choice was offered and provide opportunity for Ss to share efforts with class; demonstrate enthusiasm for effort; and incorporate results into later lessons.

One of the misconceptions of beginning teachers is the assumption that their enthusiasm for science is sufficient to generate enthusiasm for science among students. Here is another case of a necessary but not sufficient condition. The teacher must, as you can see from the strategy pattern and the illustrations given here, plan strategies at regular intervals throughout the unit to foster positive attitudes toward science. That means considerable homework on the part of the teacher to collect interesting, but not impossible, challenge problems, to propose individual or cooperative group projects, to identify library sources at the appropriate reading and interest levels, to prepare bulletin boards that pose questions, and so on. It's clear that this is another reason for storing a rich supply of ideas in your resource files.

7.3 PUTTING IT ALL TOGETHER

Just as single plans often contain a mix of concepts and rules, so psychomotor skills are frequently taught in conjunction with some rule. In other words, two or more of the instructional strategy patterns outlined earlier will typically be needed in a single lesson. The teacher must analyze the content to be taught and choose strategy patterns to match each content category. Our students have found it helpful to have all the basic strategy patterns in one place, so we have combined all into one table (Table 7.1) for easy reference.

Events of Instruction Revisited

In Chapter 2 we introduced you to the Events of Instruction in order to explore the feedback relationships implied in that sequence of occurrences. However, this same set of events should be considered a capsule treatment of daily, unit, and course plans. As you study the seven steps listed below, look for connections to planning strategies at *all* levels.

The Events of Instruction

1. Gaining and controlling attention.
2. Informing the student of expected outcomes.
3. Stimulating recall of prerequisites.
4. Presenting the new material.
5. Guiding the new learning.
6. Providing feedback.
7. Appraising performance.

Do events 2 and 3 sound familiar? They have been illustrated in each sample lesson plan and the strategy patterns for each kind of learning. Unit plans and course plans should also be designed in terms of the Events of Instruction. For example, initial lessons and initial units should be high in interest—"gaining and controlling attention"—and subsequent lessons and units dependent on earlier prerequisites can be planned to take less time—"stimulating recall of prerequisites." It should now be clear that the time spanned by each event varies widely. In a daily plan, "informing the student of expected outcomes" may be effectively done in less than two minutes, whereas "presenting the new material" might span 10 to 15 minutes, with part of that time taken up by "guiding the new learning." In the actual implementation of a plan, the events will usually flow smoothly into one another *IF the teacher is able to get the process started.* Gaining and controlling attention, thus, becomes an event of more than passing importance.

Gaining and controlling attention   Some authors refer to this event as motivating the students or "turning them on" to instruction. Whatever it's called, its presence is essential to meaningful learning. Experience convinces us that the teacher must *get attention on the lesson* within the first few minutes of the period—the sooner the better. We're not referring to commands to "Pay attention." The *repeated* occurrence of these are cues that the teacher has failed to get attention *on the lesson.* One of the easiest ways to "turn off kids" is to begin every class in the same way, to conduct routine homework postmortems without concern for feedback, to announce the topic in "big-word chemistry" prior to any concrete experiences.

Table 7.1
Instructional Strategy Patterns for Science Content

Kinds of content outcomes	Examples	Instructional strategy patterns
Vocabulary	Labels of cell, nucleus, solid, solution	T shows object (or exemplifies idea); then pronounces name and spells on board; students do like-wise, repeat (practice), give name; T elicits statement of idea or description of object; T has Ss use in context.
Concepts	Cell, nucleus, solid, solution, element, force, insect, greater than, yields	T shows differentiated examples and non-examples in sequence; gets essential and nonessential characteristics identified; elicits generalization of the concepts to a variety of specific instances not previously used.
Rules/principles	LeChatelier's principle, Mendel's laws, Newton's laws, Ohm's law	T gets Ss to recall/review prerequisites; indicates nature of expected terminal performance; cues (via questions, lab work, applications) Ss to find the pattern by chaining concepts; gets rule stated (by Ss if possible); has Ss demonstrate several instances of the rule in a variety of situations. *Fixes and maintains skills by spaced and varied drill.
Novel problem solving	Energy crises, genetic engineering, overpopulation, pollution	T presents problem; may Q/A Ss to elicit alternative approaches to solution; T emphasizes desirability of a variety of search strategies; individual work or small group discussions (data collecting, data analysis, making and testing conjectures); T asks Ss to weigh advantages and disadvantages of proposals (and processes) which arose from group discussions and/or individual work.
Psychomotor learning (manipulative skills)	Use of microscope, burette, various balances, dissection instruments, soldering tools	T demonstrates (shows how) one step at a time; has Ss do each step immediately after T shows each; T watches Ss perform each step and gets and gives feedback; then T shows several steps put together; has Ss do several steps put together, practice to get closer approximations of correct performance, then practice to increase speed.
Attitude learning	Challenge ex., historical research, search for relevant cartoons	T provides opportunities for voluntary extension activities; facilitates by making initial activities relatively easy to choose; followup soon after choice was offered and provide opportunity for Ss to share efforts with class; demonstrate enthusiasm for effort; and incorporate results into later lessons.

What does get attention? We've provided you with several examples thus far—the most recent being in the two sample lesson plans that began with recently completed demonstrations of laboratory exercises using everyday objects of interest to students. Notice that each illustration was highly interwoven with the subsequent strategies and so immediately highlighted the lesson, while having potential for sustaining attention beyond the first few minutes of the class. These are the two necessary characteristics of the opening gambit: (1) to get attention focused *on the lesson* and (2) to keep attention focused on the *lesson*. Can you see why the opening joke by the comedian teacher is likely to get attention, but *not on the lesson*? Teachers who use this ploy often create a monster they can only handle with authoritarian reprimands—not a very promising start to a class, is it? However, sometimes even apparently content-related material does not get attention on the lesson. For example, a junior-high teacher decided to teach molecular models by having the students connect gumdrops with toothpicks. To his dismay, most student interest was focused on consumption of the gumdrops. Thus, the "on the lesson" aspect is critical, both as a preventive of undesired student behavior and, more important, as an initiator of learning. Once attention has been focused on the content, keeping attention should follow automatically. Right? It should, but it often doesn't! If the class begins with the presentation of a relevant problem dealing with teenage drug addiction, the teacher is likely to get attention on the science needed to solve the problem. However, if the problem is dropped and the scientific principles are presented with no cross-references to the initial problem posed, the potential for keeping attention decreases rapidly.

What kinds of things do usually elicit student attention? The following categories have proved consistently useful:

1. An unfamiliar, puzzling or unusual event or idea.

2. A familiar object (circumstance) behaving in an unfamiliar way.

3. Materials or activities with high sensory appeal (the use of color, sound, or touch, for example, or a combination of these).

4. The use of materials or circumstances matched to the students' "here-and-now" interests.

5. The use of materials or circumstances corresponding to applications in other school subjects or in the nonschool world, where these applications have potential for students' "here-and-now" interests.

In the preceding chapters, as well as in earlier sections of this one, each of these has been illustrated. The use of balloons in a bell jar to construct a working model of the lungs is another example of a familiar object being used in an unfamiliar way and a material with sensory appeal. The fifth category is a corollary to the fourth one. However, the fifth category must be applied with discretion. For example, if none of the students take industrial arts, there's not much interest potential in an introductory problem based on that subject.

What *are* some major "here-and-now" interests of students? The following list contains a sample of interests obtained from the only reliable source, junior/senior high students themselves.

Students' here-and-now interests

Acceptance by peers	Computer games	Music	Ten-speed bikes
Acne	College admissions	Pets	Telephoning
Alcohol	Hobbies	Sex (opposite)	Tobacco
Automobiles	Money	Sports	Video games and
Body (*theirs*)	Movies		shows

Your own students will help you add to this list if you listen. Where can you find source materials related to these areas of interest? Check the local and school newspapers, *Popular Mechanics*, professional journals, and source books, plus all the many other resources identified in Chapters 9, 10, 11.

One final piece of advice before we leave the topic of daily lesson plans. Write post-mortem comments on each *immediately* after implementing them in an actual classroom situation. Revise time estimates, make notes on what worked particularly well, and earmark any section in need of repair while the experience is fresh in your mind. Our student teachers who have followed this practice report that it pays big dividends when they teach the same lessons to other classes of students. They have advised us to urge you to form this habit. Consider yourself urged.

7.4 LONG-RANGE PLANNING

As we have already seen, day-to-day planning is vital to success. But isn't long-range planning also a very important part of the teacher's task? It most certainly is if the daily lessons are to fit together into a meaningful whole. In fact, logic would seem to dictate blocking out plans for the entire year-long course first, next developing the more specific treatments to be given each of the major sequential subcomponents to fit within that overall frame of reference, and then finally working out the details of each daily lesson. Yet we are directing your attention to these levels of planning in the reverse sequence. Why? Our experience has been that novice teachers find long-range planning both a hopeless and meaningless task until they have first acquired some experience in designing and implementing daily lessons—another example of how learning most often follows psychological rather than logical principles.

Unit Planning

After a couple of weeks of experience with planning and implementing daily lessons, you should be ready to try your hand at the next step—blocking out plans for the next unit. By a *unit* we mean a *major topic that will occupy approximately two to four weeks of instructional time*. One full-year course is typically composed of a sequence of eight to twelve such units.

Recall the Resource File modular assignment we asked you to begin in Chapter 4. At that time we directed you to select one unit as a point of departure for building a file of teaching ideas that would serve as a base for future plans. Obviously, you need to fill other folders (as directed in that assignment) prior to starting plans for additional units because these materials will constitute the idea base for future instructional strategies. Also recall the Learning Hierarchy and the Concept Mapping assignments given in Chapter 6. These assignments provided experience in both (1) identifying major objectives expected of all students, or concepts to be learned by all and (2) analyzing the interdependent relationships among parts of a major topic. Since there is not time to teach all possible aspects of a unit topic, selectivity is essential. In addition, prerequisite concepts must be introduced prior to the point at which related principles/rules and their applications are taught.

Concept maps   If a novice teacher has already prepared either a learning hierarchy or a concept map for a unit, then much of the task of getting acquainted with the scope and emphasis of the unit has been done. Study Figure 7.6, a typical concept map prepared by a beginning student teacher for a unit on atomic structure. It is clear that considerable thinking went into the arrangement and relationships pictured on this concept map. The student teacher found it a particularly valuable way to analyze the unit before beginning to teach. The concept map also served as a point of departure for planning sessions between student teacher and cooperating teacher. Now individual plans and the sequence of strategies within plans could be considered in the light of the concepts associated on the map.

We believe that concept maps are a valuable way to approach the planning of a unit, especially when a teacher is beginning a unit never taught before. However, until schools and school schedules are redesigned, it would be unrealistic to expect a full-time teacher to design concept maps and learning hierarchies for every unit. Some experienced teachers, after working with student teachers who have completed concept maps, have designed their own for units they have found particularly troublesome to teach. In our opinion, this is an excellent way to reflect on both your experience and the structure of the subject matter.

Unit outlines   If you have not completed either a concept map or a learning hierarchy, then you must begin by doing curriculum research on the unit. Review the course syllabus, if one is available, and relevant sections of contemporary books used as student texts. We do suggest that you go beyond the particular text used in your school. Other texts are typically available at the school where you are teaching, in the curriculum library of the university, or in the offices of the state department of science instruction. Then you will have the same background as the designer of either a concept map or a learning hierarchy.

Next, you will need to prepare a *topic* outline, in which you build in a potential sequencing scheme. You consider the first such outline as a draft that

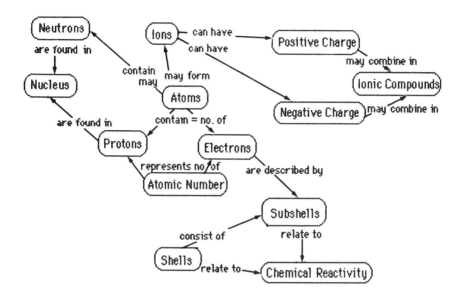

Fig. 7.6   A concept map on atomic structure.

should be modified as you rethink ideas and begin to consider relative emphasis of subtopics and ways to relate particular topics to one another. Word processing packages are particularly handy in this kind of endeavor.

The second stage in moving from a topic outline to a unit plan involves allocating the available time and listing some initial planning ideas. You will need to block out projected time allotments for parts of the outline. Next, you should begin to list (by descriptive title) potentially useful labs, demos, films, field trips, homework assignments, bulletin board ideas, and the like from your resource file. If the "cupboard is bare" for some topics, you will have to dig into the sources suggested in Chapters 9, 10 and 11 to fill these voids. Otherwise, the unit plan will *not* serve its intended purpose of providing an adequate base for more detailed day-to-day planning. Projecting time estimates is always a problem for the novice, and there is no use in pretending that there is any substitute for the experience of having taught the unit several times to varying groups of students. However, the problem must be faced squarely by every novice, and we can make suggestions that will alleviate the task to some extent. Attempt to identify topics that are either extensions or modifications of ideas previously presented. These, along with content ideas familiar to students as a result of extensive experience outside of school, can be assigned shorter instructional time than totally new work. Longer time periods should be planned for new ideas that will provide a base for more sophisticated notions to occur in future units.

Arrange the unit plan in three columns as shown in the partially completed sample of a unit plan on Sound for Ninth-Grade Physical Science (Figure 7.7). Column 1 lists topics in the sequence determined by the teacher while column 2 contains the estimated number of instructional periods to be devoted to each topic. Column 3 contains the gold-mine entries, selected instructional resources from the teacher's resource file described in a phrase as well as by a coded entry. The phrase provides immediate information for the reader and the coded entry (for example, A-BB #1 for the first [Ath] folder of the unit, the first bulletin board item) shortens the retrieval time as the teacher moves from the unit plan to daily plans. (Computer-wise teachers will recognize the importance of filing as many of your resource ideas as possible on computer disks.) You should provide your cooperating teacher with copies of (1) the unit plan and (2) all the related resources identified in the learning activities column. Schedule a conference after your cooperating teacher has had time to review these materials but far enough in advance of the time when you must begin developing the first few daily plans of the unit. At least several days of lead time are desirable. Heed the advice given and ask questions to help in thinking through various possible approaches. Examine further learning activities that may be suggested, talk out potential problems that may arise, and discuss details that might be added or deleted, in case time requirements deviate from those projected. Having done all this, you are bound to feel much more confident in developing detailed day-to-day plans, and smooth transitions within the unit will be more easily achieved. As in the case of daily lesson plans, notes to yourself written on the unit plan as implementation proceeds will prove valuable in future years.

We advocate treating the final topic outline as a guide and source of stimulation for your own thinking rather than as a requirement to be followed blindly. Experience convinces us that the final outline must make maximum sense to you, the teacher, if it is to serve as a frame of reference for daily lessons which will make sense to your students.

Course Planning

Speaking of years, 365 days does seem like a lot of time. But is it, in terms of how many full periods of 40 to 50 minutes are actually available for instruction? State regulations, school calendars, and administrators frequently refer to a 180± day school year. (This figure takes into account weekends, various holidays, and summer vacation periods when school is not in session.) Does this mean one should plan a course based on the assumption of 180 full periods available for instruction in new content? Not quite. Further time reductions must be planned to account for the realities such as the half-days of school before major holidays, standardized tests that all of your eighth graders must take during your science class, public address announcements that interrupt your class, assembly programs during class time, and mass illnesses during the winter flu season. Your own

Unit 2: SOUND
NINTH-GRADE PHYSICAL SCIENCE

Topics	Time estimates in periods	Learning activities
A. Kinds in daily life		Bulletin bd.—photos of sound
1. Musical	7/8	products (A-BB #1)
		Demo—stereo tape (A-D #6)
2. Noise	1/8	Demo—saw and wood, hammer and nail
		(A-D #7)
		HW—clipping "World of the Deaf" (A-C #3)
B. Sources		
1. Vibrations	1/4	Lab—vibrating speaker, cones, string
2. Energy	3/4	(B-L #2)
		Demo—pith ball and tuning fork
		(B-D #7)
		Demo—tuning fork & water
		(B-D #10)
C. Media		
1. Air	1/8	Whispering demo (C-D #12)
2. Solids	1/8	Lab—sound through wood and metal
a) Wood		(C-L #6)
b) Metal		
3. Water	1/8	Illustrations of sounds under water (C-C #3)
4. Vacuum	1/8	Bell in evacuated bell jar demo (C-D #3)
D. Characteristics		
1. Loudness	1	Lab—making sounds louder (D-L #3)
2. Speed	3/4	"Speed of Sound" (D-F #1)
3. Pitch	1	Demo—toothed wheel on variable
4. Quality	1/2	speed motor (D-D #15)
		Filmstrip (frames 17–23 only)
		"Science of Music" (D-F #3)
E. Thought model		
1. Waves	1	—
2. Wavelength	1/4	—
3. —	—	—
4. —	—	—
5. —	—	—
F. Applications	—	—
1. —	—	—
2. —	—	—
3. —	—	—

Fig. 7.7 Part of a unit plan.

schedule of tests/quizzes and related activities will also deduct from time available for instruction in new content. It is reasonable to assume that 8 to 10 full-period tests and 25 to 35 quizzes (10 to 20 minutes each) will be given during the year. These are essential uses of instructional time, but is it really defensible to add fuel to this fire by routinely coupling a full-period review and a half-period post-mortem to each of the big tests? Review the recommendations in Chapter 2 and 8 aimed at minimizing these problems.

So much for the myth of the 180 day school year! We have found 140 periods a much more realistic target when planning a year-long course. Eight units would thus *average* about 17 full class periods each. Obviously some could take longer, but you would then have to compensate with less time for others in the long-range plans.

Course planning schema   Is a course plan, then, merely a list of unit plans designed to fit within a 140 day school year? There are basic flaws in that approach even when each individual unit has been thoughtfully designed. Yes, sequencing may be out of whack, interconnections may be ignored, and mindless redundancy may take the place of meaningful spiraling. There's only one way to avoid these disasters and that way begins with a thorough study of all available course materials. We recommend that you select an overarching unifying theme or conceptual schema. Such a theme ought to (1) reflect a contemporary view of the particular discipline of science being taught, (2) subsume all the unit topics, (3) clarify the interrelationships among major ideas to be developed within and across unit topics, and (4) be rich in potential relevance for the prospective student population. The selection and use of a unifying theme will assist you with the development of a meaningful sequence of units, help establish reasoned priorities for treatment of subtopics, and greatly facilitate the development of advance organizers.

One student teacher's attempt to develop such a frame of reference for a tenth-grade biology course is shown in Figure 7.8. The schema, or thought model, was designed to depict her own synthesis of the course as she envisioned it. "All living things are interdependent on each other and on the non-living environment" was selected as the unifying theme and advance organizer for the entire course. Eight content topics represented by pie-shaped sectors were subsumed by this overarching theme. They are identified here by titles such as "Genetics" and "Evolution." Each of these titles was, in turn, stated as a subordinate unifying theme on an appended page in the form of one or two sentences each. Note the dotted lines used as borders between the designated units. This indicates the intent to plan instruction taught in a sequence starting with **Unity and Diversity** (note the arrow) and ending with **Ecology**. Concentric circular regions overlaying all units were used to indicate stress on science process aspects throughout the course topics. The sequential arrangements with **Observing** as the largest and **Theorizing/Model Building** as the smallest, most central process tell us something else about how this student teacher viewed science and science instruction!

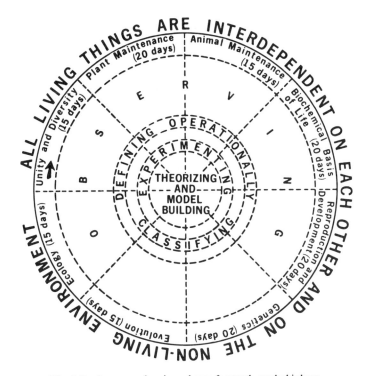

Fig. 7.8   A course planning schema for tenth-grade biology.

Now turn to the time allotments for each unit. Why were some planned for 15 days while others were given as much as 20 days? Was this strictly a function of relative importance to the overall unifying theme for the whole course? No, the thinking behind the model went further and also gave consideration to prerequisites that would be established by earlier units in the planned sequence. Fundamental concepts of **Maintenance** learned with regard to plants would be *built upon* during **Animal Maintenance**—a decision which should increase instructional efficiency. On the other hand, the absence of prerequisites from earlier courses and/or life experience seemed to dictate a longer time allotment for **Biochemical Basis of Life** than its importance to the overall course theme alone would justify. Are you still a bit puzzled about why **Ecology**, obviously so central to the main theme, was given only 15 instead of 30 or perhaps 25 days? Think of it this way. All possible course material in all seven preceding units would have been consistently related to the overarching **Ecology** theme. Therefore this final unit would consist largely of tying together and finding further interrelationships rather than being heavily ladened with concepts totally novel to the learners. All time allotments were arrived at by this kind of balancing of sequence, prerequisites, extent of novelty, and nature of objectives. There is nothing sacrosanct about these figures. They represent the best thinking of this teacher. As always, feedback during instruction may result in some differences between the actual and estimated times. Such information should be recorded and appropriate modifications made for future years. But any change must continue to reflect the conceptual framework designed by the teacher.

Now reflect on your own reactions to this particular overall course-planning guide. Does it provide a frame of reference for planning the sequence of the units it subsumes? Does it represent an accurate view of contemporary biology and yet have high potential relevance for tenth-grade students? Are interrelationships among ideas within and across units clarified? We answered yes to all these questions after studying the fully completed schema and the list of unit theme statements that was appended. Further, we judged it to have excellent potential for its intended purpose. Does this mean that this specific schema is *the correct one* to use for a tenth-grade biology course? No, we would make no such claim—only that it ought to be a highly usable one for the person who created the schema and could implement it effectively. Personally, we would use the same main unifying theme but subdivide the units somewhat differently and use a variation of the proposed sequence. These changes wouldn't necessarily make our schema superior for *your* use, though it should for *our* use.

7.5 SUMMARY AND SELF-CHECK

In this synthesis of all the previous chapters, we presented strategy patterns for vocabulary, concept, rule/principle, novel problem-solving, psychomotor and attitude planning. Sample daily plans were analyzed both in terms of the related strategy patterns and the earlier work on objectives, modes, feedback, adolescent reasoning, research on human learning, and the structure of science. In addition, the unique characteristics and problems of lessons involving type word problems were outlined. Then, the sequence of the *events of instruction* were reconsidered with particular emphasis on getting and keeping attention. Finally, we turned from daily planning to guidelines for constructing unit and course plans.

Now you should be able to:

1. Operationally define instructional strategy.

2. Describe in sequence, the major steps in the strategy patterns for vocabulary, concept, rule/principle, novel problem solving, psychomotor and attitude instruction.

3. Distinguish between the strategies essential for teaching type word problem solving and those essential for the teaching of novel problem solving and identify the bases for the differences.

4. Describe the use of 3–4 heuristics that might be useful in a novel problem solving lesson.

5. Construct or modify science problems so that they will be suitable for a junior/senior high science lesson aimed at novel problem solving.

6. Write a daily plan for a lesson in your major teaching field that corresponds in format to the plan outline, and in structure to the strategy patterns appropriate to the content, as well as to all components of the instructional model treated in the first six chapters.

7. Critique both a unit plan and a course plan for correspondence to the characteristics of sequence, time estimates, and use of resources.

8. Write a unit plan and a course plan that correspond to the sample outlines in this chapter *if you have taught*, and justify the choices of topic, sequence, and timing made.

9. Critique the opening five minutes in a "live" or video lesson for its attention-getting and -keeping potential.

10. Design an "attention getter" for any given lesson and outline its projected use throughout the lesson.

11. Identify the process skills used during a novel problem-solving lesson.

The next section contains exercises related to some of these objectives and simultaneously provides additional samples of instructional activities.

7.6 SIMULATION/PRACTICE ACTIVITIES

A. The Introductory Activity of this chapter included a partially inadequate response to a quiz question. You were asked to critique that response. Now compare your judgments against Tony's more adequate response to the same question. Tony's two objectives were just rephrasings of those written by Mary, but here is his sequence of modes:

Tony's response to the sequence of modes portion of the question

1. Do a demo of the ruler lab with the assistance of two Ss.

2. Divide Ss into groups and have them perform the lab.

3. Have small groups record data on board.

4. Have Ss in small groups discuss optimum way(s) to display total class data.

5. Ask group leaders to report on consensus and use Q/A and lecture to reach a decision.

6. Have each S graph data.

After identifying the favorable characteristics of Tony's response, reread the objectives and compare his response with the objectives. What else would you add in order to match the instruction to the objectives?

B. Construct a lesson plan designed to introduce junior high or senior high science students to one or more concept(s) and/or rule(s). Be sure to check your choice of topic with your instructor.

C. Provide a pair of students with a novel problem to solve and direct them to think aloud as they attempt to solve the problem. Identify any heuristics that the students use as well as science process skills.

D. Consult professional journals for problem solving articles that focus on the use of novel problems and/or provide insights into ways to have students generate problems based on their interests. Two examples to get you started are:

Good, R., & Smith, M. (1987). "How do we make students better problem solvers?" *The Science Teacher*, **54** (4), 31–36.

and

Pizzini, E. L., Abell, S. K., & Shephardson, D. S. (1988). "Rethinking thinking in the science classroom." *The Science Teacher*, **55** (9), 22–25.

E. Locate four articles in recent issues of *The Science Teacher* or *School Science and Mathematics* in which the authors suggest approaches to instruction on some secondary school concept or rule. Write reviews of all four articles. Be sure to give attention to the extent to which the suggested approaches seem to match the instructional strategy patterns in this chapter, correspond to the probable reasoning levels of the students, and emphasize the structure of the science model.

F. Design a problem suitable for initiating a novel problem-solving lesson based on the information below:

In Raleigh, N.C., rats have been found able to survive 2 1/2 to 6 times the normal killing dose of a commonly used rat poison. Apparently a genetic trait is involved. In Scotland about half the farms have rats, and 40 percent of them are resistant to this same poison. (*The New York Times*, October 17, 1971.)

G. Outline way(s) in which each set of objects in column 2 might be used to *get* attention on the corresponding topic in column 1.

Column 1	*Column 2*
(A) Friction	(a) Sneakers, skis, hiking boots, roller skates, auto tires
(B) Sound	(b) Hydrometer jars, water, band instruments, rubber bands, cigar box, popular tape or compact disc
(C) Heat	(c) Thermal underwear, plastic ice chest
(D) Digestion	(d) Audio tapes of radio/TV commercials for antacids and samples of each advertised product

SUGGESTIONS FOR FURTHER STUDY

Biological Sciences Curriculum Study. (1963). *Research problems in biology*. New York: Doubleday.

This series of four paperback books was produced under the Gifted Students Committee of the BSCS. The topics represent the total spectrum of biological inquiry and include such titles as *Breaking Dormancy in Seeds*, *Communication by Trail-Laying in Ants*, and *Experiments in Tissue Culture*. Each of the over 100 topics begins with a concise statement regarding existing knowledge written by a scientist working in that special area. General approaches and suggested problems are raised, but no cookbook directions are given. Rather the student is left to design and carry out inquiries at the cutting edge of science, for these are novel problems of contemporary science. No elaborate equipment is needed, and a brief bibliography of further reading is included for each topic.

Bybee, R., Peterson, R., Bowyer, J., & Butts, D. (1984). *Teaching about science and society: Activities for elementary and junior high school*. Columbus, OH: Merrill.

This series of lesson plans provides science teachers with activities in physical science, earth/environmental sciences, and environmental biology. In addition to science products and processes, societal implications are provided for each activity (more on this in chapter 9).

Gabel, D. L. (Ed.). (1989). *What research says to the science teacher* (Vol. 5). Washington, DC: National Science Teachers Association.

Seven researchers treat the subject of problem solving at different grade levels and in the various science disciplines. In addition to relating how students typically solve problems, the various writers provide practical suggestions for the teaching of problem solving in science.

Lunetta, V. N., & Novick, S. (1982). *Inquiring and problem solving in the physical sciences: A sourcebook*. Dubuque, IO: Kendall/Hunt.

With this series of activities in the physical sciences, the authors have attempted to tie scientific phenomena to everyday experiences in students' lives. The inclusion of numerous references related to the activities is an added bonus.

CHAPTER EIGHT

EVALUATION
OF INSTRUCTION
The Proof of the Pudding

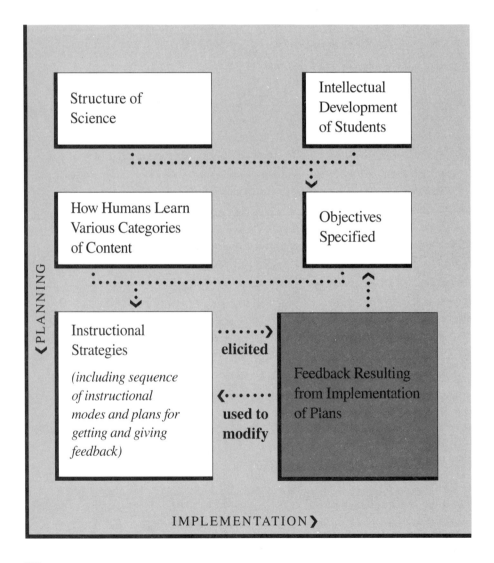

Yes, we are again back to the feedback box portion of the instructional model! Our previous treatment of this aspect in Chapter 2 focused on the minute-to-minute and day-to-day concerns of instruction. The emphasis was on getting data on which to base immediate decisions such as whether to speed up, slow down, stop, provide more or varying examples, or present a concept in a different way. Similarly, we explored ways and means of providing learners with information on their progress toward attainment of the objectives set for today's lesson, last night's assignment, or yesterday's laboratory exercise. Much dependence was placed on quick and informal means to these ends—spreading oral responses among a wide sampling of students, taking straw votes (followed by verbal expression of the "hows" and "whys"), observing student written work in progress, and giving verbal praise for correct answers and productive approaches to problems. All of this background is prerequisite to the longer-range view and the more formal means of assessment to which we now turn our attention.

Note the two feedback loops depicted on the schematic. One leads to and from the key component "Instructional Strategies," which is the summation of the planning dimension of the instructional model. If indeed "The proof of the pudding is in the eating," then crucial decisions as to what worked and why, and what didn't work and why must be made intelligently on the basis of evaluation of results. Then and only then are we in a position to redesign instructional inputs with realistic hopes of improved success. Similarly, the other feedback loop to the "Objectives Specified" component points to the need for a firm data base upon which to judge the degree to which important objectives have been realized. Initial objectives may need to be revised in the light of this experience.

Haven't all of you been evaluated throughout your lives both within the school setting and in the broader context of all life's activities? After all, you have spent a good bit of time on the receiving end during some 16 years of formal schooling. Shouldn't this experience equip you to deal with the topic on the sending end of the process? Without a doubt, you do bring some background to the task. Student teachers with whom we've worked can quickly reel off a list of ineffective techniques and practices. However, they are frequently at a loss when asked to provide the remedy: examples of good models.

Moreover, there is no sense trying to wish the problems away. Within a week to ten days of student teaching, the novice teacher typically constructs, administers, and scores one or two short quizzes. By the end of three or four weeks of student teaching, a full-period test will have to be prepared, duplicated, administered, and scored. These tasks are formidable enough, but soon come even tougher jobs—interpreting results and making a host of decisions regarding future instruction, mid-marking period warning reports, remedial instruction, and marking-period grades. All of these have to be defensible in the eyes of students, parents, school administrators, and, most important, yourself! You will hear claims that the test wasn't "objective." A parent who is an ex-teacher may question its "validity." These and other bits of jargon are abused in both everyday speech and dictionary definitions. Yet there is no hope of communicating feed-back to students, parents, or administrators without some clear understanding of the language associated with the topic of evaluation. The next section provides you with the background for the understanding of several relevant terms. It is up to you to communicate that understanding to those who receive the results of evaluation.

8.1 EVALUATION VERSUS TESTING

Evaluation and *testing* are often used synonymously but, in fact, they refer to closely related but distinct processes. The root word *value* is clearly central to the concept of evaluation. Thus, by *evaluation* we mean *any process of making judgments against selected criteria as to the worth of things or ideas, based on relevant data.* Relevant data? That's where the notion of testing comes in. *Testing* will be used to label *any procedure designed to collect evidence that indicates degree of attainment of objectives.* Note that we do not limit testing to paper-and-pencil in-struments and that the results of testing are not viewed as evaluations but rather as data upon which judgments (evaluations) will be based. For example, Jill's record shows percentage scores of 85, 99, 80, 76, and 92 on a set of written tests/quizzes over a ten-week period, but the 85 refers to a pretest given prior to instruction on the unit. As a result of that score, Jill was placed in the group of students who were to work on individualized learning activity packages. All of the remaining scores were attained on quizzes or tests administered after certain periods of instruction. How should her teacher evaluate these data for purposes of deciding her report card grade? If your response is, "I can't tell because you still haven't told me all of the criteria against which to judge these data," you are catching a good part of the idea.

Jill's first test was given for purposes of *diagnostic evaluation. Diagnostic evaluation* is *characterized by one of two purposes: (1) to place a student at the proper instructional starting point or (2) to find out the causes of instructional de-fects that have been isolated during instruction.* So Jill's score on the pretest would not properly be included in the data her teacher is evaluating for purposes of re-porting a grade. Jill's teacher had administered the second type of diagnostic quiz to a group in the class who had been making repeated errors on three of the rules in the unit. By including diverse examples at varied levels of rule application, the teacher had tried to pinpoint the *causes* of the errors. Should these scores be included in the report card evaluation? Absolutely not! However, each of Jill's other scores will be included in some fashion (more on that in the next section!) in the final evaluation. Thus, all of these test scores will serve the purpose of *summative evaluation, the use of data to make judgments as to the extent to which instructional objectives have been achieved by the students.* All final course exams fall in the category of testing solely for the purpose of summative evaluation. Re-gardless of error patterns now identified by the teacher, instruction is over and these data cannot be used to affect the instruction of that group of students (see

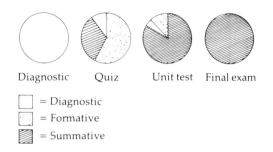

Diagnostic   Quiz   Unit test   Final exam

☐ = Diagnostic
☐ = Formative
▨ = Summative

Fig. 8.1   Relative emphasis on the three kinds of evaluation in various types of tests.

Figure 8.1). Such data can and should be used to plan instruction for future students in this course. A third kind of evaluation, *formative evaluation*, is regularly used in systematic instruction. The chief purpose of *formative evaluation* is *to assess the extent to which progress is being made on the instructional objectives and to identify those objectives that need further instructional attention.* Note that data from a short quiz serves two purposes: summative and formative evaluation. So does data from a unit test, but the emphasis from such data is now primarily on summative evaluation. The circle graphs in Figure 8.1 depict this changed evaluative emphasis as one moves from quiz to unit test to final exam. (The sectors in these graphs should not be interpreted as exact matches to the evaluation emphasis in any particular test/quiz. They should be thought of as representing a ball-park figure.) Notice the small sectors designated as diagnostic evaluation in both the quiz and unit test circle graphs. Although these kinds of tests are not *constructed* so as to discover causes of known errors, data from them sometimes yield this kind of information. You will be making judgments based on data gathered for all three types of evaluation. Knowing the what, when, and why of the process is a paramount aspect of those judgments.

Objective vs. subjective and reliable vs. valid   Another commonly expressed concern is to what extent the data gathered on the written tests were objective as opposed to subjective. *Objective* literally means that *no judgment entered into the process.* We take the position that no quiz or test could possibly meet this definition! Why? Didn't someone have to *decide* (judge) such matters as (1) which questions to include, (2) how to phrase the questions, (3) the answer or range of acceptable responses, (4) the credit value of each item, and (5) the time limit for responding to the test? Thus we will not speak of objective tests or of objective test items. It seems more honest to refer to *objectively scored test items* as *those that would be scored identically by anyone using the same answer key.* Similarly, *subjectively scored test items are those that are constructed to allow judgment of the rater to enter into the scoring process.* A word of caution is in order at this point. Do not automatically equate "objectively scored" with "good" testing technique nor "subjectively scored" with "poor" testing technique. The nature of the subject matter at stake and the particular kinds of objectives being assessed help determine which approach makes the most sense.

But don't objectively scored items lead to increased test reliability? Generally, yes. However, let's not fall into the trap of confusing reliability with validity. *Reliability is the extent to which a test yields repeatable results* (tells a consistent story) whereas *validity is the extent to which a test measures what it is supposed to measure* (tells the truth). Assume that a manufacturer inadvertently produced a batch of metric rulers 11 cm long which were each calibrated into 100 equal segments labeled mm and 10 equal segments marked cm. Skillful students using these devices would get consistent (reliable) but incorrect (invalid) measurements! Obviously we want both valid *and* reliable tests so that the data they produce can be trusted as a base for educational decision making. Fortunately for us, it turns out that highly valid tests typically turn out to yield respectable reliability. (Warning: the reverse is *not* true!) How does one insure validity? Obtaining a close match of well-structured test items to carefully specified objectives is the best way to achieve content validity. It is with this last task in mind that we direct your attention to the Introductory Activity that follows.

8.2 INTRODUCTORY ACTIVITY

Step right up and take a chance!

Test taking shouldn't resemble a carnival game of chance but, sadly, it sometimes does. Very often, this is due to poorly constructed test items. This activity places you in the role of a critic of a set of such test items. Assume that clear directions on the recording of responses have been given but that each item in the following set is defective in some way—for example, might be incorrectly answered by capable students or might be correctly answered by poor students who guess well. For each item, identify the defect(s) and rewrite the item so as to eliminate the problem(s).

Selected items from eighth-grade physical science tests

Completion

1. The man who invented the telescope was _____ .

2. _____ light has a _____ wave length than _____ light.

Multiple choice

11. A lever with an effort arm of 8 cm and a resistance arm of 2 cm has an IMA of
    (1) 16   (2) 2   (3) 4   (4) 8

12. Substances that turn litmus red and taste sour are called
    (1) acids   (2) bases   (3) neutrals   (4) salts   (5) liquids

True-false

16. *g* is equal to 32.

17. Certain solids sometimes change directly into a gas without passing through the liquid state.

After you have completed your analysis of these items, compare your corrected versions with those produced by another student. Then check on your thinking as you interact with the material in the next section.

8.3 ASSESSMENT OF COGNITIVE OBJECTIVES

The first objectives you will encounter in assessment situations in student teaching will be those belonging to the cognitive domain. For better or worse, this kind of outcome is what schools emphasize above all others. Further, the means of assessing these are often limited almost exclusively to paper-and-pencil instruments called quizzes and tests. This doesn't need to be the case, since there are several other ways to gather evidence of achievement of this kind of objective. More importantly, this shouldn't be the case if processes of science, other than procedural knowledge, are to be emphasized. Furthermore, it shouldn't be the case if the teacher wishes to collect the kind of data in either diagnostic or formative evaluation that represents the best promise for improving instruction. If the collected data include information on students' strategies, error patterns, or the rationale for the application of a procedure, the teacher will have specific evidence on which to individualize instruction and to improve instruction for the larger group. Thus, although we devote considerable attention to paper-and-pencil tests as an ongoing and important part of assessment, we first turn our attention to the more qualitative types of assessment, represented by tasks other than paper-and-pencil tests.

Assessment Other Than by Paper-and-Pencil Tests

The need for students to understand and experience science processes and the interrelationships of these to the development of scientific products is one of the goals of science instruction found in Chapter 4 of this text. Similar goals have been emphasized recently on the national level in such reports as *Science for All Americans: Project 2061* (American Association for the Advancement of Science, 1989). Along with these goals has been a call for tests to include hands-on science experiments and computer simulations in addition to paper-and-pencil items (Murname & Raizen, 1988). The process emphasis of the above goal is one example of the kind of competency that might be assessed by tasks other than paper-and-pencil. Data for assessment of process skills might be obtained by systematic observation of groups of students working on a problem-solving task with manipulatives or by sampling audiotaped verbalizations of a laboratory activity. Data could be recorded in a simple anecdotal report for each student with such reports stored on a computer file. Anecdotal reports are just that—comments about observed student behavior—with the date and lesson type or objectives recorded. Recall the crabapple lab that was used in the sample lesson plan on flower, fruit, and vegetable in Chapter 7. Teacher observation of student work with the crabapple specimens might later lead to comments, such as the following:

> *Barry seemed to have great trouble in sequencing the crabapple specimens and kept referring to his handout of flower and fruit which he had only partially completed.*

or

> *Eileen quickly ordered the crabapple specimens correctly and proceeded to question other students in her group as to why her sequence was correct before T arrived.*

It should be obvious that these students stood out because of the quality of their behavior. The teacher cannot expect to collect sufficient data to write anecdotal records for each student in class after a single lesson. However, over time, the entire class should be sampled and data recorded. Gross judgments of student progress could be recorded in a grade book type format, by symbols such as $+\sqrt{}$ or $-\sqrt{}$. This kind of data collection can be completed more quickly than the anecdotal reports, but does not provide the teacher with specifics for later use in diagnosis and future instruction. A combination of assessment types should be considered when evaluating complex behaviors.

Oral reports of library research can be presented and assessed on a written critique sheet. It is important to let the students know, ahead of time, the criteria on which they will be assessed and to share the written critique with them after the oral reports have been completed. The criteria in this case might include evidence of thoroughness of the library study, and organization and clarity of the oral report. Similarly, written reports on take-home labs and in-class projects can be assigned and analyzed for evidence of learning. Moreover, don't the actual products produced in laboratory work and bulletin board design sessions yield relevant data? Also consider the potential use of anecdotal records made by the teacher as students participate in question/answer, small-group discussion, interactive computer sessions, supervised practice, and laboratory work.

Other types of written work provide data that are rich in potential for assessing progress toward higher-level cognitive objectives. The analysis of hurricane paths, the mathematical aspects of population growth, the science of soap bubbles, and mathematics in nature are examples of topics suitable for research papers in science. Students can also be asked to write a story using science concepts correctly, given a topic such as naming and describing the atmospheric and landscape features of a planet they have just discovered (Lchman & Yarbrough, 1983). Again the teacher must be sure neither to ignore the extent to which grammar and spelling are correct, nor to allow these two components to overshadow the correct use of scientific relationships. Illustrative examples of other non-paper-and-pencil tasks were provided in Chapter 1. For further help on ways of deriving assessment data from such tasks, see the Suggestions for Further Study at the end of this chapter.

Types of Paper-and-Pencil Items

In the following section, we consider each of five types of short response items and the essay, or long response, item-type. In each case a set of clear directions to students must be our first concern, since we have to be sure that the answers reflect an understanding of the content being tested rather than the students' skill in guessing the nature of the task. Ambiguous directions not only promote undesirable guessing, but also frequently confound the teacher's work when the completed tests are being scored. Yet one of the major advantages of short response items is supposed to be ease and speed of scoring. Therefore, we will begin our consideration of each item-type by providing you with good models of directions. We suggest that you type each model direction on a separate card for inclusion in your resource file. Second, we will list a set of sample items, but these will be a mixed bag of acceptable and defective items that you will be asked to analyze with the help of some cues. Advantages and disadvantages inherent in the item-type under consideration will be treated next. Finally, some "rules of thumb" to follow when constructing the item-type will be suggested.

True-false   Most test construction experts classify this item-type as one of the most abused. Let's see why as we analyze the sample items that follow. (Remember to type the model directions on a card for your resource file.)

Directions: Circle "T" if the statement is true. Circle "F" if the statement is false.

1. Water expands when heated.   1.   T   F

2. Heat and temperature are synonomous.   2.   T   F

3. Mendel was the first known person to record the observation that
   variations in plants appear in an orderly fashion.   3.   T   F

What answers would you accept for these? Item 1 is generally true except for the 0° C to 4° C range. How, then, would you interpret the instructional implications of a response of "false"? Would you infer that (1) the student knows about the atypical behavior of water in that temperature range or that (2) the student believes that water contracts when heated from 10° C to 20° C? Why do students have trouble differentiating the two concepts in item 2? The problem of interpretation of true-false results is further complicated by the fact that the probability of guessing the correct response for each item is 50 percent.

There are other problems, too. Try writing a number of statements that are unequivocally true or false, and you will soon discover that your efforts fall into one or both of two categories. The items either test *only* recall of specific facts and/or contain key words that act as clues to the correct responses. Test-wise students have learned that words such as *may, generally, usually, sometimes,* and *probably* correlate with true statements while *never, none, always,* and *all* usually indicate false statements about science.

Is there *any* advantage to be claimed for using this type of test item? The one most frequently cited is that many items can be answered in a short time, thus increasing the sampling of knowledge. However, this feature quickly loses its attractiveness in view of the fact that what is typically sampled is simple recall of factual information. In our view, the true-false item-type is better suited for review/discussion purposes than it is for testing use. Thus, no rules of thumb for constructing this type are included.

Modified true-false   This item-type is sometimes considered an improvement over true-false items, since the student must do more than circle T or F. How much better is this item-type for sampling student achievement? Consider the set of items that follows.

Directions: Circle "T" if the statement is true. If the statement is false, fill in the blank with the word or number that would make the statement true when substituted for the underlined term.

1. Salamanders belong to the class Reptilia.   1. T _____

2. Spiders are insects.   2. T _____

3. When a cold front passes through an area, the wind
    direction changes.   3. T _____

Item 1 is a good example of this type of item. The underlined word is the label of a concept often confused with the right response, and the statement clearly calls for the substitution of the correct class name. Now contrast this with the second item. Start listing the range of literally correct responses that could be made by the students who know that spiders are not insects. How would you interpret responses such as *animals, cold-blooded, eight-legged, abundant,* and *important?* Another kind of problem is built into item 3. Did you spot the fact that it really describes a two-tailed situation? Obviously, the wind direction either changes or does not change, thus making this item a true-false type in disguise! This example would be much improved by amending it to read " ... changes from *south to north."*

Good modified true-false items are not easy to construct, even when aimed at lower levels of the cognitive taxonomy. Another limitation inherent in modified true-false is student lack of experience with this type of item. For this reason we suggest using modified true-false items on homework or worksheets prior to using them on tests. Students have to be taught that no credit will be given for (1) substitutions of equally correct terms in true statements or (2) simply writing *false* after incorrect statements.

Two advantages of the modified true-false over straight true-false can be claimed. The guessing factor is reduced substantially from 50 percent if the items are well structured and if approximately half of the statements are false. Also, it is more nearly possible to construct items that measure learning at levels II and III of the cognitive taxonomy. You may find this advantage to be more theoretical than practical because many teachers find such items difficult to construct.

Rules of thumb for constructing modified true-false items include:

1. Construct "true" statements that are absolutely correct.
2. Use approximately the same number of true as false statements.
3. Underscore a word that limits the range of substitutions in false statements.
4. Avoid where possible the use of specific determiners.
5. Avoid negative statements.
6. Keep all true and false statements approximately the same length.

Completion or fill-in-the-blank   This item-type often brings out unsuspected creativity in students, much to the teacher's chagrin. Try your own hand at the items in the sample set.

Directions: Read the sentences below and determine the word(s) or number(s) that would have to be substituted for the blank to make each sentence complete and correct. Then write these words or numbers in the correspondingly numbered blanks on the right.

1. The man who invented the microscope
   was _____(1)_____ .   1. _____

2. Lines on a weather map that join points of the same
   barometric pressure are called _____(2)_____ .   2. _____

3. _____(3)_____ exists at room temperature as   3. _____
   a _____(4)_____ and boils at _____(5)_____ .   4. _____
                                                                5. _____

6. A substance has a volume of 3.3 cc and a density of
   8.7 grams/cc. Its mass in grams is _____(6)_____ .   6. _____

Do you want to demoralize a class and start a near riot? A surefire way to accomplish both is to include items such as 1 and 3 on a quiz. Then go into class the next day and tell the students you marked their plausible, but non-keyed, answers as incorrect because they were not "what I wanted." Students who completed item 1 with an appropriate descriptor of the man's age, occupation, nationality, or mental ability cannot reasonably be marked wrong, since the question does not specify that his name is the desired response. Note how examples 2 and 6 avoid this common error, which shows up even in many published texts and workbooks! Can you guess the process that generates such monsters as that illustrated by item 3? Typically such ill-conceived guessing games result from teachers "lifting" a sentence (out of context) from the textbook and compounding the felony by replacing several key words with blanks. Fortunately this type of gross error is becoming rare in published textbook and workbook examples, but watch out for it in exercise material you assign. Yes, a serious limitation of the fill-in-the-blank item-type is the difficulty of constructing unambiguous items. You will also find it difficult to write items of this type that go beyond level II of the cognitive taxonomy—another serious limitation.

Is this type of item ever useful? Some kinds of science content, such as recalling concept labels and formulas and solving type problems, do lend themselves to this format. In fact, many science tests contain a number of items such as item 6 in order to test ability to respond accurately to basic rules and principles. However, consider the limited interpretive value of knowing *only* the answer a student arrived at and not seeing steps in the student's work that led to the response. Thus, during the early stages of formative evaluation, it makes sense to use completion for single-step computational problems and to test multi-step problems by other means. Subsequently, science teachers may wish to include some slightly more complicated examples as completion items, especially those where many of the steps are based on skills learned much earlier. An item like the one that follows, worth two credits with no partial credit allowed, falls into this category for eleventh grade chemistry students.

7.   120 grams of carbon were completely burned in air.
     The number of grams of carbon dioxide produced
     was _____?_____ .   7.   _____

At a later stage of formative evaluation, the teacher may not be seeking feedback on process errors, but instead may be emphasizing accuracy via this item-type with its "all or nothing" credit format. Science teachers would be well advised to combine this valid emphasis on accuracy with an equal (or greater) emphasis on process that must be achieved by means of other item-types.

Some useful rules of thumb follow:

1. Use only *one* blank per item.

2. Type a question mark on the blank within the item to avoid Ss writing the response there rather than on the numbered blank at the right.

3. Put all blanks at the end of the sentence.

4. Make all blanks the same length.

5. Be sure the statement clearly delimits the range of potential responses (*e.g.* include degree of specificity of numerical answers).

6. Avoid the temptation to copy out-of-context sentences from texts and then substitute a blank for a key term within the sentence.

7. In the case of computational problems, restrict use to the single-step type during the early stages of formative evaluation.

Multiple choice   This type of short response item is *the* one most favored by professional test writers. They find that well-structured multiple-choice items can more effectively assess many of the lower level outcomes often measured by other short response items. Additionally, this item-type can also measure a variety of objectives at levels III and above of the cognitive domain. As is the case with all other item-types, good items require careful attention to construction details. However, the inherent advantages of multiple-choice items over the types considered so far make for higher payoff in terms of time invested. Now check out each of the following examples for structural soundness and make mental note of any changes you might propose.

Directions: Write in the blank provided the capital letter preceding the expression that best completes *each* statement or answers each question.

1. Who wrote *Origin of Species*?

    A. Darwin

    B. De Vries

    C. Lamarck

    D. Watson   1. _____

2. Which pair of terms is correctly matched?

    A. longer string—higher pitch

    B. heavier string—higher pitch

    C. slower vibration—lower pitch

    D. faster vibration—lower pitch   2. _____

3. The principle that accounts for the operation of a hot-air balloon is the same one that accounts for the operation of a(n)

    A. airplane

    B. bird in flight

    C. kite

    D. submarine   3. _____

4. Birds

    A. can all fly

    B. are all warm-blooded animals with four-chambered hearts

    C. live only in either temperate or tropical climates

    D. build nests only in bushes or trees   4. _____

5. If carbon deposits in rocks were produced by living things, and if these deposits occur in rocks that are calculated to be older than any known fossil-bearing rocks, then life existed on earth prior to the time any now known fossil-bearing rocks were formed. The underlined portion of the foregoing statement is classified as a(n)

    A. assumption underlying the concept of evolution

    B. deduction from postulates

    C. generalization from empirical evidence

    D. conclusion not supported by empirical evidence

    E. analogy comparing a known with an unknown   5. _____

Did you spot one weak alternative among the four supplied in item 1? Watson is a poor distractor, because he is a contemporary scientist and because he is not particularly identified with the topic of evolution. A sound item always includes only plausible alternatives (distractors) plus one correct response (keyed answer) among the alternatives. The net effect of one poor distractor in a list of four alternatives is to increase the guessing factor from 25 percent to $33\frac{1}{3}$ percent. Note that none of the other sample items suffer from this type of error. In fact, you may have wondered if item 5 would be considered to be superior on this account since it contains five plausible alternatives. The five-alternative type does reduce the guessing factor 5 percent (from 25 percent to 20 percent) but the trade-off is both (1) the difficulty of finding that extra distractor and (2) increased reading time, thus reducing the number of questions students can answer in the time available. For these reasons test experts usually recommend use of the four-alternative type. You must have noticed that item 4 looks different from the others because the alternatives are all long in comparison to the one-word stem of the question—just the opposite of what is considered sound structure. Each of the other sample items contains a stem that is either a clear question or a completion-type statement followed by shorter alternatives parallel to each other in construction. This practice makes the task more explicit to students— always a desirable feature of a test.

Are there any other limitations in addition to the care needed in item construction? Yes. Multiple-choice items emphasize recognition of the correct response. Thus this item-type is a weak match for objectives that specify outcomes such as *recall* or *synthesizing* an original response. We must use other means of assessment to match these objectives.

Obvious advantages inherent in use of multiple choice include the sampling of many objectives in a short time, speed and ease of scoring, and reduction of the guessing factor to 25 percent. But don't overlook additional good features that may not be so obvious. The fact that a student has been attracted to a particular distractor has diagnostic value and also tells the teacher something about the functioning of the questions included in the test. Both of these desirable features are explored in detail in a later section on item analysis. Items 3 and 5 illustrate the potential of assessing level III and above objectives with multiple-choice questions.

Rules of thumb to follow in constructing multiple-choice questions include these:

1. Write the stem so that it presents a single, specific problem in either question or completion statement form.

2. If the stem incorporates an exception, emphasize it by solid caps and underscoring (<u>EXCEPT</u>).

3. Include in the stem all words that would otherwise be common to all alternative phrases.

4. Make the alternatives as brief as possible and in no case any longer than the stem.

5. Keep alternatives within an item parallel in form and grammatically consistent with the stem.

6. Use distractors that are plausible and incorporate typical errors and misconceptions.

7. Sequence alternatives in alphabetical or numerical order.

8. Place alternatives in a vertical column, not in a horizontal row.

Matching   In our view, this is really a special case of multiple choice. Two columns are presented, and the task is to match items from one column with items from the other column. Multiple stems are to be matched with multiple alternatives. Thus you should apply what you just learned about multiple choice as you analyze the examples that follow.

1. Directions: On the line to the right of each quantity in Column B, write the letter of the phrase in Column A that most closely corresponds.

Column A	*Column B*	
A. Acceleration due to gravity in cm/sec^2	1. 1	1. _____
B. Acceleration due to gravity in ft/sec^2	2. 20	2. _____
C. Length of one meter in inches	3. 32	3. _____
D. Length of one meter in microns	4. 39.37	4. _____
E. Length of one kilometer in meters	5. 62.4	5. _____
F. Density of fresh water in lbs/ft^3	6. 980	6. _____
G. Mass of one cc of water in grams	7. 1,000	7. _____
H. Percent of the earth's surface covered by water		
I. Percent by weight of hydrogen in water		
J. Percent by volume of oxygen in the atmosphere		

2. Directions: On the line to the right of each expression in Column B, write the letter of the expression in Column A that fits it. Each expression in Column A may be used *only ONCE*.

Column A	*Column B*	
A. Respiration	1. Chlorophyll	1. _____
B. Transpiration	2. Photosynthesis	2. _____
C. Carbon dioxide used	3. Water given off	3. _____
D. Green plants	4. Oxygen used	4. _____

No doubt you have surmised that one of these two examples is intended as an illustration of correct performance, while the other suffers from several defects. How many defects did you spot in example 2? Did you catch on to the fact that the use of short and equal columns guarantees that achievement of three correct matches will assure the fourth match (since each Column A expression can be used only once)? If the directions hadn't included this restriction, the teacher would have even a bigger mess to contend with. Green plants are correctly associated with every one of the expressions in Column B! Note that example 1 avoids these kinds of problems in a number of ways. Recommended practice was followed in that (1) unequal length columns were used, (2) the shorter column lists five to seven items, and (3) the longer column includes a maximum of ten alternatives. Yes, it is difficult to construct items that meet these criteria, and that is an important limitation of matching questions This limitation becomes even more severe when you attempt to avoid the problem of multiple combinations of matches illustrated by example 2. Homogeneity of the type of expression within each column is the best way to eliminate this particular difficulty. For instance, Column A could be limited to descriptions of various kinds of data, with Column B listing the names of the instruments. But doesn't this process then restrict matching questions to the assessment of fairly low-level objectives? Yes, it frequently does just that—another limitation of this item-type.

Aside from quick and easy scoring, it is difficult to conceive of other advantages of matching questions. Even the advantage of quick and easy scoring pales in view of the fact that other types of short-response items will accomplish that and more. No doubt this explains why matching questions are rarely used by professional testmakers.

Rules of thumb for matching questions include the following:

1. Include, in the directions, the basis for matching and state whether or not responses may be used more than once (if either is needed for clarity).

2. Place the briefer expressions in the right-hand column (easy to scan) and in alphabetical or numeric order.

3. Use unequal length columns with a range of five to seven items in the shorter, right-hand column and seven to ten in the longer, left-hand column.

4. Make the material within each list homogeneous. For example:

Column A	Column B
Achievements	Names of persons
Events	Dates
Definitions	Concept names
Functions	Names of parts
Concepts or rules	Symbols or formulas
Plants or animals	Classification categories

Long response   This item-type is also often referred to as essay, although some teachers use the term *essay* to indicate that the response desired is in the form of one or more paragraphs. Long-response items of various kinds are needed in order to test important objectives that are difficult or impossible to assess by means of short-response items. They are also required in order to get feedback on students' ability to function at the highest levels of the cognitive domain. Just as is the case with all other item-types, considerable care in construction is essential if such questions are to serve their intended purposes. Study the following examples and decide if each is likely to achieve its purpose.

1. Write in order the three rules for writing balanced chemical equations.

2. Write operational definitions of each of the following terms:

   A. Electrical current

   B. Electromotive force

   C. Electrical resistance

3. Write complete and balanced equations for each of the following reactions:

   A. Zinc and hydrochloric acid

   B. Electrolysis of water

   C. Sodium hydroxide and sulfuric acid

4. Plot the following chicken growth data on a graph and connect the points with a smooth curve.

Time in days	Percent of adult wt.
21 (hatching)	4
30	4.5
40	5
50	7
75	20
100	38
125	55
150	65
175	78
200	82

5. Can you explain why a man, a grasshopper, and a flea can all jump approximately the same height?

6. Write an essay on the importance of geology to everyday life.

7. Black Bart guided his drag racer through the standing one-quarter mile strip in 5.95 seconds. However, Wonderful Willie beat him by .025 seconds. How much faster was the average acceleration of Willie's car in ft/sec^2? Show all work.

8. "The altitude of the celestial pole is equal to the geographic latitude of the observer." Describe any assumptions one would have to make and/or any special conditions that would have to prevail for this assertion to be correct. Justify your answer. Labeled diagrams or sketches may be used to supplement your written response.

Would you have a difficult time grading responses to item 6? We would! This question as stated is so broad as to provide for a virtually limitless range of student responses. The item could be vastly improved by indicating a narrower frame of reference that would focus responses more directly on a cluster of specific objectives the teacher wishes to assess. Unless you can list the main points or key ideas that should be included in a complete and accurate answer, the question requires reworking. Otherwise that item will have very low reliability. Did you spot the error in item 5, or is it so simple a fault that you overlooked it? The answer to that question as phrased is a simple yes or no (another true-false item in disguise). Eliminating the first two words and replacing the question mark with a period would repair the item quite well. Care in item construction is needed in order to overcome the two big potential limitations of long-response items—low validity and low reliability.

The other six examples are intended to illustrate well-constructed items that assess objectives that cannot be assessed by short-response items. Outcomes that have to do with abilities such as writing definitions, stating rules, applying rules, constructing graphs, describing unstated assumptions underlying assertions, and using logic and evidence to justify answers all require long responses if the assessment means are to match objectives. But why not cast item 7 into a completion or multiple-choice format? The cue here is in the direction to "show all work." The long-response format of this question allows the teacher to find out more than just who was able to obtain the correct numerical answer and to assign partial credit to responses that indicate varying degrees of comprehension.

Rules of thumb for constructing/scoring long-response items include:

1. Use long-response questions to assess *only* those outcomes that cannot be satisfactorily measured by short-response item-types.

2. Limit the scope so that the task is clear and the time required to respond is reasonable in terms of both credit and time to be allotted to each question.

3. Prepare a key that includes all major points of information, ideas, and steps that should appear in correct and complete responses. Be sure that the part of the response involving major principles and/or concepts is assigned more credit than simple computation aspects.

4. Plan the credit distribution within each question (in terms of guideline 3) **prior to** administering the test.

5. Do *not* use "optional" questions. (Otherwise, not all students have taken the same test.)

Credit Assignment for Items

"How much does this count?" the student asks. If you are ready to ask the same question, then you are probably hampered by experience as a test-taker in which the tests seemed to consist of only one or two item-types. In general, it is common practice to assign one credit for recall items and two credits for short-response items that do not simply involve recall. Although it seems reasonable to assign more than two credits to short-response items that involve multiple processes and principles, there is a problem with this. The inability to give partial credit since no work is to be shown puts a heavy burden on complete accuracy, or lucky guessing in the case of all but completion items. Thus, we would recommend that short-response items be consistently scored 1 credit for recall only and 2 credits for items beyond recall. Obviously, we would also recommend that when complex processes are to be tested, the teacher include some other item-types that can be scored with credit related to recall, other credit to choice of correct process or to concepts and correct use of principles, and still other credit for accuracy in computation.

Storage and Retrieval of Test Items

Busy teachers need a system that allows for quick location and retrieval of a large number of test items. Contemporary computer systems are especially useful as a management tool for this purpose. The particular microcomputer and software available to you will differentially affect some of the data input procedures. However, regardless of system, you will want to begin storing potential items (with keyed answer and credit assigned) using the guidelines presented in this section. Retrieval will be facilitated if each item can be coded by item-type, science topic and subtopic, domain assessed and taxonomic level for all but psychomotor domain. After an item has been used on a quiz or test, it would be important to add codes for the difficulty level and discrimination index of the item, characteristics treated later in this chapter.

Don't wait until you begin teaching to start writing items. As you find apparently useful items in any course you are likely to teach, create appropriate files and begin to store items. Don't overlook the possibilities of creating an item based on a cartoon in which science concepts are embedded. For example, in one panel of the *Far Side*, a male mosquito is seen entering his home and informing his wife that he must have spread malaria across half the country. A relevant test item might ask students to identify and explain any content inaccuracies in the cartoon. If your computer system includes access to a scanner, maps, pictures and the like could also be stored for use with items for class work, homework, as well as for testing purposes. Warning! Some test bank software includes a set of items that cannot be modified, as well as information on credit distribution for long-response items. Before you purchase software of this type, be sure that you are able to modify the original set of items as desired. What do you do if you don't have access to a computer? Write items on index cards and code these.

The Unit Test

Within a week you will be completing instruction in a major unit in physics. Feedback obtained during group problem-solving sessions, supervised practice, lab work, and on the results of a few short quizzes is convincing evidence of the class progress to date. But can they put it all together? It's time to draft the BIG ONE!

Designing the unit test   Unfortunately, some unit tests are patchwork quilts of earlier quiz or textbook questions with no apparent parallel to instructional emphasis or sequence. If you've been victimized by such unit tests, you probably

UNIT ON LIGHT

Units of Content	Objectives by Cognitive Level			
	I	II	III	Above III
Nature of light				
Interference				
Diffraction				
Polarization				
Reflection				
Refraction				
Optical instruments				
Color				

Fig. 8.2   A partially completed table of specifications.

learned to play the game of school in order to reap the rewards of second-guessing the teacher. However, a comprehensive assessment of objectives ought not to be a capricious collection of items, but a thoughtful, integrated part of instruction. That can only happen as a result of thorough planning.

What are you assessing? It should be the extent to which the students can meet the objectives of the unit. If your instruction was directed toward the mastery of objectives at levels I and II of the cognitive domain, then your *test results* should *report whether students did or didn't achieve each objective (criterion-referenced testing)*. If you included low-level objectives that all or most students should master as well as higher-level objectives that fewer students might attain, you would be more likely to report *test results in terms of each student's relative position in the group (norm-referenced testing)*. Each of these types of testing is characterized by specific test construction principles. Since the secondary school teacher's test more often is modeled after norm-referenced instruments, we have chosen to examine testing from that vantage point. In either case, test planning begins with the consideration of the selected objectives.

Mr. Zidonis, an eleventh-grade teacher, began his test planning by completing the margins of what is called a *table of specifications*. He listed major content topics of the unit in the vertical margin and the taxonomic levels of the cognitive objectives in the horizontal margin (see Figure 8.2).

Why not list each cognitive objective? Just imagine the size of the resulting table! Such a table of specifications would become an unmanageable monster rather than a guide to test design. Mr. Zidonis apparently included all levels of the cognitive taxonomy in his instruction, and he intends to sample the effectiveness of that instruction at each level. But levels of the affective domain and objectives in the psychomotor domain are not included. Did he ignore these domains in his instruction? Definitely not, but he chose to assess them by means of

UNIT ON LIGHT

Units of Content	I	Objectives by Cognitive Level II	III	Above III	Credit
Nature of light	2	8^2	19^3		6
Interference	1		10	$21A^4$	6
Diffraction	3	15^2		$21B^3$	6
Polarization	5,6	14^2		$22A^3$	7
Reflection	7	$13^2,16^2$			5
Refraction		17^2	$22B^3$		5
Optical instruments		$11^2,12^2,18^2$	$22C^5$		11
Color	4	$9^2,20^2$			5
Credit Totals	7	22	12	10	51

Fig. 8.3   A completed table of specifications.

long-term projects and anecdotal records during lab work rather than as part of the unit test. (Other ways of assessing objectives in these domains are treated in later sections of this chapter.) Decisions! Decisions! There's no getting around it. The decisions that result in the completed margins of the table of specifications have already framed in the future test. But the professional testmaker wouldn't stop there. Next, each box of the table would be filled in with a decimal representing the instructional emphasis given the topic and the matching objectives. "You must be kidding!" Well, *they* aren't, but then their purpose and skills differ from those of the beginning teacher. Your next step is considerably different. You begin selecting and/or generating items.

You already know quite a bit about the need to match items to objectives, the pitfalls inherent in some kinds of items, the advantages of others, the scoring of varied types of items. Where do you begin? The suggestions that follow have been found useful by both novice and experienced classroom teachers.

Even if you do work on a computer system, experienced teachers have found it useful to begin with two pencilled starter sheets. One sheet contains a table of specifications, similar to the one created by Mr. Zidonis. As you create an item or choose one from your resource file, you give each a temporary number and write that number in the appropriate cell of the table of specifications. You also pencil in the credit for that item as a superscript. Thus, the 19^3 in the third column and first row of Figure 8.3 represents the nineteenth item selected so far and the assignment of 3 credits to that item.

The second starter sheet is typically divided by a horizontal line into two sections—the top section for material that could probably be tested as short-response items and the bottom section for that more adapted to long-response items. Many teachers also divide the top section into columns for item-types they would like to include on the test. Then, you need to quickly scan the text material, your lesson plans, quiz sheets, homework assignments and other handouts for particular concepts and rules and the relative emphasis on processes and products of science. As you do this, pencil in a key word or phrase in the appropriate section on your second starter sheet. Now you have an additional guide for the item-types you need.

Next comes the writing, searching and re-writing process. As items are written or located and the entries begin to fill the matrix, stop and "eyeball" both the number of items in each box and the percent of the total credit thus far assigned to each box. You may need to begin writing items in different areas of content and for neglected levels of objectives. The test emphasis represented by credit assignment may need adjusting if the test emphasis is to match the instructional emphasis. A pencil with an eraser will come in handy!

When, in your judgment, the completed matrix seems satisfactory, prepare a typed copy of the entire test. It is generally good practice to start with all short-response items. They should be clustered by type, with each type preceded by appropriate directions for that type and with credit for each item in that section indicated. Now is the time to cut and paste from your resource file the standard directions that were provided earlier in this chapter. The long-response items follow next and there are no hard and fast rules for sequence here. Again, be sure that credit for each item is indicated. Obviously, this means that the temporary numbers assigned the items in the preparation stage may need to be changed. Before you do this, examine the short-response items in each group. In particular, write down the letters designating the correct responses for the sequence of multiple-choice items. Does there appear to be a built-in pattern? If so, don't change the choices. (Remember, these should be kept in numerical or alphabetical order !) Instead rearrange the sequence of the items to eliminate the apparent pattern. Also consider the adjacent items within each cluster of items. The answer to question 4 should not "give away" the answer to question 5.

Finally, before you leave the keyboard, add headings for the test, with a space for the student's name, and numbered spaces in a column at the right of each short-response item. (Why might reading specialists approve of the answer spaces in a right margin, rather than a left margin?) Now, print a draft of your test and take it yourself. When this caution is ignored, the powerful word processing imp has a way of deleting important parts of questions to be found during the test by a smart student, or not at all by confused students.

Did you notice that Mr. Zidonis's completed table of specifications indicates a test that (1) loads almost equally on all units of content except optical instruments, (2) provides minimal rewards for straight recall, and (3) gives equal and heavy weighting to level II and to levels III and above III combined. This picture of the test would satisfy Mr. Zidonis if it matched closely the objectives and instructional emphasis of the unit. The total credits don't add up to 100! There is no reason, other than superstition, to suppose that it should. What sense would there be in juggling credits to obtain this magic number? This might destroy the match of test-to-objectives emphasis he had worked hard to achieve. It would be far better to use a conversion table or calculator to translate raw scores into percentages if that is desirable in terms of local custom or school policy.

As you work on varied stages of test preparation, be sure to share your attempts with your cooperating teacher. Modifications based on thoughtful experience will simplify your job.

To review or not to review?   Since you decided, on the basis of positive feedback, that the time for a comprehensive test had arrived, the students must be "ready" for the test. So why review? If your feedback sampling has been adequate, the answer is that typical review days are often a waste of valuable instructional time. Remember those mythical 180 days and the ways the total gets reduced? Suppose your feedback sampling was spotty. In that case the chances are that a review day will become a hurried and ineffective attempt to repair several weeks of instruction.

Don't students need some guidance in how to study for a test? Yes, and they also need information on the parameters of the test you have designed. After all, you made selective decisions as to the scope of the objectives to be tested. You may have decided to extend the test over two class periods or to include laboratory work as well as paper-and-pencil items. These decisions should not be secrets. The students should know what will be expected of them and the nature of the testing conditions.

At least four to five days prior to the test date, announce the scheduled test. If your instruction has consistently been based on the spiraling of objectives, your class will profit from a structured working session where you help them highlight major concepts. That condition is not to be passed over lightly. You must teach students how to approach a mixed collection of content topics— no easy task, since most textbooks encourage students to expect that all items in the same section will deal with the same task. Furthermore, well-managed supervised practice may have given students the false impression that they are ready to "ace" a test. What a surprise when the teacher refuses to answer questions during the test! Test preparation throughout the unit should include some simulated test sessions where no teacher or student-to-student help is given. This kind of preparation cannot be left until the day before the unit test, or it is doomed to failure. However, a summing up of all earlier practice sessions, a planned review work session focusing on areas the teacher has diagnosed as needing special attention, and a summary lecture in which the teacher outlines the format of the test, its scope and any special conditions are not only desirable, but necessary. Watch out for poorly planned review sessions that depend heavily on student-initiated questions. This frequently degenerates into a "fishing expedition" as students cast about blindly trying to locate specific items that are to appear on the test. Some characteristics of pretest work sessions that teachers and students have found successful include:

1. Short periods of supervised practice interspersed with student demonstrations, board work, or quick recall Q/A.

2. Carefully sequenced sets of written questions, where the concepts, rules, and problems most in need of review are placed first in the set, where there are more questions than can be completed in class, and where separate answer keys are distributed at the end of the session to those who wish to complete the set.

3. Tactics that allow more capable students to assist the teacher or to spend this time on a project of their choice.

Some teachers use review games very successfully. Others warn that games in which chance dictates the order and kind of question to be answered may entrap the class into experiencing a pleasurable today and a painful tomorrow when test questions fail to match game questions.

Administration of the test   Because testing periods that are badly managed lead to control problems, the basic routines for administering a test are outlined in Section 12.3 under "Effective and Efficient Handling of Routines." You may wish to look ahead at that short section right now. In that section, we allude to the problem of student cheating. Why do some students cheat? You know, from your own experience, that external pressures of varying kinds tempt even some bright, but tense, students to engage in dishonest practices. We know of no magic way to eliminate the very real pressures of college admissions, parental expectations, peer mores, and the like. There are, however, some specific suggestions that have proved useful in (1) convincing students that their chances of "getting away with it" are minimal and (2) demonstrating that built-in self-administered penalties are likely to result for culprits.

Copying from an adjacent classmate is probably the simplest and most frequently used tactic of cheaters, and even the most vigilant teacher may fail to spot occurrences in a crowded classroom. In Section 12.5, "A Pound of Cure," we describe a classroom where the teacher suspects copying has occurred during a test. Three courses of follow-up behavior are outlined, and you are asked to react to the relative effectiveness of each. Take the time to read ahead in that brief section now. Of course, we'd all prefer to **avoid** discipline problems so that a "pound of cure" wouldn't be needed. We'd recommend as an "ounce of prevention" in test administration that the first unit test be prepared in two parallel forms and distributed to the class in accordance with the directions in Section 12.5. There are several ways to concoct question papers that look alike when one glances over a shoulder. You might (1) scramble the order of the choices for each multiple-choice question (as suggested in Section 12.5), (2) reorder individual questions within each cluster of items, (3) include items that are open-ended and require a variety of responses, and (4) alter the details of explanations students are to give in the open-response items. Be sure to read the details of distributing papers, proctoring, scoring, and returning papers in Section 12.5. If you have more than one class section taking a test on the unit, you will have to construct parallel forms unless you are willing to give an automatic handicap to the first class. If you have a single section taking the test, must you always construct parallel forms? Those teachers who have used unannounced parallel forms for the first unit test find that only sporadic subsequent use is necessary. The students are now never sure whether their neighbor's test is the same form as theirs. An effective preventive? You bet it is!

How can a teacher prevent the successful use of "crib" notes? The best defense against crib notes is the construction of test items that cannot be answered solely on the basis of any kind of notes. Questions above level II are guaranteed to frustrate the student who is depending on hidden notes. The next level of defense is constant vigilance on the part of the teacher and adherence to the routines recommended in Section 12.3.

Remember, the whole point of constructing a test is to sample what students have learned about the unit, not to assess their eyesight. You should be basing future instruction on the analysis of these results. If the results are a mixed bag of half-truths, who suffers most? The successful cheater now may be tempted to cheat even more on the next unit test.

Assessing test results   Before any student's paper is scored, a key should be prepared for each form of the test. The form of the key depends on the form of the test, but it should be constructed with efficiency of scoring built in. If the students have been instructed to write answers or the capital letter of the keyed choice in a space in the right margin, the teacher's key can be constructed by correctly filling in all spaces on a copy of the test. It also helps to write the total possible credit for each cluster of items in the right margin of the key at the end of each cluster. With the key beside a student's paper, the teacher can locate and mark errors and begin the recording of credit obtained by that student. Figure 8.4 illustrates a portion of such a key, one student's responses to the first two sets of short-response items (multiple-choice—level II; completion—level I) and the teacher's scoring notations thus far.

Since Sam received 16 credits for his responses to the multiple-choice items, he must have correctly answered items 4–9. Notice how the teacher lined up the key on top of Sam's paper so that corresponding responses could be quickly checked, marked only the wrong responses, and indicated the credit accumulated for each section of the test above the slash line and the total credit accumulated thus far below the slash line.

It is good policy to score all short-response answers on each paper before addressing student efforts on open-ended questions. However, it is *not* good policy to score all open-ended responses on one paper before going on. Do you see why? Let's assume that the test on Weather included two items in which students were asked to write two essay questions in paragraph form. Even though your prepared key would include the optimum responses to each question, together with the credit to be assigned to varied portions of a response, you would find

EARTH SCIENCE TEST ON WEATHER

Period: _____3_____   Name: _____Sam Aronson_____
                                 Date: _____2-17-88_____

KEY

1.	C	1.	C
2.	D	2.	D
3.	A	3.	D √
10.	B	10.	A √
	+20		+16/ +16
11.	30	11.	32 √
12.	warm	12.	cold √
13.	Ns	13.	Ns
14.	cirrus	14.	cirrus
15.	stratus	15.	stratus
	+5		+3/ +19

Fig. 8.4   A partially scored unit test.

enough variability among responses to make judgments about scoring difficult. After carefully reading and assessing Sam's response to the first essay question, you will compound the problem of keeping the scoring reliable if you now move on to a different item on Sam's paper. That makes sense, doesn't it? What makes even more sense is the advantage gained in scoring efficiency. By the time the fifth student's response to the same essay item has been read, particular scoring decisions begin to repeat and thus can be made more easily.

At last all papers are scored and you are ready to record the grades in your grade book (computer-based, where available). An additional step may be needed at this point in the case of schools that require the reporting of letter grades. Remember, the raw scores represent *data* that will be used in *evaluating* student achievement. Whether raw scores alone are reported, or whether you need to report letter grade plus raw score or percentage plus raw score, you must make a judgment as to the meaning of the reported grade. Follow the suggestions of department head or cooperating teacher if it is necessary to translate raw scores into letter grades. In the absence of clear written or unwritten guidance as to the quantitative and qualitative match of raw scores to letter grades, we recommend that you determine a cutoff score to represent the lower limit of the D's. This is a judgment based on the total possible credit assigned to the test and the nature of the content topics and objectives it was designed to sample. If you haven't already done so, arrange the papers in rank order and write all total scores in order in a vertical array. A consideration of clusters of scores will help you make further decisions about cutoff scores in the case of A, B, C, and D papers.

Notice that we haven't suggested "curving" the grades! Why not? What does "curving" the grades mean? Every one of you is familiar enough with statistics to know that "curve" in this case relates to the normal curve. If the population being tested is normally distributed—an assumption hard to defend with class-size groups—then the mean and standard deviation can be calculated and grades of A, B, C, D, and E can be awarded on the basis of the number of deviations of a raw score from the mean. That means that a little over 2 percent of the class must be assigned an A, but another 2 percent must be assigned an E. Is that what happens when your professors tell you they've "curved" the grades? We'd bet it usually doesn't. What does happen? We'd bet that variable numbers of points are added to raw scores to make the total picture congruent with what the professor wants. A more honest term for this procedure would be "fudging" the grades. The correct use of the standard deviation to transform raw scores is described in any standard test and measurement text and will not be treated here.

Why do teachers resort to "fudging" the grades? They may have found themselves in the predicament faced by Mrs. Rely. Her scores on a unit test consisted of a few high grades, but most were dismayingly low. What should she do? Teachers have responded to similar situations in *each* of the following ways: (1) tell the class that most of the scores were so bad that the test won't count and a makeup test will be given to all students, (2) "fudge" the grades by adding an increment to the low scores, (3) tell the class the test is over, the scores are in the grade book, and that's all there is to it, or (4) carefully analyze details of test results to identify the possible source of poor student achievement and then share this information and the decisions based on it with the class. Which of these approaches is likely to increase student confidence in the evaluation process and the teacher? To us, the fourth choice is the only reasonable alternative, particularly if the teacher has followed earlier suggestions on test preparation. But after carefully constructing the test and accurately scoring all the papers, what is left to analyze? That's exactly what we need to consider next.

Item analysis   Even the trained and experienced test constructors at the Educational Testing Service (ETS) regularly reject items after analyzing the scores of a sample population. Why would they reject well-written items that match the objectives in terms of *logical* analysis? *Logical* does not equal *psychological* here any more than it does in the areas of intellectual development and human learning. Students may "read into" an item a meaning not intended by the teacher. If this happens in a random way, the teacher might well discount it. But if a number of students misread an item in exactly the same way, the item needs to be studied for the source of the error. Suppose a number of high-scoring students got a particular item wrong, while a similar number of low-scoring students got the same item correct? You'd check that item very carefully. Would you be suspicious of an item's wording on the basis of the score of one student? Two students? More than half the class? How do you decide? Here we are guided by the professional test constructor who uses, among other things, two indices: item difficulty and item discrimination.

The usual unit test (unless all the unit objectives are to be mastered by all students) is designed to differentiate the more capable students from the less capable. The teacher intends to include items of varying degrees of difficulty. Is that what happened? It's easy to ascertain. The *item difficulty* (or *difficulty index*) is defined as the *percentage of the class who succeeded on that item*. The computation of the difficulty index for two different scoring cases is illustrated in examples 1 and 2 below.

> **Example 1:**   Item 7 is a multiple-choice item worth one credit. No partial credit was given. Twenty-four students in a class of 36 students answered item 7 correctly.

$$D_f = \frac{Ns}{T} = \frac{24}{36} \approx .67 \quad \text{or} \quad 67\%$$

(D_f = difficulty index; Ns = number of successful students; T = total number of students taking the test.)

> **Example 2:**   Item 20 is worth 10 credits, but partial credit was given. In the same class of 36 students, some students received 10 credits; some 8 credits; some 5 credits; and so on. The sum of the credit obtained by the entire class on the item was 183 credits.

$$D_f = \frac{\Sigma_c}{T \times I_c} = \frac{183}{36 \times 10} = \frac{183}{360} \approx .51 \quad \text{or} \quad 51\%$$

(Σ_c = sum of the credits and I_c = credit for the item.)

The two items in examples 1 and 2 would be considered moderately difficult. In general, you should expect the difficulty index of many items to range between 60 percent and 70 percent. It is often appropriate for a teacher-made test to include a number of items with higher or lower indices. The teacher is the final judge of this, and that judgment depends in part on the original objectives set for the unit. In any case, test designers would recommend a long, hard look at items where $D_f \geq 90\%$ or $D_f \leq 30\%$. Notice the apparent anomaly. Professional test constructors call this index *item difficulty*, even though the higher percents represent easier items. As you read further, remember a D_f of 92 percent represents a very easy item for that group of students, while a D_f of 21 percent represents an item to which few students were able to respond successfully.

We also have need of another kind of index to help with analysis of items. Why? What else might we want to know? Study the information given in example 3 and try to identify one further area of potential concern.

> **Example 3:**   Item 7 described in example 1 was successfully answered by 6 of the 12 students in the top third of the class, by 8 of the middle group of 12, and by 10 of the 12 lowest scoring students.

What did you infer from the data in example 3? If you red-flagged the scoring results of the highest and lowest students on this item, you're on the right track. A test is supposed to differentiate those who have met the instructional objectives from those who haven't. Yet in this case half of the top scorers, the "haves," got the item wrong while more than three-fourths of the low scorers, the "have nots," got the item right. Why did this happen? The wording of the stem may be at fault, or the nature of the distractors may suggest erroneous information to the brighter student. So even though this item seemed to be acceptable from the point of view of item difficulty ($D_f \approx 67$ percent), it is providing false information as to the "haves" versus the "have nots." The data provided in example 3 are that used in determining the second index, *item discrimination*. In example 4, we illustrate the computation of item discrimination for the item referred to in examples 1 and 3.

Example 4:   In a class of 36, $1/3 \times 36 = 12$. Therefore, there are 12 highest scorers (H) and 12 lowest scorers (L) on the total test.

$$D_c = H_s - L_s = 6 - 10 = -4$$

(D_c = discrimination index; H_s = number of H students who successfully answered this item; L_s = number of L students who successfully answered this item.)

The negative number is an immediate signal that this item is discriminating in the reverse direction from that desired. The use of the top third and bottom third of the class is a modification of the 27 percent used by professional testwriters—a modification that works fairly well for a class size of 20 or more. If the class size is less than 20, the top and bottom halves of the class should be used with the middle scorer ignored in the case of an odd number. How is the discrimination index computed for an open-ended item worth partial credit. In example 5, we illustrate the computation for item 20 referred to in example 2.

Example 5:   Students could obtain 0 to 10 credits on item 20. The H group (12 students) in this class of 36 accumulated 96 credits, while the L group (12 students) accumulated 36 credits.

$$D_c = (H_\Sigma - L_\Sigma)/I_c = (96 - 36)/10 = 60/10 = 6.$$

(H_Σ = sum of credits obtained by H group; L_Σ = sum of the credits obtained by the L group; I_c = total possible credit value of the item, as before.)

Notice that the formula has been adjusted in example 5 to obtain, as before, an integer. In the case of item 20, where item difficulty was 51 percent, this positive discrimination index of 6 characterizes this item as discriminating in favor of the top scorers. On the basis of these two indices, item 20 appears to be doing the job it was designed to accomplish.

Although both discrimination and difficulty indices can be obtained from a computer program, most of the commercially prepared programs are not adapted to small class sizes. It is an easy matter to check a program available to you with the calculation rules provided here for several special cases. Be sure to check such a program for the kind of data entry it can handle. For example, in the case of multiple-choice items, it is useful to enter the actual distractor (O for omitted response and S for correct choice) and not just a code for success and failure. Do you see why? Remember, this analysis of items has two functions: (1) the improvement of future tests and (2) the diagnosis of individual student errors. Figure 8.5 depicts a completed set of data from a test in Mrs. Bowden's class. Each student's complete set of data was entered and then the entire set was sorted in order from highest to lowest total score. Without a computer, the papers would have been arranged in appropriate order first. The column headed N_s or Σ_c contains the number of students who succeeded on the short-response items (N_s) or the total number of points obtained by the class for the long-response items (Σ_c). The difficulty index and the discrimination index head each of the next columns. Six students got example 2 correct. Therefore, $D_f = 6/26 \approx .23 = 23\%$. Item 2 has a discrimination index of 4 since $H_s - L_s = 4 - 0 = 4$. Now it's time to check your understanding of the two indices. First, check Mrs. Bowden's figures where given. Then complete the rest of the table. You'll find our results in Simulation Exercise D.

Does the work Mrs. Bowden must have done after the test seem like "closing the barn door *after* the horse has wandered away"? It will be just that if she files the analysis sheets neatly in a file drawer and does nothing further with them. But she had much more in mind. Think back to the test post-mortem suggestions of Chapter 2. *Before* Mrs. Bowden returns these tests, she will have completed the item analysis in order to (1) identify error patterns and (2) identify students who need individual help or a differentiated follow-up assignment. The test post-mortem will be planned on the basis of this information and structured according to suggestions given in Section 2.3, Chapter 2. If Mrs. Bowden has isolated some "poor" items, identified items that many students got wrong or omitted, or identified items in which one distractor was chosen above others, she can share that information with the entire class. As a result, her questions can focus on these distractors and items. There's nothing more deadly than a test post-mortem in which the teacher or a student recites each and every answer and tells why it's correct, item by item. The "haves" are bored by the repetition, and the "have nots" are discouraged. Often the "have nots" had some reason for making an error and they are likely to repeat the same error if the limitations of that reason are never explored. However, if Mrs. Bowden structures her lesson by drawing attention to the data from particular items, the entire class can be meaningfully absorbed in questioning the results. Consider the ways the data from item 5 might be analyzed.

S_{s26} / Item #	1	2	3	4	5	30$_a$(7)	30$_b$(3)	Total (50) raw score	
D_c	7	4	—	—	—	—	—		
D_f %	54	23	15	—	—	—	—		
N_s or Σ_c	14	6	4	15	7	128	35		
Rob	O	A	E	O	B	0	0	24	⎫
Tod	E	C	E		E	1	0	24	
Milly	E	B	E	O	B	2	0	24	
Walt	O	O	O		C	2	0	25	
Rachel	D	O	E		B	4	0	26	⎬ L
Sara	O	A	A	B	B	5	0	28	
Jack		O	E	B	B	4	0	28	
Mike	D	A	E	B	O	4	0	29	⎭
Debby		O	D		O	6	0	30	
Shelly	O	O	D	C	B	6	0	30	
Alice		E	C	C	B	6	0	32	
Karen	C	B	A		B	4	2	32	
Barb	A	O	D			4	1	33	
Barry	A	E	D		O	6	1	34	
Ted			C		A	5	2	36	
Tom	A	E	O	D	B	5	3	37	
Mary				B	B	6	2	38	
Dee		B	A			6	2	39	
Jo			A	B	B	4	2	40	⎫
Mitzi		E	C		B	7	3	40	
Saul		B	A			7	2	42	
Ann		E	C	B		7	3	42	
Maud		E				7	3	46	⎬ H
Sue			C		B	7	3	48	
Bob						6	3	49	
Fran						7	3	50	⎭

Fig. 8.5

Item 5.   Through how many feet will a freely falling object travel during the first second after its release in the earth's gravitational field? (Neglect air resistance.)

A. 64   B. 32   C. 24   D. 16   E. 8

Data from the Test

Choices	A	B	C	D*	E	Omit
# of Ss	1	13	1	7	1	3

Question/answer and straw poll techniques can be used to get students thinking about *why* half of the class members were misled by distractor B while so few selected A, C, or E. Mrs. Bowden might also profitably explore the reasons for the three omitted answers. Such an analysis not only has attention-getting and -keeping potential, but helps to convince the students that the test and the test post-mortem are parts of instruction. Mrs. Bowden may subsequently decide that the multiple-choice format is not the best way to test this objective. If she wants to avoid reinventing the wheel each year, she'll record that kind of change when she adds information on these test items to her test bank file.

8.4 ASSESSMENT OF AFFECTIVE OBJECTIVES

Complying, choosing to participate, exhibiting stable and consistent attitudes—these were the three levels of the affective domain described in Chapter 5. How does the teacher evaluate such objectives? There are two chief types of assessment that teachers have found useful: (1) self-evaluation forms (that is, student response forms intended to reflect their beliefs, attitudes, opinions) and (2) observation instruments.

Student self-evaluations that are honestly completed represent a student's *perceptions* of likes, dislikes, ability, and beliefs. It is well to keep in mind that how a person perceives he or she will behave is frequently inconsistent with actual behavior. Yet, taken as a whole, the direction and intensity of likes and dislikes are a key to attitudes and so, to behavior. Students are sometimes asked to react to a collection of statements by checking or circling a numeral representing the extent to which one of two polar words represents their attitude. Such a scale consisting of polar descriptors listed in two columns is called a *semantic differential*. The scale depicted in Figure 8.6 requires the student to identify an overall attitude toward science.

A scale such as this is easily constructed. All you do is list polar words or phrases characterizing the extremes of the attitude being assessed in two columns. One caution! All the verbal cues that tend in the same attitudinal direction should *not* be listed in the same column. For example, "Valuable to Me" and "Valuable to Society" are listed in opposite columns in Figure 8.6. This construction feature will tend to identify the careless reader who circles numerals without reading each pair of descriptors. If students have had no experience with a

I THINK SCIENCE IS

Simple	1	2	3	4	5	Complex
Easy to learn	1	2	3	4	5	Difficult to learn
Boring	1	2	3	4	5	Interesting
Impractical	1	2	3	4	5	Practical
For everyone	1	2	3	4	5	For scholars only
About real things	1	2	3	4	5	About theories
Valuable to society	1	2	3	4	5	Worthless to society
Worthless to me	1	2	3	4	5	Valuable to me
Related to math	1	2	3	4	5	Unrelated to math
Related to music	1	2	3	4	5	Unrelated to music
Unrelated to art	1	2	3	4	5	Related to art

Fig. 8.6   Semantic differential.

semantic differential, the teacher will have to spend some time on the meanings associated with the numerals. Typically, one extreme end will represent strong agreement and the other extreme end, strong disagreement. Some teachers prefer to keep these ideas before the students by placing a + over one end of the scale and a − over the opposite end. Middle school teachers may be well-advised to use cartoon faces with a wide smile at one end of the scale and an extreme frown at the other. Why are the students directed *not* to put their names on the response sheet? Anonymous responses are more likely to be honest, especially when attitudes perceived as undesirable from the teacher's point of view could be revealed. Student teachers have used this type of scale early in their teaching experience to assess student attitudes toward biology and chemistry as well as toward the broader area of science in general. The results can be helpful to the teacher. For example, if most of the students' responses indicate little or no correlation between mathematics and science, the science teacher can begin to work cooperatively with the mathematics teacher to emphasize such interconnections as the kinds of symmetry exhibited by living things or the surface area versus volume relationships so important to cell size and function. A readministration of the scale at the end of the course is a way of assessing changes in attitude. But don't expect a *massive* shift in attitude despite your concentrated efforts! Experience and research results indicate that attitudes are not easily changed and sometimes decline from the beginning to end of a school year (Simpson & Oliver, 1985).

It is not easy for the teacher to identify unintentional affective instruction without systematic feedback from the students. One way of obtaining such feedback is by means of a short teacher-constructed inventory that focuses on what the teacher hoped was included in instruction. These instructional features, often in the form of questions, might be rated on a three-point scale (agree, disagree, or uncertain) or on a five-point scale. Such scales are fashioned after that developed by Likert and are thus called Likert-type scales (LaForgia, 1988). Figure 8.7 illustrates one such scale.

Answer each of the following questions by circling one of the numerals after each question.

	Definitely Not	I Don't Think So	I Can't Decide	I Think So	Definitely Yes
A. Do you understand most of the biology in the unit just completed?	1	2	3	4	5
B. Do you see any way to apply the content in this unit to real-life situations?	1	2	3	4	5
C. Were the homework assignments usually too long?	1	2	3	4	5
D. Were the homework assignments usually interesting?	1	2	3	4	5
E. Was the biology presented in a way that interested you?	1	2	3	4	5
F. Do you think too much was expected of you?	1	2	3	4	5
G. Would you like to study further on this topic?	1	2	3	4	5

Fig. 8.7   Sample Likert-type scale.

Scales such as this one can be modified by providing a "comments" space after each item. For instance, a student who circles 1 or 2 on item A might then list areas or topics that seemed most difficult. Notice the use of the pronoun *you.* It is important to emphasize that each student should reflect personal reactions rather than what "a lot of kids say." It's strange how "a lot of kids" boils down to two or three individuals when all students have a chance to express themselves without fear of peer pressure. On the other side of the coin, it's well to avoid the pronoun *I.* Item F, for example, was designed to avoid this problem. The reader often reacts differently to the same item if phrased: "Do you think I expected too much of you?" Should this kind of inventory be administered immediately after the students have been given test grades? Can you imagine the effect on responses of the student who was coasting along and got a failing grade in this test? Generally, such inventories prove most useful if administered after the students have taken the test, but before the test grades are reported. Could the inventory be administered on the test day after the students have handed in the completed test. If *all* students have the five to eight minutes needed to complete the inventory, this is an effective use of time. Otherwise, it can be administered at the beginning of the next class. In any event, inventories should not be completed by some students on one day and by others at another time, and *never* ask students to complete these outside of class time. In both cases, responses are more likely to reflect peer group comments than individual perceptions, although forms taken out of class may just disappear—to be found in the cafeteria, on the school bus, or tucked in a library book. A carefully thought-out inventory that is administered with due regard for these cautions is more apt to be taken seriously by the students, especially if feedback is shared with them later. Be warned;

overkill can destroy the impact! An inventory administered after *every* test becomes a routine.

Another type of student self-evaluation of attitudes involves the writing of open-ended essays. The students may be asked to write an essay on the topic "What Chemistry Means to Me" or to expand on a topic sentence or question, such as: "Physics is only applied mathematics. Do you agree or disagree with this statement? Give reasons to support your position." Again students need to be told why the teacher is asking them to write these essays and what use will be made of them. Feedback on areas of major agreement and disagreement should be shared with the class. This particular device has enormous possibilities for identifying and affecting attitudes as to the nature of science. (Remember the "invented versus discovered" question raised in Chapter 4?)

Essay statements might be used in structured small-group discussions or expanded on by the teacher, who could present data from the history of science or about the nature of scientific processes and products. The teacher who has specified objectives dealing with attitudes about the structure of science can use phrases from those objectives as topics, topic sentences, or questions. The essay device used in this way becomes a powerful technique for getting feedback and for using that feedback in subsequent instruction. This is another instance in which the cognitive domain is closely meshed with the affective domain. An essay on the real-life applicability of science may disclose strong biases based on erroneous or completely missing information.

The second of the assessment types listed at the beginning of this section, observation, does input individual data. Systematic observation shares with the essay technique the ability to focus on higher-level affective objectives. Moreover, observation has an advantage over all types of student self-analysis because actual behavior, rather than perceptions as to likely behavior, can be identified and recorded. The form shown in Figure 8.8 was designed by a teacher who had specified seven affective objectives to be aimed at during a lab-oriented approach to a unit on minerals. Observation must be conducted on a scheduled basis so that no students are inadvertently ignored. Hours after the event, selective recall takes over and much relevant data are lost.

8.5 ASSESSMENT OF PSYCHOMOTOR OBJECTIVES

A quick review of the psychomotor objectives listed in Section 5.3 of Chapter 5 will convince you that there is *one* valid way of assessing such objectives: systematic observation. The teacher must observe each individual perform the motor skill. An observational recording sheet analogous to that illustrated in Section 8.4 can be constructed for this purpose. Then the teacher can set up a lab practicum test in such a way that small numbers of students perform a task at lab stations with the teacher observing and recording behavior while the rest of the students work at pencil-and-paper tasks at their seats.

Students

Behavior	Paul	Barry	Lisa	Allan	→
1. Works cooperatively with other students.					
2. Treats equipment with care.					
3. Tries some of the "extra" challenge problems.					
4. Volunteers to add real-life pictures, clippings, etc., to display on minerals.					
5. Works extensively on labs when given a choice between these and free time.					
6. Asks for reference books.					
7. Chooses to do a math-related project.					

Fig. 8.8   A sample observation record form.

8.6 REPORT CARDS AND FINAL GRADES

Scores on paper-and-pencil tests of cognitive objectives are by far the most commonly used ingredient in arriving at report card grades. Such grades, which are intended to represent student achievement over a marking period or entire course, are indicators of summative evaluation. Shouldn't degree of attainment of affective and psychomotor objectives also be incorporated into such grades? That depends partly on the overall objectives of the course and partly on the definition of the report card grade used by a particular school. As a student teacher or a teacher starting out in a new school, be sure to check both written policy and unwritten tradition on these matters with the cooperating teacher or department head. Also find out if class participation and work on out-of-class projects are to be quantified and, if so, how. Suppose some diagnostic quizzes were given solely to determine the future course of instruction. Clearly these should be omitted from the calculation of a composite score. Were the unit tests designed to assess units of varied importance? If so, these scores cannot be treated as if each unit was of equal worth. Figure 8.9 depicts part of a page from Mr. Means's grade book. Since Mr. Means has recorded raw scores, he may simply obtain the sum of the raw scores of all quizzes and tests, except that given on October 31. (We hope you noticed that.) For the four weeks, depicted here, he would obtain 141 for K. Abrams. If a percentage grade is to be reported, that would be calculated by dividing each student's total by 150. Notice the difference in total possible scores on the atomic structure test and the bonding test. If Mr. Means averaged

CHEMISTRY—PERIOD 4 CLASS

Week 6

	10/10-10/14					10/17-10/21					10/24-10/28					10/31-11/4				
	M	T	W	Th	F	M	T	W	Th	F	M	T	W	Th	F	M	T	W	Th	F
1. Abrams, K.	8				88					10					35	15				
2. Anthony, R.	7				78					6					30	15				
3. Butler, A.	10				85					9					38	18				
⬇																				
23. Zeh, T.	2				55					5					25	10				

Column labels: Quiz—Particles (10); Test—Atomic structure (90); Quiz—Molecular forces (10); Test—Bonding (40); Diag. quiz—Chem. math (20)

Fig. 8.9 Sample entries from a grade book.

88 and 35 (K. Abrams's scores), K. Abrams would be assessed as achieving 62 percent of the work on these two units. If K. Abrams is as alert as her actual cumulative score on these two tests ($123/130 \approx 95\%$) indicates, she'd be complaining loud and clear! And she should! What if Mr. Means had converted individual raw scores into percentages, a common practice, and then averaged all unit tests? Would the students have been treated fairly? Let's see what happens to K. Abrams. She'd receive 98 percent (88/90) on the first test and 88 percent (35/40) on the second. Her average on the two would be 93 percent. A fluke? Well, teachers-to-be, you know how to find out. Is

$$[(a/b + (c/d)] \div 2 = [(a + c)/(b + d)]?$$

You'd be amazed at the number of teachers who behave as if they are! Of course, all this concern for conversions that maintain the initial emphasis of instruction and related assessment is based on the assumption that the teacher took this into consideration in planning and test construction. Moreover, if Mr. Means had identified ambiguous items after item analysis—items which substantially altered final test scores—and did nothing to indicate the lesser degree of validity of that test, then all bets are off.

Mr. Means has a number of other decisions to make. He also required a construction/design project of each student. How should this assessment count? Whenever psychomotor objectives are part of instruction, their assessment should be part of evaluation. In most cases, the report card grade referred to as *achievement* includes assessment of all instructional objectives. Once more the teacher has to make a policy decision. How much shall performance on these related psychomotor tasks count? The answer, as always, is based on the overall set of objectives and the emphasis of instruction.

In addition, several students volunteered to construct a large demonstration model after engaging in the required construction design project. If Mr. Means's school reporting system includes a space for "effort" or "attitude," he has a specific way to report such results. As in all other school reporting systems, the operational definition of "effort" must be gleaned from faculty handbooks and tradition. The particular interpretation placed on that definition by Mr. Means, as with any teacher, should be communicated to the students early in the year. This category of reporting is perhaps the most abused in the evaluation process. It is not unheard of for Mike to receive an A in the achievement column for biology and a 1 (inadequate effort) in the effort column for that subject. Discerning parents will rightly question that teacher's understanding of evaluation and the objectives of instruction. Mike will undoubtedly continue sliding through biology class when he can meet the objectives set by the teacher at the A-level without half trying. In the same class, Eileen received an E in achievement and a 5 (top of the scale) in effort. Do you see any reason for a parent-teacher-guidance counselor conference before sending such a report home? Considerable care is always called for in reporting affective assessments.

There are no easy answers to the questions posed here. However, it is important to keep three principles in mind:

1. Report card grades always represent a *value* judgment. (Don't let the use of numbers fool you or anyone else into believing they are objective results.)

2. Decisions as to weighting of varied projects, quizzes, tests, activities, and so on, must reflect instructional emphasis. (The die is cast after you report results on the first project—perhaps during construction of the first test.)

3. Overall principles guiding the decisions you've made must be shared with the students as early in the game as possible. (Past experience may cause them to mistrust assessment.)

The last principle is not as easy as it sounds. A good practice is to introduce the students to the teacher's task in marking report cards. Have each student keep a record of his or her individual scores and let each use a calculator during a class period to compute composite quiz and test scores according to the principles you've decided to follow. Marvin who had a string of 8s on seven of nine 10-credit quizzes and a pair of 2s begins to see what those low scores do to a composite score. You can explain how projects, laboratory work, and the like are included and then have each student submit (1) the individual computations, (2) the final grade deserved (in his or her judgment), and (3) the reasons why that grade is deserved. Teachers who use the above practice are often pleasantly surprised by the students' discerning judgment. The success of the venture depends largely on the respect the teacher has engendered thus far in evaluation and the realization that while the final *judgment (evaluation)* is the teacher's responsibility, any new data will be studied carefully before that decision is made.

8.7 SUMMARY AND SELF-CHECK

Repeatedly throughout this text, the importance of feedback getting, giving, and using has been emphasized. In this chapter, the formal feedback process known as evaluation was explored. The reader was introduced to a variety of assessment techniques, including the observational scale and the student checklist, for each of the domains. For the cognitive domain, special attention was given to the advantages and disadvantages of various types of paper-and-pencil test items. The classroom test process was outlined from table of specifications through to the reporting of grades.

In focusing on evaluation, we are once again emphasizing the need to continually and systematically assess your teaching. All the popularity contests may be ignored if the "most pleasing" teacher never achieves the objectives of instruction.

After interacting with the material in this chapter, you should be able to:

1. Operationally define evaluation, testing, formative, summative and diagnostic evaluation, objectively scored items, subjectively scored items, norm-referenced testing, and criterion-referenced testing, reliability and validity.

2. Identify the common defects in test items and revise such items in accordance with the rules of thumb in this chapter.

3. Construct test items that match specified objectives and correspond to the rules of thumb in this chapter.

4. Critique a completed table of specifications for match of items to the indicators in each margin, given a copy of the corresponding test.

5. Construct a table of specifications given a unit test.

6. Complete an item analysis sheet (including the calculation of item discrimination and item difficulty), given a set of scored test papers.

7. Critique individual test items, identify error patterns, and outline the major components to be included in a test post-mortem, given a copy of the test, the corresponding table of specifications, and the completed item analysis sheet.

8. Convert a set of raw scores into letter grades and justify your evaluation decisions.

9. Design an inventory checklist or observational scale to assess given attitudinal objectives.

10. Design an observational scale to assess given psychomotor objectives.

Check your own mastery of these objectives as you respond to the exercises that follow. Both student teaching and regular contractual teaching will offer repeated opportunities to further develop your evaluation skills.

8.8 SIMULATION/PRACTICE ACTIVITIES

A. Each of the following questions is defective in some respect. Identify the defect and revise the question so as to correspond to the rules of thumb in this chapter.

Group 1: Completion items

1. A _____(1)_____ is a warm-blooded animal
    with one pair of legs.   1. _____

2. The velocity of a bullet is 2350 ft/sec. In 1.5
    seconds, it will travel _____(2)_____ .   2. _____

3. Litmus turns _____(3)_____ in the presence   3. _____
    of a(an) _____(4)_____ .   4. _____

Group 2: Multiple-choice

5. Compared to the average thickness of the oceanic crust,
    the average thickness of the continental crust is

    A. the same   C. less

    B. greater   D. none of these   5. _____

6. Which of the following forms covalent bonds?

    A. carbon   C. sodium

    B. chlorine   D. tin   6. _____

7. Gases

    A. are colorless

    B. are lighter than air

    C. expand in direct proportion to absolute
        temperature at constant pressure

    D. expand in direct proportion to pressure under
        constant temperature conditions   7. _____

B. Refer to the Learning Hierarchy Modular assignment in the Appendix. For each objective included in your response to that assignment, construct a matching assessment item.

C. In a student teacher's table of specifications, items 3, 10, and 22 were listed under level III of the cognitive domain. The cooperating teacher agreed with the classification of item 22 but questioned the designation of the other two items as level III. Help the student teacher reclassify items 3 and 10 and justify your decisions in terms of the criteria for each appropriate level of the taxonomy.

3. A characteristic that mammals, birds, reptiles, amphibians,
    and bony fishes all have in common is

    A. a three-chambered heart

    B. a four-chambered heart

C. a hollow dorsal nerve tube

D. variable body temperature   3. _____

10. Compound X breaks down the mitotic spindle but does *NOT* interfere with growth or with duplication of cell organelles. An application of compound X should result in

A. cancer

B. cells without nuclei

C. identical daughter cells

D. polyphoids   10. _____

22. Both trout and trees are often classified as renewable resources. Give three (3) reasons why the word "renewable" does *NOT* apply equally to both organisms.

D.   In Section 8.3 you were asked to compute the values of the indices missing from Mrs. Bowden's Item Analysis sheet. The correct results are listed here.

Item #	3	4	5	30a	30b
$D_f(\%)$	15	58	27	70	45
D_c	3	3	5	4	7

With this information, the data on choices from the Item Analysis sheet, and the items themselves, Mrs. Bowden can now decide whether particular items need re-structuring before storing them in her test file and whether certain error patterns provide an answer to learning problems. Item 5 has already been subjected to this kind of analysis. For items 3 and 4, reproduced here:

a)   Identify distractors that contributed little or nothing to the item and rewrite these. (Be sure to arrange choices correctly. Mrs. Bowden didn't.)

b)   Analyze the major error patterns and conjecture the probable learning problem that led to those errors. Suggest way(s) of remediating this learning problem.

3.   Which of the following is *NOT* a flowering plant?

A. duckweed

B. pine tree

*C. mushroom

D. lawn grass

E. maple tree

4.   Most of the volume of atoms is composed of

A. electrons

B. neutrons

C. protons

*D. empty space

E. nucleus

E. On a unit test with a total possible raw score of 105, the following raw scores were obtained for a class of 31 students. Assume no problems with defective test items or test administration.

105–1	91–1	84–2	80–2	73–1	68–1
101–2	90–1	83–3	76–3	72–1	59–1
100–1	87–1	82–1	75–1	71–1	57–1
92–2	86–1	81–1	74–1	69–1	

Your school has a fixed scale to be used when assigning letter grades to test scores. Raw scores must first be converted to percentages.

Scale	A	B	C	D	E
Percentages	100–91	90–83	82–71	70–65	below 65

1. Assign letter grades to the above set of scores by using this fixed scale.

2. Find the median score (the score above or below which one-half of all scores lie). Assume that the median score should be assigned a C and assign letter grades to other scores based on "natural" clusters.

3. Contrast the results of these two methods of assigning letter grades. On what assumptions are each of these methods based? What are the advantages and disadvantages of each?

SUGGESTIONS FOR FURTHER STUDY

Hedges, W. (1966). *Testing and evaluation for the sciences.* Belmont, CA: Wadsworth.

In this paperback, Hedges gives guidelines for matching test items to objectives. Examples of items at different levels of Bloom's taxonomy for the different science disciplines, as well as examples of different types of items (*e.g.* matching), are provided.

Mullis, I. V., & Jenkins, L. B. (1988). *The science report card: Elements of risk and recovery.* Princeton, NJ: Educational Testing Service.

In this report, the authors summarize results and give illustrative items in both the cognitive and affective domains from the 1986 National Assessment of Educational Progress in science.

Schafer, L. F. (1980). "Finding lunacy (and logic) in science cartoons." *The Science Teacher*, **47** (6), 32–36.

Schafer illustrates how cartoons can be used to introduce new topics, present problems, address the nature of science, and assess science objectives. Science teachers will find the references that list sources of cartoons especially helpful.

Sund, R. B., & Picard, A. J. (1972). *Behavioral objectives and educational measures: Science and mathematics.* Columbus, Ohio: Charles E. Merrill.

We encourage you to use this text as a source of sample test items and assessment tasks in the cognitive domain and of various assessment techniques for objectives in the affective and psychomotor domains. For some unknown reason, the authors chose not to highlight the psychomotor domain, but careful readers will find illustrative assessment items hidden in observational record sheets, such as that found on page 119.

Wall, J. (1981). *Compendium of standardized science tests.* Washington, DC: National Science Teachers Association.

Wall has compiled descriptive data on nearly 50 science tests for students in grades K–12 along with information on item banks of science items.

Yager, R. E. (1987). "Assess all five domains of science." *The Science Teacher*, 54 (7), 33–37.

Yager addresses the issue of assessing different domains of goals in science education. He supports his position by including representative items and sources of assessment pools for assessing process skills, creativity, attitudes, and science and society understandings.

CHAPTER NINE

PERSPECTIVES
OF SCIENCE EDUCATION

Learning From the Past

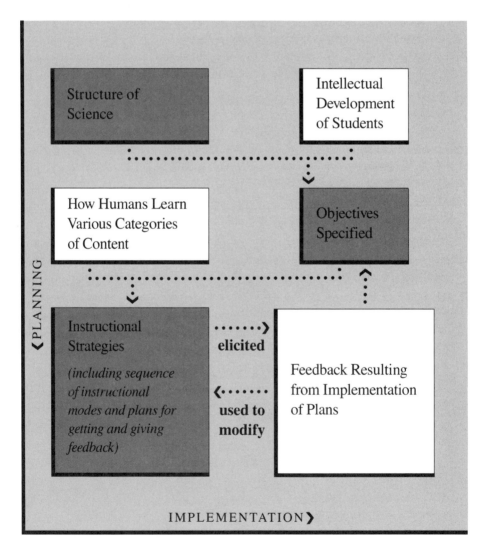

By this time you have learned that the instructional model on the facing page of each chapter depicts a dynamic interaction of multiple perspectives to be considered when you plan, and later implement, lessons. We have focused on **how** instructional objectives can be attained and much less on **what** texts, course materials and syllabi might be used to attain objectives. After all, a teacher's first concern is with appropriate instruction. Furthermore, don't text writers consider these same perspectives when they prepare materials? Well, they should, but all too often, they are influenced by other forces, such as parental cries for more emphasis on basic skills or press reports on the need for technological applications. In fact, choice of topics has even been determined by needs of a country at war. Examine physics and chemistry texts from the 1940s and early 50s and you'll find sections on radar, rockets, war gases, and speed of warplanes.

Why should contemporary science teachers be aware of textbooks used by past groups of students? Aren't our newest materials the most highly developed, somewhat like the latest model car? Well, like the latest model car, our newest materials may look sophisticated in appearance compared to many of the older black and white texts. However, the latest model car's light frame crumples on the slightest contact. Was something important sacrificed to gain speed and ease of handling? Is it possible that the text materials of the past contain some gems that a contemporary teacher would delight in using? We think so and we think you will agree!

We also believe that it is important to study the ways science instruction and curriculum have evolved, the forces that have affected their evolution, and the issues that have been concerns of science educators. Our students have found that some new "bandwagons" are old themes in disguise. Why was that particular bandwagon abandoned? What were its failures? Are we ignoring those problems again and dooming the present movement to failure? We can only begin to touch on these matters in this chapter.

A brief study of the trends of the past, which have culminated in issues of the present, will help provide a frame of reference for the contemporary scene and also give some direction to your own search for worthwhile ideas. In the following section you will be engaged in an activity designed to start you thinking along these lines.

9.1 INTRODUCTORY ACTIVITY

Those who fail to study the past are condemned to repeat it.

Choose biology, chemistry, earth science, or physics as the subject matter for this activity. Then obtain a copy of one of the texts listed below:

Biological science: An inquiry into life, Harcourt, Brace and Jovanovich, 1963.
Chemistry: An experimental science, W. H. Freeman, 1963.
Investigating the earth, Houghton Mifflin, 1967.
Physics, D. C. Heath, 1960.

Then select another secondary text and accompanying laboratory manual in the *same* field that was published during the period 1939–1959.

Respond to the following questions on the basis of a comparison of the contents of the two texts and accompanying laboratory guides.

1. What amount of space is devoted to technology (applied science)?
2. Are there major differences, other than technology, in the topics treated? If so, what are they?
3. In which text(s) is attention given to the ways knowledge in the discipline is generated?
4. Do the authors of one of the two texts seem to place more emphasis on differentiating facts and observations from theories and models?
5. Are there differences in the levels of questions included in the exercise material at the end of chapters? If so, describe them.
6. Describe any differences in what appear to be the nature and role of laboratory work. Consider such aspects as qualitative versus quantitative, investigatory versus "cookbook" type, designed to be done prior to or after correct results have been learned in class sessions, and degree of integration of laboratory and text treatment.

Then compare your results with those obtained by other classmates who chose the same science field and with the findings of several who selected a different science discipline.

Were you surprised to find such differences in texts in the same field all written just 10 to 25 years apart? Were you also surprised to learn that the 1960 texts, even though they were in different fields of science, shared so many common characteristics? There are explanations for the similarities and differences you noted, and a good part of those explanations lies in events that occurred prior to and during the time periods in which the texts were published. Think about your responses to this activity as you read about some of those events of past eras.

9.2 FROM THE THREE R'S TO PROJECT 2061

In the sections that follow, we briefly outline the history of science education from colonial America to the present (Rosen, 1963). Our emphasis is on forces and issues affecting what was taught, to whom, why, and how.

Although colonial America began to place some emphasis on the importance of formal education in the middle of the seventeenth century, only two of the three R's (reading, [w]riting and [a]rithmetic) received much attention at the precollegiate level. Massachusetts, for example, passed two education laws during the seventeenth century. The law of 1642 mandated instruction in reading and the catechism, as well as apprenticeship in a trade, while the law of 1647 required that each town of 50 families provide an elementary school teacher and each town of 100 families provide a Latin grammar school. Reading was required for admission to the Latin grammar school. These Latin grammar schools were modeled on those of England. The clientele consisted of a very small segment of the population—boys between the ages of 8 and 15 whose families could afford to have them out of economic production for as long as seven years. The typical seven-year course included *no* specific attention to mathematics, history, or the sciences. Instead the students read the classics in Latin, and presumably learned to speak Latin. Both accomplishments were considered useful in a variety of occupations and were required for admission to college.

When did science begin to appear in the schools? In 1750, the first academy, called Franklin's Academy, opened in Philadelphia. This practically oriented institution offered the first recognizable science course, natural philosophy—a forerunner of physics. Academies grew in number and served a more diverse and larger segment of the school-age population than the Latin grammar schools. The academy movement continued to flourish until the middle of the nineteenth century. It was eventually replaced by schools after the model of the English high school, which opened in Boston in 1821. In this school and later high schools, several science courses were offered; chemistry and natural history—the precursor of biology—joined natural philosophy as standard parts of the curriculum.

Colleges began to list science courses among the acceptable college entrance courses toward the last quarter of the nineteenth century. Harvard, in 1872, was the first to accept work in the sciences for college entrance. Other colleges quickly followed suit and the period of college domination of secondary school science was launched. College teachers prepared high school science outlines of study and authored most of the texts, which tended to be simplified and condensed versions of college courses. Then, Harvard published the Harvard Descriptive List in 1887, which identified 46 physics "experiments" acceptable for college entrance. This development accelerated the trend toward laboratory work in school science.

By mid-nineteenth century, Horace Mann had started America on the road to free public education, which was to alter the character of the schools, increase the need for teachers, and raise unending questions as to the kind of instruction needed by this vast and diverse citizenry. None of this happened overnight. At the beginning of the twentieth century, men such as Joseph Mayer Rice, a pediatrician with an interest in education, wrote articles deploring the state of the schools, the plight of illiterate child laborers, and the lack of concern over the education of the increasing number of non-English-speaking immigrant children. Even compulsory education laws did not dramatically increase the number of students who went to high school. Children simply continued to attend the grade school or rural one-room school until they reached the legal "leaving" age.

For all practical purposes, the bulk of our heritage in science curriculum and instruction can be found by reviewing the texts, reports, and history of the nineteenth and twentieth centuries. This is what we propose to outline as we seek answers to the questions. Where have we been? Where are we now? And where are we headed?

From the Three R's

The records of science instruction in the early nineteenth century portray a classroom where lecture and recitation (in the literal sense of the word) were the primary modes of instruction. Science was taught for informational and practical values and the methodology used by the teachers stressed memorization of the facts presented in the text. Demonstrations were rare and laboratory work was nonexistent in the early high school courses. However, as the number of high schools increased and began to serve a more diverse student body, questions arose regarding the kind of curriculum and the type of instruction that were most appropriate. By the 1860s, laboratory work on a limited scale had been instituted in many schools.

By the turn of the century it was common for high schools to offer a number of short-term courses in many sciences, including astronomy, botany, chemistry, geology, physics, physiology, and zoology. Influential committees of the National Education Association condemned this development and recommended full-year treatment of a smaller number of courses arranged in a given sequence (National Education Association, 1894). Subsequently, the pattern of physical geography in the ninth grade, biology in the tenth grade, physics in the eleventh grade, and chemistry in the twelfth grade became common in the first decades of the twentieth century. By 1920, more and more schools organized on the basis of a six-three-three plan; the junior high school movement was in full sway. As a result, general science replaced physical geography as the typical ninth-grade offering. Its functions were to provide a terminal science experience for students not going on to college and to give other students an introduction to the more specialized sciences. Soon general science also began to appear in both the eighth and seventh grades.

Over the next three decades, changes in secondary school science were minimal despite the urgings of committees of scientists, as well as those of various groups of educators (Commission on Secondary School Curriculum, 1938). These committees recommended broadening the goals of science instruction to include contributions to general education and the development of scientific or reflective thinking. Sounds very contemporary, doesn't it? The organization of science curricula around broad principles of science was recommended, and the need for functionality of science content was stressed. One recommendation that received very little attention was the need for a K–12 science sequence. How many of you were taught science in elementary school? If you were, you were one of the lucky ones. If you weren't, what might have been some possible obstacles to implementing elementary school science instruction?

At the beginning of World War II, Admiral Rickover (1960), among others, roundly criticized the teaching of mathematics and science. Not only were large numbers of recruits deficient in basic skills, but that segment of the population who **had** been educated in high-school and even college science were generally incapable of applying what they had learned in the various technological fields important to the war effort. Other critics deplored the outdated nature of school science content. To add to these problems, the already existing shortage of well-trained science teachers was intensified by World War II. Both men and women of all ages with science and/or mathematics backgrounds were badly needed for war-related efforts in government and industry. Secondary school science education was reduced to a badly disarticulated skeleton during the early and mid-1940s. Its recovery was slow and incomplete in the decade that followed the war.

Industrial demands for science-trained personnel continued as the conversion from tank and radar to auto and television production took place; and whole new industries based on new technologies were developed. The rate of development of science-based knowledge was accelerating at a tremendous pace, but little of this was being reflected in school science texts. Even though the number of science teachers was in the process of doubling during the two decades after the war, many did not have strong and contemporary science backgrounds.

The situation described in the preceding section appalled a good many people, but it was not news to many science educators. For decades, journal articles, lectures at professional meetings, and committee activity of organizations such as the National Science Teachers Association (NSTA) and the American Association for the Advancement of Science (AAAS) had identified the shortcomings of the system and recommended changes. The relatively few changes that did occur took place in an extraordinarily leisurely fashion. In the long run, change would only occur when implemented by teachers, and most teachers were not educated for change. Did World War II act as a catalyst? Not really. It took a Russian spaceship called Sputnik to jolt the nation.

The Curriculum Revolution

In the Cold War era of the late 1950s, an advance like Sputnik I frightened the nation into pushing for massive strides in science and mathematics education. The National Defense Education Act (NDEA) of 1958 made it possible for agencies such as the National Science Foundation (NSF) to distribute large sums of money to implement changes in curriculum. The number of curriculum-writing projects mushroomed and the scope of their activities increased tremendously. Institutes, both summer and academic year, were designed to update the content background of tens of thousands of teachers. Demonstration classes, often involving talented high-school students, were incorporated into some of these institutes. Scientists from both industry and universities figured heavily in all projects. Science educators and science classroom teachers were involved on a somewhat less critical basis. After all, the content was to be updated and brought into line with the contemporary status of scientific knowledge. And it was!

The committees of scientists who began to examine the status of their disciplines as reflected in secondary school textbooks and laboratory manuals were both surprised and displeased. Recent advances in knowledge had not found their way into the curriculum, and up to 50 percent or more of the space in textbooks was devoted to technology—not science. Furthermore, a great deal of the technology found there was outmoded. Moreover, the school laboratory work of the time angered scientists because it emphasized verification of what teacher and/or text had already told, instead of being inquiry oriented. The response of syllabi writers to the knowledge explosion in the natural sciences seemed to be a cursory treatment of many topics and subtopics. As a result, school science courses had become ill-articulated and lacked identifiable focus on the major ideas central to contemporary science. Much would have to change, and change fast!

A flurry of curriculum projects were begun at the senior high level. Why not begin with grade seven and build upward? Recall that professional scientists were the major force in this curriculum revolution. Not only were they likely to be primarily interested in quickly improving the quality of budding scientists, but they were specialists themselves—biologists, chemists, physicists, astronomers, and geologists. Thus, it is not surprising that they identified more closely with the traditional science courses taught at the high school level, than with the general science taught in the junior high schools.

So the die was cast and work was begun on biology, chemistry, and physics curriculum revisions with earth science following some five to six years later. There were some commonalities and differences in both approach and emphasis among these early curriculum projects. Common attributes included (1) emphasis on pure versus applied science, (2) depth of treatment of selected topics and central ideas as opposed to an encyclopedic approach, (3) courses structured around one or several unifying themes, (4) a central role for laboratory work designed to help students experience sciencing, (5) attempts to teach both the process and products aspects of the discipline, (6) a total package approach that included specially designed laboratory apparatus, audiovisual aids, tests, and supplementary reading material in addition to the textbook and laboratory guide, and (7) support of teacher retraining institutes to provide teachers with the academic background, philosophy, and techniques needed to use the curriculum materials as intended.

The picture as of 1970 was not a success story, but neither was it a complete failure. For the first time texts contained "better" science and reflected a clearer picture of the nature of science (Hurd, 1969). Science educators, such as Bingham, Hurd, Klopfer, and Pella, wrote articles and lectured to teachers on creative ideas and meaningful approaches to science. Thus, in addition to the potential resource ideas in curriculum projects, writers/teachers developed a wealth of curricular resource ideas in articles written for professional journals and in softbound "idea" books.

Curriculum projects   By 1970, 59 American projects in secondary science (15 in biology, 9 in chemistry, 9 in earth science, 14 in physics, and 12 in physical science) and 114 international projects had developed sufficiently to be outlined in the *Seventh Report of the International Clearinghouse on Science and Curricular Developments* (Lockhard, 1970). Of these, we have selected the work of seven project groups as representative of the diverse curricular trends of the time.

The Physical Science Study Committee (PSSC) was the first reform project to get underway on a large scale, and it set the tone for those to follow. Funding began in 1956 and an early decision was to start afresh rather than to repair the existing model of high school physics. By 1960 the first commercial version of the text was completed and made available by D. C. Heath. Much traditional content was omitted to make room for in-depth treatment of the modern topics physicists felt most accurately represented their discipline. The book was organized into four major parts: The Universe, Optics and Waves, Mechanics, and Electricity and Modern Physics. Two central ideas of physics, the wave-particle duality and the modern concept of the atom, served as foci for sequencing. Laboratory exercises were designed to confront the student with phenomena before encountering theoretical explanations in class sessions or text readings. Stress was placed on fostering the attitude that physics is an inquiry activity to be pursued for its own sake and on developing an understanding of the structure of modern physics. Unique films and laboratory equipment were developed as integral parts of a total curriculum package that also included tests and a series of over 50 paperback monographs designed for optional supplementary reading. Clearly the PSSC course was designed to be intellectually demanding and to appeal to no more than the upper 25 percent of the twelfth-grade population (those who typically elected the subject in 1960).

Soon the chemists were hard at work on two curriculum projects, which differed significantly from existing secondary school courses and from each other. The Chemical Education Materials Study (CHEM) writers developed the text *Chemistry: An Experimental Science*, published by W. H. Freeman in 1963. The target population was those eleventh graders (the upper 40 percent) who typically enrolled in a college preparatory chemistry course. The laboratory exercises were designed to raise, as well as answer, questions and to precede related class work. Emphasis was placed on the predictive and explanatory value of thought models in modern chemistry. The intent was that an atmosphere of inquiry should permeate every class and laboratory session. Specially produced films, tests, and programmed learning materials were key parts of the curriculum package.

In contrast, the Chemical Bond Approach (CBA) group did not produce its own film series, but rather cross-referenced its topics to both selected CHEM and PSSC films. Like CHEM, this alternative approach was a reaction against existing courses that presented a reactants' and products' view of chemistry. As the name suggests, CBA writers stressed the central role of the chemical bond. The laboratory exercises were designed as a graded set with considerable guidance provided for early experiences, less direction for those done in the middle of the course, and very little structure given to the final set of "open-ended" exercises. Success in both CBA and CHEM depended on students being able to use deductive as well as inductive reasoning. However, CBA was found to be the more difficult course—a fact many observers attributed to the heavier load of abstractions included in the course.

Meanwhile the Biological Science Curriculum Study (BSCS) group had developed three alternative approaches to tenth-grade biology. Each viewed contemporary biology through a differently colored pair of glasses and all became commercially available in 1963. The BSCS yellow version text, *Biological Science: An Inquiry into Life* (published by Harcourt, Brace and Jovanovich), emphasized the cellular/developmental view—an approach closer to pre-existing biology courses than either of its sister curricula. The BSCS green version text, *High School Biology* (published by Rand McNally), presented the ecological/evolutionary view and used Ausubelian advance organizers. The third option, known as the BSCS blue version, stressed the molecular/biochemical approach, which characterized the recent breakthrough in biological science. Its text, *Biological Science: Molecules to Man* (published by Houghton Mifflin), quickly gained a reputation as the most difficult of the three approaches. Although the treatment differed markedly within topics, all three versions showed a 79 percent overlap of topics and used the same nine unifying themes. Like their companion physics and chemistry curricula, these used laboratory work of the quantitative and explanatory type. Furthermore, it was recommended that approximately 50 percent of the course time be allotted to laboratory instruction. The curriculum package, initially available for each course, included laboratory guides, sets of special equipment, teacher handbooks, tests, and films. Later, some highly innovative audiovisual aids, such as loop films and inquiry slide sets, were added.

Then in 1965, the work of the BSCS group on a second-level course for advanced students was published by Prentice-Hall under the title *Biological Science: Interaction of Experiments and Ideas*. This advanced placement course was built upon the background produced by the regular BSCS versions and was based on the assumption that additional work would have been done by students in mathematics and physical sciences. The course incorporated a series of 38 investigations to be completed prior to studying a group of essays written by outstanding scientists.

Although the earth scientists had started work on a source book for teachers in 1959, they did not begin work on a curriculum project until 1962. Thus, it was not until 1967 that the Earth Science Curriculum Project (ESCP) had a course ready for commercial publication by Houghton Mifflin. *Investigating the Earth* was more of an interdisciplinary course than any of its predecessors. The approach was to stress the unity of the subdisciplines of astronomy, geology, meteorology, oceanography, soil science, and physical geography and to incorporate relevant concepts from biology, chemistry, mathematics, and physics as needed forces and processes. The course began by treating the earth as a dynamic system, moved to examining the cyclic nature of relevant processes, then considered the earth as an historical record, and culminated with the study of earth's interrelationships to the rest of the universe. Laboratory work was of two kinds. Some exercises were designed to introduce new concepts, while others led to application and extension of content previously learned. Unlike any of the previously developed national curriculum projects, the teacher's guide listed specific behavioral objectives for each chapter. Like the other projects, ESCP fostered an inquiry approach and produced a complete curriculum package with films, maps, transparencies, sets of equipment, and tests. Although initially aimed at the ninth grade (where earth science had found a niche as an elective for students interested in science), the course developers deemed it appropriate for use in the ninth through twelfth grades.

By the mid-1960s it was obvious that these early national curriculum materials were not suitable for as wide a student audience as originally proposed. The BSCS special materials for slower learners were developed under the title *Biological Science: Patterns and Processes* and marketed in 1966 by Holt, Rinehart and Winston. In this course, the authors sought to retain much of the flavor of the three previous versions while reducing the dependency on the ability to read at or near grade level. The major topics were reduced to five in number; special multisensory aids were developed; some programmed learning materials were incorporated in the text; and graphic illustrations were liberally used.

About this time, junior high school science began to share some of the spotlight (Hurd, 1970). Too many students in the newly developed high school courses (BSCS, CBA, CHEM, and PSSC) were having trouble. It was asserted that a major source of the trouble was that students entering these courses lacked both basic science skills and an understanding of the meaning of science. Consequently two courses designed to correct these intellectual ills were devised as suitable for either eighth or ninth grade. *Introductory Physical Science* (IPS) was published in 1967 by Prentice-Hall. Its emphasis was on the roles of operational definitions, thought models, laboratory skills, and inquiry training. Laboratory work using simplified equipment and requiring facilities no more elaborate than flat surfaces and a sink was a key part of the course. The teacher's role was that of inquiry guide, and the curriculum package included sets of equipment, a teacher's guide, tests, and four films recommended from the PSSC series.

Just as IPS was designed to form a basis for the high school physical science curricula, *Interaction of Matter and Energy* (IME) was supposed to prepare students for BSCS biology. Published commercially in 1968 by Rand McNally, this junior high school physical science course was also inquiry oriented. Again laboratory work was to be the heart of the course. The content emphases were scientific processes, interactions (chemical and physical), and energy flow in both nonliving and living systems. Its curriculum package included sets of low-cost equipment, a teacher's guide, and tests.

Did you notice the diversity, as well as the commonality in the projects just described? Variations in approach among the projects of the early 1960s were more of degree than of kind. For example, the Physical Science Study Curriculum eliminated virtually all references to technological applications, while the Biological Sciences Curriculum Study used ecology as a frame of reference for one of its three versions. There was continual emphasis on "good" science—both products and processes. There was also much emphasis on the college-bound student with an occasional interlude in favor of the slower learner, and at least one major project specifically directed at the talented student.

Recall that the impetus for the curriculum revolution was the space race that began with Sputnik. The emphasis of most of the curriculum projects produced in the decade following Sputnik clearly reflects attention to educating future scientists, engineers, and mathematicians. Yet by the middle of the same decade, the attention of the American public was diverted from the space race to riots in the cities and school desegregation issues. Consequently, the limelight began to shift to the low achiever and the disadvantaged student. Federal funds were no longer available for any and all curriculum projects. The American taxpayer began demanding that schools be held accountable for teaching *all* the students.

The Reaction

There are more chapters to the story of the reaction than can be told in a few short paragraphs.

In July 1969 Americans were the first to walk on the moon, thus signaling our clear lead over the Russians in the space race. A technological crisis had ended and, as a result, a good deal of the rationale for the "new" science evaporated. A counterculture had begun to emerge at about the same time, with youth not only questioning the relevance of their education but also the entire American way of life. Science and technology were both put on trial as enemies of the natural environment and instruments in the dehumanization of mankind. Fuel shortages, accompanied by the doubling of energy costs, brought pressure on science and technology to wave a magic wand. When they could not, scientifically illiterate citizens turned further away from viewing science as the potential savior of mankind.

When these same citizens read about the results of SAT tests and National Assessment tests—both of which showed significant declines not only in mean scores, but also in the number of **high** scores, in science and in the three R's—, they lost confidence in the "new science" and the "new math" and called for a return to the basics. It should be noted that very few bothered to specify what they meant by either *basic* or *new*.

Did all the work on curriculum development come to an end during the turmoil of the 70s? No, but the pace slowed down markedly and the direction of the movement was altered considerably. Three major projects begun in the late 60s, but completed in 1970–1971, heralded these new directions.

The first, led by a group of physicists and science educators, known as the Harvard Project Physics group (HPP), was a reaction against the narrow appeal of PSSC. These writers cited the drop in the percentage of twelfth graders electing physics since the advent of PSSC as evidence of need. No doubt they were also aware of the fact that the public school population was in the process of nearly doubling during the 1960s, thus creating a more diverse clientele. Holt, Rinehart and Winston published the first commercial version of their efforts in 1970 under the shortened title *Project Physics*. This course was designed to depict physics as a human endeavor within a cultural context. Considerable attention was devoted to the historical development of several important ideas of physics, and a philosophical view of the discipline was included. The content was broadened to encompass some of the interactions among astronomy, chemistry, and technology, and a story line was built around the broad conceptual themes of physics. The curriculum package included both basic and extension (optional) laboratory exercises, sets of special equipment, a teacher's guide, supplementary readers and self-instructional booklets, tests, and a variety of audiovisual aids.

In 1971, McGraw Hill published another response to the continuing decline in enrollments in the physical sciences—*The Man Made World* produced by the Engineering Concepts Curriculum Project (ECCP). The writers were guided by the beliefs that learning should be fun, science should be easy, and that applied science (modern technology) touches the lives of people much more directly than does theoretical science. It is important to note that it was the rare textbook writer of that time period who was aware of the disparate enrollments of girls in the sciences. Thus, the chosen title, which today would be decried as sexist, was in the 70s praised for its emphasis on the human enterprise. The project authors wished to develop technological literacy among future citizens destined to live in the age of technology. Thus, they designed a course based on information systems and incorporated topics such as decision making, modeling, dynamics, feedback, stability, and logical design. The computer was incorporated in some aspects of the course and a set of equipment was specially designed to match the 30 laboratory exercises. The package also included a teacher's guide, 300 transparency masters, tape cassettes, workbooks, tests, observation checklists, and a student attitude survey.

The third transition, in 1971, was the development of the Intermediate Science Curriculum Study (ISCS) as an integrated three-year series of courses designed primarily for use in grades seven, eight and nine. These courses were comprised almost entirely of guided discovery laboratory exercises that were to be self-paced for the most part. Excursions of two types, remediation and enrichment, enabled student and teacher to tailor the work around the central core of the curriculum. The Level 1 course content included selected concepts and rules of physics (energy) while that of Level 2 was drawn from chemistry (matter) and built on Level 1. Level 3 consisted of a set of modular units from the biological and earth sciences, which provided for application of concepts and rules developed in the first two years of the program. Attention was paid to the process aspects of science throughout and an attempt to use notions of contemporary developmental and learning psychologists was evident. The overall purpose was to serve the general education function of junior high school science by developing scientific literacy rather than to develop skills and understandings particularly needed in BSCS, CBA, CHEM, or PSSC high school courses. Sets of special equipment, teacher training modules, and tests were included in the curriculum package. All printed materials (including *Probing the Natural World 1, 2*, and *Modules*) were produced commercially by Silver Burdett.

Thus, Project Physics was an attempt to appeal to students other than those planning to pursue the subject on the college level. ECCP revolted against an academic treatment of "pure" science in favor of a contemporary technology approach more in touch with daily life and ISCS was the first to adopt a multi-year, integrated course approach. It was also the first to incorporate major provisions for individualized instruction into the main texts.

A much sharper reaction against the general direction of the pioneer curricula was evident in *Ideas and Investigations in Science* (IIS) published by Prentice-Hall in 1971. Like ISCS, this curriculum was based on almost daily use of short laboratory activities. However, unlike any of the previous projects this one (1) was not funded by any grant, (2) was produced by a team of two secondary school science teachers (Harry Wong and Malvin Dolmatz), (3) was designed for the potential school dropout (including racial minorities), (4) was written in terms of the slang used by the target population, (5) was profusely illustrated by photographs, sketches, and cartoon characters (including Fat Albert and Peanuts), and (6) was structured around "here-and-now" interests of youth, such as alcohol, drugs, smoking, pollution, sex, and venereal disease. Ten units, evenly divided among biological and physical science topics, were included in the course and dependency upon learning by reading and writing was minimized.

Reactions were also apparent among those concerned with secondary school chemistry instruction. A group of college professors and high school teachers, led by Marjorie Gardner at the University of Maryland, perceived a need for new ideas and materials for high school chemistry. They sought to popularize chemistry and extend chemical education to a larger audience of adolescents than those attracted to CBA, CHEM, or the hybrids spawned by the earlier projects. Their efforts were directed toward developing a new course that would be inquiry oriented but more flexible and more fun than the existing academic courses. Without the aid of foundation funding, a modular chemistry course was written; it was marketed in 1973 by Harper and Row under the title *Interdisciplinary Approaches to Chemistry* (IAC). Eight interchangeable modules in paperback form were supplemented by a teacher's guide, tests, media packages, laboratory kits, and enrichment readings for student and teacher. Teachers could use all eight modular units for a year's course or could use only selected modules in combination with other text materials. Teachers were also encouraged to try self-pacing some or all parts of the work. Laboratory work was incorporated into the text and the subject matter focused on the relevance of chemistry to everyday events and the concerns of society. Among the unique features was clear specification in behavioral terms of objectives in the cognitive, affective, and psychomotor domains.

A later and more far-reaching reaction against the inflexibility of most of the science curricula of the revolution was published in 1976 by Ginn and Company. The *Individualized Science Instructional System* (ISIS) consisted of a large number of minicourses in self-contained modular format. The modules were designed to be clustered into many different types of 9–12 science courses, which could be tailored to local needs. Each minicourse provided a number of activities in its "core" section plus several others in the "advanced" and "excursions" sections. Except for the planning activities, which were designed as prerequisites, the activities in each section could be done in any order. Cassette tapes were produced to accompany many of the minicourses, and both specific objectives and sample test items were included. The subject matter treated in this NSF-funded project ranged across youth and society in general. The developers of ISIS were concerned with the large number of students who were rejecting high school science courses. Hence, their project was designed to appeal to a wide range of student interests and abilities.

Yes, there definitely were reactions to the curriculum revolution of the 1960s. It is true that some were negative reactions *against* parts of the emphasis of the early projects. However, it should also be clear that many reactions actually built on what had been developed in the early 1960s and tended to broaden and modify the original prototypes. Then, in the mid 1970s, the National Science Foundation, in keeping with the educational accountability theme of the 70s, funded three studies to assess the impact of the curriculum development efforts of the preceding two decades (Helgeson, Blosser, & Howe, 1977; Stake & Easley, 1978; Weiss, 1978). At the same time, data from the third National Assessment of Educational Progress (1978) revealed declining achievement scores and relatively poor student attitudes toward science. All of these results were used in the late 1970s as the foundation for *Project Synthesis*, an attempt to determine the present and future state of science education (Harms & Yager, 1981). One of the outcomes of the project was the identification of four goal clusters that provided a rationale for including science in school programs. These goal clusters were identified as (1) personal needs, (2) societal issues, (3) academic preparation, and (4) career awareness. Thus, the stage was set for redefining science education in the 1980s.

A Crisis of Mediocrity

In the early 1980s, the National Science Teachers Association (NSTA) recommended that science should be taught to **all** students, not just the elite, every single school day. At the same time, NSTA began national searches to identify and disseminate information about exemplary science curricula (Yager, 1986) that most closely matched the desired conditions put forth in *Project Synthesis* (see the NSTA's *Focus on Excellence Series*). Thus, the move was underway to find curricula that were more personally relevant to students and that stressed societal issues and career awareness.

Meanwhile, the public became more aware of the problems of education as a result of a widely published report, *A Nation at Risk* (1983). Although the committee was commenting on education in general, their characterization of American education, as a "rising tide of mediocrity," captured the headlines. Other national reports followed, with one specifically devoted to the need for citizens literate in mathematics and science. This last report, *Educating Americans for the 21st Century* (1983), was sponsored by the National Science Board and read almost like a call to return to the early post-Sputnik days, in terms of its emphasis on content. Some reactors warned the science and mathematics education community not to forget the lessons of the post-Sputnik period. Overemphasis on good science had produced texts that scientists found acceptable. However, projects that did not include emphasis on research on human learning, cognitive development of students, and education of teachers in strategies based on this interface had led to little change in the classroom.

Responses   At the national level, Congress began to approve legislation that increased the funding available to develop curriculum, create inservice science teacher education programs, and initiate research programs. However, the grants were not of the same magnitude as that of the immediate post-Sputnik era. Thus, large-scale national projects have not been the norm. Instead there have been many smaller curriculum projects, often aimed at a unit within a course, some innovative materials financed by industry, state-funded curriculum projects, and sourcebooks and curricular modules published commercially and by the National Science Teachers Association. We briefly describe some representative projects here.

Several of these curriculum projects focused on the science, technology, society theme. The importance of this theme in the 1980s is evidenced by the National Science Teachers Association's publication of three yearbooks related to this topic (Butts & Brown, 1983; Bybee, 1985; Bybee, Carlson, & McCormack, 1984). In addition, a project at the Pennsylvania State University, Science through Science/Technology/Society (S-STS), led to the development of a network of educators interested in STS. Activities from this group have included inventorying and reviewing STS curriculum materials, holding annual conferences, and distributing relevant STS information in newsletters. One such is the *S-STS Reporter*. Modules reviewed and developed by members of this network are on topics such as acid rain, biomedical technology, land use, water quality, food and agriculture, energy, space, and solid waste management.

Staff at the Lawrence Hall of Science have been involved in science curriculum development for over two decades. An ongoing series of curriculum booklets, the Great Explorations in Math and Science (GEMS) project, provide teachers with "guided discovery" activities to supplement both elementary and secondary curricula. Booklets typically contain materials for 4–6 class sessions as well as extension activities. Topics include *Mapping Animal Movements, Discovering Density, Chemical Reactions, Earth, Moon, and Stars, Paper Towel Testing,* and *Bubble-ology*. The publication of these materials was supported by grants from the A. W. Mellon Foundation and the Carnegie Corporation of New York.

Two innovative projects funded by Phillips Petroleum Company are titled *The Search for Solutions* and *The Challenge of the Unknown*. *The Search for Solutions* focuses on the process of science and consists of a set of nine films *(Prediction, Modeling, Theory, Adaptation, Trial and Error, Context, Evidence, Patterns,* and *Investigation*). The films (also available on videotape) portray science as a problem-solving activity of humans. For example, on the *Evidence* film, segments include Kowal's possible discovery of a tenth planet, Gajdusek's hunt for the cause of the Kuru disease, and a physician listening for a lack of abnormality in a heart-beat as evidence for a healthy heart. In addition to the tapes, the trade-book *The Search for Solutions* by Judson (1980), a teacher's guide, and teaching notes are available.

The second project *The Challenge of the Unknown*, although originally conceived for use in mathematics classrooms, complements *The Search for Solutions* and can be used by science teachers as well. The project consists of a series of seven films, available on videotape, and a teaching guide. The entire set of films is aimed at teaching problem-solving skills, by reference to the real applications and the use of zany cartoon characters. The teaching guide contains specific teaching suggestions, additional background reading for the teacher, interesting exercises and projects for the students and an annotated bibliography. As an example, the film *Estimation* contains a segment called *Sharks: One if by air ... Two if by sea*, another called *China census: Everyone counts* and a third titled *Avalanche: Snow job*. It is easy to teach students about the interface of science and mathematics with these films. The films can be borrowed from Phillips by a school district, for the purpose of dubbing on videotape. There is no charge for the loan. The guide is available from W. W. Norton at a small cost.

Information technology and science   By 1980, personal computers were being touted as the tool that would transform teaching. There was a flurry of activity at school and college levels to train teachers, usually mathematics and science teachers, so that they might teach courses in computer literacy, computer programming, and computer math. School districts, through small grant programs, purchased microcomputers and set up computer labs—in many cases, with little idea of what to do with the technology once it was in place. By the end of the 1980s, microcomputers had become more sophisticated, educational software had moved beyond the "drill and practice" variety, and a generation of students were already familiar with joysticks, keyboarding, mouses, and the like.

However, change takes place very slowly in classrooms. In a survey of microcomputer use in science classrooms, Lehman (1985) found that only 23 percent of the science teachers ($n = 1470$) in his study reported that they used microcomputers, while an even smaller group (6 percent) reported that they used them on a regular basis. Teachers cited lack of training, the inaccessibility of microcomputers for classroom use, and the quality of some software as major factors impeding the progress of this technology.

Authors in special technology issues of the *Journal of Research in Science Teaching* (April 1987; May 1987) and *School Science and Mathematics* (October 1987) have addressed the issue of the integration of technology (usually microcomputers) into the science curriculum in a variety of ways—theoretical considerations, the results of empirical studies, or practical suggestions. One area of potential integration for all science disciplines is the interfacing of probes and the use of accompanying computer software to collect, record, and graph data during laboratory investigations. Referred to as microcomputer-based laboratory (MBL) materials, the Technical Education Research Center (TERC) in Cambridge, MA has undertaken a five-year effort to develop these curriculum materials (Mokros & Tinker, 1987). By using such materials, students can ask "What if ... " questions, collect and display data from additional investigations, and analyze data in ways and time frames not previously available to them.

A non-computer application of technology in the classroom is the use of videocassette recorders to provide students with a macro-context for problem solving. For instance, Sherwood, Kinzer, Bransford, and Franks (1987) reported using short segments of films like *Raiders of the Lost Ark* and *Star Wars* on videotape with students. The use of such films, they suggest, will provide students with a context that makes the learning of science more meaningful. Furthermore, they assert that students will perceive science as a means to an end, instead of an end in itself, thus increasing students' motivation for learning science.

It seems clear that the vision of the authors in these special technology issues, as well as the view of other science educators, is that information technology can and will affect the curriculum and instruction of the future. When? As we have seen in the brief history of science education presented thus far, forces outside the education community can either hinder or promote that vision.

Controversial issues and science   Many controversial issues in science relate to the theme of Science/Technology/Society outlined earlier. While not new to the 1980s, issues with implications for school science—the definition of animal rights, conservation of the environment, and evolution versus creationism—received widespread attention in the popular press, the courts and the schools. Each of these issues has been articulated by organized groups, within and outside the education community, and provides a contemporary example of the influence of societal forces on school science.

Animal rights activists have engaged in debate over the raising of animals for fur, the control of animal populations by the application of hunting and gaming laws, and the dissection and use of animals in research and teaching. All of these issues interface with concerns of science education. The place of living creatures, other than humans, in the food chain, their function as an economic commodity, and their role as a sportsperson's trophy—all have implications for science and society, and thus, for the study of science. How are creatures added to the endangered species list? What is the purpose of restricting hunting times and locations? What happens to some elements in the food chain when a particular type of predator becomes extinct? All of these questions raise a host of others that are often raised outside the science classroom, but that clearly relate to the process and product model of science. Equally important, and often more controversial among certain animal rights activists, is the issue of the use of animals in the science laboratory. Recently, a high school student's refusal to dissect a frog in biology class with the subsequent lowering of her biology grade became a cause célèbre. The California student sued the school district on moral grounds. Meanwhile, the California legislature adopted a law that requires schools to provide alternatives to students who object to dissection on moral or religious grounds. Massachusetts already has such a law. Some scientists and science educators worry that attacks on dissection will erode the quality of science research and science education. Others believe that dissection shouldn't be mandatory, except for college students who intend to study medicine or do biological research. Most states have produced legislative regulations on the use of animals in school programs. Thus, science teachers who plan to use animals in their classroom activities should obtain a copy of the pertinent state regulations. Science teachers can also be important expert witnesses when such regulations are rewritten and should be aware of the guidelines for animal use and treatment developed by the National Science Teachers Association (1978), as well as those developed by the American Humane Association (1980).

Environmental issues, from the pollution of our air to the burial of radioactive waste, have political, health, economic and educational ramifications. Debate over the construction of a new atomic plant, the depletion of the ozone layer, the reduction of the number of private cars on the freeways and in the cities, antipollution devices, world famine, trash recycling, and the cleanup of the rivers and streams affects the school curriculum by focusing classroom attention on the effects of science and technology, the ethics and values relative to certain developments made possible by science and technology, and ultimately, the nature of science itself. There is no neighborhood free from examination of this kind of issue. Trash recycling may be occurring in the suburbs; a mountain community may be battling developers or legislators over the proposed takeover of forest land; a farming community is likely to be confronting the results of irresponsible dumping in a local river by mill-hands. Once again, the implications for the food chain, the resulting effects on health of a community, and the long-term economic and environmental results are appropriate material for discussion in the science classroom. Contemporary science curricula and projects (for example, *The Search for Solutions* noted earlier) not only include content on environmental background knowledge, but also engage the students in an examination of the responsibility of the scientist vis-à-vis society.

Debate over the study of evolution in schools is not new. In the famous Scopes trial of 1925, captured in a film version, *Inherit the Wind*, John Scopes was tried for teaching evolution as a theory of science. The silver-tongued orator, William Jennings Bryan, and the defendant's lawyer, Clarence Darrow, made legal history with their arguments. At the end of the emotional trial, Scopes was convicted and fined. As has happened so often throughout history, the theories of science were being *subjected to a legal test*, rather than to empirical verification. In the decade of the 1980s, opposition to the teaching of evolution in science classes has once again become highly vocal in the form of organized groups, who generally call themselves *Creationists*. As defined by these groups, creationism is based on a **literal** interpretation of the account of creation recorded in the Book of Genesis. In some states and at the national level, adherents of creationism have lobbied for legislation that would label creationism a scientific theory and make it part of the science curriculum. In the view of some of these adherents, creationism should replace evolution in the curriculum. Others have argued that creationism should be given as much emphasis as evolution in the curriculum. Science teachers have countered these arguments, often in the popular press, by discourses on the nature of science, the nature of a scientific theory, and the role of verification of a theory. They have attempted to distinguish between religion and science, to show that acceptance of evolution as a scientific theory does not preclude belief in a God who creates, and that science by its nature cannot address the same issues as religion, which is based on faith. Yet, to the public-at-large, the labels of *creationism* and *evolution* are all-too-often associated with conclusions based on emotional responses, rather than those associated with knowledge or data. Thus, the battle rages on, in parent-teacher association meetings, school board meetings, and legislatures.

Project 2061 and the Future

One of the most ambitious projects to be undertaken since the reform movement of the 1960s is *Project 2061* by the American Association for the Advancement of Science (1989). This three-phase endeavor is directed at reforming science, mathematics, and technology education and emphasizes the need for ALL students to be both scientifically and technologically literate. Architects of the completed Phase I have identified knowledge, skills, and attitudes that ALL students should acquire from their pre-college school experiences. The project writers emphasized the need to reduce the amount of content in science courses, to stress more clearly the connections between science, mathematics, and technology while softening the distinction between the various science disciplines, to encourage higher-order thinking skills, and to present science as influencing and being influenced by society.

During Phase II of the project, to be completed by 1992, several curriculum models will be implemented in selected schools across the United States in an attempt to implement the suggestions from Phase I. Finally in Phase III, which will continue into the 21st century, the resources from the first two phases will be implemented on a larger scale. The development of the projected curriculum models and materials could have a dramatic impact on the science you will teach in the next decade. Much depends on the commitment of schools and the public to a significant change in their schools.

9.3 IMPLICATIONS FOR THE SCIENCE TEACHER

Think back to the Introductory Activity. You were asked to compare a text published between 1940 and 1960 with a text typical of the curriculum revolution. You should have found the threads of emphasis on unifying themes, laboratory work to help students experience sciencing, structure of the discipline, and so on throughout the newer text. In like manner, contemporary science curricula bear unmistakable marks of the revolution. All *claim* a conceptual base, give some attention to the processes and products of science and tend to use laboratory work to foster inquiry. Furthermore, that caricature of science as a body of organized facts has been banished—or at least driven underground. Thus, the first major implication of the curriculum reforms of recent decades resides in their impact on all curricular materials produced since 1970. There is no turning back, despite the cry of "Back to Basics," but modifications of the emphases of varying projects are possible and already in full swing.

This means that the texts you may be expected to use should correspond to a contemporary view of science, a view your own science background ought to reflect. Hence, you'll understand the basic science well enough to reinterpret it for the students you teach. Right? Wrong! Under the best of circumstances, the *learning* of college science does not require that the student translate scientific concepts and principles into everyday situations, rephrase definitions in his or her own words, or explain the reasonableness of a theory. Moreover, the typical "block-and-gap" structure of a college major sequence may well have left you with some gaps! Why? Think back to the last time you took a course in general biology, chemistry, earth science, or physics. Was it during the freshman year of college or back in your high school days? That's right. Your experiences for the last three years have been with separate courses such as plant physiology, genetics, biochemistry, physical chemistry, oceanography, geology, mechanics, and nuclear physics. Thus, you will lack recent experience in putting together all of these separate inputs into the "whole cloth" of the curriculum to be taught (such as general science, biology, and earth science). Thus, you need to start reeducating yourself, and some of the best sourcebooks for that purpose are those of curriculum projects such as BSCS Yellow and BSCS Green (biology majors), CBA and CHEM (chemistry majors), ESCP (earth science majors), PSSC and HPP (physics majors), or ISCS and IPS (general science majors). Read the text material, think about the sequencing of ideas, and constantly seek answers to "why?" as well as "how?" Try to make connections between your college science learning and that in the corresponding secondary school text. For example, the biology major might ask: What is the correspondence between the sophisticated concepts you may have learned in a genetics course and the way concepts and principles are presented in the BSCS texts? Study the teacher's guides accompanying the text you selected; they are an important source of potential help. Finally, while novice teachers are rarely in a position to select new texts for a class, they should be constantly seeking resource ideas to add life and meaning to lessons, and the texts of the past can be a rich source of such ideas.

Don't overlook texts from the nineteenth or early twentieth century. (See Greenslade [1976] for examples of nineteenth-century science text illustrations.) Many of our students are so convinced of the value of these old texts that they haunt second-hand book stores and look for old natural philosophy and other science texts. Next, take note of the curricular projects of the revolution. They are a gold mine of ideas, to be selectively extracted from the project and modified as necessary.

For instance, note the easy-to-make physical models developed by ISCS and IPS to help students formulate simple thought models of atoms, molecules, and systems. Browse through the tests developed for any of the alphabet curricula and locate individual items appropriate to other courses in the same science field. Examine laboratory exercises with the same thought in mind. By all means, read descriptions of unique audiovisual aids, such as films, loop films, and inquiry slide sets produced by BSCS, CHEM, ESCP, and PSSC. Preview these when possible to separate out the real gems from those that are a waste of time and money (such as a motion picture film of a scientist writing on a chalkboard). Check catalogs of scientific supply companies for unique and relatively inexpensive demonstration/laboratory apparatus, such as stream tables, hand-held stroboscopes, ripple tanks, and force measurers. Yes, there is *gold* in the project curricula—and plenty of it. Find it, store it in your resource file, and it will be available to you at crucial moments such as lesson planning and test construction sessions. It is our opinion that *selective adaptation* of the products of the curriculum revolution is, and will continue to be, a valuable approach for classroom teachers.

A large number of paperback pamphlets, hardcover texts, and articles in professional journals have focused on activities suitable for laboratories or demonstrations. The *Journal of Chemical Education* has a regular feature on demonstrations using the overhead projector, while *School Science and Mathematics* has a lesson plan in each issue aimed at integrating mathematics and science (more of this in the next chapter). Many professional journals also have monthly computer sections with software reviews and classroom teaching ideas along with science book reviews that both teachers and students can read as sources for information.

These are just a few of the ideas to be found in curriculum materials. We encourage you to investigate your college library to locate ones mentioned in this chapter. Then browse thoughtfully for ideas, presentations, interesting problems, information on history of science, laboratory activities and demonstrations that might be useful when you are teaching. Don't ignore cartoons to be found in some texts, the daily newspaper, professional journals, or even science calendars. For example, Larson's (1989) *Prehistory of the Far Side* not only contains many cartoon panels, but also some of the background, anecdotes, and letters from scientists about some of the cartoons.

9.4 SUMMARY AND SELF-CHECK

In this chapter we identified the major milestones in the history of school science, the forces behind some events, and the issues that continue to affect science teaching. The characteristics of the curriculum revolution of the 1960s were delineated and the work of seven curriculum project groups of that era was outlined. We examined the reaction to the curriculum revolution and the swing of the pendulum back to emphasis on "basic skills." Then we referred to reports of comparatively low achievement of American youngsters, the spate of national reports criticizing education, and the call to reform science education so that **all** students would be scientifically and technologically literate. We briefly considered the potential that information technology has to offer science education and the impact it could have on science curriculum. Finally, we examined some of the recommendations from Project 2061 and future directions of that project.

The title of this chapter has the subtitle: Learning from the Past. To the beginning teacher, the fact that changes in school science have sometimes been made on the basis of powerful public reaction is startling. *"You mean that the texts I'm teaching from may not be based on our expanding knowledge base and on a consideration of an instructional model such as the one the we have been studying?"* It surely is possible, if past history is an indication. Thus, we have emphasized the importance of a rich bank of ideas in your resource file. Ideas that do correspond to the instructional model in this text will help you get beyond a static, outdated text. Here the past can assist you again. For the project materials, old textbooks, journal articles, and paperback resource books are sources of those ideas. We gave examples of a few of these. Many more can be found within the covers of each of the sources cited in this chapter.

At this point you should be able to:

1. Identify some of the forces and issues that have repeatedly affected school science.

2. Describe the major characteristics of *at least four* major projects of the curriculum revolution.

3. Compare the "new" science of the 1960s with science educators' views of science for the 1980s and 1990s.

4. Identify two specific ways information technology may affect science curriculum and instruction.

5. Select ideas from curriculum projects, yearbooks, and other sources cited in this chapter that would be appropriate supplements to any curriculum that you are assigned to teach.

9.5 SIMULATION/PRACTICE ACTIVITIES

A. Choose a topic from your major field of science. Research the approach to that topic in *one* of the curriculum projects described in Section 9.2. Then answer the following questions:

   1. What prerequisites do the authors of the chosen text assume as a basis for the selected topic?

   2. In what ways and to what extent are the processes and products of science illustrated by the text presentation?

B. Read **two** of the following and write a summary of the author's position.

   Brunkhorst, H. K., & Yager, R. E. (1986). "A new rationale for science education—1985." *School Science and Mathematics, 86*, 364–374.

Bybee, R. W. (1985). "The restoration of confidence in science and technology education." *School Science and Mathematics*, **85**, 95–108.

Tinker, R. F. (1987). "Educational technology and the future of science education." *School Science and Mathematics*, **87**, 466–476.

Yager, R. E. (1988). "A new focus for school science: S/T/S." *School Science and Mathematics*. **88**, 181–190.

C. Read the following and compare each author's ideas/position from the 1960s with those you summarized in Simulation Activity B.

American Institute of Biological Sciences (1960). The Biological Sciences Curriculum Study. *Science Teacher*, **27** (3), 41–48.

Hurd, P. D. (1962). "The new curriculum movement in science: An interpretive summary." *Science Teacher*, **29** (1), 6–9.

D. Read the National Science Teachers Association's *Focus on Excellence* volume in your content area (Biology, 1984; Chemistry, 1985; Earth Science, 1986; Middle School/-Junior High Science, 1985; Physical Science; 1984; Physics, 1985). Examine the criteria for excellent programs as well as program descriptions and consider how well your beliefs and background match these criteria.

E. Locate two or more exercises in pre-1950 textbooks that would be interesting to today's students.

F. Peruse recent issues of the *Journal of Research in Science Teaching* and *Science Education* to find descriptions of recent curriculum development activities in other countries. Compare your findings with the developments in American education cited in this chapter. One example is:

Nishikawa, J., & Kobayashi, M. (1986). "Recent revision of the science curriculum for upper-secondary schools in Japan." *Science Education*, **70**, 123–128.

SUGGESTIONS FOR FURTHER STUDY

Bybee, R. W. (Ed.) (1985). *Science, technology, society*. Washington, DC: National Science Teachers Association.

In this yearbook, science teachers are provided with background, rationale, and instructional strategies (including some lesson starters) for implementing the STS focus in the science curriculum.

Judson, H. (1980). *The search for solutions*. New York: Holt, Rinehart & Winston.

This book is designed to accompany the film series described in this chapter. Science teachers will be able to use the material to generate new teaching ideas in the content areas represented by the films. Judson also included strategies related to the discussion of ethics in science.

Staver, J. R. (Ed.). (1981). *An analysis of the secondary school science curriculum and directions for action in the 1980s* (Yearbook of the Association for the Education of Teachers in Science). Columbus, OH: ERIC Clearinghouse for Science, Mathematics, and Environmental Education.

In this yearbook, several writers examine the science curriculum from the perspective of Ralph Tyler's rationale. The status of science education around 1980, social/political forces that affect the curriculum, and new directions for science education are delineated.

Addresses of Some of the Sources Cited in this Chapter

The Search for Solutions Film Series (free)
The Search for Solutions Teaching Guide
The Challenge of the Unknown Film Series (free)
Phillips Petroleum Company
Bartlesville, OK 74003

The Challenge of the Unknown Teaching Guide (minimal cost)
W.W. Norton
500 Fifth Avenue
New York, NY 10110

LHS GEMS
Lawrence Hall of Science
University of California
Berkeley, CA 94720

National Association for Science, Technology, and Society
117 Willard Building
University Park, PA 16802

National Science Teachers Association
1742 Connecticut Avenue NW
Washington, D.C. 20009

Send to NSTA for publications and membership catalog for a listing of available resource materials. Members receive a discount.

CHAPTER TEN

THE SCIENCE, MATHEMATICS, AND EVERY-DAY WORLD INTERFACE

Communication and Cooperation

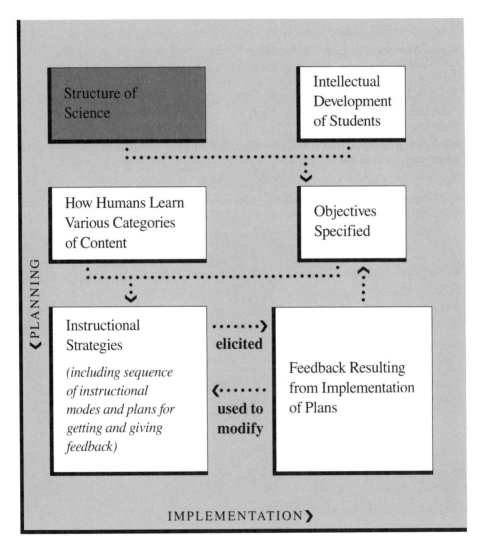

Few who are alert to the temper of the times and the needs of contemporary society recommend treating school science as an island unto itself. Fewer yet of those aware of the recent history of science in the secondary school propose that it be taught primarily for the very few students who will become professional scientists. In fact, the goal of scientific literacy for every citizen has been steadily gaining support among science educators for over a decade. Not all who cherish this goal agree on the exact meaning of the term *scientific literacy*. However, there are common grounds of agreement that are likely to persist and these merit the attention of all science teachers.

Students, as well as teachers, agree that it makes sense to consider the implications of science for everyday life, but why single out the interrelationships with mathematics? Doesn't science have some important connections with many other school subjects? We think it does, and in this chapter we sketch a few of them. However, we have chosen to concentrate on mathematics for a number of reasons. First, modern science cannot exist without mathematics. Its concepts and thought models are the lifeblood of our discipline. You will find mathematical concepts and models interwoven in every secondary school science course that *your* students will be studying. You and your students will be consciously or unconsciously using (or abusing) mathematics on a regular basis. Second, the history of science and the history of mathematics illustrate the long and fruitful union of mathematics and science. The contributions of Newton, Kepler, and others were cited in Chapter 4 as sources of teaching ideas for the science class; but the work of these men also could be a basis for a mathematics lesson. Third, your own academic background typically includes a substantial amount of mathematics. This ought to facilitate talking to, and working cooperatively with, colleagues in mathematics education. You should be able to depend on their expertise to help you to convey needed mathematical ideas in ways consistent with those taught in mathematics classes. Fourth, mathematics teachers also need *your* help in finding ways to design interesting and relevant lessons with a science basis. Thus, a profitable *quid pro quo* arrangement is highly feasible. Finally, one has to start somewhere in helping students cross those artificial watertight compartments that too often isolate one school subject from another and separate school learning from out-of-school life.

Successful cooperation with mathematics teachers can lead you to explore similar possibilities with those who teach your students subjects such as social studies, physical education, industrial arts, and fine arts. Communication and cooperation among teachers can go a long way toward overcoming the feelings of isolation and frustration that too frequently engulf teachers and students alike.

We have shaded in the "Structure of Science" portion of the instructional schema to call attention to the science/ mathematics interface so often overlooked in the literature. Authors of many journal articles that deal with the use of mathematics in science instruction treat it as interesting, supplementary material to incorporate in lessons, if time allows. We recommend a more serious and deliberate approach based on a careful analysis of the nature of the two disciplines, the structure of school curricula, and applications to out-of-school life. Both the Introductory Activity and other sections of the chapter are designed to start you thinking along these lines.

10.1 INTRODUCTORY ACTIVITY

Ivory towers are lonely places these days.

A. Table 10.1 contains some typical science topics and the mathematics concepts or rules that are used in these topics. Study the table and respond to the questions that follow:

1. Choose *two* of the science topics from the life sciences section and *two* from the physical sciences section and investigate the depth of the corresponding mathematical knowledge needed. Ask a mathematics major to help you identify the way that topic would have been presented in mathematics class.

2. For each of the related mathematics topics, identify any potential areas of confusion for students—*i.e.*, differences in the way the label or rule is used in science class.

3. Ask three to four science majors and the same number of mathematics majors what they understand to be the meaning of the following: line graph versus graph of a line, solving an equation versus balancing an equation, function versus relation.

B. Table 10.2 contains a set of questions that can be used to introduce or develop understanding of science concepts or principles. These questions are drawn from the everyday world of potential interests of the students.

1. Answer questions 1, 4, and 5 from the table.

2. List the steps a class would need to take to obtain prerequisite information related to questions 2 and 3.

3. For *each* question in Table 10.2, write additional spinoff questions that could be used to enhance the science being taught.

After comparing your responses to these activities with those of other classmates, you may find that you need additional background references on certain questions. If so, check through the references provided in the final section of this chapter.

10.2 SCIENCE AND MATHEMATICS

You don't have to have a major in mathematics in order to use mathematical language, concepts, and models to teach science. You do have to understand the *concept* of a mathematical model. In all of science—theoretical or applied, elementary school level to graduate school, biological or physical—mathematical models are used to describe something going on in the world, to explain and predict events, and to suggest solutions to complicated problems. Thus, the natural (counting) numbers are appropriate mathematical models for describing the number of planets but inadequate models for describing the size of bacteria, a virus, or a molecule. Does that use of mathematical model seem to be a far cry

Table 10.1
Mathematics in Typical Science Courses

Selected Science Topics	Mathematics Concepts/Rules
Life Sciences	
Water loss by leaves; Limits on cell size	Area and volume
Inherited traits; Variations in nature	Probability/Statistics; Combinations
Growth curves	Functions
Population studies	Graphing; Percentage
Enzyme action rates	Rate and ratio
Classification of organisms	Symmetry
Physical Sciences	
Chemical equations	Equations
Crystal structure; Shells in model of atom	Symmetry; Geometric structures
Wave phenomena	Periodic functions
Kinematics	Vectors
Boyle's law; Charles law	Volume
Lenses; Mirrors	Properties of curves
Distances to planets; Sizes and numbers of cells	Scientific notation

from the sophisticated mathematical models found in college-level physics texts and advanced biology texts? It should. However, it's exactly that simpler view of modeling that is the key to the ideas presented in this section.

Let's start with an activity based on the life style of a honeybee. In a junior high class, the teacher can show the students a picture of a cross-section of a honeycomb or, better yet, pass around (or project on the overhead) a portion of a real honeycomb. Don't assume that all the students have seen a honeycomb. Many supermarkets sell only jars of honey, minus honeycomb. Honeybees make these structures out of wax, and the honey they subsequently produce is stored in the cells. Is the regular hexagonal shape of these cells the most efficient arrangement in terms of least wax used per volume of honey stored and least volume of space wasted? Would the bees do better if they changed their habits and used equilateral triangles, squares, regular pentagons, or circles as basic geometric shapes? (Here is a good place to seek assistance from a mathematics colleague directly in class, or indirectly as a resource person. Students may need

Table 10.2
Selected Everyday-World Questions for the Science Classroom

Questions	Everyday world of:
1. What kinds of data appear on cereal boxes, candy wrappers, and medicine containers? What units are associated with any numbers related to these data?	the home
2. If all the litter found in one week in the square block area around the school were recycled, how much and how many different kinds of trash could be salvaged?	ecology and the school
3. Compare the balls used in various sports, e.g., golf, football, tennis, baseball. How fast can your school's best pitcher throw a baseball? Why are there dimples on a golf ball?	sports
4. Some linemen in football use a three-point stance, while others use an upright, or two-point, stance. What are the advantages of each? What kinds of stances are used (and why?) in other sports?	sports
5. Select a toy, such as a yo-yo, and use science concepts to explain how the toy works.	hobbies

help in recalling that regular polygons are figures with congruent sides and congruent angles; that a square is a regular quadrilateral; and that an equilateral triangle has three congruent angles as well as three congruent sides and, thus, is regular. If you're not sure, have a mathematics colleague explain the different meanings of *equal* and *congruent*. Don't feel guilty about asking for this kind of assistance since your mathematics colleagues will certainly need your help in assisting students to make proper use of science in their mathematics classes.)

The "efficiency" question needs to be examined from a biological point of view, as well as from a mathematical point of view. Sometimes this is accomplished most easily by beginning with a demonstration, using the only non-polygonal shape listed earlier, the circle. Use pennies on the overhead to simulate a honeycomb cross-section; then ask the students to consider the hypothetical structure and its advantages and disadvantages as a habitat and working environment for the bees. Remind them that the opaque regions represent the cells filled with honey, while the transparent regions represent air space. The students will quickly realize that a circular honeycomb would be subject to cold drafts and not likely to sustain the population over a cold spell. Now students can be helped to see that the efficiency question really consists of two main issues:

1. Which other shape(s) leaves no air spaces, or "fills the plane"?

2. Given a fixed surface area to use for a cell wall, which of the plane-filling shapes provide for maximum volume of the enclosed space?

Table 10.3
A Completed Data Table

Shape of cell	No. of sides	Air spaces?	No. of angles around a pt.	Measure of one angle
Equilateral triangle	3	No	6	60°
Square	4	No	4	90°
Regular pentagon	5	Yes	3+	108°
Regular hexagon	6	No	3	120°

Multiple congruent cutouts of equilateral triangles, squares, regular pentagons, and regular hexagons could be used to answer Question 1. The students might be asked to make a plane cross-section of a comb out of the cut-out shapes and, as a result, to identify those shapes that make good cells and to determine the number of such cells needed around a point. It is a good idea to include large (such as 10 cm on an edge) and small (such as 4 cm on an edge) sets of each shape. Then, elicit from the students conclusions, such as "six equilateral triangles fit around a point whether the triangles enclose a large or a small region." One class recorded their data in the form shown in Table 10.3.

Protractors can be made available if students have forgotten (or are just beginning to investigate) the angle measures of some of the shapes. The students can be encouraged to find patterns in the data, such as the recurring product of 360° ($6 \times 60°, 4 \times 90°, 3 \times 120°$), and the increasing number of sides coupled with the decreasing number of cells around a point. Ask the students to look at the pattern under the "No. of cells around a point" column and explain why that pattern "tells" us to end the investigation. If the pattern of a product of 360° holds, then no wonder the regular pentagon wasn't a useful cell: 108° would have to be a factor of 360° and it isn't. Don't miss the opportunity to point out the inexactness of measurement and the differences between the cell of the comb, the cutout hexagonal shape, and the mathematical thought model, the hexagon.

The results of this part of the investigation make the bees' construction of the comb even more puzzling. Surely, it would have been easier to build a three- or four-walled cell rather than a six-walled cell! Perhaps the solution to the second question we posed originally will help here. Although the students could use the same cutout shapes and simply compute areas, we've found that a laboratory activity designed to produce a three-dimensional visual solution is far more productive. You can use old manila folders (or other suitable substitutes), which you will need to cut into strips 2 cm by 12 cm. Students working in groups of two or three should be asked to construct a cross-sectional slice of a comb. Some groups should construct a comb with hexagonal cells; others, a comb with square cells; and the rest, a comb with triangular cells. In *all* cases, the surface area of the wall of any *single* cell will be the same, 2 cm × 12 cm. Each group will need a supply of strips (8 to 10), tape, a scissors, and a metric ruler. (The group constructing square cells won't need a ruler. Why not?) The teacher needs to remind

Fig. 10.1   Models of combs.

the class that combs do not contain double-walled cells. Furthermore, the teacher will need to precede this laboratory with a demonstration of the construction of a single cell and the subsequent attachment of an adjacent cell. As students work through the laboratory, and then compare results visually by placing one kind of honeycomb cell over another, the capacity-advantage of the hexagonal cell over either of the others should be unmistakable. Moreover, the advantage of having a constant surface area for each cell wall becomes clear. The science teacher must be especially careful when explaining the basis of this adaptation. Anthropomorphic comments about the bees' "desire to conserve wax" are non-scientific and may result in a lost opportunity for a discussion of the true nature of evolutionary fitness. This is also a good opportunity to illustrate the way in which form and function are so often interrelated in nature. In this case, students can be asked to elaborate on the bees' use of the comb, not only for the storage of honey, but also as a site for the development of eggs.

The "combs" in Figure 10.1 were produced by groups in one class. The combs were taped to the board, and all of the students observed the structural problem, which had been commented on earlier by several small groups. "The triangle is a rigid figure" became a meaningful statement to all the observers. (Then, why don't the hexagonal cells droop in the honeycomb?)

Structural rigidity is an important concept in the biological, physical and engineering sciences. Have students examine the skeletons of birds and the structures of plants for evidence of triangular support components. Ask them to bring in pictures of similar support systems used in construction. Bridge designs, cross arms on telephone poles, and floor joist braces are just a few of the many examples they should find. Ask students to study photos of athletes. (Remember question 4 in Table 10.2? For more on this relationship, see Simulation Activity C.) This is also a golden opportunity to point out that physical and biological sciences are main branches of the same tree—science.

Shape, space-filling, and perimeter/area/volume relationships are also important to multiple fields of science. Consider some basic biological concepts and rules that are inherently related to shape, space-filling and the ratio of area to volume. Living things grow due to an increase in the number of their cells rather than by continuous enlargement of individual cells. Materials must be able to get in and out of the surface rapidly enough to keep the cell contents alive. Thus, the size of individual cells is limited by the ratio of surface area to volume. These ideas may seem simple to teachers, but often are difficult for students to understand unless concrete examples and physical models are provided.

The activities outlined here have proved to be another excellent way to illustrate the science/mathematics interface and to lead students to a deeper understanding of both subjects. Cardboard shoe boxes (right parallelepipeds) of various sizes can be shown as physical models to represent many types of plant cells. The most common shapes of animal cells can be represented by spherical objects, such as basketballs, softballs, baseballs, or inflated balloons. Then the teacher can introduce another common shape of animal cells, but a shape not as familiar to the students, a regular dodecahedron (Figure 10.2). The teacher might question the students about the etymology of the word, "dodecahedron," and relate that to the model. The students can be asked to count the twelve (from "dodeca") faces (from "hedron") and examine each face for other relationships. They should realize that each face is a regular pentagon and that all are congruent. Next, the teacher can ask the students to explore the space-filling property of this shape of cell. To do this, each student can be given a paper pattern (Figure 10.3), two old manila folders, a straightedge, and a pin or thumbtack, and scissors. They should be directed to place one of the manila folders under the pattern and use the sharp metal point (pin or thumbtack) to poke holes through each of the 20 vertices of the figure. When they remove the pattern, they need to use the straightedge to draw all the line segments. A second half of the model needs to be prepared in the same way. Both must be cut out and folded along the dotted lines. Finally, tape can be used to connect the two "bowl"-shaped halves. One teacher who used this activity assigned the construction of the individual models for homework. Students were given the paper pattern, the manila folders, and a set of directions. They were instructed to be very careful in preparing the final model for use in the next class. The followup to this model-construction assignment was a class activity in which the students tried to "pack" the models together. The students found that the regular dodecahedron shape, like the spherical shape, did not fill space. The teacher posed questions about the arrangement of such cells in animals and why "packing" was not a necessary quality in this case. Some of the

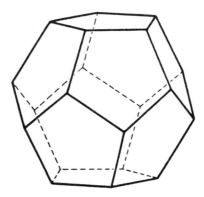

Fig. 10.2   Dodecahedron.

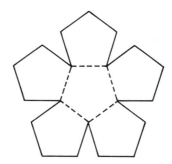

Fig. 10.3   Pattern for regular dodecahedron.

students had seen a science video show in which cells of a human were displayed under the electron microscope. Others remembered that cells had to obtain nutrients from, and discharge waste into, their surroundings. Now the teacher was able to explore further concepts such as interstitial fluid, the clusters of different types of cells in complex organisms, and the different kinds of intercellular space.

Use of these concrete models will help students envision the three-dimensional nature of cells and the types of "packing" that do and do not occur in multicellular organisms. It will also provide concrete referents for later work on surface area to volume ratios where number concepts (abstractions) are used. In a subsequent lesson, the students might first work through a simplified case where right parallelepiped cells have faces that are congruent squares (a cube). With the aid of physical models (such as a photocube), students can be reminded that the surface area is six times the area of any face (S.A. cube = $6s^2$, where s is the length of an edge) and that volume is found by cubing the length of any edge (V. cube = s^3). We suggest that you supply hypothetical edge dimensions, such

Table 10.4
Surface Area to Volume Ratios of Cells Shaped Like Cubes

Edge (in.)	S. A. (in^2)	V. (in^3)	Quotient S.A./V.	=	Ratio S.A. to V.
12	864	1728	0.5	=	1:2
9	486	729	0.666 ...	=	2:3
6	216	216	1.	=	1:1
3	54	27	2.	=	2:1
1	6	1	6.	=	6:1
.5	1.5	0.125	12.	=	12:1
* .1	0.06	0.001	60.	=	60:1
* .01	0.0006	0.000001	600.	=	600:1
* .001	0.000006	0.000000001	6000.	=	6000:1

* Range of actual sizes of most cells.

as those in Table 10.4, and assign work on different-sized cubes to small groups of students. Each group should be told to compute the surface area, volume, and the surface area to volume ratio for the assigned cube, and then enter all results in a common table on the chalkboard, or on an acetate on the overhead projector. Check to make sure that the students are using the correct order of operations on their calculators. (See Table 10.4 for an example of a completed chart.) Students may have trouble reading the volume of the smallest cube on their calculators. Ask them to compute it on paper and then ask them to explain the discrepancy between that calculation and the calculator readout. They also may need help in writing the ratios from these calculator quotients. It helps to start with the cubes with the edges of 6, 3, and 1. When the table has been filled in completely and correctly, have the students look at the last column and describe the pattern of surface area to volume ratios. Direct their attention to the last three rows of numbers—the range of size of most cells—and ask about the significance of this for the functioning of a cell. Then, later, when the teacher poses questions about the relative dissolving rates of cube sugar versus granulated sugar and the value of chewing solid food, the students should begin to understand how the surface area to volume ratio applies to other related science phenomena.

These are excellent examples of lessons that might be concurrently taught by you and a mathematics colleague. Although working together in the same classroom would be ideal, it may not be possible to arrange. Alternatively, in mathematics class, the students can spend time on development of the formulas, the order of operations used on the calculator, and the way to transform a calculator quotient to a ratio. In either class, the concrete models of cells can be made. In science class, questions can be posed as to the relevance of the differing ratios of surface area to volume in living things. Both teachers have an opportunity to explain why a ratio is a more meaningful way to compare surface

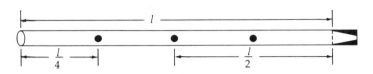

Fig. 10.4   Soda straw clarinet.

area to volume than to use a quotient. The same assignment can be assessed by both teachers.

Very large and very small numbers are constantly encountered in science, and it is essential to help students conceive of the relative sizes and distances involved if accurate thought models are to result. This is another instance of a problem that is common to both mathematics and science teachers. All too often, when scientific notation is taught in mathematics class, students are likely to give astonishing wrong answers because they have no concrete referents for the numbers and, thus, no common sense reaction to gross errors. In both cases and, we have found, for all ages of students, the construction of large- or small-scale physical models is helpful. (Recall the Piagetian nested stages model presented in Chapter 3.) In a joint, or concurrent lesson, students could be provided with the information that the size of gas molecules found in the air ranges from 2×10^{-8} cm to 4×10^{-8} cm in diameter and that they are about 3×10^{-7} cm apart under normal conditions. Then ask them to make a large physical model (to scale) of air in the room using ping pong balls taped to strings of varying lengths. Students usually express surprise at the great distance between the molecules, but they still fail to realize just how many times larger their scale model is than the phenomenon it represents. Further information can be supplied at this point to help them think along these lines. For example, a single cubic centimeter of air normally contains about 3×10^{19} molecules, and even a partial vacuum of one billionth of an atmosphere would still contain some 3×10^{10} molecules per cc. It is also important for students to understand that their model is a static one, whereas actual air molecules travel at an average speed of 4×10^4 cm/sec (the approximate speed of sound in air).

Beyond the relationships of very large and very small numbers are the manifold properties represented by a class of mathematical models known as curves. *Pitch, frequency,* and *period* are terms associated both with properties of sound and of the sine curve. For example, the trace of a vibrating tuning fork is a sine curve. The soda straw clarinet laboratory is designed to introduce the concepts of frequency and pitch and the mathematical relationship between them through the medium of music. The teacher must obtain a supply of soda straws, some single-edged razor blades, and a metric ruler. Measure a 3 cm length from one end of a straw and carefully make a horizontal crease at that point. Then flatten the shorter portion of the straw as shown in Figure 10.4. To complete the construction of the reed of the clarinet, cut two congruent right triangles out of the reed about 2.5 cm from the end of the straw. Now try the clarinet.

The reed vibrates as air is blown through the straw, which acts as a wind tunnel. The sound will not be very musical, but it represents the basic note of that clarinet. Each student's clarinet may sound slightly different (a good place to ask "Why?"). Be sure that each one is able to produce a sound before proceeding further. You may need to suggest that a sharper crease be made at the end of the reed or that the trapezoidal mouth of the reed be opened more so that air will circulate into the straw. (Paper straws may have become too wet, while some plastic straws are difficult to flatten.)

The next step is to alter the clarinets so some variable sounds can be heard. The teacher must demonstrate how to cut a hole *on the top* (this is important!) of the straw and halfway down the air column (see Figure 10.4). Then have each student "tune-up" and alternately open and close the hole with a finger to produce the basic note and the new note. The new note should sound higher; ideally, it will be pitched twice as high as the basic note. What happens when new holes are cut at the one-quarter and three-quarter marks? Let the students try these and produce the resulting sounds. The class is now ready to play their own music. They should be encouraged to do so and to listen to the effects caused by changing the length of the air column.

From here to inverse variation is an easy step. Length of air column can be related to wavelength produced by the vibrating air within that column. The *time it takes to produce a single wave* is called *the period*. The teacher can point out that time, usually expressed in seconds, is used to define period in the case of sound and time is used again to define *frequency* as *the number of complete vibrations in a second*. Experiments have demonstrated that whether executed as a loud or soft sound, a pitch of middle C on a tuning fork will result in 262 vibrations per second. Moreover, a frequency of 262 will produce a pitch of middle C for all musical sounds. For example, if 262 teeth of a steam-saw cut into a log every second, middle C is produced. Many more examples of the relationship of frequency to pitch are given in Jeans's essay "Mathematics of Music" in Volume 4 of *The World of Mathematics* (see Newman [1956] in the Suggestions for Further Study). The relationship of frequency, and thus pitch, to wavelength is equal to the velocity of sound. Is the amplitude of the sound curve somehow related to what we hear? Definitely, and your students who know about amplifiers can probably guess how. That's right—a louder sound will result in higher curves. A middle C on the piano will sound like middle C as long as that key is played but as the pressure on the key changes, the sound curve reflects this in a shifting amplitude.

There are many additional questions that are spinoffs from the clarinet laboratory.

1. Who in class plays a drum, a violin, or a trumpet? Where is the vibrating air column in each of these instruments? How are changes in pitch created? (This is an excellent place to use the expertise of the music teacher.)

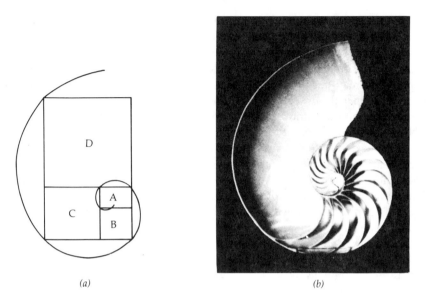

(a)   (b)

Fig. 10.5   Examples of the equiangular, or logarithmic, spiral.

2. According to the *Guinness Book of World Records* (McWhirter & McWhirter, 1976), the amplification for the rock group Deep Purple attained 117 decibels in London's Rainbow Theatre in 1972. Three members of the audience were said to become unconscious as a result. What is a decibel? What kind of input power is required to produce an output of 117 decibels? What is the relation of energy to perception of loudness? See Jeans's essay (Newman,1956) for information on loudness, the threshold of pain, and the scale of sound intensity.

The clarinet laboratory is one with long-term possibilities—for interrelating science and mathematics and for interrelating science and music. This kind of triple benefit is not unusual. The dodecahedron-cell lab may lead to additional excursions into crystallography and the various polyhedra that have been found to be models for crystals. For example, the crystal of pyrite (FeS_2) resembles a regular dodecahedron.

The well-known Fibonacci sequence $(1,1,2,3,5,8,...)$ can be introduced by sketching the family tree of a male bee. (Why *male?*) The same sequence can be related to the golden rectangle, a rectangle whose sides are in the ratio of 1 to $(1+\sqrt{5})/2$, and to the uses of that rectangle in architecture and art. The spiral illustrated in a family of golden rectangles (Figure 10.5a) is an example of an equiangular, or logarithmic, spiral, which is vividly displayed in the shell of the chambered Nautilus (Figure 10.5b). In fact, the logarithmic spiral *is* the best fit model for the shell of the chambered Nautilus as is evident from an analysis of its structure. See Simulation Exercise B for more information and further exploration of this fascinating topic.

Notice how many of the activities suggested thus far have interfaced with everyday world interests of students. Questions about musical groups the kids enjoy are likely to capture their attention. Avid beachgoers and shell-collectors are usually interested in the relationship of the Fibonacci sequence to the chambered Nautilus if the shell is displayed and questions are raised about the shapes of other shells that they have collected. Don't be worried about needing to be an instant expert. Learn together by consulting a field guide, such as Abbott, R. T. (1968). *A guide to field identification: Seashells of North America.* New York: Golden Press. Ask students to voluntarily explore the possible relationships for other shells. These are classroom-tested ways to instruct so as to work toward affective objectives.

It is easy to capitalize on students' interest in their bodies by having them gather data on the ratio of head to total height of various age groups. They can measure teachers and parents to obtain an adult category and compare this ratio with that of other groups such as young adults (twelfth-graders), young adolescents (their own grade), young children (first graders), and newborn babies. All categories except the last one are readily available in sufficient numbers to yield an excellent data base. Photographs of newborn infants can be measured to supplement data collected by measuring actual babies. This is a good opportunity to explain the power of a ratio—when students wonder why they can use the scaled-down measurements in the photograph as a replacement for measurements of a full-size infant. The striking differences in ratios obtained for various age groups generate student interest in investigating other body ratios. We suggest foot and hand to height, and distance between fingertips (with arms held outstretched horizontally at the sides of the body) to height. In all cases, students can gain further experience in measuring, calculating a ratio, using the metric system, and graphing data while learning a considerable amount about growth rates of the human body and its parts.

In like manner, the laboratory lesson described in the following paragraphs exploits student interest in muscular prowess. The lesson, entitled Muscle Fatigue, is fully described in the SMSG text *Mathematics and living things* (see the Suggestions for Further Study for the complete reference). The class is challenged, perhaps by the latest feats of school athletes or by stories of national champion weight lifters or interviews with winners of international events. They've probably seen TV coverage of the exhausted marathon runners as they stagger across the finish line. All of these familiar experiences are the basis for introducing the question of the effect of a simple exercise on fatigue, of a brief rest on the quality of subsequent performance, and of differences in the quality of performance from student to student. The teacher demonstrates the exercise in question. With one arm on the desk, elbow to hand touching the desk and palm of that hand facing up, the teacher clasps and unclasps the hand. Each time the fingers must touch the palm and then the desk, while the entire arm remains on

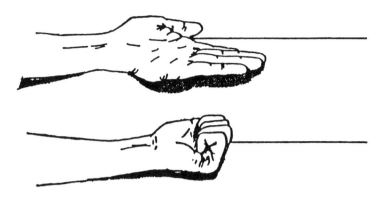

Fig. 10.6   Muscle fatigue laboratory.

Table 10.5
Lab Sheet for Muscle Fatigue Activity

Name _____   Rt. or left-handed _____

Time Period	Time in Seconds	Total Count Rt. Hand	Right Hand	Total Count Lt. Hand	Left Hand
1st	30				
2nd	30				
3rd	30				
Rest	30				
4th	30				
5th	30				
6th	30				

the desk (Figure 10.6). The goal is to do this as fast as possible within a period of 90 seconds, rest for 30 seconds, and resume the exercise for another 90 seconds.

The only equipment needed for this activity is one large wall clock with a second hand (or sufficient watches with second hands for each lab group) and lab sheets for each student (See Table 10.5).

The class is divided into groups of three. One person does the exercise for the right hand, and then for the left; one counts aloud the number of flexes from the starting to the stopping signal; the third person starts and stops the exercise and records the number of flexes at 30 second intervals on a lab sheet. The teacher will have to tour to be sure that students are performing the exercise correctly. As soon as one member of a lab group completes the exercise for both hands, a second member of that lab group begins the exercise. When all members of the class have completed the exercise, the teacher should ask the students to compare the individual data from the first 30 seconds to the second and then to the third 30 second period, and for the periods after the rest. Finally, each student can compare the data for the left hand to the data for the right hand. Each student can then be asked to compute a mean of the data for each hand before and after the rest period. Individual data and the means of the class can be graphed. The students may expect the performance of the boys to exceed the performance of the girls. Collect the means by gender and graph these data. Percent of increase and decrease, range, and extrapolation of the data beyond that collected—all of these are potential topics that can be explored. Have the students talk about the location of the muscles that tired. Ask the following questions: "How might a physical therapist use data of this kind to be able to better help a patient?" "Did you "recover" fully in the 30-second rest period?" "Did right-handed people show an advantage for use of the right hand?" This activity is a good example of the use of mathematical techniques and models to interpret biological data.

As the foregoing illustrations demonstrate, the world around us provides us with a limitless source of data that can be used to teach science. Moreover, the mathematics teacher can become a key resource person if you ask the right questions. Most science teachers are aware that their subjects are interlaced with mathematics; however, they generally consider only the computational or algorithmic aspects of mathematics. They very seldom think of the concepts of shape, geometric relationships, properties of curves, space-filling and numerous other concepts and rules that are essential prerequisites for a full appreciation of science. Mathematics teachers are just as vague about the kinds of mathematics concepts that play such a large part in understanding science concepts. Thus, the result of misguided attempts to communicate is often frustration. We've found that both parties are amazed by data such as that displayed in Table 10.1. After examining such a table, the science teacher might ask a mathematics colleague one of the following questions.

1. Let me show you some problems my students have had with balancing chemical equations. I suspect they're confusing them with algebraic equations. Maybe you can help me identify the problem.

2. We're studying crystals next week. Any chance your class would be working on symmetry? What kinds of symmetry will they be learning? How about planning a back-to-back lesson on the symmetry of crystals?

It will help if the science teacher would share with the mathematics teacher the frustration when students automatically divide the sheet of graph paper into four quadrants. What kind of relationships might result in the use of more than one quadrant in graphs? Temperature problems or problems involving distances above and below sea level come to mind immediately. These are just a few examples of the potential for science/mathematics cooperation. One excellent source of ideas related to the science/mathematics interface is the SSMILES (School Science and Mathematics Integrated Lessons) section of the journal *School Science*

Table 10.6
Maximum Power Generated by Selected Sources of Music

Source of Music	Power in Watts
Orchestra	70
Bass drum	25
Snare drum	12
Trombone	6
Piano	0.4
Bass saxophone	0.3
Bass tuba	0.2
Flute	0.06
Bass voice	0.03
Alto voice	0.001

and Mathematics. Recent issues have included lessons on *sampling with replacement, modeling natural selection, temperature measurement, and food labels.* In addition, examine the sources listed at the end of this chapter as you begin to add teaching ideas to each of the folders in your resource file.

10.3 SCIENCE AND THE EVERYDAY WORLD

As we have seen, lessons designed to emphasize the interface of science and mathematics often include attention to the everyday world. However, it is possible to interface science with the everyday world in ways that do not necessarily emphasize mathematics. When we talk about the "everyday world," we mean the *here-and-now* world of *the students.* Recall the list of potential interests of teenagers given in Chapter 7. These areas represent starting points, with your own future students providing clues as to additional areas of interest. Although attention-getting and -keeping alone would be sufficient reasons to concentrate on the everyday world, there is another reason. The vast majority of your students (98 percent or more) will *not* be majors in science or engineering (Brunkhorst & Yager, 1986) but they *will* be citizens in a world whose events are increasingly entwined in science or technology. Thus, the everyday world of school, home, hobbies, sports, summer jobs, music, design, and the like makes sense to the teenager and helps give meaning to science as a school subject.

The soda straw clarinet activity described in the previous section interests almost every student. Why? For one thing, students enjoy making something with their hands. Then, too, just think of how many phonograph records, tapes, and compact discs are sold to teenagers and how many teenagers play musical instruments. Music is very much a part of both the in- and out-of-school lives of young people. An effective follow-up activity to the soda straw clarinet is to invite a music teacher to the next class session. Ask that teacher to demonstrate various instruments, explain their functioning, and answer questions about the applications of science and mathematics to music. Another tie to music is provided by data such as that supplied in Table 10.6.

Students quickly notice the vast differences in sound power generated by the cited musical sources. What they fail to realize, however, is that humans do not perceive the bass drum as being some 800 times as loud as the bass voice. In fact, it takes a ten-fold increase in sound radiation to register a doubling of our perception. For example, it would take only 3 alto voices to balance the volume of 1 bass voice—not 30. A graph will display the logarithmic nature of this relationship. Conversations with vocal and instrumental music teachers will reveal many additional opportunities for mutually beneficial learning activities.

Many opportunities exist for crossing the natural science/social science barrier, as previously indicated within the S/T/S theme in Chapter 9. Teachers of both disciplines deal with controversial issues that incorporate science-based data and/or science concepts, principles, and theories. Prime examples include population control, protection of the environment, and use of energy sources. Social studies teachers are typically strong where science teachers are weak (economics, government) and weak where science teachers are strong (natural science content). Social studies teachers have learned to use debates, role playing, and value clarification techniques in their classes—techniques that science teachers might adopt when teaching about controversial issues. We can also follow up on what students have been taught about propaganda techniques in social studies class by asking students to identify the same basic tactics when used in pseudoscientific-based advertising. Thus, both science and social studies teachers can gain from seeking ways to pool students, ideas and resources.

Do any science-related activities take place in the fine arts and industrial arts courses in which many of your students will be enrolled? Yes—and it will be well worth your time and effort to find out the specifics. Drawing and painting classes typically include learning to produce various colors by mixing pigments of the primary colors, sketching animals in ways that accurately reflect internal anatomical structure, and using the lines and colors of living things to stimulate impressionistic interpretations. Shop lessons often include the tempering of metals, construction of strong structures from light-weight materials, shaping of wood to obtain maximum beauty of annual ring structure, and achieving etching effects by the action of acid on metal. Each of these activities involves some aspect of science. One way to elaborate on that science is to ask the student who constructed the project to explain its construction to the rest of the science class. Then all can be asked to identify the aspects of science processes and products involved in the project. For example, one student was asked to display and talk about the construction of a homemade anemometer. It was constructed from paper cups, two thin strips of wood (each 30 cm long), and a piece of broomstick with a nail embedded in one end (Figure 10.7). The student calibrated it against a commercial instrument and reported that the following rule of thumb seemed to work: "Count the number of revolutions the black cup makes in 30 seconds and then divide by 5 to obtain the wind speed in miles per hour." The

Fig. 10.7   Homemade anemometer.

science teacher asked a series of questions designed to stimulate the thinking of the entire class. "Why does the rule give reasonably accurate results?" "Would increasing or decreasing the length of the arms by 2 cm make any difference in accuracy?" "Why or why not?" "To what extent would doubling arm length affect the result?" "How do you know?"

The out-of-school world of youth is also replete with science applications. Wind-chill equivalent temperatures are regularly reported in the mass media since they affect many daily activities. Research on how best to protect soldiers in cold and windy environments supplied the original data that led to the development of graphs such as those shown in Figure 10.8. Correct interpretation of these graphs has implications for maintaining human comfort and safety under very warm, as well as very cold, conditions. Moreover, everyone is interested in remaining comfortable!

Everyone is also in daily contact with many devices that have reflectors designed to control the path of energy. Flashlights, floodlights, photoflash units, automobile headlights, mirrors in telescopes, special-purpose microphones, and radar antennae are some examples of devices that use parabolic surfaces. Why parabolic?

Give each student a piece of wax paper approximately 30 cm on each edge. Tell them to perform each manipulation *after* you demonstrate it on the stage of the overhead projector. Begin by drawing a line, *l*, and a point *P*, not on the line. Then fold the paper sharply so that *P* coincides with any point on *l* (Figure 10.9a). Open the paper and tell the students to put arrowheads on the ends of *l* so that this drawn line will not become confused with the folds they are about to make. Then tell them to match *P* to a different point on *l*, fold sharply, and open the paper. They should continue matching to different points along *l* with a fold being made each time. Instruct the students to keep folding until the pattern shown in Figure 10.9b is developed. Then ask why the folds were trapped into the outline of a parabola.

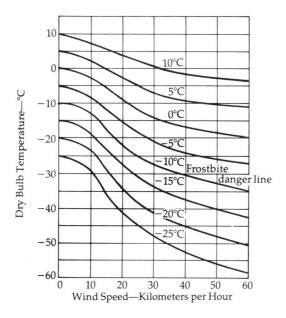

Fig. 10.8   Wind-chill graph.

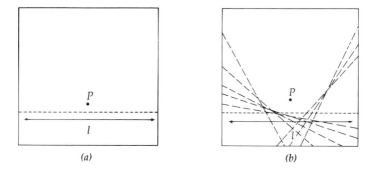

(a)   (b)

Fig. 10.9   Wax paper parabola construction.

If your students have taken a second-year algebra course, they should be able to state the locus definition: "A parabola is the locus of all points equidistant from a fixed line and a given point not on that line." Have the students examine the geometric relationship of a fold to P and a particular point to which P was matched. If necessary, have them connect P and the corresponding point. They should realize that the fold is the perpendicular bisector of the line segment and be able to make a convincing argument why the folding process yields the parabola. Someone may remember that the point P is called the *focus* (from the Latin for hearth or burning place). Perhaps a student will remember setting paper on fire by placing it at the focus of a parabolic mirror that was reflecting the sun's rays. Similarly, the focusing of light rays enables us to see objects far off in space, as with a telescope. The focusing property is used in the reverse, as in the case with loudspeakers when sound waves emanate at the focus and are reflected off the parabolic surface (all of these are actually paraboloidal surfaces) to reach a large audience. Each of these examples is an adaptation of the property of a parabolic reflecting surface—that all light rays emanating from the focus are reflected out parallel to the axis of the parabola and to each other. Why does this happen? For a start, identify the angles of incidence and reflection for a light ray and try to show that these are congruent. (For geometry students interested in a proof of this property, refer them to pages 561–563 of Fremont, 1969.)

These examples of "light" paths of reflecting surfaces should remind you of the Introductory Activity in Chapter 3 when you worked with a plane mirror. The property of plane mirror reflection can be extended to strategies for aiming a billiard ball on a pool table or for striking a golf ball so it will fall into the cup in miniature golf. In each case, the eyeballing of congruent angles of incidence and reflection and dependence on the physics of rebounding objects lead to success. Before we leave this fascinating subject of light paths, we urge you to talk with an area stage designer about the uses of various reflecting surfaces, plane and each of the conical forms, to achieve certain stage effects.

For better or worse, automobiles are of high interest to nearly every teenager, and sources of relevant information are readily available. Several popular automobile magazines regularly publish acceleration and stopping distance curves for current models. These can be used to teach interpretation of graphs and the use of controls in comparative testing, as well as to lead to exploration of those design features that can be manipulated to improve results. Newspaper advertising proclaiming EPA estimates for gasoline mileage can be compared with actual road-test results reported in automobile magazines. The disparate figures will stimulate consideration of the effects of various test conditions and point out the dangers of trying to interpret data in the absence of firm knowledge of the conditions under which the data were obtained. Data on the efficiency, cost and emission dangers from various kinds of fuel can be used as a lead-in for discussion of a contemporary S/T/S theme, air pollution on our highways.

Younger students, who are not yet ready for driver education class and the attendant responsibilities, can examine testing conditions in a different way—by designing and constructing paper airplanes, **with** the teacher's permission. Why not set up a contest to see whose plane will fly the longest time and/or follow the straightest glide path? A great deal of applied science can be used in deciding on the rules (such as standardizing launch conditions or limiting the kinds and amounts of construction materials) as well as in designing the planes. Arrangements can usually be made to hold the contest in the gymnasium while the physical education class is using outdoor facilities. Just be sure that no litter is left there after the contest.

Sports are a rich source of science ideas. We've already alluded to that in questions 3 and 4 in Table 10.2, and the use of reflection properties in sports involving bouncing a ball off some kind of backboard. What has perspiration got to do with sports or with science? Anyone who engages in any kind of athletic activity, whether team sports or individual fitness activity, has experienced the smarting sensation and salty taste when perspiration runs into the eyes and onto the lips. It is also common knowledge that one gets thirsty after perspiring for a while. However, it is a rare student who knows much about the importance of the water and dissolved salts in this substance. For example, a 2 percent water loss initiates the thirst sensation, while a 5 percent loss generates intense thirst, elevated body temperature, and a rapid rise in pulse rate. Circulatory failure and subsequent death are consequences of losses of 7 percent. The salt component is equally significant, since losses of 37 grams per 45 kilograms of body weight are associated with shock and a drop in systolic blood pressure.

After this type of information has been presented, other relevant questions are likely to be raised. "How much of the perspiration is water and how much of it is salt?" "What kinds of salt are involved?" "How much lag time is involved in replacing perspired water and salts by ingested equivalents?" "How many sweat glands are there in the body?" "How are these glands distributed over the body?" "Is it true that dogs perspire only through their tongues?" Questions such as these lead to consideration of many important aspects of human physiology. An excellent attention-sustainer is to list the percentage composition of perspiration on the chalkboard. Then do the same for urine in a column next to the one for perspiration. Finally, ask if there are any questions as to why regular bathing is highly recommended!

There is really no end to the possibilities for teaching science by using the everyday world. Table 10.7 lists additional types of everyday ideas and questions to introduce or review some related science concepts/principles.

By this point you should have noticed that sources of everyday materials are all around us *if* we are diligent observers. Those data tables and graphs in the local newspaper, photos of nature found in last year's calendar or taken on your last vacation trip, the cartoon on a science/technology/society topic, the pine cones you found outside (Count the bracts and look at the spirals!)—all of these are potential sources of teaching ideas. If they are to be on hand when you need them, they must be systematically stored in your resource file, annotated as to potential use, and able to be readily retrieved when needed. *Now* is the time to start!

10.4 SUMMARY AND SELF-CHECK

Although constant references to students' interests have been made throughout this chapter, the authors chose to shade in only the "Structure of Science" portion of the instructional schema. Why? We wanted to emphasize the products and processes of science in their relation to other subjects and other areas of everyday life. Thus, attention was drawn to the shape, size, and function of animal and plant cells in the dodecahedron space-packing question. Moreover, we suggested strategies designed to *introduce* science concepts and rules, as well as

Table 10.7

Selected Everyday Ideas as Sources of Science Instruction

Everyday ideas	Science-related questions
1. Obtain advertisements for several brands of paper towels (or other products).	1. Have students design and carry out experimental procedures to determine which brand of towel absorbs liquid the fastest. Which absorbs the most?
2. Obtain data on several automobiles, such as engine size, number of cylinders, amount of horsepower, fuel consumption, etc.	2. How do engines in automobiles compare to engines in other machinery? What happens chemically when fuel is "burned"?
3. My size, my height, my weight: How do I compare with my classmates? With an "average" person my own age?	3. Make out a personal chart and record your height and weight. Keep track of all you eat for a week. Determine nutritional value of your diet. Compare nutritional data with that from fast food restaurants or other snack foods.
4. Interview several sports coaches at your school and make a list of the exercises that the various athletes perform.	4. Compare the types of exercises performed in each sport. Explain the physiological and training benefits for each exercise. Are there differences in exercises for boys versus girls?

strategies designed to promote retention and transfer through applications in situations novel to the students.

We emphasized the everyday world of the students, in contrast to applications of the work world. We did so, not because the latter are unimportant, but because for many students, these adult applications are not real to them. Once again, note the influence of Piagetian theory. If we are to convince students that science is relevant for them, the connections must be concrete and familiar. Once these connections have been made, we agree on the interest-potential of applications from the field of medicine, avalanche control, the criminal justice system, genetic research, and so on. However, these must be presented in an understandable and interest-catching manner.

Throughout the various illustrations, the reader was reminded to consider the intellectual developmental stage of the students, to be alert to the dangers of overgeneralization, and to cooperate with mathematics colleagues in an intellectually honest presentation of the science/mathematics interface.

Now you should be able to:

1. Describe several ways in which science teachers can use mathematics in the teaching of science.

2. Give *at least three* reasons to support an emphasis on the science/mathematics interface in science classes.

3. Describe ways in which several areas other than mathematics can be used to teach science.

4. Cite *at least four* sources of mathematics-related materials and *at least four* sources of everyday-world materials that have potential for teaching science.

5. Add to your resource file ideas that use mathematics, other school subjects, and everyday phenomena in the teaching of science.

10.5 SIMULATION/PRACTICE ACTIVITIES

A. Common patterns often escape student attention. One such is the case of binding energies of the nuclei of isotopes. Prepare a table listing isotopes in order of increasing mass. Include one column for the calculation of binding energy and another for binding energy per particle. Graph the data and look for a pattern. What occurs for the points that represent the isotopes ^4_2He, $^{12}_6C$ and $^{16}_8O$? Infer a relationship. Identify the mathematical models used in this analysis and be ready to discuss their importance in arriving at an explanation of this scientific relationship.

B. The logarithmic, or equiangular, spiral is a property of dead tissues rather than living tissues, according to D'Arcy Thompson (1917/1961). Thompson provided details on the chambered Nautilus and listed several other examples of structures that display the equiangular spiral: a snail's shell, an elephant's tusk, a beaver's tooth, a cat's claws, a canary's claws, and a ram's horn. Study any of these structures by observing the varied lines of growth in one of the structures or in a good photograph. Compare the organism at various stages of growth with the spiral shown in Figure 10.5a. Next, look up a definition of the logarithmic spiral in a mathematics dictionary. Finally, read Thompson's explanation in Chapter 6 of *On Growth and Form* (see Suggestions for Further Study) to compare your ideas with his.

C. An easy way to help a junior high class understand that the triangle is a rigid figure is to give them equal lengths of plastic straws and straight pins. Have them construct equilateral figures of 3, 4, 5, 6, 7, and 8 sides. Project sample models on the overhead. Then display the picture of a golfer shown in Figure 10.10 and ask the students to find the triangles and to explain how these shapes help in preserving the stability needed in golf.

D. Read **two** of the science/everyday world articles listed here and write brief reviews of each:

Burger, W. (1987). "Ode to slinky on its birthday." *Science Teacher*, **54**, (7), 25–28.

Carle, M. (1988). "Olympic wrestling and angular momentum." *The Physics Teacher*, **26**, 92–94.

Greenslade, T. B. (1983). "More bicycle physics." *The Physics Teacher*, **21**, 360–363.

McGehee, J. (1988). "Physics students' day at Six Flags/Magic Mountain." *The Physics Teacher*, **26**, 12–17.

E. Find examples of photos, slides, clippings or cartoons that might be used to teach students something about the interface of science and mathematics or science and the everyday world. Write a brief explanation of the way(s) the item might be used in a lesson.

Fig. 10.10   The golfer.

SUGGESTIONS FOR FURTHER STUDY

AIMS Education Foundation. P.O. Box 7766, Fresno, CA 93747

Project AIMS (Activities for the Integration of Mathematics and Science) consists of a series of books (Grades 5–9) containing lessons on aerodynamics, the human body, foods, geology, the environment, shadows and more. A newsletter and poster series are also available.

Bell, M. S. (1972). *Mathematical uses and models in our everyday world* (Studies in Mathematics, Vol. 20). Stanford, CA: School Mathematics Study Group.

The author provides an extensive treasury of problem materials ranging from data on diets to the characteristics of precious gems. The needed mathematics may involve simple calculations, graphing, or the solution of quadratic equations. This is a prime source, which should be owned by every science teacher, for it merits repeated use.

Boehm, D. A. (Ed.). (1988). *Guinness book of world records.* New York: Sterling Publications Co., Inc.

This paperback is regularly updated to incorporate the latest records set by both pros and amateurs. The authors have more than once illustrated ways in which such data might be used to teach science. We encourage you to browse through the latest edition.

Hay, J. G. (1985). *The biomechanics of sports techniques.* Englewood Cliffs, NJ: Prentice-Hall.

In this easy-to-read text, Hay provides an analysis of science concepts and principles involved in baseball, basketball, football, golf, softball, gymnastics, swimming, and track and field events.

House, P. A. (1980). *Interactions of science and mathematics.* Columbus, OH: ERIC Clearinghouse for Science, Mathematics, and Environmental Education.

This book contains a variety of science investigations requiring minimal equipment. The investigations are designed to help the teacher respond to that typical question by students—Why do we need to know this?

Newman, J. (Ed.). (1956). *The world of mathematics* (Vol. 1, 2, 3, 4). New York: Simon and Schuster.

This set of four volumes includes essays on the mathematics of "gifted" birds, the kinetics of gases, crystals, mathematics in golf and gambling, and mathematics in war and art. Two essays, Jeans's and Haldane's, are particularly valuable as sources of science/mathematics ideas.

Ontario Science Center. (1989). *Sportsworks: More than 50 fun games and activities that explore the science of sports*. Reading, MA: Addison-Wesley.

In these simple activities for the upper elementary and middle school grades, the science of sports is explored. Activities include tests for bouncing basketballs and why cyclists attempt to stay in a draft during races.

Petit, J. (1985). *The adventures of Archibald Higgins* (Transl. by I. Stewart). Providence, RI: Janson Publications, Inc.

We recommend two books in this series as particularly appropriate in terms of the science/mathematics interface—*Everything is relative* and *The black hole*. Bright senior high students will find the cartoon approach to complex ideas from physics and mathematics both challenging and enjoyable.

Polya, G. (1963). *Mathematical methods in science* (Studies in Mathematics, Vol. 11). Stanford, CA: School Mathematics Study Group.

Polya's paperback guides the reader through the struggles of Newton, Galileo, Kepler, and others. He describes the way monumental results were developed on the basis of simple mathematical concepts. The book abounds with examples of the contiguous development of science and mathematics and is highly recommended.

SMSG. (1965). *Mathematics and living things* (Rev. ed.). Stanford, CA: School Mathematics Study Group.

A student text and teacher's commentary are available under this title. The science activities require only commonly available or homemade apparatus. The mathematics ideas are developed inductively for the most part by finding common patterns in the data. Main topic titles include: "Leaves and Natural Variation," "Natural Variation—Us," "Muscle Fatigue," and "Size of Cells." Our student teachers and cooperating teachers rate this set as A-1.

Steinhaus, H. (1969). *Mathematical snapshots* (3rd ed.). New York: Oxford Press.

Steinhaus uses photographs and diagrams to present mathematical phenomena as they relate to the real world. His illustrations include the patterns formed by dried mud, the properties of soap bubbles and the paths squirrels follow up a tree. This is a highly recommended source, which you should put at the top of your list.

Thompson, D. W. (1961). *On growth and form* (Abridged ed.). Cambridge, England: University Press. (Originally published in 1917.)

Thompson's text is an existence proof for the thesis that science is a large part of our everyday life. In masterful, clear, and even poetic fashion, Thompson talks of drops of rain, the spider's web, the forms of cells, and the shapes of snow crystals. (His discourse on the equiangular spiral was cited earlier in this chapter.)

CHAPTER ELEVEN

RESOURCES FOR SCIENCE INSTRUCTION

Gold Is Where You Find It

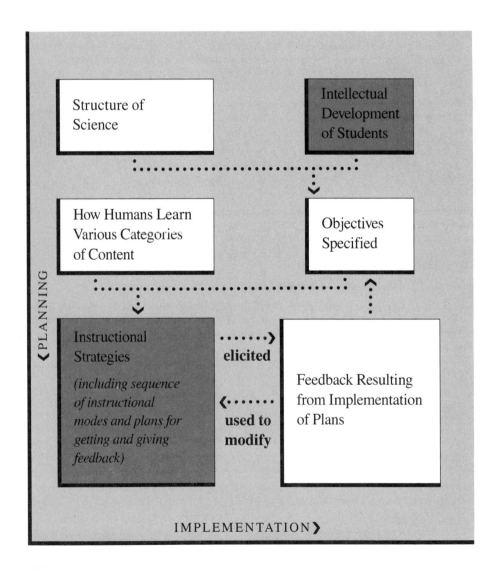

If you've been interacting with the text, you have no doubt realized that Chapters 1–8 comprise a cycle of instruction with each chapter focused on one or two components of the instructional model. Chapter 9 was designed to help provide perspective to the teacher—a perspective that at one and the same time sheds light on the past and the present and points the way to intelligent uses of contemporary curricular materials. Chapter 10 played a complementary role in that you were alerted to the instructional potential of other school subjects and non-school areas—areas outside the academic aspects of subject matter *per se*. These last two chapters were intended to add depth and breadth to the integrated approach to instruction that evolved in Chapters 1–8. Now you should be ready to use that approach in planning and teaching.

Why have we devoted an entire chapter to resources? And why so late? After all, we did recommend that you begin collecting resource ideas as early as Chapter 4. Moreover, we continually provided illustrations of a variety of references. Then what is the focus of this chapter?

In this chapter, we look at the everyday world of concrete objects, movable devices, people and issues to see how they might relate to science instruction. We know that all too often by the time the teacher sits down to plan a lesson on chemical equations, eclipses, or genetics, there is a frantic last-minute search for concrete materials that could be used in a demonstration. Then, the teacher remembers the "junk" thrown away last week that might have been used in this lesson or the TV program that could have been taped to use as an advance organizer. This chapter, then, is based on the premise that part of the long-term planning that supports meaningful instruction depends on storing in a Resource File the science teacher's collectibles. Our students have found that they become better collectors after they have had some teaching experience; thus, this chapter is presented late in the text. We are also cognizant of the life-long study of teaching in which the best inservice teachers continually engage. So in the final section of the chapter, we briefly outline some of the resources available through professional associations, through associations devoted to work on contemporary issues and through teacher participation in research.

Why did we elect to shade in the "Instructional Strategies" and the "Intellectual Development of Students" portions of the instructional model? The reason for the first choice is probably obvious to you since instructional modes are key elements in strategy design. If you recall that research on adolescent reasoning demonstrates the essential role of concrete experiences in learning abstractions, then the rationale for shading in the second box becomes clear. For this same reason, we ask you to begin your interaction with the ideas in this chapter by engaging in the concrete experience that follows.

11.1 INTRODUCTORY ACTIVITY

Seeing is not the same as observing.

Go to a multipurpose store (such as Woolworth's, K-Mart, or Korvette's). Visit the hardware, toy, notions, stationery, sewing, pet, and household departments.

A. Make a list of all inexpensive items that are potential pieces of teaching equipment. Specify the projected use of each item. For starters, think of the materials included in previous illustrations in this text.

B. Compare your list with that of two or more other classmates.

C. Keep this list handy and modify it as needed after you finish studying this chapter.

11.2 INEXPENSIVE EQUIPMENT AND SUPPLIES

If you were surprised at the length of the lists compiled by you and your classmates, you are in good company. As soon as you begin to observe the teaching potential of all you encounter, the most mundane objects take on scientific characteristics. For example, a croquet ball may be perceived as a pendulum bob and the cutoff top of a plastic bleach jug as a funnel. Table 11.1 lists items like balls and jars. Some may be purchased, but most may be found in the garage, kitchen cupboard, sewing basket, school cafeteria, art class, repair shops, and even enroute to the trash can. As you read the list in Table 11.1, try to concoct one or two ways in which each item could contribute to a lesson.

Don't be overly concerned if you draw a blank on some items at first. We have provided illustrations of the uses of a few of these. After interacting with the reading, make a second attempt to identify uses of items that stumped you on the first go-around. Then be on the alert for other potentially useful pieces of "junk" and add these to your collection.

We have not included standard science lab equipment in this list. If, as an inservice teacher, you are asked to place an order for new equipment, you'll want to consult some of the available science catalogues for ideas and prices. A list of a few of these can be found at the end of this chapter. We also have not included computers or computer-related material since these are not in the same category as the items in the list of "Usable Junk." However, the importance of such equipment in the science classroom is without question. There are grants and discounts available to schools for the purchase of computer equipment. Before a major purchase of this kind is undertaken, the teacher (and preferably the entire science department) should study the advantages and disadvantages of the proposed computer system, the kinds of educational software available for the system, and its potential for diversification in instruction. Bramble and Mason (1985) provide some specific pre-purchase ideas in their chapter "Getting started" in *Computers in schools* published by McGraw Hill. A field trip by the science teachers to one or more schools using microcomputers—to talk with other teachers, to see classroom uses and to try out the system—is one viable way of getting specific information before making a major purchase.

Table 11.1
Usable "Junk"

Bags and baggies: plastic
Bags: assorted sizes (paper)
Ball bearings
Balloons: assorted sizes
Balls: ping pong, golf, baseball
Bicycle inner tube
Bird's nest
Boxes: assorted sizes (cardboard)
Buttons: assorted sizes
Candles
Cans: assorted sizes
Cards: index (assorted sizes)
Cartons: milk (1/2 pt., pt., 1/2 gal.)
Clay: modeling or putty
Cloth: misc. pieces and colors
Clothespins: pincer type
Coat hangers: wire
Computer pinhole strips
Contact paper: transparent
Cotton: roll or balls
Corks: assorted sizes
Cups: paper
Dowels : wooden
Dress snaps
Egg cartons: colored
Elastic thread
Felt scraps
Fish line
Flashlight bulbs and receptacles
Flower pots
Foil

Funnels
Glass: flat pieces
Household chemicals: alcohol, salt
    ammonia water, baking soda, food
    coloring, iodine, lemon, lye, juice,
    mineral oil, sugar, vinegar
Jars: baby food, both sizes
    with tops
Jars: pint, quart and one gal. size
    with screw tops
Lead shot
Leaves: dried and pressed
Magnets
Magnifying glasses
Marbles

Mechanical toys
Mirrors: plane, curved
Musical instruments (toy)
Nails
Pantyhose
Paper: construction, wax
Paper clips
Paper fasteners
Pins: common and safety
Pipe cleaners: white and colored
Plastic tape
Plastic wrap
Poker chips
Razor blades
Rope
Sand
Sandpaper
Scissors
Screws: assorted sizes
Seeds
Shirt cardboards
Soda straws
Soil
Sponges: assorted sizes
Springs: assorted sizes
Stoppers: rubber
Stopwatch
Strainers: kitchen
String
Styrofoam
Tape: electrician's, masking,
    transparent
Thermometers: Celsius
Tongue depressors
Toothpicks

Tools: hammer, screwdriver, drill,
    saw, tin snips, plane
Tubes: cardboard, metal, rubber

Thread
Velcro swatches
Washers (metal): assorted sizes
Wire and wire ties
Wood
Yarn: colored

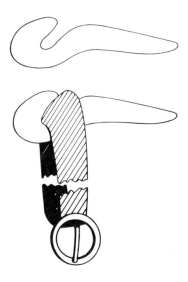

Fig. 11.1   "Sky hook" demonstration.

11.3 USES OF COLLECTIBLES IN THE SCIENCE CLASSROOM

In the paragraphs that follow, selected uses of equipment from Table 11.1 are outlined as they pertain to specific instructional modes or activities used in conjunction with one or more of these modes.

Demonstration

For example, two inflated balloons connected by a long piece of thread make a good demonstration of static electricity. Suspend them from the middle of the connecting thread and then charge each one by rubbing it on a student's hair. Then try wool and a variety of synthetic cloth. This apparatus is large enough for all to see and sensitive enough to be thoroughly convincing.

Use a styrofoam ball to throw "incurves," "outcurves," and "drops" that "break" dramatically. Ask the baseball coach to show you how to do this. Such a demonstration breathes new life into Bernoulli's principle.

Ask an industrial arts teacher to cut up a scrap piece of wood following the pattern in Figure 11.1. Keep this out of sight while you demonstrate that a meter stick will balance on your fingertip at the 50 cm mark. Then demonstrate the point of balance of the "sky hook" with and without a man's belt inserted in the slot. This has proved to be a way of stimulating level III and above thinking on the topic of leverage!

Who ever heard of boiling water in a paper bag? Assert that you can do it *over an open flame*. Remove the top and bottom from a coffee or juice can and make air slots around the bottom rim with a punch-type can opener, as shown

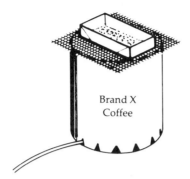

Fig. 11.2   Boiling water demonstration.

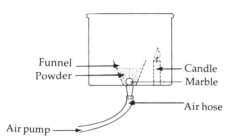

Fig. 11.3   Dust explosion.

in Figure 11.2. Cut a rectangular piece from a grocery bag and fold into a tray about 4 cm deep. Paperclips are sufficient to hold the folded corners in place. Use either a lighted Bunsen burner or candle as a heat source inside the can. Cover the can with either a piece of window screen or wire gauze. Fill the paper bag tray with water to a depth of 2 cm, place it on the screening, and bring to the boiling point. Question students about the concepts of kindling temperature, conduction, and specific heat as they watch the water continue to boil.

A coffee can with a friction top can be used for a striking demonstration of the dust explosion phenomenon. Punch a hole in the bottom and arrange it with lighted candle, plastic funnel, marble, and lycopodium powder as shown in Figure 11.3. Darken the room and then force a blast of air through the air hose **after** making sure all are at a safe distance from the can.

Laboratory

Obtain enough colorless plastic shoeboxes with friction-fit tops to supply students working in pairs. First, have one student in each pair mark off 2 cm depths on the sides of the boxes while the other makes an irregularly shaped mountain of modeling clay and fits it inside the box. Water is then added to the level of the first mark; the top is placed on the box; and a magic marker is used to trace the high-water mark on the mountain as seen from above. This is repeated until the box has been filled with water in increments of 2 cm. The resulting outlines on the top are a contour map of the mountain.

Plastic baggies are great for measuring the amount of transpiration from leaves. Students are instructed to weigh their baggie, fasten it over a group of leaves of a plant with twist-type fasteners, leave it for 24 hours, and then remove and weigh the moist baggie. The difference in weight in grams equals the weight of water lost in one day by the number of leaves enclosed. An estimate of the percent of total leaves covered makes possible an approximate calculation of total daily water loss by transpiration. This lab makes a nice followup to the respiration lessons outlined in Chapter 3 of this text.

Middle-school students can begin to form concepts of positive and negative valence by manipulating nuts and bolts as analogs of elements. It becomes obvious that one can assemble nuts to bolts but that nut-to-nut and bolt-to-bolt connections are not possible. Short bolts that accept only one nut, longer ones that accept two nuts and still longer bolts upon which three nuts can be threaded, help establish the notions of various combining capacities.

Distribute a piece of wax paper to each student and instruct the students to hold their paper flat on top of a page of print. Distribute an eyedropper and a baby food jar of water to each pair of students. Next, have the students use the eyedropper to place a single drop of water on the wax paper. As soon as all have noted the magnifying effect of a single drop of water over a lower-case letter, tell them to make separate pools of two, three, four, and five drops respectively and compare the effects on the same lower-case letter. Next, lenses salvaged from flashlights (or other discarded magnifying lenses of all types) can be used to investigate image formation. Meter sticks supported by scraps of wood with slots cut in them are useful aids for quantification of results. Index cards make satisfactory screens for location of images formed by the lenses.

Students frequently have trouble counting their own pulses before and after exercise. Pieces of smooth aluminum foil, glass, or mirror about 1 cm on each edge can be balanced on the pulse just above the wrist. Bright light reflected from the glass casts an image on the ceiling or wall that deflects as much as 15–20 cm with each pulse. An alternative technique is to insert the point of a thumbtack into a match stick and then balance the head of the tack on the pulse area. The match will bob impressively with each pulse.

Individual Projects

Some biology students are interested in dissecting a wider variety of plants and animals than can be done during class and laboratory time. Single-edge razor blades make effective scalpels. Pineboard scraps from the shop make fine dissecting boards, and cake tins partially filled with wax serve as dissecting trays. Common pins, string, household tweezers, and flashlight lenses all substitute well for their commercial counterparts. Before performing dissections, students might react to ethics issues treated in articles on the use of animals in classroom activities, such as the editorial by Orlans, entitled "Should students harm or destroy animal life" (1988). (The entire reference is listed in the References.)

Other biology students may be interested in preparing articulated skeletons. In this case, large metal cans are useful for boiling flesh off the bones. A drill with fine bits and small pieces of copper wire provide the means to reassemble the skeletons.

Those who sell competing brands of antifreeze claim to offer the best protection against freezing while providing insurance against corrosion of cooling system parts. Similarly, highly touted motor oils are promoted as preventing corrosion of vital engine parts at high temperatures while maintaining their viscosity characteristics. Water baths constructed of juice cans, polished pieces of metal scraps, and thermometers can be used to check on the validity of such claims.

The rockhounds among your students will find plastic egg containers invaluable for sorting, storing, and displaying their collections. Budding young botanists will find the same containers ideal for starting seedlings if they poke a small hole in the bottom of each compartment.

What would anyone want with discarded pantyhose? Cut off the panty part and attach the top of a leg section to a wire coat hanger bent into a circular shaped hoop. Either attach three pieces of cord to the hoop for towing behind a boat or wire the hoop to a broom handle and you have a plankton net. This piece of equipment can be useful in a number of individual projects in aquatic biology.

Individual projects have great potential for assisting in the development of process skills. One way to encourage this development is to ask the student to keep a log of the project—its construction, data collected, results, and conclusions. Communicating about science is an important goal of science instruction and writing is an invaluable way of communicating.

Did you notice that some of the suggested individual projects could have been used as laboratories for larger groups? In fact, some of the demonstrations outlined earlier can be developed as laboratories, just as most laboratory activities have promise as demonstrations. Continue thinking of multiple uses as you read the sections that follow.

Bulletin Boards

A corkboard surface, a wall, a chalkboard, or even a square of poster board can be used as the backdrop for a static or movable display. Use loops of masking tape on movable colored cutout shapes and transform an unused section of chalkboard into a vertical demonstration table. Have students bring in photographs that illustrate examples of various habitats and make a collage of their examples. Titles are readily constructed by "writing" in yarn with the aid of a stapler or by twisting pipe cleaners into the shape of letters.

A biology teacher with an abundance of chalkboard space converted the side and the rear areas into bulletin board space. Large pieces of colored paper were attached to the chalkboard with masking tape. The names of major animal phyla were used as titles for each section. Students brought in magazine photographs and glued them together to make montages of the phyla.

A feltboard (or a velcro board) is useful if you want the students (or the teacher) to move cutout materials around on the display. Cover one side of a sheet of plywood with felt or velcro. (Ask the industrial arts teacher for help.) Staple it securely to the reverse side. Use light poster paper to trace and cut out the shapes (or paste on the paper pictures of plants or animals) you want to move. Paste a piece of flannel or a piece of velcro on each piece of poster paper, depending on the type of board you've constructed. Then place the shapes on the board; move them to different positions; move them again. Some teachers use this kind of board in a classification task. First the board is separated, perhaps by two large yarn enclosures. Then the movable pieces (*e.g.*, fruits and flowers) are moved by the students into the correct enclosure.

Physical science teachers can draw large-scale circuit diagrams on plywood and then fasten actual parts next to each of the appropriate schematic representations. Similarly, earth science teachers can display mineral specimens next to index cards that include summaries of important characteristics, interesting facts, and important uses of each.

One innovative middle school teacher adapted the tree of science schema (Chapter 4 of this book) to the construction of a "tree of life" model. She supplied the basic model at the start of the year and displayed it permanently on a bulletin board. As students studied each concept, principle, or thought model, they added its labeled symbol (in the form of a leaf, flower, fruit, or subbranch) to the colorful display.

Displays do not have to be on flat surfaces, but can be in the form of three-dimensional models. For example, one of our student teachers got his students interested in making mobile models of the atomic structures of key elements. These were hung from ceiling tile frames and frequently referred to by teacher and students during chemistry lessons. Notice that this display could have started as individual student projects and then become a display. Think about the relative advantages and disadvantages of having the display done in class as a group project, versus being primarily done outside of class by individuals. What differences in directions would be needed? What feedback strategies would be needed in each case to assess student understanding?

There is also a place for current event clippings relative to topics under study or to emerging issues, discoveries, or new applications of science. Attention can be directed to such items by arranging them on a bulletin board so the items look important. For example, incorporate large index cards that have questions written on them with magic marker. "Were the data collected under controlled conditions?" "What other inferences could be drawn from the same data?" "What is the unstated assumption in this report?" Pieces of colored yarn can be stapled to the question cards and to relevant sections of the clippings. Students should be encouraged to look for such news items and add to the display. They can also help identify the questions that need to be asked about the substance of the clipping.

We encourage you to *use* bulletin board displays as a basis for demonstrations, as a basis for a problem-solving lesson, as a cue card for review lessons, or as an attention-getter for a unit. Bulletin board displays should not be merely decorative additions to the room; they should be incorporated into lessons and serve as a basis for evaluation.

Games and Competitions

Perhaps pleasant past experiences cause students to equate a game with fun. Whatever the reason, a well-designed and well-organized game has the potential for getting and keeping attention. When you visited the toy and games department as part of the Introductory Activity, you probably noted a few commercial games and kits that could be used in the science classroom. Some that we have found useful are:

1. Clean Waters
2. Evolution
3. Pollution

4. Predator Prey
5. Space Hop
6. Weather Slam

Most of the above games are suitable for use by at most two or three students at a time. Keep them in mind when you plan diversified activities but be prepared to modify them for class-size groups. Be alert to the fact that some science concepts and principles may have been bent a bit in the process of fitting into the game format. These cases should be pointed out to students to prevent misunderstandings.

In similar fashion, you can modify other games not originally designed for the classroom. Watch any of the popular game shows on television and take notes as to the essential features of the game—the rules, the penalties, the kind of game board, and so on. Cross-wits becomes a combination of a crossword puzzle and a "less than 20-questions" game. If your puzzle were projected on the overhead, the entire class could follow the game. The contestants might be filling in names of concepts, formulas, or principles, or citing reasons for some assertions. There are no holds barred on the content of the individual items or the key question related to the individual clues. Moreover, the entire class could play the game if two teams were designated and appropriate rules for deciding the order of the contestants were outlined.

The game of Trivia can be adapted for use in the classroom with the help of the students. Ask each one to prepare trivia cards, by topic, about scientists and their contributions, or perhaps about the relationship of a concept or rule to some real world application. A student committee might take the responsibility of screening all cards and getting decks ready for classroom use. More cards or decks could be added during the year.

Finally, don't forget the games of childhood. Twenty questions, Who dunnit? and What's my question? are always ready to be adapted for a quick review or a probing, challenging exploration.

11.4 NONTYPICAL USES OF AUDIOVISUAL AND TECHNOLOGICAL AIDS

Cassette audiotape recorders can be used to bring a wide variety of sounds into the classroom, such as the sounds of the countdown at a space center, bird songs, parts of a speech by a famous scientist, and radio commercials. Some teachers have also recorded their own mini-lectures designed to accompany a demonstration, filmstrip, or slide presentation. Recall the student teacher's use of a tape recorder to give directions in a lesson on slide preparation in Chapter 7. The unusual use of a tape recorder not only got attention, but also freed the teacher to move about the class observing individual student psychomotor learning. Furthermore, if repetition of instructions is needed, the tape recorder will faithfully repeat verbatim. Teacher preparation needs to include (1) speaking slowly and clearly with pauses built in and (2) asking someone else to listen to the tape and try to follow the instructions.

Homemade charts are easy to make and valuable to have. Obtain some of those outdated pull-down maps from the social studies department. Turn them over and you have blank charts that one of your artistically inclined students can convert into custom-designed visuals.

If you have access to a microcomputer with a scanner, you can scan cartoons, pictures, graphs and the like and transfer these to class handouts to be photocopied.

The uninterrupted and unaltered viewing of a motion picture film is not always the most effective use of this medium. Shut off the projector at key points and question students as to (1) the major points developed thus far and (2) their predictions of what will happen next. Turn off the sound and supply your own audio when the commentary is either too sophisticated or too childish for your students. Reverse the film, start it again, and ask students to observe a sequence a second time. Moreover, don't overlook the possibility of making a motion picture of your own design. Many schools own a good quality motion picture or video camera. Typically it is signed out to the athletic department on a semipermanent basis, but since it is school property, you should be able to arrange to use it.

Filmstrips and slides also lend themselves to imaginative use. Students who have been absent for several days can be put in one corner of the room with projector, filmstrip, and teacher's guide while you are busy with other students. After viewing the strip and reading the guide, the catch-up session with the teacher will be facilitated. Some filmstrips may contain only a dozen relevant frames. Cut these out and mount them in empty 35 mm slide mounts available from any photographic supply store. Homemade filmstrips are easily produced by turning a 35 mm camera on its side while photographing the scenes. Then simply instruct

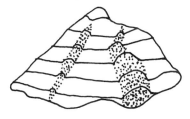

Fig. 11.4 Projected contour lines.

the developing house to "Develop only. Do not cut into separate frames." Making your own sets of instructional slides is even easier. The yearbook advisor is the likely custodian of a school-owned 35 mm camera, which you can arrange to borrow. Students in the photography club can be enlisted to instruct you in its use or to supply both the camera and skilled labor to get the job done. Also, investigate some of the slide sets available from science supply houses. Some can be projected on the chalkboard with room lights on so teacher and students can add labels, auxiliary segments and graph lines with chalk. These are designed to promote an inquiry approach and many of them are quite effective.

In addition, a slide projector may be used as a light source for all kinds of demonstrations. Get an outdated globe of the earth from the social studies department, paint it with dull black paint, and use white chalk to mark on it the Arctic Circle, the Antarctic Circle, the equator, and both tropics. Darken the room and set up the slide projector in the position of the sun. Day and night and the seasons are demonstrated by manipulating the earth model. Add a tennis ball tacked to a string and eclipses can also be shown. Another use requires a small piece of acetate cut and mounted in a 35 mm slide frame. Draw parallel lines horizontally on the acetate and project them on a white cloth covering an irregular pile of objects (See Figure 11.4). Arrange the cloth to show contour lines representing a wide variety of geological features.

Overhead projectors have become the most common visual aid in the schools. Typically their use is limited to projecting acetate-based images on a screen, but they do have additional uses. Trace or "bake" (use a thermofax or photocopy machine) a complicated diagram on acetate, project it on the chalkboard after school, go to the board, and trace the lines with a soft lead pencil. The lines will be visible to you, but not to the students, as you chalk over each in turn during a lecture and question/answer session in class the next day. Also, some demonstrations are more effective if projected on a screen. For example,

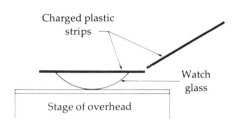

Fig. 11.5   Static electricity demonstration.

place bar magnets on the stage. Cover them with an acetate sheet, sprinkle on iron filings, and tap the sheet gently. Another example involves static electricity and is set up as shown in Figure 11.5. The amount of friction between the bottom of the curved glass and the stage is small and an impressive degree of motion is projected on the screen. Overhead projectors can be used to project large screen computer displays when the appropriate hardware is wired to the computer and placed on the stage. The MacViewFrame is one such example of liquid crystal display (LCD) technology. An image as large as 15 feet can be projected onto a wall or screen. Color changes in various demonstrations are also easier to see if the glass containers are set on the lighted stage of an overhead projector. In this case it is helpful to cover the projection lens with dark cloth or a cardboard mask.

Television equipment is now available in almost every school and offers many unique opportunities for teachers. Science-related programs can be recorded from commercial television during evenings or weekends for class viewing during regular school hours. (Care must be taken not to violate copyright laws.) It is also easy to record phenomena from field trips and laboratory work and play the tape back in slow or stop motion. One experienced teacher used a camcorder to film animal behaviors at a zoo and then used the tape to introduce a unit on animals. Another videotaped the slide preparation demonstration outlined in Chapter 7.

These are just a few ideas to start you thinking about seldom-used audiovisual and technological techniques. We made no attempt to tell you how to thread, set up, or focus these devices. Each make is a bit different, and each comes with instructions for its use. The easiest way to learn the mechanics of these devices is to have someone show you how and supervise your first attempt.

11.5 FIELD TRIPS

Field trips have high potential for contributing to important goals of science instruction *if* they are carefully planned and effectively executed. Among the possible goals are generating interest in the subject, collecting data for further study in class, and observing the use of science in an applied area.

Trips to oil refineries, power plants, drug manufacturing companies, college laboratories, electronics industries, and telephone companies have proved worthwhile for physical science classes. Some examples of field trips oriented toward biology students are (1) visiting various habitats to identify and count organisms, (2) demonstrating the use of soil auger, increment borer, and soil- and water-testing kits, (3) touring the pathology laboratory of a large hospital, and (4) studying the natural history exhibits of a museum. Other types of informal settings, such as science centers, zoos, aquaria and nature centers, are additional sources of exhibits, printed curriculum material, and human resources. Some museums provide enrichment programs for students by taking them behind the scenes to meet with one of the museum's curators and to view stored collections. Other museums provide camp-ins, overnight stays that provide a unique way to generate interest towards science. Whatever the trip, thorough and detailed planning far in advance of the trip is essential. In fact, program coordinators at many informal science institutions now require teachers to meet with their educational staff prior to student visits to cooperatively plan the visit and pre- and post-visit activities.

Safety rules, appropriate clothing, and any special student behaviors need to be specified on a guide sheet and reinforced verbally. These rules and the purposes of the trip should also be included in the parental permission slips that are to be signed and returned prior to the day of the trip. Such slips carry little legal status in a court of law but they do establish consent and often generate parental understanding and support for your efforts. Don't forget to consult the principal's office about arrangements for students who forget to return permission slips. Every school has its own set of regulations governing field trips, and these must be followed from the earliest planning stage through the culmination of the trip.

All trips must be carefully supervised. Here's the time to enlist parental assistance and wider support of your efforts. Followup activities include written reports, laboratory work on collected data, class discussions, and letters of appreciation to those who made the trip possible. A brief oral report to the principal and department chairperson is in order and may well insure cooperation when future trips are planned.

11.6 HUMAN RESOURCES

Don't overlook the human resources available to you for the asking. We have repeatedly referred to the mathematics teacher as a resource person and we encourage you to seek out that expertise and to reciprocate as needed. All of the other staff in the school are also potential human resources. For example, the school nurse can demonstrate and explain the use of a sphygmomanometer. A parent who is a medical doctor can furnish both the actual X-rays, or EKGs, and the information needed for you to construct a bulletin board display. A student's older sister home for a college vacation may be willing to talk about her chemistry major requirements with interested students. A local research scientist or college professor might be willing to consult with a talented student pursuing a science fair project. Someone from the area chapter of the American Chemical Society could be asked to advise on potential laboratory hazards. The president of the area chapter of Trout Unlimited could put you in contact with a person who is an expert in the field of aquatic insect life. A beekeeper might be persuaded to present a lecture-demonstration on the life cycle and habits of honey bees. There are many laboratory technicians in nearby industries and hospitals who could talk about their work and the training required for such careers.

Then, too, don't forget your students. Many of them will have hobbies and skilled training in science-related areas. Musicians, amateur radio operators, electronic-kit builders, photographers, orienteerers, sailing enthusiasts, and readers of science fiction are but a few of the many human resources often overlooked. It is probably obvious that electronic hobbyists could be used to help assemble science equipment purchased in kit form, but what can be done with future sailors? Think in terms of vectors and forces!

11.7 SAFETY AND LEGAL ASPECTS

Teachers are legally responsible for the welfare of students under their supervision. Attendance books have been subpoenaed for evidence in courts of law and teachers have been called upon to testify as to the accuracy of these records. Teachers have been sued for liability when injuries were sustained while the teacher stepped out in the hall for a few moments. Negligence actions have been won against teachers who allowed students to use faulty equipment, perform laboratory exercises that included undue safety hazards, or work without using proper safety devices.

We are not lawyers and thus cannot give legal advice. However, we are experienced teachers and supervisors and can offer tips about how to avoid trouble:

1. Keep accurate attendance records for every class period. Put a written reminder in the "Routines" section of each lesson plan and put a checkmark next to the notation after you do it.

2. Place laboratory safety posters around the classroom and laboratory. Leave these in place permanently and call attention to them frequently.

3. Present a model of correct performance while doing demonstrations. Call attention to both the techniques used and the reasons for using them.

4. Write specific safety precautions (as needed) on each laboratory guide sheet and verbally remind students of these before they begin work.

5. Check all equipment before distributing it to students and instruct them to notify you at once if anything seems to malfunction.

6. Know your state safety laws thoroughly and enforce them religiously. For instance, some states require that *approved* safety glasses be worn by *all* in the room any time hot or corrosive liquids are in use. This includes boiling

water and means glasses covering the eyes—not the hair as some careless students are prone to wear them!

7. Never allow students to clean up broken glassware or chemical spills without your supervision.

8. Train the students to report *all* accidents to you immediately. You, in turn, should report these in writing according to the established policy in your school.

9. Establish a policy that no unauthorized "experiments" are to be attempted by anyone at any time.

10. Supervise actively and thoroughly. No one expects you to be standing next to every student at the same instant, but correcting papers while youngsters work unattended is an invitation to trouble.

11. When you obtain your first teaching position, ask your department chair for permission to contact the local chapter of the American Chemical Society (if not done previously). A member of their safety committee will inspect your classroom and laboratory facilities. Notify your immediate supervisor in *writing* of any unsafe conditions or recommendations.

In the eyes of the law, you are held accountable to behave as a "reasonably prudent adult" and as someone with expert knowledge of science. Fortunately, the record of the science teaching profession has been very good. Unfortunately, some serious accidents have resulted in the loss of life or limb. We recommend that you consider obtaining liability insurance coverage for professional activities as soon as you accept your first teaching position. Some professional organizations include such coverage as part of their package of membership benefits. We also encourage you to begin collecting safety articles for your resource file. Particularly good sources are professional journals, like the *Journal of Chemical Education*, *Science Teacher*, and *The American Biology Teacher*.

11.8 DIFFERENTIATING INSTRUCTION

Sometimes teachers or administrators try to make the best of the difference in needs, interests, and abilities of the human resources of their students by diverse grouping arrangements. Many secondary schools use some kind of homogeneous grouping system, for example, sections for the college-bound and noncollege-bound or classes designated as honors, average, and basic. Regardless of these attempts to subdivide students according to such criteria as IQ scores, reading test scores, grade-point averages, or teacher recommendations, even a casual observer soon notices wide differences in a supposedly homogeneous group of students. For this reason, we believe that differentiation of instruction must take place in *every* class. Again we call attention to the saying: "Different strokes for different folks!" On a day-to-day basis, the teacher can work at this by (1) assigning individual projects that span a wide range of interests and skills, (2) dividing the class into several heterogeneous groups so that a variety of talents may be shared, or using more homogeneous groups, each assigned different activities, (3) initiating a "buddy" system where pairs of students work together at stated times (seek the advice of your cooperating teacher before deciding who will be paired with whom), (4) designing homework assignments with built-in choices, and (5) allowing individual students to browse through science-related reading on a classroom shelf, work on a project, spend more time with challenging problem solving activities, and so on while the teacher and the rest of the class continue a lesson. Doesn't that kind of instruction require a lot of planning time? You bet it does! However, if the payoff for the time and energy you've expended is student learning, then the extra effort is worth it.

If you've realized that the success of such activities also depends heavily on the accurate diagnosis of student talents and weaknesses, then you've taken the first step toward differentiating instruction. Thoughtful observation of selected students followed by conferences with their other teachers will help to sharpen your observation skills. At the same time you need some broad guidelines relative to atypical students. Novice teachers generally find it most helpful to focus on those who are labeled the "slow learner" and the "academically talented."

We remind you that characteristics of these categories of students were outlined in Chapter 3. Moreover, other individual differences in reasoning and approaches to problems were presented in that chapter. It is a good idea to return to that section when you are faced with the diagnosis of learning difficulties of one or more of your students.

An increasingly popular way to individualize instruction within a heterogeneous classroom is by the use of structured small groups working within the guidelines of cooperative learning (Humphreys, Johnson, & Johnson, 1982). In cooperative learning groups, students share ideas and take responsibility for their own learning and for their teammates' learning. Some teachers have used such groups for a single lesson, or a group of lessons. In the next section, we describe an approach to individualization that uses individual laboratory work as well as work in pairs or small groups over the course of a single unit.

The Learning Activity Package Although the novice teacher normally needs to find ways to accommodate atypical students within the usual instructional pattern, there is no doubt that instruction designed to allow students to work at varied rates and on varied materials would be a far better long-term solution to the needs of *all* students. This is the purpose of the instructional materials that we call a Learning Activity Package (LAP).

The three initials in LAP denote the major components of the learning activity package. The *L* in learning is seen as the learning of concepts, rules/principles, and other cognitive objectives plus the learning of related affective and psychomotor objectives. The *A* in activity denotes major emphasis on laboratory activities and constant attention to interaction via visual images, relevant everyday experiences, and thought-provoking questions. The *P* in package denotes a total instructional unit complete with reading material, laboratory directions, projects, instructions to work with other students, hints, feedback (including praise), test(s), answer keys, and more. The package is the student's personal instructional guide. Now the teacher is freed to deal with individuals, to offer the extra cues, challenges, and guidance needed, and to collect extensive feedback and modify individual use of the LAP based on that feedback. Students engaged in a LAP will be working at lab tables, looking at filmstrips, listening to tapes, reading and writing in personal LAP booklets, and working with other students or with the teacher. A highly structured, well-organized, thoughtful LAP plus an observant and resourceful teacher are clearly prerequisites.

11.9 THE SCIENCE TEACHER IS A LEARNER, TOO

There is life after student teaching! and after graduation! However, as you will soon realize, there is always more to learn about the teaching of science. Much will be learned from your colleagues; perhaps more, from your students. In this section we emphasize three other kinds of resources that are of great help to the career teacher of science.

Professional associations   Throughout this text we have referenced many sources published by the National Science Teachers Association, the major professional association for the United States. We encourage you to take out a membership in this association and your state or regional association as early as possible. Members get discounts on publications, receive free copies of position papers, and receive journals and newsletters as part of the dues. Find out when and where the annual or regional meeting of these associations are being held. Find out school policy on attending such meetings and whether some or all of your expenses might be paid. Teachers repeatedly sing the praises of such meetings for the learning and sharing of ideas that takes place and the renewed vigor with which they return to classes. We also believe that one of the first steps toward helping teaching become a profession is for teachers to be active members of their professional associations.

Exploring issues   In Chapter 3, we referred to some of the research on gender differences in achievement in science and some of the possible factors affecting differential achievement and differential attitudes. Both gender and equity issues continue to be an important area of concern for all teachers, although they seem to be particularly of concern to science and mathematics teachers. This is one area that might be addressed through inservice education, or even in science department meetings. The activities of the newly formed Association for Multicultural Science Education (NSTA, 1990) might be reviewed and a departmental project developed. The science faculty might discuss a presentation on equity issues from a recent regional or national conference, or discuss an article that includes attention to gender issues, such as that by Smith and Erb (1986). Smith and Erb studied the effects of the *Career Oriented Modules to Explore Topics in Science* (COMETS) listed in the Suggestions for Further Study section of Chapter 4. For a list of resource groups related to the gender issue, see the Suggestions for Further Study in this chapter.

In Chapter 9, we outlined some of the curricular issues facing science teachers. Among these were the curricular revisions that would be possible if technology were integrated into the classroom. The science teacher needs to read about this issue, study the implications for change, and be open to potential major changes in the curriculum. We identified major sources of reading in Chapter 9. Frequent updates will be found in the journals of the professional organizations—the National Science Teachers Association, the American Association of Physics Teachers, the American Chemical Society, the National Association of Biology Teachers, and the National Association of Geology Teachers. Related to the integration of technology into the classroom are a host of social, ethical and equity issues. See, for example, articles by Troutner (1986) or Kreidler (1986) listed in the References. Such articles can serve as a starting point for a faculty discussion of ways these issues affect their own classroom instruction.

Also in Chapter 9, we highlighted the increased emphasis of science/technology/society issues—issues that, in some instances, are highly controversial in nature. To update their background in the S/T/S area and to familiarize themselves with the everchanging nature of the issues, the science faculty might spend a department meeting discussing taped segments from a television show like *Nova*. If the department members were revising curriculum to reflect S/T/S interrelationships, subgroups of faculty might examine one of several state curriculum guides, such as New York State's *Science, technology and society: Block J*. A third activity might be to schedule an inservice day on local or national environmental issues. Area chapters of groups, such as the Audubon Society or the Nature Conservancy, could be asked to send representatives to talk with faculty about regional problems and needed actions as they see them. Faculty would also find it useful to learn about the environmental education activities of two national projects, *Project Wild* and *Project Learning Tree*.

Two other controversial issues were treated in Chapter 9—questions dealing with the humane treatment of animals and the teaching of evolution versus creationism. Guidelines and sources related to the first issue were cited in Chapter 9. Faculty might discuss such guidelines and ways to implement them. They might also profit from a departmental seminar, led by a representative from the American Humane Association. The second issue, the teaching of evolution versus creationism, has received widespread attention in the media. Professional organizations, in particular the National Association of Biology Teachers and the National Science Teachers Association, are excellent sources of background materials for teachers. One available book from the latter association is *Modern science and the Book of Genesis* (Skehan, 1986), which might serve as the focus of an inservice day.

Teacher partners in research   Inservice teachers are sometimes asked to collect data, administer tests, or release students for interviews by college faculty researchers. However, more and more often, there are opportunities for interested teachers to be active members of research teams. Research networks have been started in some parts of the country, expressly to encourage cooperative efforts across disciplines, between faculty at different colleges and between faculty in schools and colleges. Such a group, called the Mathematics and Science Education Research Network (MASERN), was formed in New York State in 1986. Interested colleagues support these groups because all wish to explore one particular area of concern. In meetings, existing research background, special problems of conducting research in schools, appropriate collection methods and the like are discussed. Some teacher participants want to learn interview techniques and become the skilled collectors of data; others are interested in analysis of data; and still others prefer to work on the managerial tasks associated with a project. Team presentations at professional meetings are an exciting way of sharing the team's experiences with other teachers. For those who like to write, jointly authored articles or project booklets are a satisfying result of thoughtful collaboration. If you are teaching in New York State and are interested in working on such a team, see the address in the Suggestions for Further Study. In other areas, consult your regional or state professional association or science education faculty at a nearby college for opportunities.

11.10 SUMMARY AND SELF-CHECK

In the present chapter we extended the earlier work on the importance of a rich collection of resources. We emphasized the use of simple and inexpensive materials in innovative ways, atypical uses of Audiovisual and Technological Aids (ATA's), guidelines for field trips, safety in science teaching, and the human resource pool. Then we turned to the need to individualize or differentiate instruction for the various levels of students in the same class. We referred to the use of cooperative learning teams and outlined the design of a learning activity package (LAP) to accomplish this goal. Finally, we asked you to look beyond student teaching to the continual learning characteristic of effective teachers. We highlighted the resources available through membership in science education professional associations, faculty discussions and work on contemporary issues and involvement in research teams.

Now you should be able to:

1. Collect a wide variety of free and inexpensive materials and project specific uses for each item in science instruction.

2. Cite atypical uses of ATA's in teaching science.

3. Identify specific human resources and the ways in which they might assist in science instruction.

4. Expand your resource file to include the total range of resources needed to teach both typical and atypical students.

5. Plan and conduct field trips in a manner consistent with both safety and educational considerations.

6. Plan and conduct science learning experiences that are in accord with sound safety procedures.

7. Identify two or more ways practicing science teachers can use resources to continue their education.

11.11 SIMULATION/PRACTICE ACTIVITIES

A. Obtain one of the sources of ideas listed in the final section of this chapter.

1. Locate *two* common, hands-on materials, *not* specifically described in this chapter, that have potential use in a junior high class. Outline projected use. Indicate topic, specific subject matter content objectives, and teacher and/or student use.

2. Locate *two* common, hands-on materials that would enhance a lesson in density, radioactivity, or mitosis and outline the use of each as indicated in A.1.

B. Each of the films/videos/slide sets in the following list has been successfully used in science instruction. Locate *each* in the appropriate film catalogue. List, for each, the cost of rental or purchase, color or black and white, time, the content, and the grade level toward which the visual is directed. Preview each of these.

Film	Company
1. Adventure in Science: The Size of Things	Bailey Film Associates
2. The AHA! Box	W. H. Freeman and Co.
3. The Paradox Box	W. H. Freeman and Co.

C. The major national professional association for science teachers is the National Science Teachers Association (NSTA). Active state and regional organizations also exist throughout the country. Each of these associations can be of service to beginning teachers.

1. Research the purposes, membership fees, publications and services of the NSTA.

a. What special student membership and conference registration fees are offered?

b. What types of publications are provided and at what costs? Specify the titles of *at least one* of each type.

c. Obtain information on the location and scope of all NSTA meetings being held during this academic year.

d. What employment/placement services are offered to members?

2. Answer all of the above questions for one other science teaching organization in your state or region.

D. In Section 11.3 we included a short list of commercially produced games. Obtain *two* such games and read and follow the instructions. (You may need to obtain one or more coplayers.) After playing the games, respond to the following questions for *each* game.

1. What science topics might be appropriate ones for use of the game? Explain.

2. What grade level(s) and type of students seem most appropriate for use of the game? Defend your decision.

3. Estimate the time needed to both learn and play the game. For you? For your students?

4. What problems might be encountered if this game were used, as directed, in a classroom? What revisions or modifications might alleviate these problems?

E. Research some sources aimed at the talented and the slow learner. Prepare *at least five* cards (for your resource file) directed at enrichment for the talented student and *at least five* others directed at adapting instruction for the slow learner.

F. Identify *two* locations in your geographical region that would be appropriate places for a field trip in your content area. For each location, outline:

1. the instructional objectives of such a trip,

2. the preparation the students would need prior to the trip,

3. the followup classroom activities related to the objectives, and

4. anticipated problems relative to this field trip.

G. Read one of the following articles and report on the ideas presented and the way in which they could be used in science instruction.

Demoura, J. D., & Darrington, R. W. (1990). "The great margarine meltdown." *Science Teacher*, **57** (1), 30–32.

Dolan, A. W. (1987). "What's the big deal about an empty bottle." *Science Teacher*, **54** (7), 50–51.

Edge, R. (Ed.). (1988). "Coefficient of restitution." *Physics Teacher*, **26**, 540–541.

(The Edge citation is from the *String and Sticky Tape Experiments* section, a regular feature)

SUGGESTIONS FOR FURTHER STUDY

Catalogues of equipment, hands-on and visual resource material

Arbor Scientific
P.O. Box 2750, 415 W. Ellsworth, Ann Arbor, MI 48106

Carolina Biological Supply Co.
2700 York Road, Burlington, NC 27215

Creative Publications
Order Department: 5005 West 110th St., Oak Lawn, IL 60453

Cuisenaire Co. of America, Inc.
12 Church St., Box D, New Rochelle, NY 10802

Dale Seymour Publications
P.O. Box 10888, Palo Alto, CA 94303

W. H. Freeman and Co.
660 Market St., San Francisco, CA 94104

Janson Publications, Inc.
222 Richmond St., Suite 105, Providence, RI 02903

Ward's Natural Science
5100 W. Henrietta Rd., P.O. Box 92912, Rochester, NY 14692

For a more complete list of catalogues and other resource material, obtain a copy of:

National Science Teachers Association. (1990). *NSTA supplement of science education suppliers 1990.* Washington, DC: NSTA.

Computers

Ellis, J. D., & Keurbis, P. J. (1989). *ENLIST micros.* Colorado Springs, CO: BSCS.

This project is designed to help teachers integrate the use of computers into their science teaching.

Petit, J. P. (1985). *The adventures of Archibald Higgins: Computer magic.* (Trans. by I. Stewart). Providence, RI: Janson Publications, Inc. (Originally published in 1980).

This is another of the clever Archibald Higgins series in which Archibald learns about computers.

Demonstrations and laboratory idea sources

Liem, T. K. (1987). *Invitations to science inquiry.* Lexington, MA: Ginn.

Approximately 400 discrepant events from each of the science disciplines are found in this source. Many use simple or easy-to-find materials.

McKenna, H. J., & Hand, M. (1985). *A guidebook for teaching biology.* Newton, MA: Allyn and Bacon.

In addition to demonstrations and laboratory ideas, this source includes reproducible masters and lists of teacher resources.

Schmidt, V., & Rockcastle, V. (1982). *Teaching science with everyday things.* New York, NY: McGraw-Hill.

Though targeted for the elementary school, the many hands-on activities have proved to be especially effective with middle school students who need additional concrete activities.

Yurkewicz, W. (1985). *A guidebook for teaching physics.* Newton, MA: Allyn and Bacon.

This source contains both demonstrations and laboratories. For the most part, the author has used simple and inexpensive equipment.

Exploring Issues: computers

Ellis, J. D. (Ed.). (1988). *AETS yearbook: Information technology and science education.* Columbus, OH: ERIC Clearinghouse for Science, Mathematics, and Environmental Education.

In this yearbook, issues related to the application of technology to the teaching of science are explored.

Taylor, R. (Ed.). (1980). *The computer in the school: Tutor, tool, tutee.* New York: Teachers College Press, Columbia University.

This book of readings contains sometimes provocative essays by early leaders in computer education: Alfred Bork, Thomas Dwyer, Arthur Luehrmann, Seymour Papert and Patrick Suppes.

Resource Organizations

CONDUIT, P.O. Box 388, Iowa City, IA 52244

Minnesota Educational Computing Consortium (MECC), 520 Broadway Drive, Saint Paul, MN 55113

Project SERAPHIM, Department of Chemistry, Eastern Michigan Univ., Ypsilanti, MI 48197

Exploring issues: controversial issues

Hampton, C., Hampton, C., & Kramer, D. (1986). *Classroom creature culture: Algae to anoles.* Washington, DC: NSTA.

This collection of ideas, drawn from a series of articles that appeared in *Science and Children*, provides the teacher with background information on the collection, caring, and investigation of simple plants and animals.

Skehan, J. W. (1986). *Modern science and the Book of Genesis.* Washington, DC: NSTA.

A geologist, a geophysicist, a philosopher, and a theologian report on the dialogue between faith and science.

Exploring issues: gender and equity

Malcolm, S. M., Hall, P. Q., & Brown, J. W. (1975). *The double bind: The price of being a minority woman in science.* Washington, DC: American Association for the Advancement of Science.

The authors summarize the findings and recommendations of the first conference of minority women scientists.

Skolnick, J., Langbort, C., & Day, L. (1982). *How to encourage girls in math and science.* Englewood Cliffs, NJ: Prentice Hall.

This source includes research results on the reasons why girls avoid mathematics and science. The authors also suggest instructional strategies for preventing the avoidance syndrome, or reducing its effects.

Truely, W. G., & Bilski, V. (n.d.) *A winning formula: A program to promote sex equity in mathematics and science.* Brooklyn, NY: New York City Board of Education.

This program guide contains ideas for the classroom teacher and essays on the underrepresented minorities. Valuable lists of resources—materials, ATAs, and human—are included in the guide.

Resource Organizations

Math/Science Network, c/o Math Science Resource Center, Mills College, Oakland, CA 94613

Women's Educational Equity Act Publishing Center, Education Development Center, Inc., 55 Chapel St. Newton, MA 02160. (Send for their current catalogue of resources for educational equity.)

Games, problems, puzzles

Gardner, M. (1960). *Science puzzlers.* New York, NY: Viking Press.

Simple equipment can be used by middle school students to solve these common problems.

Hounshell, P. B., & Trollinger, I. R. (1977). *Games for the science classroom: An annotated bibliography.* Washington, DC: NSTA.

The annotations for some 200 games include ordering information, description of the games, preparation by the teacher, and evaluative comments by the authors.

Informal settings

Druger, M. (Ed.). (1988). *Science for the fun of it: A guide to informal science education.* Washington, DC: NSTA.

Among the many ideas presented for extending science outside of the classroom are the use of zoos, museums, and science competitions.

Resource Organizations

Contact the following for lists of available, educational material:

Franklin Institute Museum-To-Go, 20th and The Parkway, Philadelphia, PA 19103

Lawrence Hall of Science, University of California, Berkeley, CA 94720

New York Zoological Society, Education Dept., Bronx Zoo, Bronx, NY 10460

Smithsonian Institution Press, 955 L'Enfant Plaza, Rm. 2100, Washington, DC 20560

Safety

(na). (1986). *Safety hazards in science classrooms* (Science education digest: no. 1). Columbus, OH: ERIC Clearinghouse for Science, Mathematics, and Environmental Education.

and

(na). (1980). *Safety in the science classroom* (Information bulletin no. 3). Columbus, OH: ERIC Clearinghouse for Science, Mathematics, and Environmental Education.

These two publications are part of ERIC SMEAC's efforts to disseminate important information to science educators.

Virkus, R. N. (Ed.). (1978). *Safety in the secondary science classroom.* Washington, DC: National Science Teachers Association.

This publication of the NSTA Subcommittee on Safety provides essential information on safety aspects of school science programs.

Science/Technology/Society

American Chemical Society. (1984). *Chemcom.* Washington, DC: ACS.

This project consists of a series of modules for a full-year course that emphasizes the interaction of chemistry with society.

Biological Sciences Curriculum Study. (1984). *Social consequences of science and technology program.* Dubuque, IA: Kendall-Hunt.

This series consists of five modules that contain material on topics such as human reproduction and biomedical technology.

Bybee, R. W. (Ed.). (1985). *Science, technology, society.* Washington, DC: NSTA.

See abstract in Suggestions for Further Study, Chapter 9.

Resource Organizations

Project Wild, PO Box 18060, Boulder, CO 80308

Project Learning Tree, 1250 Connecticut Avenue NW, Washington, DC 20036

Selected Journals

Published by the Association for the Education of Teachers in Science:

Science Education contains position papers and reports of research.

Published by the National Association for Research in Science Teaching:

The *Journal of Research in Science Teaching* will be of most interest to inservice teachers who wish to learn more about, or become involved in, research.

Published by the National Science Teachers Association:

Science and Children, Science Scope, Science Teacher

These three journals, designed for elementary, middle, and secondary school teachers respectively, are devoted to the improvement of science teaching through idea articles, issue essays, sample lessons, and special columns. Many of t ie ideas can be used across several grade levels with minor modifications.

Published by the School Science and Mathematics Association:

School Science and Mathematics features articles on the teaching of the two separate disciplines, as well as articles/lessons on the integration of mathematics and science.

*The following subject-specific journals contain issue articles, teaching idea articles, and special columns:

American Association of Physics Teachers: *Physics Teacher*; the American Chemical Society: *Journal of Chemical Education*; the National Association of Biology Teachers: *The American Biology Teacher*; and the National Association of Geology Teachers: *Journal of Geological Education*.

**There are also some excellent journals published by state science teachers associations, as well as a number of international journals that are devoted to theoretical or research articles.

***In addition to the articles and columns on technology and information processing to be found in any of the journals listed above, there are also some recent journals devoted to computers and education. Two of these are listed here:

Computing Teacher, and *Journal of Computers in Mathematics and Science Teaching*.

Television

The following programs have aired for several years and provide teachers with content updates and ideas for teaching activities.

Mr. Wizard's World—Nickelodeon

Newton's Apple—PBS

Nova—PBS

Check all other chapters, but especially Chapters 9 and 10 for additional idea references.

CHAPTER TWELVE

DISCIPLINE

Control or Chaos in Your Classroom

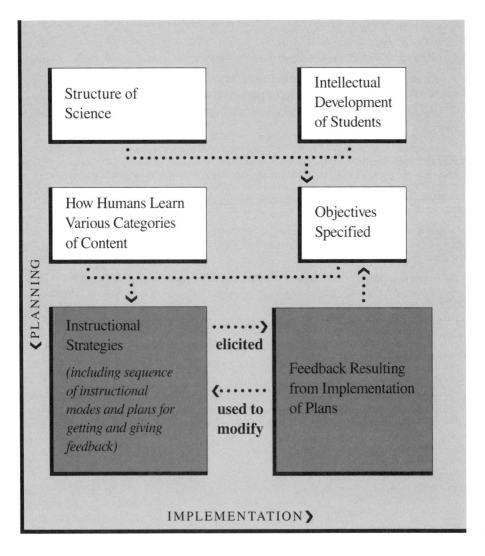

Some prefer to call this topic *pupil management*, while others insist that *instructional leadership* is the proper term. Choose whichever title pleases you most, but what they all boil down to is **control or chaos in your classroom.** Yes, yours. After all, you, the teacher, are supposed to be the adult in charge—the one legally responsible for the safety of students and professionally accountable for providing an environment for learning.

Make *no* mistake. Someone will be the leader in your class, and the choice is up to you as to whether it is you or one or more of the students. Some type of atmosphere for learning will prevail as a result of that leadership. The question here is the suitability of that climate for learning, both in the sense of promoting intellectual understanding and as a positive response to reasonable rules designed to protect the rights of all. These two goals, intellectual understanding and the protection of the rights of all, are the keys to the two boxes shaded in on the opening page of this chapter. The emphasis intended by shading the boxes "Instructional Strategies" and "Feedback" is that a positive classroom atmosphere depends on careful planning and consistent, thoughtful responses to feedback during the class period. What should and can be done about this problem?

In general, there are two approaches that work in the classroom; in the real world of the classroom *both* are needed. The first, like preventive medicine, must be employed whenever possible; the second, like surgery, is effective only in specific cases and for limited time spans. But before going into the details of either of these approaches, we should first agree on operational definitions of terms used frequently to characterize "good" versus "poor" discipline.

12.1 ATTENTION VERSUS NOISE

An *absolute* prerequisite to comprehending most of the terms used to describe classroom management is firm knowledge of the operational definitions of instructional modes as found in Chapter 1. Why is this the case? It should be fairly obvious that specific expectations for student behavior vary according to the mode being used at the moment. Thus it will be well worth the effort to run a quick self-check on these prerequisites prior to reading any further. Be aware of the fact that the classroom management terms considered in this section are limited to those that seem to be most useful to the novice teacher.

Appropriate noise level   Immediately after a classroom observation we are frequently asked, "Was my class too noisy today?" In our judgment, the *kind* of noise should be the primary concern, but more on that later. The noise level is appropriate for a lecture or a quiz if *the sounds from students approach zero (very, very closely)* and the noise level is appropriate for Q/A if *students speak one at a time with volume enough for all to hear.* Why does this description of appropriate noise level make sense? Note the specific ties to the particular mode being used at given points in the class period, and proceed to construct your own operational definitions of appropriate noise levels for each of the other common modes of instruction. An obvious nonexample would be if students in a small discussion group were screaming to each other in order to communicate over the shouting level being used by another group. Suppose that the inappropriate noise level of this group had been, in turn, caused by their need to hear each other over the alternately loud and quiet conversations of yet another group. Some novices fail to recognize this as a problem if all talk is relevant to the task at hand. Then they are surprised that one group is soon forced to escalate its volume further to hear themselves over the other groups.

Appropriate kind of noise   Like the previous set of operational definitions, this one is tied specifically to the particular instructional mode being used at various points in the class period. During lecture there should be *only the sound of the teacher's voice.* However, during Q/A *one-at-a-time talk on the topic by both teacher and students is desired.* During laboratory work appropriate kinds of noises include *the sound of footsteps, student-to-student and teacher-to-student conversation on procedures and content topics, the manipulation of equipment, and clean-up sounds.* Obvious nonexamples include talk about dates and the sounds of breaking glassware, equipment falling on the floor, or chairs being knocked over. Now consider the other instructional modes and construct your own operational definitions for the kind of noise appropriate for each.

Positive student attention signs   What would be some kinds of feedback which a trained observer in your classroom would characterize as positive student attention signs? *Students facing front, being quiet, and occasionally writing in notebooks would be positive attention signs during that portion of a class period when the teacher is lecturing from the front of the room.* Similarly, *many hands raised with relevant questions and answers being volunteered are positive signs during a question/answer session.*

Negative student attention signs   Quiet may be very desirable during a lecture, quiz, or while viewing a motion picture, but *silence should be interpreted as a negative attention sign during certain modes such as discussion, question/answer, and small-group laboratory work.* Similarly, *spitball throwing, manufacturing paper airplanes (with accompanying test flights), note passing, students eyeing the clock, reading of books hidden from the teacher's view, eating lunches, or sticking neighbors with pins can rarely be considered anything other than negative attention signs regardless of the instructional mode in use.* Now extend the list to include more of the subtle varieties and ask an experienced teacher to check it out for completeness. Be sure to include such signs as *students' gaze fixed on the spot where the teacher used to be* and *many requests that the teacher repeat questions.*

We have observed examples of student behavior listed in this section in many classrooms. In our experience, it is fatal for a teacher to overlook or ignore repeated instances of inappropriate level and kind of noise or negative student attention signs. The introductory activity, which follows, is designed to start you thinking seriously about teacher behaviors characteristic of both effectively and ineffectively managed classrooms.

12.2 INTRODUCTORY ACTIVITY

Get it straight from the horse's mouth.

In order to perform this activity, you will need to locate three to five secondary school students. Interview each of them individually to get their perceptions regarding the characteristics of good and bad teaching. Ask each student to record reactions on a form such as the one in Figure 12.1.

After collecting your data, compare it with that collected by your classmates who have interviewed different students. Look for patterns in the data, talk about these patterns with your classmates, and be prepared to discuss the matter further with your instructor.

A successful interview requires preparation as well as follow-up. One does not just walk into a secondary school and stop students in the hallway. You should talk with your instructor, who is knowledgeable about local school and college/university policies, regarding any permissions and protocol. Once the arrangements for interviewing have been made, you must duplicate the form in a neat, easily readable fashion. During the interview, you may need to give operational definitions of terms which may not be clear to younger students. Encourage them to ask questions about any statement that is not clear to them. *Refuse to allow the student to use the name of any particular teacher, either on the form or in conversation with you.* Observe closely to be sure that the directions are being followed and be sure to thank the students and all school personnel who made the interviews possible.

12.3 AN OUNCE OF PREVENTION

If the data that you obtained in the introductory activity match that which students have given us, then the notion of trying to survive in a poorly managed class probably frightens you as much as it does us. We know of no teacher who is pleased about the possibility of being in a chaotic class. It's clear that the wise teacher does all in his or her power to *prevent* such a situation, and the first line of defense is to be found in the quality of the lesson!

Planning and Implementation of the Lesson

Getting student attention *on the lesson* is a prime consideration in the development of any lesson plan. The number and variety of ways to accomplish this are limited only by the teacher's imagination. An interesting demonstration is one of the most productive ways to accomplish this end. What makes an interest-catching demonstration? Seek one that seems to defy "common sense" or one that focuses attention on an unfamiliar (to the student) aspect of a common phenomenon. If you can locate one that combines both ingredients, so much the better. Other serviceable ideas include laboratory activity (Remember we mean by this *student manipulation of materials*!) having the same characteristics as described for demonstration, a controversial statement written on the chalkboard

TO THE STUDENT

I am interested in learning to be a good teacher. I believe that student judgments about good and poor teaching can be helpful to me. Thus, I am asking you to record your honest reactions on this form. Do not sign your name. Your reactions will be kept confidential and will be added to those of other students to give me a picture of what many students think about good and poor teaching.

First, think in terms of one or two of the very best teachers *YOU* have had. Use the column on the left under the word BEST and place a check mark in one of the five boxes to indicate whether your best teacher(s) had a particular characteristic never, rarely, sometimes, often or always. Do this for each of the ten characteristics listed.

After you have finished rating all ten characteristics in terms of your best teacher(s), start again at the top of the list and place a check in the boxes in the right column that describe the worst teacher(s) *YOU* have had.

MY BEST   MY WORST
TEACHER(S)   TEACHER(S)

Never Rarely Sometimes Often Always   Never Rarely Sometimes Often Always

☐☐☐☐☐   1. Made the subject interesting.   ☐☐☐☐☐

☐☐☐☐☐   2. Made the subject easy to learn.   ☐☐☐☐☐

☐☐☐☐☐   3. Kept many students participating in class.   ☐☐☐☐☐

☐☐☐☐☐   4. Had only a few rules for student behavior in class. ☐☐☐☐☐

☐☐☐☐☐   5. Had many rules for student behavior in class.   ☐☐☐☐☐

☐☐☐☐☐   6. Enforced whatever rules he or she had for student behavior in class. ☐☐☐☐☐

☐☐☐☐☐   7. Treated all students fairly.   ☐☐☐☐☐

☐☐☐☐☐   8. Threatened students.   ☐☐☐☐☐

☐☐☐☐☐   9. Punished only those who misbehaved.   ☐☐☐☐☐

☐☐☐☐☐   10. Punished the whole class for the misbehavior of a few students. ☐☐☐☐☐

Fig. 12.1 Student reaction form.

prior to class, or a totally restructured classroom environment that connects to the lesson (chairs and desks arranged in a circle or small clusters). The illustrations found in Chapters 1–11, as well as the references cited in Chapters 9, 10, and 11, are rich sources of ideas for such activities.

Keeping student attention on the lesson is a more difficult task. This cannot even be approached unless the teacher *first gets attention*. Let us assume that this has been done. One obvious way to keep attention is to vary the teaching modes. If the class began with a teacher-performed demonstration coupled with question/answer, the teacher might switch to short lecture, then small-group discussion or short lecture with note-taking and/or a combination of student board work and seat work. Relevance to the "here-and-now" interests of students should be worked in as quickly as possible and emphasized throughout the class period. The increasing use of divergent questions as the period progresses will also help maintain attention. "Dead time" in the lesson is an invitation to trouble. When planning the lesson keep asking yourself, "Is there something constructive for every student to be doing every minute of the class period?" If the teacher cannot answer "yes," potential problems surely lie ahead. In addition, many novices beg for trouble by not informing students what they should be doing every minute of the class period. Even more make the error of not informing students *how* they are to perform the instructional tasks. Now might be a good time to refer back to "The Events of Instruction" in Chapters 2 and 7. Here our emphasis is prevention of management problems; in those chapters the emphasis was on ways to plan and implement a meaningful lesson. Notice how one depends on the other.

Students will work just so long without feedback on their efforts. They need to know how they are doing. Nothing is quite so satisfying as success coupled with knowledge of success. What can be more frustrating than failure or thinking you are doing a task correctly only to find out too late that you have been practicing errors? Refer back to Chapter 2 on feedback; that chapter contains many specific suggestions on this point.

"It is a smart person who knows when to give up." Many students get lost when the teacher has failed either to control the pace or to ensure that each step in the lesson is based upon prerequisite learnings actually achieved by the students. This kind of teacher behavior breeds frustration, then a "what's the use" attitude, followed by student activities of their own design—often at odds with what the teacher had in mind. The work of many researchers on the reasoning of adolescents and the conditions affecting learning provide important guidelines on how to avoid these problems and are well worth referring to once again (see Chapters 3 and 6).

Effective and Efficient Handling of Routines

Attendance must be taken every class period. The class attendance records of a teacher are legal documents subject to examination in a court of law. The teacher must take care of this detail daily without allowing the procedure to constitute "dead time." It is important that the class session get off to a fast and interesting beginning. A seating chart is a must until the teacher knows at a glance who is absent and can record the same without taking any class time for this important routine. Useful techniques include checking attendance at the start of the period while (1) some students put answers to homework on the board and others check answers at their seats, (2) all take a quiz, or (3) the teacher conducts a five-minute question/answer review of yesterday's lesson. Sometimes a student volunteer can perform the mechanics of attendance taking, but the teacher must check the accuracy of the record at some convenient point during the period.

Collecting and passing out papers must also be reduced to a routine. Students respond readily to habit in this regard if the teacher establishes a set procedure at the beginning of the year and consistently uses it. For example, the teacher might hand all papers for a given row to the student sitting on the right end of that row. That student passes the papers to the left. Likewise, papers might always be collected by having students pass them to the left end of the row and then to the front left seat. Some teachers have a box near the door for routine collection of homework papers as students enter class. The main idea is to establish a procedure and make it automatic so that it does not interrupt the flow of the lesson.

The distribution and collection of working materials should be similarly handled. A key consideration here is preventing jam-ups (and consequent pushing, arguing, and so on) by planning efficient distribution patterns. Dividing materials into four sets available at the four corners of a classroom makes much sense. On the other hand, asking an entire class to clean up materials at one desk during the final three minutes of class is an invitation to chaos.

Administration of a quiz or test should begin by getting complete attention from all students and following the routines for passing out papers. Then the teacher belongs in the rear of the room, on his or her feet with eyes and ears alert. Do you see why? If a student were to cheat, what is the first thing that student would have to do? That student would have to look around to find out where the teacher is—thus attracting the teacher's attention. Students with questions should be instructed to raise their hands and the teacher should follow procedures designed to avoid disturbing nearby students when attending to individual requests for clarification. As in supervised practice, the teacher must listen to a question while glancing around frequently at other students, whisper in response to a question, and insist that students speak at the same quiet level. Unlike supervised practice, during a test, the teacher must refuse to respond to students who seek assistance with the content. Beginning teachers are often trapped into giving the cues they would have provided in a supervised practice situation. Students soon learn that those who ask, receive! The complaints of unfair treatment are well deserved and the teacher is on the road to a self-imposed discipline problem. See the section on **Administration of the test** in Chapter 8 for further details on preventing undesirable behavior on the part of the test-takers.

Teaching students to respond to nonverbal signals is relatively easy and quite effective. Try switching the lights on and off in a class or laboratory where students are talking and/or working away at some activity. It works the first time and will work on successive occasions *if it is taught* as a signal that (1) it is time to stop work and clean up, (2) the noise has inadvertently gotten a bit too loud for the present activity, and (3) it is not used for every little disturbance. Effective instructors teach students to respond to a whole range of other nonverbal signals such as a snap of the fingers, the closing of the classroom door, or a finger touched to the lips of the teacher. Observe a real "pro" to pick up a whole repertoire of other signals to which students can be taught to respond.

Praise/Reward for Correct Behavior

Few teachers give enough attention to praising and rewarding students for behavior they wish to foster. Most attend only to inappropriate behavior and ignore that which they would like to promote. To be effective, the praise must be sincere, justly deserved, and not embarrassing to student recipients. Effective teachers use techniques such as (1) telling the entire group what a good job they did with today's lesson, (2) congratulating all for the fine results on yesterday's unit test, (3) calling attention to the thought-provoking quality of the question just raised by one student, and (4) asking a student's permission to read a particularly outstanding homework answer to the rest of the class. Also, nonverbal praise in the form of teacher smiles, hand signals, and gestures is very effective.

Other rewards often further increase the effects of praise. For example, the teacher can point out that because work progressed so effectively during the first 30 minutes today, the class can devote the final 15 minutes to an interesting educational game. Similarly, at the end of a particularly effective supervised study or practice session, the teacher can announce cancellation of the previously announced written homework problems "as there now appears to be no need for further practice." It is quite important to insure that students understand that the reward is a consequence of their good work, not a capricious act on the teacher's part.

One of the biggest mistakes we all tend to make in using praise/reward is the tendency to withhold these until student performance reaches some peak of perfection. We must learn to give encouragement for small steps in the right direction without overdoing it (and thus finding nothing left to connect with the final level of performance desired). Another all-too-common error of novices is to mistake a punishment for a reward. The typical student does not view doing problems 11–20 as much of a reward for having correctly solved problems 1–10 faster than the rest of the class! Sometimes the teacher can offer an incentive to the class when attention to the task begins to lag. One way to do this is by application of "Grandma's Rule. "

What rule is that? Grandma might have said, "Yes, you certainly may have a portion of ice cream, as soon as you finish your meat and vegetables." Thus, Grandma's Rule occurs when you make the satisfaction of someone else's wants dependent upon first achieving what you desire. When the teacher tells the class that those who complete the set of practice problems in class will have no homework tonight while everyone else will have to complete the exercises and hand them in tomorrow, that teacher is using Grandma's Rule. Another example of a teacher using Grandma's Rule was the response of Mr. Norris to his seventh-graders. As the students entered his classroom, they began coaxing him to let them continue playing the educational game in progress at the end of yesterday's lesson. Mr. Norris's response was that if all students worked effectively on the new lesson, they should have 10 to 15 minutes left for the game. Every teacher needs to master this approach because it works and because students react positively to its use when properly employed.

Conveying the Teacher's Enthusiasm for the Subject

It is a truism that one can't convey what one does not have. Some prospective teachers have learned science as a stagnant body of "facts" and complicated rules or principles. They can recite these flawlessly to the class (provided they re-memorized the details the night before) and can work stereotype problems faster than all but their brightest students. But that is it; there isn't any more! Those who recognize the above as a self-description are in deep trouble in trying to deal with students. "Death-warmed-over" won't work. What are these prospective teachers to do?

Self-education here and now is the *only* way out. Understanding the structure of ideas and processes for generating knowledge in science can be gleaned from the sources cited and activities suggested in Chapter 4. A rich store of interesting applications to the real world and the "here-and-now" interests of students is to be found in Chapters 10 and 11. Once the teacher becomes enthusiastic about the subject matter, then it is probable that he or she will find ways to demonstrate it to students. The obvious techniques include incorporating a wide variety of atypical examples, television commercials, labels from food and drug packages, newspaper articles, cartoons, and other objects brought in from the outside world. Appropriate nonverbal signals such as the gleam in the eye, spring in the step, or excited tone in the voice of the teacher are hard to describe and prescribe; but these are very important. Observe an enthusiastic teacher at work and try to incorporate some of these aspects that are compatible with your own personality and classroom style.

The Quiet, Insistent, Consistent, Business-like Approach

Screaming simply does not work! In fact, some students make a game out of seeing how quickly and often they can elicit this kind of response from their teachers. They will respect the calm, cool approach if the lesson is well planned and interesting. Students expect the teacher to act like an adult, not a tantrum-throwing child or an insecure teenager. This quiet approach, used consistently, has the same certain results as erosion that reduces boulders to sand grains over time.

Business-like does not mean the teacher never smiles or laughs with the students when something genuinely humorous happens. On the other hand, when we have all enjoyed our laugh, it's time to get back to work. Incidentally, it is unpardonable to laugh if it is at the expense of a student or group of students. No student respects a teacher who does this, but all admire a teacher who is big enough to laugh at himself or herself on occasion.

Neither this nor any other approach will work, however, if you, the teacher, present poorly prepared lessons that students perceive as dull or disjointed. A firm prerequisite to effective long-term classroom management is the planning and implementation of lessons that are both interesting and understandable. You will find that one of the most potent forces at work in the classroom is *peer pressure*. If the majority of the students are convinced that something worthwhile and interesting happens in your class, they will use very effective sanctions against the one or two whose actions tend to get out of line.

Remember that *consistency is imperative*. Words and deeds must match, and the teacher cannot allow rules to be violated for the first half of the lesson and then come on with thunder and lightning about the same breaches in conduct during the final minutes of the period. Appearances to the contrary, teenagers are really very conservative in many respects. They are creatures of habit and like to know which rules are to be enforced.

Establishing a Few, Simple, Reasonable Rules

If there are too many rules, the class atmosphere is repressive and students can't remember half of them in any case. If the rules are too complicated, most students will find avoidance behavior a more appealing alternative than trying to follow the rules. If the rules seem arbitrary and codifications of the teacher's whims, it will take more time and effort to enforce them than any teacher of an academic subject can afford to devote to nonacademic matters.

Some advocate spelling out all rules the first day, but our experience suggests a different approach in order to emphasize the "no rule without a good reason" guideline. For example, on the first day of class students usually will enter and automatically take a seat. Suppose at the instant the bell rings, a cartoon relevant to science is projected on the overhead and students are asked to raise their hands if they cannot see. They are then told they can keep their chosen seats as long as they can see, hear, and behave where they are today. They are also requested to keep the same seat for at least the first few weeks so the teacher can learn all of their names quickly. Suppose, too, that a question/answer session is woven in with the opening attention-getter. Then the first time several students call out in a mixed chorus, one nonparticipating student is asked if he or she agrees with the answer given and why. After he or she admits confusion, the request for hand raising is made. Then students will understand that the rule is for the benefit of all. As the question/answer continues, another mixed chorus response is likely to occur and this time the teacher should call on someone who raised a hand and did not shout out. Consistent teacher behavior leads quickly to desired student behavior without recourse to threats, screams, or punishment. Other simple rules, such as that no one talks while another (student or teacher) has the floor, are similarly taught as the occasion arises. Nonverbal signals, such as those described earlier, are very helpful both in establishing and maintaining the reasonable, rule-governed behavior that sets humans apart from lower animals.

12.4 THE BIG CULPRITS

The suggestions in the previous section are designed to help you eliminate the major sources of discipline problems faced by the novice. We call these sources the "big culprits" because we have seen them trap and destroy student teachers. In many situations the student teacher is deceived as to the destructive nature of these teacher behaviors because they see no apparent disastrous effects in the classrooms of experienced teachers. What novices fail to observe are the many counterbalancing moves by experienced teachers. If you want to avoid the usually impossible task of regaining control once it has been lost, you must learn to recognize and avoid the big culprits.

Accepting responses of students who do not raise their hands   The teacher tells the students to raise their hands and wait to be called upon prior to answering or asking questions. Shortly thereafter, someone calls out a correct answer and the teacher says "Right." What effect does this action have on the students who did raise their hands and did wait for the teacher's signal to answer? What would you do if you held your hand up while others who ignored the teacher's directions were rewarded by being recognized? The slowest student quickly realizes that the teacher's actions and words do not match. This realization leads to an increasing number of students who shout out in response to the teacher's questions. Finally, the teacher gets upset, "reams-out" the class, and proceeds further down the road to disaster by going right back to inconsistency of words and deeds. This reaction often is paired with the second big culprit.

Inviting the chorus response   Sometimes there are several students calling out the *same answer* at the same time (if the teacher is lucky or everyone knows the material anyway). There are two big problems with this unison chorus.

First, it is inevitable that only the vocal segment of the class will continue to respond while the majority sits quietly. But will the quiet ones think along with the teacher and the minority, or will they find some other quiet activity to engage in while the show goes on?

Second, how long can this situation continue before it becomes a mixed chorus of shouts? Soon two or three different responses occur at once. How does the teacher pick the one to respond to with "Right," "O.K.," or "Good"? Typically the teacher only hears what is expected and ignores the other responses.

Imagine the plight of the quiet and attentive student who wonders which of three answers is being identified as "Good." Now put yourself in the role of the teacher who wants to get feedback on group thinking and reinforce correct responses. Certainly, inadvertent promotion of the second big culprit is not the way to do it. Furthermore, the resultant student confusion fostered by this type of teacher behavior frequently leads to the third big culprit.

Teacher talks over student-to-student talk Inviting the chorus response not only results in student boredom but is the leading correlate of student-to-student (S ↔ S) talk. Students ask neighbors, "What did he say?" "How can that be if this is … ?" "I thought she told us yesterday …," and so on. Typically, the teacher caught in his or her own web either remains unaware of the S ↔ S talk or ignores it so as not to squelch the responsiveness of the class (perhaps only 4 to 10 students out of 25). When the murmur becomes a roar, the novice teacher senses that all is not well with the class and comes down hard with recriminations, threats, or slogans that are the direct opposite of what has been reinforced by previous events. Good luck to this teacher! Experienced supervisors call this practice "pushing the self-destruct button." Some novice teachers insist on continually pressing this button, and their supervisor's unhappy dilemma becomes the identification of the kindest and gentlest way to counsel them out of teaching.

Threats the teacher cannot or will not carry out "If you do not … immediately, I will … ." Is the teacher sure he or she can carry out the threat? Too often the novice teacher hasn't the foggiest idea how he or she can make good while the students are reasonably sure that the teacher can't or won't make the ultimate decision. Usually the students know more than the novice teacher about a particular school's policies. After all, they have been playing the game of school for 8 to 11 years in this very system while the teacher has been here only a few weeks and *doesn't even know that the principal never sees troublemakers who are sent to the office.* Those foresighted novice teachers who look up the school policy may find out that the vice-principal sees discipline cases. The student is thoroughly chastised by the vice-principal and returns to class a reformed student, right? Wrong! In more cases than we'd care to count, the student cools his or her heels in an outer office and continues the disruptive behavior for the benefit of the school secretary and visitors and peers who stroll by. When, at last, he or she confronts the vice-principal, there may be a brief heart-to-heart talk with a finale in which the student glibly promises to do better. Now who has punished whom? The student returns from the wars as a veteran with a story to tell, and you may be sure that it will be told.

There may be a time when one student must be removed from the class for the benefit of others, but the teacher must determine where that student can be sent, follow up the removal, and treat this kind of action as a final step with serious consequences.

Musical chairs   This variation of the popular child's party game is often played by teachers who are really a bit old for this game. The game begins when the teacher moves a troublesome student to another seat away from his or her friends. If the character in question is the class clown, the typical move to a front seat provides a wider audience for future antics. Who has fooled whom? Then, too, what has the teacher unwittingly done to the cooperative student who previously enjoyed the front seat? One could hardly say that this student was rewarded for good behavior by being forced to change seats. What is the teacher's next move when Charley's (the clown's) behavior deteriorates again? Too often another student is forced out of his or her seat in order to relocate Charley a second time. Frequently other students now join in the sport, the game gets more complicated, and the class slips further away from the control of the teacher.

This is *not* to say that judicious moving of one or two students is valueless. A move can be quite effective if the teacher (1) separates students who can't seem to get along together, (2) avoids creating even worse combinations (usually requires teacher homework ahead of time such as a trip to the guidance office and/or consultation with other teachers of these same students), and (3) makes clear to all concerned that their next seat change will have to be to somewhere other than in this classroom. Obviously the teacher must check the school policy thoroughly and be prepared to follow through.

Rewarding inappropriate behavior   The sixth big culprit creeps in when the teacher inadvertently reinforces the very behavior he or she is trying to extinguish. For example, one teacher told the class that those who worked effectively and efficiently on the worksheet during the period would have time to manipulate the periscope and begin construction of one of their own. Sam wasted time and distracted others. The teacher reprimanded him several times during the first 30 minutes of class time. Finally the teacher took away Sam's half-finished worksheet and told him to begin work on the periscope. What did this teacher's action tell those students who had worked diligently at the assigned task? What did it tell Sam?

Suppose the teacher has some students who do not wish to be in class. They are there only because (1) they had too many study halls and thus the guidance officer put them in chemistry class or (2) parents insisted that they take earth science. Is it reward or punishment for these students to be expelled from a class they have tried to escape taking in the first place? There is no denying that it may occasionally be in the best interest of all concerned to remove such a student from class. However, let's neither mislead ourselves that this is a punishment nor try to sell the students on this as a punitive measure. They simply won't buy it!

Inconsistent teacher behavior   Yesterday the teacher angrily reprimanded the class when several students poked neighbors and disturbed other students during laboratory work. Today, the teacher ignored this same behavior without so much as a verbal reminder. What will be the teacher's reaction to similar student behavior tomorrow? Is it any great wonder that inconsistent student behavior develops and that students come to view rules of order as capricious whims of their teacher?

Teacher's words and deeds do not match   This culprit is very closely related to inconsistent teacher behavior, but it is common and important enough to deserve special emphasis. It also overlaps many other categories of culprits identified here. For example, minutes after stating that students must raise their hands and wait to be recognized, the teacher falls into the pattern of accepting shouted-out answers. Another common error occurs when the teacher announces that there will be absolute quiet during the test and then finds it necessary to make numerous oral announcements, corrections, and clarifications throughout the period. A third common invitation to breakdown in morale is the practice of admonishing students to do neat and accurate work and then passing out teacher-made handouts that are almost impossible to read.

Using subject matter as punishment or threat of punishment   "If this class doesn't quiet down immediately, we will have three extra homework problems for tonight." Such a statement has the same effect on student attitude toward the subject as "Because there's so much noise, we'll have a quiz right now." It is a well-known truism that students who are interested in the subject matter or "turned on" by the way the teacher presents ideas attend to the lesson and *not* to disruptive activities. Now the harassed teacher has destroyed the goal toward which he or she is working. What must students think of quizzes that are planned on the basis of noise rather than on teacher assessment of feedback on lessons? The predictable reaction of the students is undisguised grumbling, comments on the lack of fairness of the teacher, and an increased dislike for science that must be practiced for punishment, rather than need.

Pleading for personal favors   One of the most difficult roles for the novice teacher is that of acting like a thoughtful, responsible leader in the classroom. During initial lessons, the beginning teacher's unwillingness to accept this responsibility is exhibited by verbal patterns such as "Would you please be quiet?" or "Keep it down, please," usually offered in a pleading, hesitant tone. The students quickly sense the teacher's failure to lead and begin taking over the reins of the classroom. Such a teacher tends to describe the situation by statements such as *"They* were very good today" or *"They* were noisy so I couldn't accomplish anything!" The students have been given the decision-making role here and have not been helped to greater self-control. Student caprice determines the days of apparent cooperation. If this initial behavior of the teacher isn't altered fast, the observer soon is treated to the spectacle of abject pleading: "Please be quiet!" "Help me out, please!" The teacher who reaches this stage must change or withdraw from teaching, for he or she is doing irreparable harm to the students in the process of losing his or her own human dignity.

Punishing all students for the misdeeds of a few   "If the person who threw the spitball doesn't confess, everyone will stay after school for one hour." What does this treatment tell students who have been behaving as desired? They might as well get into the act, since it is likely they will be punished anyway! This also tells students that the teacher is not capable of controlling the situation. This teacher has convicted all students as accessories to the misbehavior. Students cry "Foul play" deservedly. The teacher has gained many enemies and has helped to solidify the class in opposition to him or her. The odds of 25 students to 1 teacher are very difficult ones for any teacher to overcome.

The inappropriate teacher behaviors illustrated in these sections are those that seem to occur repeatedly and with immediate negative consequences in the classrooms of those who are unable or unwilling to accept their responsibility for ensuring a positive atmosphere. But suppose a teacher has been attending to all the suggestions and has been alert to early signs of erosion—does that teacher ever find it necessary to react to disorder? If so, what are some alternatives? Some of the ills for which you may need a cure and some classroom-tested cures are described in the following section.

12.5 A POUND OF CURE

The day of the hickory stick in public-school classrooms is long gone. It is true that some teachers lament its demise and a few attribute many of our present educational problems to its passing. Nonetheless, the fact of the matter is that there are very few schools today (public or private) where teachers are allowed to punish students with either fists or physical objects—the substitutes for the bygone hickory stick. Contemporary teachers must find more appropriate ways to get and maintain control over events in their classrooms.

The experiences of effective teachers, department chairpersons and student teachers indicate that the approach to take is the *elimination of the need* for punishment. Careful and consistent attention to the recommendations made previously in Sections 12.3 and 12.4 have proved to be 90 to 95 percent effective. But aren't there situations where punishment is called for in spite of the best efforts of the teacher? Yes, unfortunately. Remember above all else that any alternative will work if and only if the teacher has been trying, and continues to try, to implement the positive approach. We can hold out little or no hope that anything will work out for the teacher who has consistently, and over a period of time, ignored the "ounce of prevention" approach.

What is and is not considered punishment? *Punishment is the presentation of aversive stimuli.* Aversive to whom? The offender, of course. Anyone who hopes to use punishment effectively must remain alert to the fact that what is aversive to one student may actually be perceived as positively reinforcing to another. A loud and stern lecture on proper behavior delivered to the boy who craves attention is hardly punishment for him—particularly if it is done in the presence of his peers. Similarly, the lonely and lovesick girl sentenced to spend an hour after school with a handsome young male teacher doesn't perceive her predicament as the worst of all possible fates. Effective use of punishment, like so many other aspects of instruction, is dependent on the teacher's knowledge of individual differences among students.

Be forewarned. Punishment, negative reinforcement, seems to have less predictable effects on behavior than a positive, preventive approach (Skinner, 1953) and it often results in fostering poor attitudes toward school, science, and the teacher. "O.K., but what am I to do when I *must* punish?" Let's consider some general guidelines and their application within the framework of realities set by typical school situations.

The first order of business is to *find out both the school and the department policy on discipline.* It is a rare school that doesn't have such policy statements written down somewhere. Often the department has more specific guidelines designed to fit within the general school policy. Seek these out and learn them before the first day you teach a class. Armed with this knowledge you should then be able to question experienced teachers regarding those all-important "unwritten" policies that everyone, including the students, knows—that is, everyone except you. It is too late to find out these things after you have embarked on a course of disciplinary action and find yourself in the embarrassing position of having to back down.

Warn only once. Then act. This is easy to carry out provided you catch "little things" that, if ignored, will rapidly grow into major problems. For example, if you notice Paul is writing definitions for his English vocabulary list during supervised practice in science class, tell him in a whisper to put away that assignment and work on the assigned problems. The next time you see him exhibit this type of misbehavior, either during the same or any subsequent class session, don't say anything to him. Simply pick up his paper, put it in your desk drawer, and refuse to discuss the matter during class. When he appears at the end of the period to plead for his paper, tell him you will deliver his paper to the English teacher with an explanation of how it got into your hands. If Paul repeats this type of behavior a third time, immediately tear up the paper, drop it in the wastebasket, and refuse to discuss the matter.

Immediacy is vital if the consequence (punishment) is to be connected in the student's mind to the cause (the act of misbehavior). Note in the illustration in the preceding paragraph that the punishment was initiated within seconds of the time the offense came to the teacher's attention. Suppose you had opted for telling Paul a second time not to do other homework in this class and you had sentenced him to stay after school to make up one period of class time. The time span between the undesired act and its consequence now becomes hours instead of seconds. Further, you are now punishing yourself by giving up after-school time needed to help slower students and to prepare materials for tomorrow's lesson. Also consider that staying after school may not be much punishment for Paul if he normally just hangs around after school with little to occupy his time. Then, too, in many school situations it is impossible to keep certain students the same day. For example, bus students must have a day's advance notice, band students cannot be kept from after-school rehearsals on Tuesdays and Thursdays, and varsity athletes are immune on game dates. By the time you get some students in after school, both you and they will barely remember the purpose! Experienced teachers learn to use staying-after-school punishment with discretion.

"Praise in public and punish in private" is an old slogan that retains quite a bit of applicability to the contemporary school scene. For example, once you have told Sue and Kathy (persistent whisperers) to see you immediately after class, go right on with the lesson. Steadfastly refuse to respond to their pleas of "We weren't doing anything." Such a conversation in the presence of other students will only serve to waste class time, divert other students' attention from the lesson, and provide an audience for whom Sue and Kathy feel compelled to provide an "act." Further, this matter is no one's business except yours and the offending students. Experienced teachers also know that Tommy Tough Guy frequently becomes reasonable when dealt with in private and Mary Martyr climbs down from her cross when no audience of peers is around to appreciate her performance.

The punishment must fit the crime—both in kind and in severity—if it is to achieve maximum effect. An effective consequence of littering the floor with bits of paper is to arrange for the offender to spend some of his or her own spare time picking up similar debris by hand in several classrooms. Similarly, more than one desk carver has been cured by the experience of hand-sanding and refinishing the object back to its original condition (by all means, check school policy first on this one). Consider also the case of Spitting Sam, who was caught doing his act from the front row of the balcony during an assembly program. Immediately after school he was handed a beaker, informed of the biology classes' need for 100 cc of saliva for tomorrow's laboratory experiment, and told he could leave when that need had been fulfilled. Interim drinks of water could not be allowed since the need was for saliva, not water. One nonexample of the point being made here is the practice of having students write "I must not talk out of turn during class" some horrendous number of times. Typically this serves more to develop an aversion to writing than anything else!

It is the act that must be punished, not the person. All of us must make certain we communicate this message to students when we administer punishment. Words alone help some, and making the kind of punishment match the kind of behavior at issue often helps even more. But it is the teacher's behavior toward the offending student *after* the punishment that can clinch the point. Every effort and means must be used to project attitudes such as "Your mistake is over and done with, and I bear you no grudge" and "I expect you have changed and no recurrence of the problem is anticipated." A student who is left with the impression that he or she is a marked person whom the teacher will seek opportunities to pick on is very likely to become a repeated offender due to a "what's the use" attitude.

Consider three different approaches to handling collusion during a test. One approach is to tear up the offenders' papers and record zeros in the grade book. A second is to allow the offenders to complete the test believing they are undetected, score their papers, take the higher score, and award half to each paper in question—justifying this in private conversation with these students as the fairest way you could devise since you don't know who contributed which proportion of the correct information. A third approach is to do or say nothing about it this time and prepare two identical-looking but varying forms of the next test. The easiest way to do this is to vary the order of choices for each multiple-choice question. Identify the two test versions only by a period after the test title on one form, stack the papers so alternate forms are distributed to students sitting next to each other, proctor as usual; then collect, sort, score, and return the papers. Which of the three approaches best matches what has been pointed out about punishment thus far? In which do guilty students catch and punish themselves? If you chose the third approach, you agree with us. You should also have noticed that the third approach avoids the trap of requiring that the teacher "prove" the students cheated if irate parents phone the principal.

Consistency from day to day and from student to student is vital. You must learn to resist the tendency to overlook an infraction when perpetrated by Bright Bill and yet to come down hard on Slow Sally for the same breach of conduct. Student morale suffers badly if they even suspect their teacher is playing favorites. Likewise, tolerating loud and boisterous behavior during laboratory work one day and punishing it the next confuses students about the teacher's expectations. Developing a consistent approach takes a conscious effort on the part of most teachers, but the results are well worth the effort.

Suppose you have tried various means to deal with Terrible Tim, but nothing seems to work in his case. You have reached the end of your rope. He simply cannot be allowed to continue disrupting the lessons. Should you call for help, or would this be admitting to students, parents, and school administrators that you are incapable of handling the class? If you have done everything expected of a competent teacher, you should appeal to your cooperating teacher first and next, through the cooperating teacher, to the department chairperson. A regular teacher who has this problem has some additional options to explore if the problem persists. He or she could go for outside assistance at this point. A recommended sequence of actions would be to phone the parents, describe the evolution of the problem, tell them what he or she has tried to do to date, impress upon them the teacher's responsibility to others in the class, and ask for their assistance in correcting the situation. If this doesn't lead to resolution of the problem, the teacher could ask the guidance counselor to schedule a conference including the parents, the teacher, and the counselor. Should these measures fail, the next step is to remove the student from class and turn the matter over to the department chairperson for resolution with the vice-principal or principal. Many school systems now have access to the services of a school psychologist, who may be called into the situation at various points in the process. A student teacher may proceed through all of these steps but only in concert with the cooperating teacher. The cooperating teacher is ultimately responsible for the learning of the students and needs to be perceived by the parents as a continuing force in the education of their children. In any case, the phone call or conference is bound to be more effective if it is a cooperative effort of two colleagues, the cooperating teacher and the student teacher. Above all else, doublecheck the school policy *before* you initiate the first steps that could utlimately lead to the removal of a student from class, as this is a very serious matter.

In any case involving punishment it is critical to be sure you have first identified the right student(s) as targets for corrective action. This seems obvious, doesn't it? For example, Ms. Smith turned from writing on the board just in time to see Marge slap Walt, who sat behind her. Marge was kept after class and lectured to on everything from the evils of distracting others to standards of ladylike behavior. Ms. Smith raved on at such a pace that Marge could not get a word in edgewise. By the time Marge was given a chance to speak, she was so angry that she refused to say anything. Her anger flared even more when, after being dismissed by Ms. Smith, she heard Wiley Walt bragging to his friends about how he had gotten away with jabbing her with a compass. What a difference it would have made if Ms. Smith had asked Marge the reason for her behavior prior to starting the aversive lecture!

Some techniques for catching those guilty of copying neighbors' test answers have already been described. But how can the teacher catch litterbugs and desk carvers when five different classes use the same room during a day? Let's assume Mr. Johnson finds carving on a certain desk as he is trying out a demonstration activity after school. Which of the five students who sit at that desk is the guilty one? Mr. Johnson need only take a quick tour of the area during the last minute of *each* class period for a day or so to find out. When additional embellishments are added, his question is answered. Think through other possible instances when it may not be obvious which student or students are the actual offenders and consider alternative ways of identifying the individuals at fault. This kind of thinking ahead should be excellent preparation for the moment when actual decisions will have to be made.

12.6 SO YOU'RE A TEACHER

Are you sure you want to be a science teacher? What kind of person will you become? Must you stop smiling, never make mistakes, always behave in the "proper" way? In the early twentieth century citizens required their teachers to adhere to certain rules and regulations. One list given to New York City teachers admonished them against courting on weekdays, frequenting barbershops, and using curses or other foul language. Today it's a rare community that has written rules of behavior for teachers, although some still cling to unwritten rules. You should check out such unwritten rules with experienced teachers before you accept a job in the community.

But, more important than any rules are the human characteristics that encourage that positive atmosphere in which students are able to learn. We've said often that you must be able and willing to be effective and consistent. Are you willing, or are you plagued by doubts about the teacher image? Let no one tell you that students and parents will ignore the teacher who gets noisily drunk in the local inn as they ignore the similar behavior of their favorite auto mechanic. The mechanic will often service the family car with no loss of effectiveness, but the teacher may be forced to deal with in-class misbehavior as a consequence of the teacher's actions outside of school. How strange! Authors of some articles in popular magazines seem to imply that teachers don't have to worry about serving as adult models, that today's students don't want their teachers to play this role. Ask a student teacher who has just given an anonymous attitudinal survey to the class about the nature of student responses to class management. The great majority of students regularly reiterate their desire to have a class environment suitable for learning and their belief that the teacher is the one to ensure that this is the case. Statements such as the following are often made: "You should have told the kids who talk to shut up," "You let the kids get away with too much noise," "It's not fair to the ones who are trying to work when other kids clown around. You should stop them," or "I study for tests, but you let other kids cheat." These statements speak loud and clear. *You* are supposed to be the leader. It's your job to see that all are given an equal chance. The students look to you to exercise that leadership.

A little thought will also convince you that teenagers want adult models desperately and are sometimes deprived of them by well-meaning, confused parents and teachers—the two classes of adults who have the most contact with teenagers. Both parents and teachers sometimes try to be friends, just like Lynn or Carolyn. But most teenagers have plenty of friends their own age with whom they can share secrets, exploits, and misdeeds. They occasionally want the very advice they seem to ignore—for example, the firm decision about curfew and the consequences that follow when that curfew is ignored. Jeff, a sophisticated eleventh-grader who never did any homework and had a record of numerous "cuts" and failing grades, was inspired to do one unusual homework assignment by a thoughtful student teacher. The next day he told that student teacher how both his parents expressed pleasure that he had brought a schoolbook home and was doing homework. "But," said Jeff, "they never told me before that they cared whether I did homework. If they'd told me how upset they were, I would have done it earlier." There's a moral in the above true story for all who work with teenagers. Attempting to reduce the barriers between student and teacher by becoming "just one of the gals or guys" may actually create a barrier so high that no student will seek out your advice, accept your leadership, or try to attain the goals you set.

Will you accord your students the same measure of respect that you want demonstrated toward you? Will you listen thoughtfully when students are responding to a question even when they are stumbling with both ideas and words? Will you encouage students to try without fear of a verbal put-down if they make an honest error? Some teachers mistakenly believe that they are preserving the integrity of science by insisting on precision and exact answers even during the early stages of the development of a topic. In fact they discourage insight, do harm to the understanding of the content, and present an uncompromising personality.

Students have bad days, too! When Bonnie, usually a cooperative, pleasant student, suddenly erupts and spits out a defensive remark, the thinking teacher won't lash out in return, but may quietly, and for Bonnie's eyes only, signal a "calm down." That teacher will probably remember to unobtrusively seek Bonnie out at the end of class—not as a punishment, but to find out if help is needed. But beware! We all have an aversion to the classic "do-gooder." A teacher's help *cannot* be forced on a student.

If students have a right to make an honest error, to try different approaches to a problem, and to expect that there should be a reason why they are required to learn something, then teachers also have a right to make an honest mistake, to admit they don't have all the answers, or to say that question never occurred to them. None of the above teacher behaviors will diminish the respect of the students for him or her if such behaviors are appropriately followed up. Ms. Steyer says she has no idea why the chemical symbol for tungsten is W, but admits that that's a reasonable question and says that she will find out and answer it tomorrow. Mr. Mapes was asked the same question, but he countered with, "That's a question you should all be able to answer! Since you asked, Barry, your assignment is to look up the answer and report to all of us tomorrow." Which response adds to the teacher's stature? You may be sure that Barry has learned not to ask curious, relevant questions of this teacher. Notice that the word *relevant* was used in the previous sentence. Students come in all flavors, and you'll be missing the spice of life if you are never faced with one or more good-humored clowns, with their irrelevant and funny questions. It is up to you to discriminate between the good-humored clown and the so-called troublemaker. Neither one must be allowed to steal the time of other students, but your response to each differs significantly. Reread Section 12.5 and try to identify differences. In no case should you try the game of one-upmanship! Once a teacher begins to respond to a funny remark with a funny remark, the class is off in a contest of wits which has nothing to do with the lesson. Nine times out of ten the teacher is no match for the student, and even the one time the teacher wins, he or she has lost. The students have learned that the teacher is fair game and the traps will be set with repeated frequency.

Are you sure you want to be a teacher? Yes, you *can* smile and you *will* make mistakes, but you must realize that you will be seen as a model. If you are able to roll with the punches, to keep your enthusiasm for teaching science despite long, hard hours of work, and to find satisfaction in the long-term accomplishments of your students, then you are the kind of person who can help your students become all they are capable of becoming.

12.7 SUMMARY AND SELF-CHECK

Whether we use the words *control*, *discipline*, or *management*, we are labeling a set of competencies that is a necessary but not a sufficient prerequisite to instruction. In other words, if a teacher is unable to promote and maintain an environment for learning, no other instructional competencies the teacher may possess will be realized. However, the reverse is not true! The ability to stave off chaos does not automatically include the ability to instruct in an interesting and meaningful manner. The development of worthwhile lessons will require further work on all the components of the instructional model.

You would be well advised to remind yourself of the "big culprits" as you gain experience in teaching. Experienced teachers have told us that this chapter is a gold mine of practical ideas that they have found helpful. All of us at times fall into a comfortable rut of bad habits—habits that may prove to be disastrous in a new class.

At this point you should be able to:

1. Give illustrations of negative and positive student attention signs—indicators of time-on task.

2. Identify instances of negative and positive student attention signs and of appropriate or inappropriate kind and amount of noise level during either a "live" or recorded lesson and state reasons for your judgments.

3. Identify instances of the "big culprits" during either a "live" or recorded lesson and describe the teacher reactions to the "big culprits" and consequences that occurred as a result of those teacher behaviors.

4. List four to five preventive measures that should be part of each teacher's behavior pattern.

5. Explain how you could apply Grandma's Rule, given a specific description of a class situation.

6. Describe remedial steps you would take to solve a specific misbehavior problem and be able to justify your decisions.

In the following exercises you are given an opportunity to test your ability to meet some of the above objectives. Be sure to check your responses with those of your classmates and your instructor. Perhaps more than any other area treated in this text, management requires more than an intellectual response. You must learn to know yourself, the attitudes you project in the classroom, and the effects of your behavior on students. You must respect both yourself and your students. It is a lifelong study for those who want to be students of teaching.

12.8 SIMULATION/PRACTICE ACTIVITIES

A. The first day Mr. Atkinson met his class, two students arrived a half-minute late. On the second day three students were a minute late and Mr. Atkinson waited to begin class until they were in their seats. By the end of the week he was delaying the start of class until five minutes after the bell because the students continued to trickle in throughout this time interval.

1. What do you predict will be the situation by the end of the second week? Why?

2. What alternatives are open to Mr. Atkinson for Monday of the second week?

3. Which of the alternatives identified in your response to 2 are likely to lead to a worse situation? Why?

4. Which of the alternatives identified in your response to 2 are likely to lead to improvement? Why?

B. Ms. Brown complains that her class sessions begin quite promptly but that trouble starts about the middle of the period and the situation rapidly degenerates to obvious chaos by the end of the class. When asked to specify the nature of the problem, she replies that the students have no manners and such poor attention spans that even frequent switches of teaching modes get her nowhere. A check of her lesson plans reveals well-sequenced lessons, frequent change of modes, adequate plans for getting and giving feedback, many practical applications, and good relevance to the "here-and-now" interests of students. Plans for pacing seem adequate and there is an excellent match of strategies and stated objectives. On paper she looks great!

1. Assume you are going to observe Ms. Brown in action. What would you focus on in this observation? Why?

2. What is (or are) the most likely problem(s) you would expect to find?

3. Cite specific suggestions you would make based upon the data you would expect to gather in 1.

C. Mr. Forgette's class proceeds smoothly as long as the modes employed are short lectures, question/answer, or teacher demonstration. Whenever he uses laboratory or small-group discussion, or sends students to the board, discipline disintegrates.

1. What are possible causes of the problem?

2. Which of the possible causes is the most probable? Why?

3. What is the basic cure for the cause cited in 2?

D. The students in Ms. Klutz's class are busily working—that is, all but Pete and Harry. Ms. Klutz, a pretty first-year teacher, hears a sound and glances up just in time to see a note being passed from Pete to Harry. She stalks down the aisle and loudly demands the note. The rest of the students stop work and watch as Harry obsequiously hands Ms. Klutz a folded paper. Ms. Klutz threatens, "If this note is so important, maybe I should read it to the entire class!" Pete smirks and says, "Go ahead." When Ms. Klutz looks at the paper, she is horrified to find an obscene remark directed at her.

1. It is clear that Ms. Klutz has already firmly entrapped herself. Describe the best alternative(s) at this point.

2. If Ms. Klutz had it to do over, what effective approach(es) could she have used from the instant she spotted the note? Be sure to consider the limitations of each alternative approach you suggest.

E. Barbara approached Mr. Zillis after class and invited him to attend a party at her house following the Friday night pep rally and bonfire. Mr. Zillis is a young unmarried teacher with no previous commitment for that evening.

1. Describe a few potentially troublesome situations Mr. Zillis might be getting into if he accepts this invitation.

2. What further information should he seek, and from whom, prior to deciding whether to attend?

SUGGESTIONS FOR FURTHER STUDY

Charles, C. M. (1989). *Building classroom discipline: From models to practice*. White Plains, NY: Longman.

The author presents eight models of classroom discipline. Each model is illustrated by applying aspects of that model to common classroom management problems. Following the description of the model is a set of Application Exercises. These include descriptions of two classroom cases (the same two for each model) and sets of questions designed to help the reader identify the advantages and disadvantages of applying the model to each case. A careful reading of this book will yield many useful ideas for the inservice and preservice teacher in need of alternative management strategies.

Sanford, J. P. (1984). "Management and organization in science classrooms." *Journal of Research in Science Teaching*, **21** (6), 575–587.

Data from observations of 26 junior high and middle school science classes were analyzed for relationships between science teacher management behaviors and student behaviors. Preservice teachers should find especially helpful the examples in the following three sections: *Effective Classroom Procedures and Rules, Organizing and Presenting Instruction*, and *Student Work Procedures*.

APPENDIX
Modular Assignments

RESOURCE FILE MODULE

A. Objectives

    1. To build an organized resource file for *one* of the major units in a course you will teach (or for a course you are presently teaching).

    2. To begin an organized resource file for *each* of the other units in the course selected in A-1.

    3. To devise an organizational scheme that will serve as a pattern for developing resource files for other courses.

B. Enabling activities

    1. Study the syllabus, a widely used text, and teacher's handbook for the chosen course, in order to identify the major objectives for the unit selected for A-1 and for the entire course referred to in A-2.

    2. Consult the annotated references in the Suggestions for Further Study section at the end of each chapter in this text.

    3. Look for additional idea sources in the college or university library, the public library, the professional and school libraries at the secondary school where you will student-teach (or are teaching), supermarkets, department stores, garages, newspapers, and popular magazines. Some suggested areas where you will need resource ideas are educational games, pictures and sketches of bulletin boards, ideas for projects, supplementary readings on a range of reading levels, transparency ideas, directions for constructing homemade equipment or models, field trip possibilities, and laboratory activities.

C. Directions

    1. Whether you are storing your resource file on a computer disk or in a file drawer, you will need to prepare 8–12 file folders. Label each with the topic of a unit in the selected course. As the storehouse of ideas increases, you will find it helpful to add subtopics to each folder. (If you

Burger, W. (1987). "Ode to slinky on its birthday." *Science Teacher*, **54** (7), 25–28.

Materials: one slinky, one stopwatch for each pair of Ss

Idea: Give each team of two Ss a slinky and have them estimate and then record the time that it takes the slinky to "walk" down a flight of stairs. Have the Ss then take opposite ends of the slinky and move apart so the slinky sags under its own weight. (You might ask students if they could think of conditions under which the elongated slinky would not sag.) Have each student move the hand holding the slinky vertically and observe the motion. Repeat the action but move the slinky horizontally. Finally have students record data in diagram form.

Purpose: Lab to introduce topic of wave properties and to continue to explore the physics of toys.

Modification: Show video segment from NASA's *Toys in Space* project and have students compare slinky's behavior in gravity and zero gravity conditions.

Fig. A-1   Sample card from a resource file folder.

are using manila folders, subdivide within a folder via colored divider sheets as the store of ideas increases.) Even with a computer system, you will need to provide for storage of adjunct materials, such as physical models in labeled boxes or a file cabinet.

2. As you find a potentially useful idea, record the bibliographic data, any needed materials, and a **summary** under **Idea** on a resource file card (see Figure A-1). It is seldom productive to simply copy pages of an article and file them. A resource file is not very helpful if, at a later date, you must go back to the original source, reread it to see why you selected it, and then try to retrieve your original intent. Make exact copies of only those diagrams, reading material, and references that would be lost in a summary.

3. Return to the cards you have begun and now identify projected classroom **purpose(s)** of the idea (for example, an attention getter in a lesson on _____ , an enrichment assignment in _____ for more capable Ss, a lab to introduce the rule _____ , and so on). Be sure to briefly summarize details of that use. For example, indicate whether the lab, demo or other mode will be used to **introduce** a concept or **give practice in** a rule.

4. Finally, be sure to note any **modifications** needed for the class you will be teaching (for example, rewriting at a lower reading level). Sometimes you will add modifications after testing out the idea with one class.

5. The set of 8–12 folders should be sprinkled liberally with items that emphasize:

a) Science/mathematics interrelationships, as well as those to other content areas.

b) Content related to the Ss "here and now" interests.

c) Ideas from *at least two* national and/or international curriculum projects.

d) Ideas from *at least three* different teaching journals in your content area (as well as the interrelated science/mathematics journals).

LEARNING HIERARCHY MODULE

According to scientists, experienced teachers, and cognitive psychologists, the discipline of science is a tightly hierarchical structure. Unfortunately many novice teachers view their subject matter discipline as a massive collection of facts and an arbitrary set of rules with few connections. Moreover, secondary school students are unlikely to learn anything about the structure of the subject matter unless relationships and connections are made explicit by their teacher often and in various ways. Thus, the planning of instruction consistent with the structure of the subject matter requires serious homework by the novice teacher. It is to that end that this module is directed.

A. Objectives

   1. To construct a learning hierarchy for one of the major units you will teach.

   2. To write a sample test item for each objective in the learning hierarchy.

B. Enabling activities

   1. Study both content sequences and exercises in the syllabus, a widely used text, and teacher's handbook and identify the major objectives of the unit and some of the assessment measures found in those sources.

   2. Study the learning hierarchies diagrammed in Chapter 6 of this text.

   3. Study the guidelines proposed in the "Task Analysis" section of Chapter 6 to sequence the set of objectives listed in the same section.

C. Directions

   1. Select a unit comprising two to three weeks of instruction.

   2. Write five to seven *major (important)* cognitive instructional objectives and one sample corresponding test/quiz item per objective. Each objective and its corresponding test item should appear on a separate index card. Arrange these in a learning hierarchy by clipping or taping cards to a large sheet and adding appropriate arrows.

   3. Then analyze *each* of the major objectives to identify prerequisite objectives not already written. (It is possible that one of the major objectives may be prerequisite to another major objective.) Write these additional

instructional objectives and corresponding sample test/quiz items on index cards. Insert these in appropriate locations in the learning hierarchy
and change arrows as needed.

4. Finally, write four to six *future* objectives (that is, from units to be taught
   after the selected one), for which the original major objectives are prerequisites. Write corresponding sample test items. Again adjust the
   learning hierarchy arrangement and arrows so as to correctly depict the
   overall sequence. Key the three types of objectives by a color code or
   diverse shapes. Identify the unit and grade level on the final chart.

REFERENCES

American Association for the Advancement of Science. (1989). *Project 2061: Science for all Americans*. Washington, DC: AAAS.

American Association for the Advancement of Science. (1965). *The psychological basis of science—A process approach*. Washington, DC: AAAS.

American Humane Association. (1980). *Guiding principles for the use of animals by secondary school students and science club members*. Denver, CO: American Humane Association.

Allen, L. (1973). "An examination of the ability of third-grade children from the Science Curriculum Improvement Study to identify experimental variables and to recognize change." *Science Education*, 57, 135–151.

Ault, C. R. (1985). "Concept mapping as a study strategy in earth science." *Journal of College Science Teaching*, 15, 38–44.

Ausubel, D. P. (1963). *The psychology of meaningful verbal learning: An introduction to school learning*. New York: Grune & Stratton.

Ausubel, D. P. (1968). *Educational psychology: A cognitive view*. New York: Holt, Rinehart & Winston.

Ausubel, D. P. (1979). "Education for rational thinking: A critique." In A. E. Lawson (Ed.), *The psychology of teaching for thinking and creativity* (pp. 174–190). Columbus, OH: ERIC Clearinghouse for Science, Mathematics and Environmental Education, The Ohio State University.

Bandura, A. (1969). *Principles of behavior modification*. New York: Holt, Rinehart & Winston.

Bell, M. S. (1972). *Mathematical uses and models in our everyday world*. (Studies in Mathematics, Vol. 20). Stanford, CA: School Mathematics Study Group.

Bloom, B. S. (Ed.). (1956). *Taxonomy of educational objectives, Handbook I: Cognitive domain*. New York: David McKay.

Bramble, W. J., & Mason, E. J. (1985). *Computers in schools*. New York: McGraw-Hill Book Co.

Bruner, J. S. (1960). *The process of education*. Cambridge, MA: Harvard University Press.

Bruner, J. S. (1966). *Toward a theory of instruction*. New York: W. W. Norton.

Brunkhorst, H. K., & Yager, R. E. (1986). "A new rationale for science education—1985." *School Science and Mathematics*, 86, 364–374.

Budd-Rowe, M. (1973). *Teaching science as continuous inquiry*. New York: McGraw Hill.

Budd-Rowe, M. (1978). "Wait, wait, wait, ..." *School Science and Mathematics*, 78, 207–216.

Buerk, D. (1982). "An experience with some able women who avoid mathematics." *For the Learning of Mathematics*, 3 (2), 19–24.

Butts, D. P., & Brown, F. K. (Eds.). (1983). *Science teaching: A profession speaks* (NSTA Yearbook). Washington, DC: National Science Teachers Association.

Bybee, R. W. (Ed.). (1985). *Science/technology/society* (NSTA Yearbook). Washington, DC: National Science Teachers Association.

Bybee, R. W., Carlson, J., & McCormack, A. (Eds.). (1984). *Redesigning science and technology education* (NSTA Yearbook). Washington, DC: National Science Teachers Association.

CASDA. (1985–1986). "High school students discuss attitudes of young women toward the study of math and science." Albany, NY: *CASDA/DS Newsletter*, 24 (1), 6–7.

Center for Educational Research and Evaluation. (1981). *The status of middle school and junior high science* (Vol. II). Louisville, CO: Biological Sciences Curriculum Study.

Clough, E., & Wood-Robinson, C. (1985). "How secondary students interpret instances of biological adaptation." *Journal of Biological Education*, 19, 125–130.

Commission on Secondary School Curriculum. (1938). *Science in general education*. New York: D. Appleton-Century Co.

Davidson, N. (Ed.). (1990). *Cooperative learning in mathematics: A handbook for teachers*. Menlo Park, CA: Addison-Wesley.

DeBoer, G. E. (1984). "Factors related to the decision of men and women to continue taking science courses in college." *Journal of Research in Science Teaching*, 21, 325–329.

Dewey, J. (1910). *How we think*. Boston, MA: Heath.

Dewey, J. (1965). *Democracy and education*. New York: The Macmillan Co. (Originally published in 1916).

Doran, R. L., & Ngoi, M. K. (1979). "Retention and transfer of selected science concepts in elementary school students." *Journal of Research in Science Teaching*, 16, 211–216.

Driver, R., & Erickson, G. (1983). "Theories-in-action: Some theoretical and empirical issues in the study of students' conceptual frameworks in science." *Studies in Science Education*, 10, 37–60.

Duncker, K. (1945). "On problem-solving." *Psychological Monographs*, 58 (5), 1–111.

Fajemidagba, O. (1983). "The relationship between Piagetian cognitive developmental stages of concrete and formal operations and achievement on mathematical ratio and proportion problems." (Doctoral dissertation, State University of New York at Albany, 1983). *Dissertation Abstracts International*, 43, 3497A.

Farmer, W. A. (1983). *Cognitive development of gifted middle school students*. Paper presented at the Regional Conference of Association for the Education of Teachers in Science, Teaneck, NJ.

Farmer, W. A., & Farrell, M. A. (1989). *Activities for teaching K–6 math/science concepts*. Bowling Green, OH: School Science and Mathematics Association.

Farrell, M. A., & Farmer, W. A. (1985). "Adolescents' performance on a sequence of proportional reasoning tasks." *Journal of Research in Science Teaching*, 22, 503–518.

Fremont, H. (1969). *How to teach mathematics in secondary schools*. Philadelphia, PA: W. B. Saunders Company.

Gabel, D. L., & Sherwood, R. D. (1982). "Facilitating problem solving in high school chemistry." *Journal of Research in Science Teaching*, 20, 163–177.

Gagné, R. M. (1970). *The conditions of learning* (2nd ed.). New York: Holt, Rinehart & Winston.

Gagné, R. M. (1977). *The conditions of learning* (3rd ed.). New York: Holt, Rinehart & Winston.

Gagné, R. M. (1979). "Learnable aspects of human thinking." In A. E. Lawson (Ed.), *The psychology of teaching for thinking and creativity* (pp. 1–27). Columbus, OH: ERIC Clearinghouse for Science, Mathematics and Environmental Education, The Ohio State University.

Gagné, R. M., & Briggs, L. J. (1979). *Principles of instructional design* (2nd ed.). New York: Holt, Rinehart & Winston.

Gardner, M., & Yager, R. (1983). "Science education: Restoration at the precollege level." *Journal of College Science Teaching*, **13** (1), 44–49.

Greenslade, T. B. (1976). "Looking backward: 19th century textbook illustrations." *Science Teacher*, **43** (1), 31–33.

Hall, G. S. (1883). "The contents of children's minds." *Princeton Review*, **11**, 249–272.

Harms, N. C., & Yager, R. E. (Eds.). (1981). *What research says to the science teacher: Volume 3.* Washington, DC: National Science Teachers Association.

Hart, K. (1978). "The understanding of ratio in the secondary school." *Maths in School*, **7** (1), 4–6.

Helgeson, S. L., Blosser, P. E., & Howe, R. W. (1977). *The status of pre-college science, mathematics, and social science education: 1955–1975. Volume I: Science.* Columbus, OH: Center for Science and Mathematics Education, The Ohio State University.

Holliday, W. G. (1975). "The effects of verbal and adjunct pictorial-verbal information in science instruction." *Journal of Research in Science Teaching*, **12**, 77–83.

Humphreys, B., Johnson, R. T., & Johnson, D. W. (1982). "Effects of cooperative, competitive, and individualistic learning on students' achievement in science classes." *Journal of Research in Science Teaching*, **19**, 351–356.

Hurd, P. D. (1969). *New directions in teaching secondary school science.* Chicago, IL: Rand McNally.

Hurd, P. D. (Ed.). (1970). *New curriculum perspectives for junior high school science.* Belmont, CA: Wadsworth.

Inhelder, B., & Piaget, J. (1958). *The growth of logical thinking from childhood to adolescence.* New York: Basic Books.

Judson, H. (1980). *The search for solutions.* New York: Holt, Rinehart & Winston.

Kahle, J. B. (1982). *Double dilemma: Minorities and women in science education.* West Lafayette, IN: Purdue Research Foundation.

Kahle, J. B., & Lakes, M. K. (1983). "The myth of equality in science classrooms." *Journal of Research in Science Teaching*, **20**, 131–140.

Karplus, R., & Karplus, E. (1972). "Intellectual development beyond elementary school III: Ratio: A longitudinal study." *School Science and Mathematics.* **72**, 735–742.

Karplus, R., Lawson, A. E., Wollman, W., Appel, M., Bernoff, R., Howe, A., Rusch, J. J., & Sullivan, F. (1977). *Science teaching and the development of reasoning.* (Volumes for Biology, Chemistry, Earth Science, General Science and Physics). Berkeley, CA: The University of California.

Karplus, R., Pulos, S., & Stage, E. K. (1983). "Early adolescents' proportional reasoning on 'rate' problems." *Educational Studies in Mathematics*, **14**, 219–233.

Kell, C. L., & Corts, P. R. (1980). *Fundamentals of effective group communication.* New York: Macmillan.

Kline, M. (1972). *Mathematical thought from ancient to modern times.* New York: Oxford University Press.

Krathwohl, D., Bloom, B., & Masia, B. (1964). *Taxonomy of educational objectives, Handbook II: Affective domain.* New York: David McKay.

Kreidler, W. J. (1986). "Teaching computer ethics." In D. O. Harper & J. H. Stewart (Eds.), *Run: Computer education* (pp. 223–226). Monterey, CA: Brooks/Cole Publishing Co.

Kuhn, D., & Phelphs, E. (1979). "A methodology for observing development of a formal reasoning strategy." In D. Kuhn (Ed.), *Intellectual development beyond childhood* (pp. 45–57). San Francisco, CA: Jossey-Bass.

LaForgia, J. (1988). "The affective domain related to science education and its evaluation." *Science Education*, **72**, 407–421.

Larkin, J. H. (1977). *Problem solving in physics* (Working Paper). Group in Science and Mathematics Education and Department of Physics, University of California, Berkeley, CA.

Larkin, J. H. (1983). "The role of problem presentation in physics." In D. Gentner & A. L. Stevens (Eds.), *Mental models*. Hillsdale, NJ: Lawrence Erlbaum Associates.

Larson, G. (1989). *The prehistory of the far side: A 10th anniversary exhibit*. Kansas City, MO: Andrews & McMeel.

Lawson, A. E., & Thompson, L. D. (1988). "Formal reasoning ability and misconceptions concerning genetics and natural selection." *Journal of Research in Science Teaching*, **25**, 733–746.

Lederman, N. G., & Zeidler, D. L. (1987). "Science teachers' conception of the nature of science: Do they really influence teacher behavior?" *Science Education*, **71**, 721–734.

Lehman, J. R. (1985). "Survey of microcomputer use in the science classroom." *School Science and Mathematics*, **85**, 578–582.

Lehman, J. R., Koran, J. J., & Koran, M. L. (1984). "Interaction of learner characteristics with learning from three models of the periodic table." *Journal of Research in Science Teaching*, **21**, 885–893.

Lehman, J. R., & Yarbrough, J. (1983). "25 (Scientific) writing activities." *The Science Teacher*. **50** (2), 27–29.

Linn, M. C., DeBenedictis, T., Delucchi, K., Harris, A., & Stage, E. (1987). "Gender differences in national assessment of educational progress science items: What does 'I don't know' really mean?" *Journal of Research in Science Teaching*, **24**, 267–278.

Lockhard, J. D. (Ed.). (1970). *Seventh report of the International Clearinghouse on Science and Mathematics Curricular Developments*. College Park, MD: Science Teaching Center, University of Maryland.

Lovell, K., & Ogilvie, E. (1968). "The growth of the concept of volume in junior school children." In I. E. Sigel & F. H. Hooper (Eds.), *Logical thinking in children* (pp. 30–40). New York: Holt, Rinehart and Winston, Inc.

Lovell, K., & Shayer, M. (1978). "The impact of the work of Piaget on science curriculum development." In J. McCarthy Gallagher & J. A. Easley, Jr. (Eds.), *Knowledge and development* (Vol. 2, pp. 93–138). New York: Plenum Press.

Mayer, R. E. (1983). "What have we learned about increasing the meaningfulness of science prose?" *Science Education*, **67**, 223–237.

McBride, J. W., & Chiappetta, E. L. (1978). *The relationship between the proportional reasoning ability of ninth-graders and their achievement of selected math and science concepts*. ERIC Reports (ED 167 351).

McDonald, J. L. (1982). "The role of cognitive stage in the development of cognitive structures of geometric content in the adolescent." (Doctoral dissertation, State University of New York at Albany, 1982). *Dissertation Abstracts International*, **43**, 733A.

McWhirter, N., & McWhirter, R. (1976). *Guinness book of world records*. New York: Bantam Books.

Mills, L. C., & Dean, P. M. (1960). *Problem solving methods in science teaching*. New York: Teachers College Press.

Mokros, J. R., & Tinker, R. F. (1987). "The impact of microcomputer-based labs on children's ability to interpret graphs." *Journal of Research in Science Teaching*, **24**, 369–383.

Mullis, I., & Jenkins, L. B. (1988). *The science report card: Elements of risk and recovery.* Princeton, NJ: Educational Testing Service.

Murname, R. J., & Raizen, S. A. (Eds.). (1988). *Improving indicators of the quality of science and mathematics education in grades K–12.* Washington, DC: National Research Council National Academy Press.

National Assessment of Educational Progress. (1978). *Three national assessments of science: Changes in achievement, 1969–77.* Denver, CO: Education Commission of the States.

National Commission on Excellence in Education. (1983). *A nation at risk: The imperative for educational reform.* Washington, DC: U.S. Government Printing Office.

National Education Association. (1894). *Report of the committee of ten on secondary school studies.* New York: American Book Company.

National Science Board Commission on Precollege Education in Mathematics, Science and Technology. (1983). *Educating Americans for the 21st century.* Washington, DC: National Science Foundation.

National Science Teachers Association. (1978). *Safety in the science classroom.* Washington, DC: NSTA.

National Science Teachers Association. (1987). *Criteria for excellence.* Washington, DC: NSTA.

National Science Teachers Association. (January 1990). "Multicultural science education association." *NSTA Reports*, 3.

Neimark, E. D., DeLisi, R., & Newman, J. L. (Eds.). (1985). *Moderators of competence.* Hillsdale, NJ: Lawrence Erlbaum Assoc.

Newman, J. (Ed.). (1956). *The world of mathematics* (Vols. 1, 2, 3, 4). New York: Simon & Schuster.

Novak, J. D., & Gowin, D. B. (1984). *Learning how to learn.* New York: Cambridge University Press.

O'Connell, R. O. (1984). "The influence of content organization and relevant prior knowledge on the cognitive structure and achievement of sixth grade science students." (Doctoral dissertation at the State University of New York at Albany, 1984). *Dissertation Abstracts International*, 45, 3601A.

Orlans, F. B. (1988). "Should students harm or destroy animal life." *The American Biology Teacher*, 50, 6–12.

Padilla, M. J., Okey, J. R., & Garrard, K. (1984). "The effects of instruction on integrated science process skill achievement." *Journal of Research in Science Teaching*, 21, 277–287.

Piaget, J. (1971). *Science of education and the psychology of the child.* (D. Coltman, Trans.). New York: The Viking Press. (Originally published in two parts 1935 and 1965).

Piaget, J., & Inhelder, B. (1969). *The psychology of the child.* (H. Weaver, Trans.). New York: Basic Books. (Originally published in 1966).

Posner, G. J., Strike, K. A., Hewson, P. W., & Gertzog, W. A. (1982). "Accommodation of a scientific conception: Toward a theory of conceptual change." *Science Education*, 66, 211–227.

Pouler, C., & Wright, E. (1980). "An analysis of the influence of reinforcement and knowledge of criteria on the ability of students to generate hypotheses." *Journal of Research in Science Teaching*, 17, 31–37.

Ranucci, E. R., & Teeters, J. L. (1977). *Creating Escher-type drawings.* Palo Alto, CA: Creative Pub.

Renzulli, J. S. (1979). "What makes giftedness: A re-examination of the definition." *Science and Children*, 16 (6), 14–15.

Resnick, L. B., & Ford, W. W. (1981). *The psychology of mathematics for instruction.* Hillsdale, NJ: Lawrence Erlbaum Assoc.

Rickover, H. G. (1960). *Education and freedom.* New York: E. P. Dutton & Co., Inc.

Rivers, R. H., & Vockell, E. (1987). "Computer simulations to stimulate scientific problem solving." *Journal of Research in Science Teaching*, **24**, 403–415.

Ronning, R., & McCurdy, D. W. (1982). "The role of instruction in the development of problem solving skills in science." In R. Yager (Ed.), *What research says to the science teacher* (Vol. 4, pp. 31–39). Washington, DC: National Science Teachers Association.

Rosen, S. (1963). "Innovation in science teaching: A historical view." *School Science and Mathematics*, **63**, 313–323.

Rubinstein, M. F. (1980). "A decade of experience in teaching an interdisciplinary problem solving course." In D. Tuma & F. Reif (Eds.), *Problem solving and education: Issues in teaching and research*. Hillsdale, NJ: Lawrence Erlbaum Associates.

Rumsey, S. R. (1986). "An analysis of proportional reasoning topics in high school chemistry from a cognitive development perspective." (Doctoral dissertation, State University of New York at Albany, 1986). *Dissertation Abstracts International*, **47**, 1679A.

Sacco, W., Melville, J., Copes, W., Sloyer, C., & Morningstar, K. (1983). "Glyphs: Getting the picture." *The Science Teacher*, **50** (2), 51–53.

Sagness, R. L. (1970). "A study of selected outcomes of a science pre-service teacher education project emphasizing early involvement in schools of contrasting environmental settings." (Doctoral dissertation, The Ohio State University, 1970). *Dissertation Abstracts*, **31**, 4606A.

Salunkhe, D. K. (1974). *Storage, processing, and quality of fruits and vegetables*. Cleveland, OH: CRC Press.

School Mathematics Study Group. (1965). *Mathematics and living things*. Stanford, CA: Leland Stanford Junior University.

Seymour, L. A., & Padberg, L. F. (1975). "The relative effectiveness of group and individual settings in a simulated problem-solving game." *Science Education*, **59**, 297–304.

Shavelson, R. J. (1974). "Methods for examining representations of a subject-matter structure in a student's memory." *Journal of Research in Science Teaching*, **11**, 231–249.

Shayer, M., & Wylam, H. (1978). "The distribution of Piagetian stages of thinking in British middle and secondary school children, 11–14 to 16 year olds and sex differentials." *British Journal of Educational Psychology*, **48**, 62–70.

Sherwood, R. D., Kinzer, C. K., Bransford, J. D., & Franks, J. J. (1987). "Some benefits of creating macro-contexts for science instruction: Initial findings." *Journal of Research in Science Teaching*, **24**, 417–435.

Shulman, L. S. (1970). "Psychology and mathematics education." In E. G. Begle (Ed.), *Mathematics education* (69th Yearbook of the National Society for the Study of Education, pp. 23–71). Chicago, IL: University of Chicago Press.

Simpson, R. D., & Oliver, J. S. (1985). "Attitude toward science and achievement motivation profiles of male and female science students in grades six through ten." *Science Education*, **69**, 511–526.

Sipe, H. C., & Farmer, W. A. (1982). *Summary of research in science education in 1980: Science Education*. Columbus, OH: ERIC SMEAC.

Skehan, J. W. (1986). *Modern science and the book of genesis*. Washington, DC: NSTA.

Skinner, B. F. (1953). *Science and human behavior*. New York: The Free Press.

Skinner, B. F. (1968). *The technology of teaching*. New York: Appleton.

Slavin, R. E. (1980). "Cooperative learning." *Review of Educational Research*, **50**, 315–342.

Smith, M. U., & Good, R. (1984). "Problem solving and classical genetics: Successful versus unsuccessful performance." *Journal of Research in Science Teaching*, **21**, 895–912.

Smith, W. S., & Erb, T. O. (1986). "Effects of women science career role models on early adolescents' attitude toward scientists and women in science." *Journal of Research in Science Teaching*, **23**, 667–676.

Stake, R. E., & Easley, J. A. (1978). *Case studies in science education*. Urbana, IL: Center for Instructional Research and Curriculum Evaluation.

Suchman, J. R. (1977). "Heuristic learning and science education." *Journal of Research in Science Teaching*, **14**, 263–277.

Thompson, D. W. (1961). *On growth and form* (Abridged ed.). Cambridge, England: The University Press. (Originally published in 1917).

Thorndike, E. L. (1921). *New methods in teaching arithmetic*. New York: Rand-McNally.

Thorndike, E. L. (1922). *The psychology of arithmetic*. New York: Macmillan Co.

Tobin, K., & Garnett, P. (1987). "Gender related differences in science activities." *Science Education*, **71**, 91–103.

Tomera, A. N. (1974). "Transfer and retention of transfer of the science processes of observation and comparison in junior high school students." *Science Education*, **58**, 195–203.

Troutner, J. (1986). "Computer literacy: Teaching computer ethics." *The Journal of Computers in Mathematics and Science Teaching*, **5** (3), 11–12.

Trowbridge, J., & Mintzes, J. (1985). "Students' alternative conceptions of animal and animal classification." *School Science and Mathematics*, **85**, 304–316.

Vetter, B. (1986). "The last two decades." *Science 86*, **7**, 62–63.

Vockell, E. L., & Lobonc, S. (1981). "Sex-role stereotyping by high school females in science." *Journal of Research in Science Teaching*, **18**, 209–219.

Watson, J. D. (1968). *The double helix*. New York: Atheneum.

Weber, M., & Renner, J. (1972). "How effective is the SCIS program?" *School Science and Mathematics*, **72**, 729–734.

Weiss, I. R. (1978). *Report of the 1977 national survey of science, mathematics, and social studies education*. Research Triangle Park, NC: Center for Educational Research and Evaluation.

Wertheimer, M. (1959). *Productive thinking* (Enl. ed.). New York: Harper & Row. (Original work published in 1945).

Whimbey, A., & Lochhead, J. (1982). *Problem solving and comprehension*. Philadelphia, PA: Franklin Press.

White, R. T. (1988). *Learning science*. New York: Basil Blackwell.

Winne, W. (1982). "The role of diagrammatic representation in learning sequences, identification, and classification as a function of verbal and spatial ability." *Journal of Research in Science Teaching*, **19**, 79–89.

Yager, R. E. (1986). "Searching for excellence." *Journal of Research in Science Teaching*, **23**, 209–217.

Yager, R. E. (1987). "Assess all five domains of science." *The Science Teacher*, **54** (7), 33–37.

Yager, R. E. (1989). "A rationale for using personal relevance as a science curriculum focus in schools." *School Science and Mathematics*, **89**, 144–156.

Yager, R. E., Aldrich, B. G., & Penick, J. (1983). "Science education in the United States." In F. K. Brown & D. P. Butts (Eds.), *Science teaching: A profession speaks* (pp. 3–18). Washington, DC: National Science Teachers Association.

NAME INDEX

SUBJECT INDEX